Bitcoin & Cryptocurrency Investing For Beginners: 7 In 1

The 7 In 1 Step-By-Step, Beginner Friendly Guide To Understand & Make Money With Crypto Trading, NFTs, The Metaverse & Decentralized Finance (DeFi)

MAX BANCROFT

TABLE OF CONTENTS

INTRODUCTION

In the real world, fiat currency acts as a store of value and a medium of exchange, allowing you to buy and sell whatever you desire. But how do you suppose you'll pay for your painting, land, and Taylor Swift concert in a smooth, immediate manner in your virtual world? Crypto is the answer.

It isn't easy to see the metaverse, the alternate reality, functioning without cryptocurrency.

Without cryptocurrencies, it isn't easy to imagine the metaverse, or parallel reality, functioning. Crypto has become a must rather than an option inside a society where security, speed, and transparency are nearly required. At its foundation, cryptocurrency is the suitable medium of exchange for this quickly evolving hybrid society.

Take time to think about that. To begin with, rapid, swift, and frequent transactions, such as selling your antique and purchasing a new one right away, or even gaining that NFT, demand decentralization and transparency, in which the ability to authorize and authenticate your desired transactions resides with everyone in the network collectively, rather than with a single centralized authority or hub, making it more democratic, accessible, and quick! You do not place your trust in just one individual.

Secondly, given cryptocurrencies like bitcoin depend on advanced cryptographic technology for encryption and fund security, you can be sure that your acquisitions are safe if you're using a public ledger like blockchain, where each transaction is irreversible, traceable, and secure.

The enviable lightning-fast speed would surely be the third pillar of the metaverse and a gap filled admirably by cryptocurrencies' scalability promise or their ability to process or complete a more significant number of transactions per second! So go ahead and enter the metaverse, a parallel universe that is just as real and probably even more expansive than the one we live in! Crypto is the way to go because it solidifies the concept of interoperability, which includes the ability to work across several blockchain systems, quick value transfer, and digital, permanent proof of ownership in the metaverse. And the simplest way to get started with cryptocurrencies and take the plunge is to use reputable cryptocurrency exchanges and trading platforms such as CoinSwitch Kuber.

Like some other game-changing technology applications such as artificial intelligence (AI) and the internet of things (IoT), the metaverse and blockchain are not isolated notions. Because they all contain a variety of traits and functions that complement one another, allowing them to diverge in ways that make them more excellent than the sum of their parts! When they're used together, they'll reach their full potential.

Cryptocurrencies are a type of virtual currency.

Let's begin with some of the most prominent applications of blockchain technology in the metaverse: money! The metaverse has the potential to create a virtual world like "Ready Player One," in which we can play, work, and mingle with our friends in immersive environs without ever leaving our homes. And, of course, anyone who understands anything regarding human nature can forecast one of the most prominent activities people will want to do while shopping and buying goods!

It's already possible to buy virtual real estate plots inside the Decentraland online environment using the cryptocurrency Mana – in fact, someone recently made headlines for doing so for $2.4 million. Aside from land, we'll be able to buy digital representations of everything and anything we can acquire in the actual world, as well as a lot of things we can't! Governments are also getting in on the game, with Barbados recently opening the world's first metaverse embassy utilizing Decentraland.

On the other hand, buying stuff is likely to be just the start of blockchain-based currency in the metaverse. Decentralized finance (De-Fi) is a fast-growing field that is well-suited to operate within virtual worlds and surroundings. We should expect to see more metaverse-based financing, borrowing, trading, and investing.

WHAT IS AN NFT

NFTs, also known as Nyfties, are digital assets on a blockchain. They have unique qualities that stop them from being interchangeable. That means that they are difficult to forge, so it guarantees the authenticity of the purchased item.

NFTs had helped solve the problem artists worldwide have been having when it came to getting their well-earned royalties. As technology grew, so did the ease of making forgeries, duplicating work, and so forth that have been costing artists their well-earned pay for decades. NFT ownership is recorded on the blockchain, thus preventing illegal copies from being made. That ensures that artists get paid for their work.

Hence, the different types of NFTs spring up, including music, artwork, event tickets, domain names, physical asset ownership, and collectibles. At the moment, these are sold at auctions in a similar style to how artwork is sold at a live auction. The only difference is that it is all done online.

How Does It Work?

NFTs are mostly found on the Ethereum blockchain, and Ethereum-based tokens are used to authenticate ownership of the NFT. That's because the item or asset is attached to the token so that you can copy the file from someone else's NFT, but it won't be the original, and that can be traced. Whoever owns the token owns the NFT. Each copy or reproduction is verified as not being the foremost. The token contains the ownership information, a certificate of authenticity, and copyright information.

The blockchain is the public register for ownership of a particular digital item because it can't be hacked or overwritten. A ledger entry is created the same way as with any blockchain cryptocurrency. This entry contains the address to the file, which establishes the NFT. When the NFT is sold, that token code is also transferred and noted as a ledger entry. That is how ownership is tracked on the blockchain.

The NFT owner can add metadata to the character of their new NFT. This additional information would describe whether it is art, music, and so forth and what format it is in: for example, jpeg—video, and so on.

Tokens don't have any value on their own; they are based on the media attached to them. Think of an award-winning piece of art. The artist's talent and reputation give the painting its value, which it gets priced for an auction. Value is based on market demand. It is also based on rarity or scarcity because the NFT creator can decide if they want to make copies and, if so, how many.

Something essential to bear in mind is that the artist still owns the copyright, which they use to claim their royalties.

Therefore, ensure that you know what happens to the asset should these things occur to protect your purchase.

Why Is It Popular Now?

The amount that several digital items have been sold for has turned heads. And the industry has exploded purely because cryptocurrency is on the rise, and the COVID-19 pandemic has pushed a lot of items online. People can't physically watch a concert, so they purchase a whole album online and watch it there.

People were also not spending as much money because they were stuck indoors, didn't have to drive to work, and couldn't travel, so they now had the extra cash to spend. Plus, cryptocurrencies have surged in popularity, so one could say that the stars have aligned for NFT trading.

Its popularity has also helped create several companies that facilitate the buying and selling of NFTs, called NFT Marketplaces.

Many investors are paying high rates to promote NFTs based on their belief that they will only increase profitability.

Trade is an easy process that doesn't require extra financial backing or platforms. For example, if you create a piece of digital art, you have to sell it on a marketplace. There is no need to market it, spend money on promoting it, or punt potential buyers. With all this backing, it's no wonder more people are interested.

Is It A Crypto Fad?

I have mentioned a few times that NFTs are not new and have been around for at least a decade. An example of this is CryptoKitties, digital kittens that were collectibles and very popular among those involved in cryptocurrency when they were created in 2017. Despite all the celebrity hype, NFTs aren't a fad based on how high the trading volume is and is still growing.

NFTs have been linked to a technological revolution that taps into us wanting to own rare items of high value without the worry of illegal copies. That is fantastic in an age where everything online can and is copied. NFTs, bring back value to items with security and traceability.

Even though there were record-making sales in the news, NFT prices have dropped but are staying constant even as the hype dies down, making it a much more stable market in which to invest. It's also innovative and new, which can be a pushback to many presented with something that appears too fine to be true.

But not everyone is skeptical. NFTs have been likened to the dot-com bubble when people thought the internet was a fad. In reality, it was just overly priced early projects that had caused all the excitement. That is why there are problems that the NFT market could crash and bring down investors with it.

At this point, there is a ton of hype, so prices are high, but they will drop and stabilize. That is a pleasing item because it signifies that NFT trading is here long term.

What Are Speculative Investments?

You need to research any investment, so it's essential to cover all three types of assets: saving, investing, and speculating.

You will thank me later.

Save

The first way to invest is to save by putting money aside. For example, you can put your money into a savings account to keep for a specific item. Although you have the item's value, that can change but not rapidly, and you are saving towards it. The process is slow, with very little growth in terms of interest, but your money is safe because you won't lose any in the process.

That method can be used for short-term usage if you're saving for something specific and don't want to pay the penalty for an early withdrawal from an IRA. But most retirement funds for long-term usage are included in these types of investments.

Invest

Investing your money means that you are taking on a slight risk as your money starts growing, based on where it is supported. That is a long-term process with a minimum of 3 years so that any losses can be offset when the profits increase. Anything shorter, and you won't see a good trade-off. That's because your money will rise and fall as markets do but not at an alarming rate, and by the end, you would have weathered the ups and downs and realized a good profit.

That can be done by owning a successful business because you expect its success to mean more significant returns for you. Most people will invest with companies specializing in this and put the money to grow.

Speculate

With speculation, you are looking at quick profits over brief periods. The risk is significantly higher as you hope you don't lose your money and make a high return. An example of this is day trading.

Speculation has been likened to gambling one's money, but there is an art to belief, and when done right, the rewards are fantastic. The key is to maintain an eye on the markets to determine what will bring in the most profit.

That isn't a new concept, as it is used for art, collectibles, stocks, and other tangible items. The only difference now is that the things are digital, not physical, and you can trace their authenticity in a secure environment.

NFTs fall under speculative investment because their value fluctuates, depending on popularity. It's essential to understand this concept well as you begin your journey into NFT trading because the risks are high.

What Are The Most Expensive Nfts To Date?

As the list is continuously changing, I will not list the top 10 most expensive NFTs to date but list some of the most notable NFTs based on their price, rarity, and originality.

Beeple With Every day: The First 5,000 Days

That piece of NFT art was sold at Christie's for $69 million and, to date, is the enormous amount anyone has paid for an NFT, as well as the most expensive work of art by a living artist. It comprises 500 pieces of art that were created in May 2007.

The artwork was bought by Vignesh Sundaresan, also known as MetaKovan, who has displayed it in a digital art museum in the Metaverse, a virtual space shared.

Edward Snowden with Stay Free (Edward Snowden 2021)

This piece of art depicts Edward Snowden's portrait over the court documents showing that the National Security Agency in the United States illegally masses surveyed individuals. That was a piece of charity art that benefited a company called Freedom of the Press Foundation by being sold for over $5.4 million.

Mad Dog Jones with Replicator

This artist is currently the most-expensively selling living Canadian artist because of this piece of art. It is also unique because new NFTs will come from it every 28 days, each with its resale value. That is quite a return on investment for the buyer, who could own up to 220 unique NFTs that they can sell. It's well worth the cost of $4.1 million if you can get so much more out of it.

Kevin McCoy with Quantum

That is an exceptionally unique NFT, as it is the first-ever created as far back as 2014. The artist created the token on Namecoin in May 2014 using technology he made with the coder Anil Dash. They presented this to an audience at the New Museum in New York, but they laughed.

But as the phrase goes, "Who's laughing now?" I would say $1.4 million is undoubtedly having the two creators laughing all the way to the bank.

Pak with the Switch

That artwork gives the owner the option of changing the painting to a new unknown image. That part of the artist's way of representing art is evolving digitally. However, once the new owner decides to trigger the switch, it can't be changed back.

It was sold as part of a collection of seven digital art pieces at Sotheby's for $17 million, so I can see why the owner would be hesitant to change the piece.

3LAU with Gunky's Uprising

This piece combines animated artwork and a music video to celebrate the disc jockey (DJ) and electronic musician's third anniversary of his album Ultraviolet. For $1.3 million, it's no wonder he has a couple more art pieces for sale.

These unreleased feature music with the option for the buyer to name the songs when purchased.

Don Diablo With Destination Hexagonia

This Dutch DJ, record producer, musician, and songwriter is known for his electronic music created this full-length, 1-hour concert.

Based on a Sci-Fi theme, the owner received a hard drive containing the only copy of the file. That makes it a rare collectible and worth roughly $1.2 million costs.

Don Diablo is now creating NFT comic books.

HISTORY OF NON-FUNGIBLE TOKENS

L et's delve into the history of non-fungible tokens, where we understand their functions and uses and deepen our understanding of how they are used in trade. Non-fungible tokens have been around since the start of blockchain technology. The first cryptocurrency ever established, Bitcoin, produced a digital asset entirely controlled by its developers. These assets were referred to as "bitcoins," giving their owners a particular level of importance. The coins could be possessed by a user and used to purchase or sell real-world assets (mainly BTC) via the Bitcoin network. That meant that these assets could be used to create fiat money on the blockchain, which was unprecedented at the time. That gave Bitcoin early adopters an edge over others looking to purchase cryptocurrencies because there was a straightforward way of using them to buy real-world goods. Some of the first NFT games were made with Bitcoin in mind. For example, Spells of Genesis (SoG) and CryptoKitties make it feasible to spend their cryptocurrencies in a match.

The popularity of NFTs started to expand significantly in 2017 and 2018. That was primarily because of the advanced awareness and usage of cryptocurrencies on the blockchain—games focused mainly on creating a digital asset traded for real-world assets (fiat). However, more and more users were becoming curious about using NFTs and other blockchain tools to create progressive game experiences. That resulted in the creation of CryptoKitties, which became an instant hit. By the end of 2017, it obtained more than $12 million in funds from investors. That was huge at the time, particularly for a blockchain-based game. The cost of a CryptoKitty was reportedly so high that a digital cat went for $110,000. That means it was on par with the price of a work of art! That shows just how valuable NFTs can be. They can be operated to build assets that have real-world significance, not just game value. It was after the triumph of CryptoKitties that the ERC-721 prototype was created. One of the leading causes of this standard is CryptoKitties and the point that it presented NFTs to an even larger audience. That indicated that people who had never heard about blockchain technology now comprehended what they were, how they functioned, and how they could be utilized in a game. Around this time, blockchain technology began to become additional mainstream, which also helped increase the number of developers who noticed the value in NFTs and other blockchain tools.

Today, any game can use non-fungible tokens because they are effortless to build and integrate. The popularity of NFTs has directed to many other chances for games that were formerly thought unimaginable. It's also worth mentioning that many games are now designed to increase the value of NFTs. As we believe earlier, NFTs are more beneficial and have more roles than classic digital assets. For example, CryptoKitties follows the total number of cats that have been made and even allows users to collect and trade them.

Shortly, we will start to see a lot of games that use non-fungible tokens as their core currency. That will permit players to use NFTs to purchase things, services, and other investments within the game. These assets can be of any sort, including weapons and vehicles.

Non-Fungible Tokens Myths

Several myths surround NFTs and non-fungible tokens. That is understandable, considering that most of these myths have existed for years. Here's a checklist of some of the more typical myths:

1. Myth: "Ethereum has thousands of pending transactions" is one of the most common misconceptions about Ethereum. It reveals a misconception about how blockchains work and how they process data. The number of pending transactions has nothing to do with the number of people using the network or its popularity. It only means that there are many uncertain transactions in this block, which is good because many developers and users use Ethereum. The more additional people who use Ethereum, the more beneficial it becomes. That is true in some markets, but it is not the case in most cases.

2. Myth: "NFTs are a scam" is another common misconception about NFTs. A few years ago, this was right because people were unfamiliar with the idea of non-fungible tokens. Nevertheless, as time went on and more people comprehended what they were, this myth died out. Today, many experienced traders who understand NFTs and blockchain technology's advantages start to view them as investments rather than scams. That was delivered by nine percent of all NFTs traded on the Ethereum network during 2018.

3. Myth: "NFTs are too volatile" is another typical misinterpretation about non-fungible tokens. The cost of an NFT will go up and down, just like any other coin or token. That is because it is not connected to a particular item and can be used in any number of games. That is why it can be exchanged for games and real-world assets.

4. Myth: "NFTs are too pricey" – This is not true at all. The price of NFTs alters, but the average cost is identical to that of other cryptocurrencies, which are already inexpensive compared to standard currencies. That implies you can get as many NFTs as you want for a fraction of the cost of conventional money.

5. Myth: "NFTs are too complex and hard to make" – This is not true, either. It all relies on the game developer and which blockchain platform they are using. Since there are many additional types of blockchain platforms, developers will use whichever one they prefer.

However, if they use Ethereum, they can use NFT-Crowdfund to create their own NFT token. That means they can rely on a protocol to create their NFT without learning a different programming language or building their smart contracts. They will only need some details about Ethereum and how it works.

6. Myth: "NFTs don't bring significance to the gaming industry" – This is another typical misinterpretation about non-fungible tokens. There are a lot of games that allow you to collect NFTs. That means that these components can increase the value of an NFT. After all, NFTs can be used in many different forms, including virtual items in games such as CryptoKitties and Spells of Genesis.

Problems Or Controversies

When you tear off the first layer of NFTs, some overlapping problems arise: environmental, logistical, ethical, etc.

Numerous have pointed out the effect (extreme ecological impact) of NFT formation and trade explosions on planets already destroyed by climate change (climate change-related disasters, environment, racism, inequality). What is the relationship between NFTs and climate change? Ethereum is a platform that hosts a fixed blockchain with many of these NFTs. Put, a lot of energy is used along with the process of issuing NFTs, adding tokens to the blockchain, and the wave of transactions (bidding, resale, etc.). Multiplying that by a considerable market driven by greed, we are initiating new forms of environmental destruction. That promised to transform the system into a carbon-depleting form so much that it kept it working safely, but this hasn't happened yet. The timing of this switch is still unknown.

From fairness and ethical standpoint, the choice to sell a particular art as an NFT may not have the right opportunity it has. Digital artist RJ Palmer recently warned that accounts extract art by minting tweets from fellow artists and artists and selling them as NFTs. The work of a budding artist can be severely abused if not properly enforced or investigated whether the person writing the NFT is the real artist, the actual creator, or the copyright holder. It has created an environment where the relative anonymity of cryptocurrency transactions can be exploited, stolen, and harmed.

Make Enlightened Business Decisions.

Transitioning the practice of art into cryptographic art requires careful planning as a business decision and the selection of art dealers and galleries. The crypto art industry is now valued at $445 million, with Nifty Gateway leading sales volume. Because the competition is intense, it's critical to grasp the terminology, choose the right platform, and seek out well-informed professionals for guidance. Do not focus on stable or fast profit yet. It is advisable not to allocate funds from the sale of cryptographic arts to pay the rent. Thus, it won't be different from the "old" art market.

Studies show that, given the environmental impact of Ether mining, the footprint a computer needs to create a single board NFT is the same as the total electricity usage of EU residents in a month. In comparison, for 2020, Louvre Museum consumed the same amount of electricity as 677,224 households in Paris. It would be good to invest some of the income earned from the art of cryptography to fund Jason Bailey's Green NFT grants and other attempts to decrease NFT consumption of energy.

Just as you would experiment with a new medium, experiment with one piece at a time. It's a good idea to complete, embed, or create activated encrypted art by playing it back in media, such as playing it as an animation in .mp4 or .gif format, adding sound, or converting a picture into interactive digital art. You can also create an NFTonly series to see which works are the most popular. We experiment and research what's best for your target collector and you while staying true to your values and trademark community.

Therefore, as long as the legal consequences are understood, NFT can provide an attractive alternative to the usual art market, the choice of the market and the detailed artwork to be sold result from careful consideration of commercial, practical, and legal aspects.

TYPES OF NFTS

The concept of what constitutes an NFT is still somewhat ambiguous, with the result that essentially anything may be classified as an NFT. Here is a list of the most general and reasonable NFTs currently available on the market.

Understanding The Different Types Of Non-Financial Transactions

Creating one-of-a-kind digital assets based on blockchain technology has gained considerable popularity in recent years. Non-fungible tokens, often known as NFTs, are prominent subjects that will get significant attention in 2021. Consequently, there has been a substantial increase in interest in learning more about the numerous kinds of nonlinear optical fibers.

Besides being intrigued by the potentially lucrative economic possibilities connected with NFTs, people are also intrigued by the prospect of altering traditional asset management. The progressive expansion seen in non-fungible tokens might result in a plethora of options for NFT developers and investors. As a result, having a firm understanding of the various sorts of non-fungible tickets will assist you in making smarter choices along your NFT journey.

- Art

The most often practiced type of NFT is an artistic expression. The creation of NFTs provided an excellent chance for artists to sell their greatest works online in the same way they would sell them in a physical store. At the moment, many of the costliest nonlinear optical transducers are pieces of art. "EVERYDAY'S: THE FIRST 5000 DAYS," by well-known artist Beeple, is the most value NFT ever sold, according to Luno, making it the most expensive NFT ever sold. An incredible $69 million was paid for this painting. There are additionally very costly non-financial transactions (NFTs) that are destroying the financial accounts of billionaires.

That holds for works of video art as well. Short films and even spirited GIFs have been selling like hotcakes for millions of dollars. Notably, a looping 10-second film called "Crossroad," which depicts a nude Donald Trump sprawled on the ground, went for $6.6 million and was the most expensive video ever sold on eBay. This one was created by Beeple as well.

- Music

Music is also a prominent component of the NFT spectrum. Music has been a fungible product for decades, having been produced and delivered on various media, including records, cassettes, CDs, and now digitally over the internet. NFTs, on the other hand, have become more popular with artists and DJs, resulting in some of them earning millions of dollars in a matter of hours.

Because of cutbacks made by streaming platforms and record labels, musicians often only get a percentage of the revenue generated by their work. When it comes to non-financial transactions, artists may retain around 100 percent of the money, which is why so many musicians are turning this way.

- Video Game Items

With video games, we have reached another frontier in the NFT domain. Companies are not selling whole games as non-transferable tokens. Instead, they'll sell in-game material such as skins, characters, and other accessories. At the moment, users may purchase millions of copies of DLC assets. An NFT item, on the other hand, will be unique and exclusive to a single customer. NFT allows developers to sell ordinary DLC while also selling a limited edition version of that DLC on the NFT marketplace.

- Trading Cards/Collectible Items

NFTs may be compared to digital trading cards in several ways. It is common knowledge that limited edition baseball cards can sell for thousands of dollars, and the NFT market is no exception. It is possible to purchase and exchange virtual replicas of trading cards on the market, and they may be kept in the same way that genuine trading cards are supported. And, much like the real thing, some of these replicas fetch more than a million dollars in price.

Businesses can sell various sorts of collecting things, not simply trading cards, on the NFT market. If anything is considered collectible, it can be sold on the open market.

- Big Sports Moments

NFTs provide something that cannot be replicated in the physical world: a recollection of unforgettable sporting occasions. These are brief videos of historical events in sports, such as game-changing slam dunks or game-changing touchdowns, that are worth seeing. Although these recordings may be as short as 10 seconds in length, they can fetch upwards of $200,000.

- Memes

If you were beneath the appearance that the internet couldn't get any more entertaining, the NFT market now allows you to buy and sell memes. A unique feature is that in certain circumstances, the person shown in the meme is the person who is selling the item. Several of the most well-known memes, including Nyan Cat, Bad Luck Brian, Disaster Girl, and others, appear on the list, with earnings ranging from $30,000 to $770,000 per meme. The Doge meme, the most valuable meme to date, was sold for a whopping $4 million at a recent auction.

- Domain Names

NFT fever has expanded to domain names, which are not immune to the disease. It is possible to register a domain name and then sell it on the NFT market, and this has several advantages over other options. You will often be required to pay a third-party business to administer your occupation title. If you buy one on the NFT demand, you will be capable of claiming sole ownership of the word, therefore eliminating the need for a third-party intermediary.

- Virtual Fashion

Everything purchased and sold on the NFT market has been done virtually, so why should fashion be an exception? You may pay a lot of money for a great bikini, but you won't be able to wear it properly. Instead of dressing up their real-life avatars, those who purchase fashion NFTs will do it online.

That may appear ridiculous, but keep in mind that someone paid $4 million to own the Doge meme somewhere in this world. Being the proud owner of a virtual purse or jewelry is reserved for the more lavish and fashion-forward. These, of course, will all be one-of-a-kind creations with a limited number available.

- Miscellaneous Online Items

The other elements on this list were straightforward to describe, but the NFT market is somewhat of a wild west of online business, as seen by the NFT market meltdown that occurred a few months ago. As formerly indicated, Jack Dorsey essentially sold a single tweet. That opens the door for anyone to sell whatever they want on the NFT market, which is indeed what it is for. Whether it is tweeted, Facebook statuses, articles, Snapchat Stories, or TikToks, the sky is the limit when it comes to what people may sell on the internet.

NFT - KEY CONCEPTS

NFTs have reached such a level of fame due to the celebrities who participated in creating, buying and selling them and due to something intrinsic to NFTs themselves: their ability to create value. To fully understand what NFTs are, you don't just need to know about the technology they are based on; you need to understand a few key concepts. This knowledge will reveal the beauty of NFTs, and you will be amazed at their impact on everyone's lives and their future direction.

To better understand the topic, we will start with the basics and evaluation each essential term thoroughly.

Objective Value Versus Subjective Value

People attach value to many things, including objects, activities, goals, careers, and more. If you were to question a group of people what a valuable experience or something is to them, you would receive a wide range of answers, perhaps including a luxury sports car, a nice walk on a dream beach, being with friends, listening to good music, etc. The common thread that runs through these items is desire. What tends to be considered valuable is thought of that way because of the intrinsic desire to achieve or satisfy it. We don't desire objects, experiences, or anything else because of the feeling these create, but because of the passion, they profit. And desire creates subjective value.

The concept of value is intimately tied to preferences, which tend to be arbitrary and depend on what a given person believes, desires, or perceives. Through desires, the reasons for pursuing pleasure are perpetuated. Moreover, the more desires are satisfied, the more value is produced. Subjective value, therefore, is the value that each individual is willing to assign to a good. Thus, it is arbitrary and temporary. Try to think about it: an urgent necessity can exponentially increase the value of a good concerning what might be considered regular or average.

Trying to define objective value is not as simple. Although we can speak of the temporary and not arbitrary objectivity of prices (where a central power does not fix the price of a good), there is no reasonable way to determine value objectively. Thus, were not coercive by an authority, all matter is exclusively subjective: the market price is generated by subjective evaluations.

Therefore, the value is not something intrinsic to the product. It is not one of its properties, but simply the importance that we attribute to the satisfaction of our needs about our life and our well-being.

The Market

The correlation between subjective value and market prices is one of the most invisible aspects of modern economics. It is the correlation between personal value and objective monetary prices. When referring to the subjective matter, there is no single unit of measurement.

Through the attribution of value, people estimate and classify goods according to their preferences. The concept of value creation plays a central role in management theory.

The term "marketplace" has two possible meanings. First, it is a physical place where people go to sell, buy, or trade a product or good—for example, a supermarket, a shopping mall, or a car dealership; it can also be digital, including platforms such as Amazon, eBay, Alibaba, Shopify, and many others. Second, the term "market" or "marketplace" can also describe the existence of people who desire to buy, sell, or exchange a particular type of product. There is a market in that a specific product can elicit desire and be adjusted to consumers' tastes or preferences.

A market is organized according to the following different approaches:

- Free competition occurs when the price is formed by the encounter between goods or services offered by competing firms, and consumers have the freedom to choose between different offers.

- Oligopoly occurs when a small number makes the offer of operators.

- Monopoly: occurs when there is no choice but to accept the price imposed by the offer.

The advent of the free market has produced many benefits for community life. Consumers' needs and value on goods or services are always brought to the forefront within market research and marketing. This understanding of the term is much more abstract: a market exists when many people are curious about buying or selling a specific product, service, information, or currency.

For all physical assets, the market value is determined by supply and demand and, therefore, by the relationship between the number of goods available and the order. In physical assets, we talk about the concept of scarcity of support, which has not been part of the digital world for a long time. For example, an asset that is highly sought after but scarce acquires value due to the competition between those who want it, while a purchase that is available in large quantities or total, even if highly sought after, does not acquire value because those who seek to possess it can quickly obtain it.

A market test is a tool that companies use to identify the types of people interested in a product about to be put on the market. This test helps companies determine how much money people are willing to spend to get their products. The results show that different people are interested in various products and are eager to pay a specific amount for a particular product. Today's companies listen to the needs of consumers and respond to them. Classical economics has always been based on scarcity, which often defines prices and focuses on those products that satisfy 80% of the population. Thanks to the internet, the possibilities have increased exponentially. Our web offers greater market possibilities because it reaches a global audience, meaning that practically every product or good finds its market of reference. Chris Anderson's dream was with "the long tail" strategy, a retail plan based on statistical analysis. It is preferred to sell many unique items in relatively small quantities rather than a small number of popular items in large amounts.

The web market is very often devoid of intermediaries. Thus, trust and word-of-mouth opinions are critical and represent the most current marketing methods online.

Fungible Versus Non-Fungible Assets

To better understand the difference between fungible and non-fungible, it is essential to learn about (or brush up on) the concepts of assets, tokens, tokenization, and Blockchain.

What is an asset?

The asset is a term used in finance that refers to anything assigned a monetary value and can be helpful or desirable. It can be physical, digital, abstract, or that helps generate earnings. A fungible asset is interchangeable because it possesses the same value as another. For example, a bitcoin is a fungible asset because one bitcoin has the same value as another bitcoin. Fungibility is an alluring property for a currency because it allows free exchange when there is no way to know the history of each unit. However, fungibility is not a valuable property of collectibles.

A non-fungible asset is something that is not interchangeable or even divisible. A non-fungible investment is, for example, a house, a used car, or a unique football card. These cannot be divided because they would not have the same value. A token is nothing more than the digital representation, which can be anything, as long as it has recognizable and certifiable properties.

In the world of blockchain technology, a token is a virtual token whose value is issued by an organization. Tokens are value units; they represent a digital asset (a cryptocurrency, a physical product or object, etc.).

In a broad sense, a token is an object with a particular value only within a specific context.

How about an example? Casino chips. These chips are just pieces of plastic worth nothing outside the casino's walls. In this context, their value is agreed upon, and they become the representation of an asset.

Historically, tokens have created coins with value within a given context. Therefore, the value of a token is what its creator decides to provide it.

The moment when a token is assigned that property and value are called tokenization and occurs within blockchain technology. The Blockchain is a technology that can be equated to a database that collects classified data within computers and networks. Blockchain technology is supported by three pillars: decentralization, transparency, and immutability. Blockchain allows for a decentralized model where one computer does not control the entire network. A decentralized system allows for greater clarity: every movement is recorded within the Blockchain, and everyone can maintain the log of activities and transactions. It is almost impossible in physical reality to find a model with such a level of transparency, where everything is recorded and can be seen by everyone. Moreover, this data cannot be altered in any way, and, for this reason, it is immutable.

The tokenization of a digital asset within blockchain technology can create a non-fungible token: an NFT is the unique representation of a natural or digital asset that cannot be exchanged for an equivalent because an equivalent does not exist. There is no NFT equal to another in the world. People can accomplish with NFTs is endless. The application possibilities cover all sectors, including art, online gaming, music, collectibles of various kinds, exclusive luxury goods, virtual properties, and much more. Blockchain technology adds unique properties to digital assets by providing people with ownership and management of that token and the ability to transfer it to a decentralized, transparent, and immutable platform.

What Is Blockchain?

Blockchain is a shared and immutable data chain structure. It is a digital ledger containing data grouped into blocks concatenated together in chronological order whose integrity and credibility are ensured by cryptography. Moreover, the content cannot be modified or deleted once inside it unless the entire structure is invalidated. This technology is included in the family of distributed ledgers. The blockchain system is distributed across multiple nodes, and there is no single control center. Every transaction is thus recorded. That reinforces the integrity of the process itself. The whole thing is based on a set of properties that represents the foundation of the entire system, and that can be defined as the three fundamental pillars of the Blockchain:

1. Decentralization offers the possibility of transferring assets without a unified administration; for example, it allows for the transfer of money without the intervention of a banking institution. Within a distributed system, power does not lie solely with a single authority. In the Blockchain, there are no intermediaries between actions.

2. Transparency allows people to see how simple and secure the system is. Anyone can view transactions on the Blockchain but not individual data. That allows a transparent system that will enable owners to control their data and all associated movements. In this way, users' privacy is protected.

3. Immutability can be defined as the ability of a blockchain to remain unchanged and unalterable. No data can be modified, and the database cannot be manipulated in any way because each block is uniquely identified by a value called a hash.

WHY NFT IS BECOMING SO POPULAR

NFT marketplace development is a new industry that serves as a massive income structure for tech-savvy and talented developers and artists. It encourages the development of new, one-of-a-kind technological solutions. The significance of NFTs in art and games has led to the introduction of augmented reality and virtual reality in various services.

For many, NFT marketplace development is a once-in-a-lifetime opportunity to demonstrate individual talent and creativity, creative collectibles, and display those products to facilitate effective digital asset management.

The Best Evidence Of Nft Market Growth And A Promising Future

NFT marketplace development is a fantastic trend and a promising source of income due to the following factors. We'll show that NFT marketplaces development is a lucrative business. To begin with, its market capitalization is increasing rapidly, rising from $141.56 million in 2019 to $338.04 million in 2020. Making money in this manner is not challenging.

Benefits of an NFT marketplace:

- Transactions are settled instantly

NFT developers will easily take cryptos as payment and payout options, enabling cryptocurrency owners and new mainstream users to earn and settle transactions fast and without a hitch!

- Increased participation and support

The adoption of NFT technology in NFT marketplace development makes NFT minting and trades by promoting increased participation, marketplace expansion, and support for content creators worldwide.

- A seamless user experience for participants

An NFT marketplace, created on the solid design of a blockchain network, provides a smooth user experience to both participants. Each step of the process, such as tokenization, storage, and marketplace usage, is simple to grasp.

- Future of technology and art

NFT platforms are developing a set of features targeted at providing various solutions and services. Today, the emphasis is on bringing the uniqueness of NFT to every industry imaginable, not only traditional art! NFT, presently, is the start of a fantastic collaboration between technology and art.

Solutions offered by NFT marketplace

- An NFT marketplace powered by blockchain network and the colossal power of bitcoin that eliminates any third-party intervention in the whole process of selling, purchasing, and trading NFTs.

- Blockchain network creates permanent records of authenticity and provenance, minimizing the chances of fraud and counterfeits while remaining legally compliant.

- Collectibles may be bought and sold directly on the site without any license.

- Payments are made instantaneously in the marketplace's native coin.

- A marketplace is being created to provide direct access to collectors for artists without exorbitant fees or third parties.

- Accessibility to a worldwide audience that is not limited by geography.

- A platform where artists can find out all they need to know regarding the resale of their work.

- All transactions and exchanges are carried out transparently on the forum.

Tech Stack For Nft Marketplace Development

After you've decided on all of the elements you'd like to see in your NFT marketplace, it's time to determine the tech stack you'll need to put the project into action. You'll have to decide on a blockchain network, a storage system, front-end development architecture, and the NFT standard that your platform supports.

Blockchain Network

You'll require a blockchain network to run your NFT marketplace, as it'll be the backbone of the platform. Since records and token information are publicly verifiable, Ethereum is the traditional option of NFT marketplace developers, providing extra security to NFT activities. NFT holders may readily transfer their tokens using the standard backend of all Ethereum-supported NFT markets. NFT creators use Flow because of its simple, user-friendly Cadence programming language for creating digital assets, games, and apps. Tezos is another famous option since its FA2 NFT contracts are ideal for the NFT marketplace development goal. Finally, the Cardano platform is highly secure and long-lasting.

Storage Systems

You must select where NFTs will be held whenever you plan on an NFT marketplace development. The IPFS hypermedia protocol or the decentralized Filecoin hold system will be perfect fits for this reason. Pinata is also a viable option because it is IPFS compatible and provides safe, verifiable NFT storage.

NFT Standards

ERC-721, ERC-1155, FA2, dGoods, and TRC-721 are the current NFT-bases standards. Individually of this has its collection of technological challenges, so you'll need to work with your design team to develop a suitable solution.

Front-end

Vue, Angular, and React are the most preferred front-end development frameworks for the NFT platform. They're all essential and coder-friendly, with sleek, easy-to-navigate interfaces that provide rapid results.

Elements That Distinguish NFT Marketplace

Certain essential qualities characterize, define, and explain NFTs marketplace. From the video industry to collectibles and other digital items, it's possible to base this idea on many things. Nonfungible token developers can come to develop an unlimited volume of coins. The following are the primary characteristics of NFTs marketplace that entice business runners:

- Unified tokens

- Unique tokens

- Rarity

- More power to ownership

- Clearness

- Compatibility

You have many reasons to participate in the NFT marketplace development business when you blend trustworthiness, ease of transfer, and indivisibility.

NFT Marketplace User Flow

For nonfungible token sites, the user flow appears to be the same. Visitors to the website must create an account by filling out all required information. They must either create a cryptocurrency wallet or connect a current one to keep all their tokens in one place. The development of NFTs is the next step. Those who scaled through registration must tender digital assets that reflect their work. They can make complete collections and sell individual pieces at a defined price, or they may set up a bidding scheme in which the highest bidder receives the desired item. No items will appear on the site unless checked and validated. Moderation is essential. Once the system allows NFTs, users will see them ready for sales/bidding. The auction starts afterward. You can select the crypto you want to use for your transactions. When the items are sold, both parties are informed. Finally, the service maintains track of all trades and item movements.

That is how an actual user flow works. While participating in the development of the NFT marketplace, bear this in mind.

Launching NFT Marketplace as a Business

Do you want to begin a business with an NFT marketplace? Note, you must target your audience before launching the product. Furthermore, you must identify challenges that you intend to address. The issues determine these difficulties that your potential customers are facing.

After that, make a list of the essential components of the NFT marketplace, so you don't forget anything. Select the best NFT marketplace development approach and guidelines. If you consider building an exclusive NFT marketplace from the ground up, keep the following stages in mind:

Target Niche

Specialists advise betting on a vertical market rather than a horizontal market. The first implies that its members seek to offer goods/services that meet the needs and demands of a specific customer segment. Amazon and eBay are not the most excellent examples because, as horizontal suppliers, they provide everything to everyone.

Propose User Roles

There are not usually many possibilities but consider deeply. Will they be buyers, artists, or admins?

Structure Your Platform and Design

The marketplace development process starts with project documentation. It is a routine, and you risk spending substantial time if you do not document. In-house employees do not need the same level of documentation as offshore professionals.

Move to Development

It's now time to put your design idea into action once you've finished it. Choose the structure that you think best fits your objectives. Many people may consider employing a pro-NFT developer to ensure high performance and credibility. They help you save time and money.

Integrate Smart Contract Token Generator

Back-end development takes on a different appearance during an NFT marketplace. On the blockchain network, the vast majority of information is verified. Pass internal logic to the decentralized aspect if you plan to make an application decentralized.

Examine and Implement

Testing and deployment are the final but not least essential stages. It's all about spotting and avoiding potential pitfalls. Software testing guarantees that your project is running smoothly. Post-launch support is also necessary to keep bugs at bay and ensure the system's quality of service. Please do not remove the service until you have thoroughly tested its features. Is the finished product up to par with your expectations? Consider how users would receive it. This stage is crucial for establishing a reputation and delivering outstanding results.

Keep in mind the key features that the NFT marketplace platform must have before you begin to work on it.

Essential Features of the NFT Marketplace

NFT marketplace's essential features are the characteristics that distinguish the platform as unique and appealing to both buyers and sellers.

Before going over the remaining features, consider the following principal reasons why NFTs and NFT marketplaces in general pique the public interest. Blockchain technology makes it possible to formalize rights and create digital assets much easier to work with. NFTs can also be freely traded. What's more, blockchain technology assures users that they'll get what they need. Other important characteristics include:

Storefront

It is an essential feature. It should include information like bids, glimpse, holders, and price records, among other things.

Advanced Token Search

A user must obtain reliable information on products they require quickly and with minimal effort. All products in an NFT marketplace should be classified by specific features (for instance, books, articles, videos, art). Quick searches improve customer satisfaction.

Filters

This feature is similar to the former one in that the goal is to help users fast and efficiently determine the appropriate product. Split all products into several classes that impact the buyer's decision in most cases. Prices, new items, hot deals, best-sellers, and other factors can all be considered. Users will select items they require more quickly, increasing purchasing them.

Listing Creation

Users should have the ability to create and transfer collectibles. Ascertain that they can do so quickly and without difficulty. Create a page where consumers may upload a file and type in precise item information. Title, tags, and description are all required.

Listing Status

This alternative should assist those who provide items and satisfy item verification requirements. It enables you to see how long the confirmation process is. This functionality comes in handy when it comes to implementing collectible verification.

Bidding Option

Every e-commerce platform needs to allow users to buy and bid on products. It draws more users since some people like flexible pricing and doesn't want to pay the total price for collectibles. Bidding is usually entertaining. If you're using an auction function, don't forget to provide an expiration date. Users who have enrolled should view information about the present state of their bids. It will assist them in deciding whether to purchase or continue to place new bids. Another essential feature is the auction watch list.

Wallet

Users require a secure environment in which to hold and keep nonfungible tokens. Not all alternatives are appropriate since some may pose a risk to the security of assets. That is why the

NFT marketplace service should have an initial wallet installed so that tokens may be safely saved and submitted. Rather than requiring the customers to sign up for other online wallets, create and provide a linked, "native" wallet. First and foremost, consider their comfort. It would help if you did not make a wallet from the ground up.

UNDERSTANDING THE DIFFERENT TYPES OF NFTS

One of the prominent topics in 2022 is Non-fungible tokens or NFTs. Blockchain technology is based on unique digital assets which have gained popularity in recent times. As a result, the interest in comprehending the different types of NFT has been growing recently.

Apart from a vision for altering predictable asset management, people are fascinated by the promising economic potential associated with NFTs. The endless opportunities for NFT creators and investors can be guaranteed by the steady growth visible in the domain of NFTs. Therefore, for making better decisions in your NFT journey, a deep impression of the different types of non-fungible tokens could help significantly.

Digital tokens are not something innovative in the world of technology. Once the digital artist Beeple auctioned off his artwork at a Christie's auction in March, the NFTs started to catch the world's attention. Favorable opinions have been expressed regarding the NFTs by famous names such as Twitter chief Jack Dorsey and Elon Musk. Interestingly, only six years after minting the first NFT in 2014, the NFT market cap reached nearly $2 Billion, only in the first quarter of 2021. In 2020, the total value of sales reached nearly $250 million. NFTs are digital or cryptographic tokens you can find on a blockchain that can preserve exclusivity. NFTs could be tokenized alternatives of valuable assets or native digital assets.

However, one of the protruding aspects which can confuse many beginners in NFT is the association of NFTs with art. NFTs are not limited only to the field of art. Different types of NFTs with exclusive traits and specific use cases can be found.

The primary cataloging of types of NFTs mentions the general categories. The three common types of NFTs are:

- Original or copy of work that is accepted on a blockchain network or DLT

- Digitally inherent NFTs that own rights to an artwork that account for NFTs

- NFT metadata comprises the NFT that provides a demonstration of ownership for metadata files

The usual types of non-fungible tokens propose a comprehensive description of the standards used in NFT classification. The original NFTs are created on the blockchain network, and they remain there. Digitally native NFTs involve issuing NFTs to numerous people with asset ownership rights. A significant way to classify the non-fungible tokens is the NFT metadata, as it fundamentally has a link that leads to the metadata for the NFT. Consequently, you don't get ownership of the NFT and just the rights for using it.

What Are The Different Types Of Nfts?

Important discussion topics involve the different conjectures regarding the NFT potential and the value and risks associated with them. NFTs could explain the true origin of an asset with the functionalities of blockchain. Holding, limiting, or rejecting access to the rights of a person could be helped by NFTs, thereby guaranteeing exclusiveness.

The applications of NFTs could be nurtured in various sectors by developing the infrastructure and an increased opportunity for novelty in the NFTs space. Therefore, new types of NFTs can be reasonably expected to emerge. You can look at some of the notable NFT types popular in present times.

The protuberant records in a non-fungible tokens list would include the following,

- Artwork
- Event tickets
- Music and media
- Virtual items
- Real-world assets
- Identity
- Memes
- Domain names

To understand their significance, an overview of these different non-fungible tokens or NFT variants is given below.

Collectibles

With the development of Cryptokitties, the leading example of NFTs, the collectibles emerged. As a point of fact, The first occurrence of people using NFTs are crypto kitties. Cryptokitties became popular enough in 2017 to congest the Ethereum network as a matter of interest. One of the conspicuous accompaniments to the non-fungible tokens list in the class of digital collectibles is crypto kitties. They are fundamentally digital kittens with discrete traits that make them prevalent and promising than others.

Artwork

Another projecting contender for NFTs is the artwork. The usual non-fungible tokens in this area mention programmable art, containing an exceptional blend of creativity and technology. As of now, many limited edition artwork pieces are in circulation with the scope for programmability under certain conditions. To create images represented on blockchain networks, oracles and smart contracts could be used by artists, which could help immensely. NFTs have also stimulated participation from the legacy arts industry.

The adoption of NFTs could be encouraged by the tokenization of real-world assets. The exciting prospects for scanning a code or sticker on purchases could be offered by the possibilities of combining blockchain and IoT. The NFT types in artwork could certify that ownership of real-world artwork on a blockchain network could be quickly registered. Successively, the complete history of a painting, such as former ownerships and the prices for which they were sold in the past, could be found by users,

Event Tickets

Event tickets are another promising addition among the types of NFTs. Attending events like music festivals and concerts are allowed to verify their identity and tickets by using such types of NFTs. A specific number of NFT tickets could be mined on a selected blockchain platform by the event managers. Customers could buy the tickets through an auction, and those tickets could be stored in their wallets, easily accessible through mobile devices.

Music and Media

The domain of music and media leads to another category of NFTs due to the experiments they are trying to carry out with NFTs. Music and media files could be linked to NFTs, enabling an individual to access the files with a valid ownership claim. The two noticeable platforms helping artists mint their songs as NFTs include Rarible and Mintbase.

One of the leading reasons for infusing traits of vintage vinyl records is the intellect of uniqueness in purchasing NFT music. The listeners get a quality experience, while the artists benefit from reaching out directly to their followers and new audience. Consistent projections for addressing the concerns of music piracy and intermediaries could be offered by the growth of music NFTs in the non-fungible tokens list.

Gaming

In gaming, the common types of non-fungible tokens are principally fixated on in-game items. Profound levels of interest have been aroused among game developers by NFTs. The functionality of ownership records for in-game items could be offered by NFTs, thus driving the progress of in-game economies. Most importantly, NFTs in the gaming segment also focus on announcing a comprehensive display of benefits for players.

While in-game collectibles were mutual necessities for a better gaming experience, NFTs have the prospective for changing their value Money could be quickly recovered by in-game items as NFTs by selling it outside the game. On the flip side, game developers or the creators allotting NFTs could receive a royalty for every sale of items in the open marketplace.

Real-world Assets

Many NFT types could not be found serving as tokens for real-world items; it could be possible due to the progress in the NFT domain. For instance, many NFT projects are concentrating on the tokenization of real estate alongside luxury goods. NFTs are fundamentally deeds that can familiarize the flexibility for buying a car or home with an NFT deed. Consequently, NFTs demonstrating real-world assets can capitalize on the prospects with cryptographic proof of ownership.

Identity

Non-fungible tokens have a critical trait, and that is a rarity. Every NFT is unique and cannot be substituted with any other token. The working of identity NFTs is similar to that of event tickets NFTs. They can function as unique identifiers, hence aiding as trustworthy sustenance for the identity management systems.

The commonly used applications of identity-based NFTs are unmistakable in certifications and licensing. The identity management sector for proving and verifying records of an individual could be changed by minting certificates and licenses and NFTs. Furthermore, identity-based NFTs could also ensure that individuals could store proof of their identity without risking losing it.

Memes

The most noteworthy development in the domain of NFTs recently is the sale of memes as NFTs. While being a fragment of widespread culture and a favorite among internet users, memes have also been related to NFTs. They are selling the memes as NFTS displays the prospective for unique meme creators to participate in a progressing revolutionary ecosystem.

Domain Names

Domain names are another category of NFTs which have become popular recently. The top examples of domain name NFTs are Decentralized Domain Name Services such as Unstoppable

Domains and the Ethereum Name Service (ENS). ENS aids in translating long and complex user addresses to a flexible and friendly experience for users with easier onboarding.

The prevailing admittances in the non-fungible tokens list portray the NFT ecosystem's potential. Firstly, you can have an original NFT created and stored on the blockchain. It is a new class of digital or tokenized assets; NFTs are altering the predictable concepts of asset usage and ownership. Consequently, you can find the common types of non-fungible tokens concentrating on what you get with an NFT.

The second type of NFTs denotes digital natives in which numerous NFTs serve as parts of ownership rights to specific assets. The third category of NFTs only proposes access to NFT metadata, permitting you to use the NFT rather than distribute ownership. The various kinds of NFTs that are being distributed, such as artwork, music, media, domain names, memes, also demonstrate capable prospects for the future of NFTs.

CAUSES FOR CONCERN

It's not all wine and roses. There are causes to be hesitant, even if you are well-informed and see the potential. Everything has downsides, and NFTs and cryptocurrencies are no exception to this rule. There is a lot of alarmism and exaggeration about the dangers of crypto markets. Most are overblown, but even the overstated ones have their merits. It's necessary to address these because problems aren't solved until they are acknowledged.

Energy And Pollution

Lately, a ton of recent attention has been paid to the amount of energy used to maintain blockchains. Blockchain is very clever and valuable technology, but it is energy inefficient. Whereas two banks can send a tiny bit of data to one another, the blockchain requires a lot of powerful computers using a tremendous amount of power to compete with each other.

If you've read news headlines recently, this issue probably seems noncontroversial. News makes money by eliciting clicks with enticing headlines, and nuanced discussions don't generate the same traffic as doom and gloom stories. That said, the facts of pollution are not a consensus. There is a vigorous debate on this topic, with both sides of the issue making solid points that need to be considered.

Most of this news comes from one source, an academic article in the journal Nature Climate Change. This 2018 article raised alarms that Bitcoin alone could raise the global temperature by 2 degrees Celsius within the next 30 to 60 years, enough to begin raising the ocean to catastrophic levels (Dittmar & Praktiknjo, 2019).

Because the authors are experts on climate science and not computer science, they make some assumptions that aren't reliable. For one, the authors assume that the exponential adoption of crypto will continue indefinitely. That is far from a certainty. Few things grow exponentially forever, unabated. Almost all growth has peaks and valleys and periods of flattening.

The article also makes a significant mistake in saying that the Bitcoin network processes 1 billion processes, which is several times more than what Bitcoin can do. It also assumes that each transaction equals one block. As we consider earlier, a single block contains many trades, as many as 3,000 per block for Bitcoin.

The article claims that a single Bitcoin transaction requires more electricity than 750,000 credit card swipes. That is true, but electronic banking transactions are a lot more than just signals sent by swipes at retailers. Banks and credit card companies have an infrastructure. They have offices; they have company cars, ATMs, customer service systems, and many other things that use energy but aren't factored into the calculations.

The numbers also assume that Bitcoin energy comes exclusively from fossil fuels. Many crypto mining operations use coal as their primary energy source for a considerable amount of their work. Without a doubt, that is troubling and needs to be phased out, but it isn't particular to computing. The point is that the numbers require that ALL energy is spent this way, which isn't true.

Miners are incentivized to reduce the cost of mining by reducing energy. At a certain point, if energy expenses are too high, mining profits are at a net loss, and mining would end. The energy efficiency of mining equipment has been improving, though the paper doesn't address this.

According to Cambridge, their best guess is about 130TWh (CBECI, 2021), the same as the energy spent mining gold every year.

There are also some exciting ideas about making crypto greener. Computer farms of the sort that miners use produce a considerable amount of heat from their electricity. These miners are already developing ways to use that heart as a form of energy.

Renewable energy has a lot of promise, but at this time, they have a technological chokepoint that stops them from becoming the standard. Solar and wind power can pull tremendous amounts of energy if the sun is shining and the wind is blowing, much more than is needed on the electrical grid all at once. It produces nothing when the sun isn't shining, and the wind isn't blowing. At this time, we don't have the technology to store vast amounts of energy. That amount of battery storage necessary isn't feasible yet. During those peak times, that excess energy could be directed specifically to mining, and the crypto produced could be invested back into the energy company towards expanding renewables.

Don't take this to mean that crypto has no impact on the environment. That isn't true at all. There are legitimate concerns about this issue, but it is not likely the climate doomsday scenario that news headlines imply.

Bubbles

Crypto is not regulated like banks are. We are at the later stages of a Wild West crypto economy. The market has a lot of natural volatility and can be manipulated by governments and private citizens with the money to throw their weight around.

Tweets sent by people like Elon Musk can spike or tank the crypto market by enormous margins (Kau, 2021). That can be accidental or deliberate. One way to manipulate the market for profit is for a "whale," a well-financed person or institution, to purchase a lot of cryptos. They need a lot of money to make this happen, but the price will spike if coins are being bought up quickly and in large quantities. It creates a shortage and reinforces people's confidence in the asset's value, and more people want to get in on the action, increasing the weight. The whale's portfolio will go up. When they see it leveling off, the whale can dump their portfolio for a lot of money, which tanks the price. People see it going down, and panic sells. Now that the price is low again, the whale can buy it cheaply. They can repeat this process forever. It would be naive to assume governments aren't participating.

Bubbles are an unavoidable feature of any market, but crypto especially. That is a very new thing, and it is unregulated and still in its infancy. The traditional legacy banking system has put enormous resources into learning how to calculate risk, hedge it, maximize profits, and develop a massive library of financial instruments to maximize profit and keep the market stable enough that they feel secure to operate in it with minimal risk. Crypto is not quite so mature. It is more like a young person kicking in the door and claiming that the older adults don't know what they are speaking about and trying to change everything all at once. The crypto culture is right about many things, and they're also probably wrong about a lot of things. A specific amount of time needs to go by, and learning is necessary before this thing works itself out.

Legal Grey Area

During times of great economic crisis, people are often eager to find alternatives to the financial system in crisis. During the great depression and stock market crash in America in the 1930s, there was a fear that government policies and spending would lead to hyperinflation of the kind experienced in Germany. To protect themselves from poor government monetary policy, people with the means to do so attempted to turn their cash into commodities, particularly gold. Even if the cash value is devalued, the relative price of other assets like land and gold rises by the same amount, protecting the person from having their entire savings withered away by central banks.

The value of any currency is dependent on people's trust and faith in it. Cash is similar to any other asset. It has a supply and demand curve just like anything else. When people lose faith in the solvency and profitability of a corporation, the stock value plummets. When people lose faith in the solvency and future of a country, the value of its money vanishes. If people begin to jettison cash, that country's cash value diminishes.

The United States government was not naive to this fact. In their mind, if no one had a means of exiting the United States dollar, the value of it couldn't be destabilized quite so easily. For that reason, they wanted to get ahead of the curve and decided that they had the right and responsibility to confiscate gold. They also instituted many financial regulations, some sensible, some crazy, to protect the United States dollar.

Make no mistake. If the United States dollar seems threatened by cryptocurrency, governments will intervene and shut it down. That includes NFTs. A problem with regulating digital assets is that the regulators don't know anything about computers. The middle age in the United States is 64 years old (Cillizza, 2021). Almost all of them have backgrounds in the military or law. There are few politicians with a strong experience in technology, except perhaps the 2020 presidential candidate, Andrew Yang, who is not an elected official at the time of this writing.

Without warning or a deep understanding of what is happening, other countries have begun to crack down on digital assets. In a recent case, India has outlawed cryptocurrencies entirely. That is a response to a technology that they fear the consequences and implications of, and they view banning these currencies as getting a head start on it before it gets out of their control. China has simultaneously begun to develop its cryptocurrency, outlaw competing currencies, and invest in current cryptocurrencies that are already popular and proven and in circulation. That is a sign that China has a good sense of the implications of what crypto is and wants to get a lockdown on it and control it.

There's no reason to think that United States governments or any governments in the West will not also begin investigating and regulating these things. On account of the general ignorance of these issues by the governments and by the voters, we can expect that whenever regulation does come our way will be guided by established institutions with deep pockets which have a reason to be concerned about a fledgling upstart that plans on putting them out of business through obsolescence. That is something that everyone needs to consider before going deeply into investment in NFTs or crypto. There's a lot of instability in these markets intrinsically because it is a new technology that people are still figuring out and constantly reinventing. Still, there's an additional layer of flux in the unpredictable reactions from the government. Government tends to operate at two speeds: "Do nothing" and "overreact." If senators aren't placed into a state of panic in a hurry, they usually don't do anything. When they do act, you can expect an overreaction.

Copyright And Illegal Content

Making an NFT doesn't automatically give you a copyright to the art. Likewise, tokenizing Disney's Snow White and the Seven Dwarves into a video NFT doesn't mean you have the right to it, either. There isn't much to stop people from tokenizing material they have no right to and spreading it.

DIGITAL ART AND DIGITAL CREATORS

Paints and brushes are tools that some painters utilize to produce their artwork. However, many others use contemporary creativity methods, such as video technology, television, and computers, to further their interests. Digital art is the term used to describe this kind of artwork.

Digital art is any work created or presented using digital technology, whether or not it was created using digital technology. Image types that fall under this category include pictures made entirely on a computer and hand-drawn drawings scanned into a computer and completed using software such as Adobe Illustrator. It is also possible to create digital art via animation and 3D virtual sculpting representations and projects that use many different technologies. Some digital art is created by manipulating video pictures in some way.

The phrase "digital art" was initially used in the 1980s to refer to a computer painting software developed. To be clear, this was far back when they weren't even called applications! It may potentially be seen in many different ways, including on television and the Internet, on desktops, and various social media platforms, making it a technique of art-making that lends itself to multimedia presentation. In a nutshell, digital art is a kind of fusion of the arts and technologies in specific ways. It opens them to a plethora of new possibilities for artistic expression.

Historical Development

In 1965, artist Frieder Nake used an ER 56 computer (about the size of a standard room in a home) to apply an algorithm to analyze a Paul Klee picture. That is considered to be the "beginning of digital art." The artist produced many versions of "Highroads Byroads," and he called the one that, in his opinion, was the most effective Hommage à Paul Klee. Several artists and computer scientists collaborated over the same period to develop computer-generated artworks, and the emphasis shifted to programming throughout the 1970s, allowing art to be made rather than merely copied or translated. The invention of the stylus enabled artists to use their inherent skills on computers. It distinguished work that was computer-generated from work that was computer-aided in the production of the work. As a generation of artists started to alter video, music, and graphics in the 1980s, digital media saw rapid development. By the early 2000s, the rapid expansion of computer usage has enabled artists to broaden their audience via digital technology.

What Do Digital Artists Do For A Living?

Digital artists have several different professional options from which to select. These jobs include creating visual effects and animated visuals for various media, such as videos and computer games, among others. Digital artists may find employment in multiple industries, including film production, advertising, video game development, and software creation. You will utilize computer software to bring your work to life, whether a painting or a sculpture, in any position involving digital artists. Depending on your profession, they may subsequently be transformed into 3D interactive graphics for websites or visual characters for animation. Specializations include game design, web design, multimedia, and energy, to name a few areas of interest. Whatever field you choose to work in, the ability to think creatively is essential.

How To Become A Digital Artist

Digital artists must have creative ability and a bachelor's degree in visual or commercial art, or a related area, to succeed in their careers. Even though a degree is not required, this is a competitive profession, and it is essential to include formal training in both your CV and your portfolio to stand out. It would be okay if you also maintained up with the latest creative and animation technologies developments. If you cannot transfer your creative abilities from a pen and paper to a drawing tablet, entering the digital art industry may be challenging. The opportunity to do an internship in your chosen profession is a fantastic way to acquire practical experience, develop your abilities, and network with others in the industry.

What Software Does Digital Artists Use?

Digital artists utilize a wide variety of software tools to create their works. These may vary depending on your area of expertise, but the most popular are found inside the Adobe Creative Cloud. You may use Adobe InDesign to plan up print projects such as brochures, ebooks, posters, and magazines, as well as digital projects such as websites. Photoshop is one of the most popular photo-editing applications, and it may be used to enhance the appearance of your artwork. On the other hand, Adobe Illustrator is essential for 2D art. That is the stage at which you sketch and create your designs. If you work in Maya, animation and Harmony, which are not part of the Adobe Creative Cloud, are utilized for 2D and 3D animation. Harmony and Maya are not part of the Adobe Creative Cloud. Similar to how your duties vary with your sector, so does the software you need.

What Is The Distinction Between A Digital Artist And A Graphic Designer?

It is essential to note significant distinctions between digital artists and graphic designers. A digital artist is concerned first and foremost with art. In contrast, a graphic designer is concerned first and foremost with conveying a message, which may include the use of various fonts, graphics, pictures, and sound in certain instances. Design graphic designers work in advertising or companies to develop layouts for advertisements, print projects, newsletters, and social media campaigns while keeping the target audience in mind. Being aware of your target audience impacts your decisions about color, style, and images to utilize in the project.

ARE NFTS A PASSIVE WAY OF INCOME?

NFTs allow us to come up with new financial applications that can then issue tokens that may represent anything from stocks and bonds to cars and real estate. It's all that you can think of.

The basis of the NFT technology is on Ethereum blockchain technology. The Ethereum blockchain is time and again termed as programmable money. Now, what is that? It means that it can let anyone come up with and create their tokens or NFTs using the Ethereum protocol.

Essentially there are two types of NFTs:

- Restricted NFTs

- Unrestricted NFTs

NFTs that allow you to claim ownership in buying and selling the asset is known as unrestricted NFTs.

NFTs that do not support such claims and transferability are termed restricted NFTs.

If you see, you will notice that money cannot be generated from the NFTs in their basic form. What happens is that these NFTs are used to create tokens, and then those tokens are made a part of the decentralized finance landscape.

Nft Vaults & Staking

It needs maintaining funds in a bitcoin wallet to retain the security and functionality of a blockchain network. To earn incentives from securing your assets, the process is known as staking. If you compare mining and staking, you will conclude that staking is a less resource-intensive substitute to mining.

The staking process has been implemented by various cryptocurrencies, including VeChain, Tezos, Decred, Navcoin, among others. Most NFT projects are expected to start staking as revenue of generating passive income from their platform as a result.

NFTs are the only ones that have the staking ability. It has become mandatory to acquire obligatory utility out of the NFT tokens.

NFTs can be stored in storage facilities called vaults. Issuers of vToken offer access to the token holders for their assets that are locked. Vaults are used for this purpose.

If you have an Ethereum address, you will generate a vault for any of your NFT assets. Everybody has the right to credit the eligible NFTs into the vault to create a fungible NFT-backed cryptocurrency called a "vToken."

vTokens make use of NFTs as a security to be held in escrow during a secure, peer-to-peer lending system. Decentralized exchanges assist this lending system. In a nutshell, one party leaves an asset locked up as security, and the other receives a loan from that asset at a cheap interest rate.

The person who creates the vTokens can specify the number of primary assets in a vault. He will also be able to plan the mechanism for pricing. It should be linked directly to the price of the primary asset or basket of assets. The vToken protocol has been executed on Ethereum.

A vToken allows you to generate income from any primary asset. It is a financial instrument that can generate revenue from the investment it represents. This revenue generated may be due to interest, dividends, or coupons.

If you are trying to create decentralized applications, you have to keep in mind that vTokens are crucial. VTokens allows the users to make protocol fees, trade fees as a liquidity provider, and farm as loan collateral. These can compete with the rivals with centralized counterparts in speed, efficiency, and scalability.

Protocols Designed For Passive Income

A new standard for transferring and settlement of tokens has been established. That is because the skating protocols allow better distribution and increased transparency in the delivery. The reach of those platforms will increase multiple folds that use these distribution protocols that may result from adoption.

New content may be rapidly used to generate liquid markets for virtual assets, which will get the most out of their utility.

Several skating protocols may be of use if you consider the gains of decentralization of finance.

Lending protocols provide permissions for forming financial assets that can be used as security on a decentralized lending platform.

The Peer-to-Peer lending market has great potential, but unfortunately, it is pretty under-serviced. The conditions required to progress the lending into blockchain will come from the introduction of next-generation credit scoring and asset tokenization.

Lending backed by assets could provide the borrowers with significant liquidity, low margin rates, fast compensation timeframes, and efficient risk management protocols.

An alternative class of asset tokenization that can signify the payment means and store the value for fiat currency on the Ethereum main net is collateralized stable coins.

In general, NFTs are comparatively illiquid and hard to price. Taking chances in the NFT market is more accessible due to the skating protocols. Another gain it provides to these platforms is to sell their NFTs faster. That also helps in providing the customers with an enhanced user experience.

Transaction costs are highly reduced and allow for near-instant transaction speeds.

If you consider the flexibility of the NFTs, you will notice that they are a flexible class of digital assets. It has numerous applications in art, gaming, finance, and more. Decentralized applications will be controlling their governance protocols, which will be made possible by this technology. Also, it will not be cutting down on its transparency and decentralization. A good way of passively generating revenue from digital properties is to monetize NFTs.

The collateralized stablecoins operated on the Ethereum mainnet are tremendously helpful by the businesses. Stablecoin that is used as collateral can help protect businesses from high fluctuations in the price and increase their ability to transact with customers in a quicker and well-organized way.

To create a standard of the next-gen decentralized finance applications or the DeFi, the next-gen protocols need to set the tokenization of assets as their primary objective.

FUNDAMENTAL ANALYSIS FOR NFT INVESTING

NFTs have progressed from specialist blockchain communities to everyday commercial sectors. The future potential of NFTs is far beyond imagination at this point.

The advances in blockchain technology have resulted in a revolution in the economic environment. In many ways, the arrival of cryptocurrencies such as Bitcoin, Ethereum, and Tether has disrupted the established financial industry.

Alternative assets, such as artworks or collections, are often sold through dealers or traditional auction platforms. Alternative asset classes in NFT markets, on the other hand, differ from existing markets in many ways. NFT markets are peer-to-peer auction markets driven by blockchain technology (e.g., OpenSea or Rarible).

There are no central bodies or trade intermediaries in NFT markets, allowing NFT owners or collectors to interact directly with their counterparts. Both parties can trade at an agreed price at any time if they have an Ethereum wallet (e.g., MetaMask), expanding public access to NFTs and lowering deadweight loss in illiquid asset markets.

Nft Marketplace

The use of NFTs in collectibles has brought NFTs to the forefront of the media. The market capitalization of the top 100 significant NFTs collections is roughly $14,492,390 as of this writing in July 2021. CryptoPunk and Crypto-Kitties created history in NFT technology in 2017 — the former because some of them were sold for millions of dollars, and the latter because the enormous volume of transactions initiated by their exchange rendered the Ethereum network useless for a few days. The HashMasks, Meebits, and Bored Ape Yacht Clubs are some of the most recent NFT collections from 202. They're all made up of a small number of assets with varying rarities.

Each collection is backed by a solid and cohesive community that communicates through social media channels like Twitter and Discord. Property is another potential application for NFTs. This notion has yet to be fully realized in the real world, but it has proven to be quite successful in the metaverse, where video game players may buy and sell collectible virtual universes. Even if NFTs can become a powerful example of digital personal property recognized by a decentralized body in the following years, the technology is still in its early stages.

Due to the lack of systematic summaries and the number of hype cycles, newcomers may become lost in its frantic evolution. Furthermore, logical analogies between NFT transaction networks and graphs characterize social media user interactions. It can disguise the characteristics of an engaging environment in which objects can be traded for extremely high prices, perhaps hundreds or thousands of ETH.

NFTs, like any other financial asset, can theoretically be traded on blockchain-based platforms. Although NFT marketplaces do not provide a low- or high-price estimate, anybody can evaluation historical transactions for a certain NFT, including bids, offers, sales prices, trading dates, ownership changes, and even information on the parties involved. With such trackable records, determining whether an NFT is a duplicate or an original work with such trackable records. These capabilities also allow us to investigate NFTs at the transaction level.

Transformation Of Assets

According to specific estimates, most investable assets available in private and public markets are non-fungible. For example, the estimated value of real estate, which is non-fungible, vastly outnumbers the capitalizations of both the global bond and equities markets. Perhaps more importantly, derivatives, the world's largest asset class with a notional value of $580 trillion, are also non-fungible. They can't be moved between multiple exchanges or trading platforms. Art and collectibles are non-fungible items, albeit with a far lesser value (about $2 trillion).

Because of the preceding discussion and current technological advancements, all non-fungible assets can be represented as NFTs. For a range of reasons, it is crucial to investigate this option. NFTs, for starters, boost market liquidity and price discovery. Trading assets are more efficient if ownership can be instantly proved and transferred swiftly and securely for a low charge. As a result, NFTs improve asset openness, transparency, and financial globalization. It results in increased trading volumes and market expansion on its own.

Second, NFTs do away with the functions of delayed clearing and settlement. Settlement times are currently measured in days. NFTs reduce the time it takes to decide a dispute from days to seconds. Furthermore, physical clearing is still used by some market participants. NFTs, on the other hand, rely on fraud-proof blockchains, which allow information to be validated and recorded in real-time. Third, collateral management necessitates openness, which can be severely harmed in the current financial system, as in the recent instance of Archegos9. Again, the NFT presents a clear-cut solution, removing any potential for market players to hide self-serving behavior.

Nft Liquidity Mining And Farming

NFT liquidity mining and NFT farming are two very similar concepts. NFT liquidity mining is an investing activity that entails locking an NFT in a smart contract with two primary goals, depending on the market side:

- Making NFT deposits (providing liquidity) on the NFT platform, and

- Making a return for the NFT investor who made the NFT deposit.

NFT liquidity mining, like a simple buy-and-hold method, entails making or purchasing an NFT and transferring it to a smart contract (akin to gambling activity in the PoS blockchain). Investors receive interest in exchange for providing NFT liquidity. Interest is usually paid in the network's native currency, dependent on NFT liquidity mining for survival. It's worth noting that if NFTs are fractionalized and hence directly interchangeable, mining algorithms could potentially acquire more liquidity.

Dego Finance (DEGO), for example, is an NFT-related project that focuses on NFT mining, auctioning, trading, farming, and other NFT-related applications10. Dego compensates NFT holders for converting their NFTs into the native Dego token, including voting and dividend rights. The mining efficiency and power value assigned to each NFT11 affect the staking yield. NFT farming, on the other hand, entails staking a blockchain native token in exchange for a native NFT, which can subsequently be stored, sold, or used as collateral. On some of the NFT-dedicated blockchains, NFT farming is now active (e.g., Ethernity, SuperFarm). The sealed native token can be un-farmed at any moment.

Nft Fractionalization

Unlike accredited investors and investment funds, retail clients have restricted capital access, limiting their investing options. Due to their excessive price levels, several asset classes, on the other hand, have insufficient liquidity and unbalanced markets. The preceding issues are addressed by blockchain technology, which allows for asset fractionalization or the division of an enormous asset into smaller pieces. This notion has been considered in the literature in artwork and is known as securitization.

Investors can buy a portion of the NFT through fractionalization. As a result, it is an opportunity to gain exposure to premium and well-known NFT at high absolute prices. For example, an NFT by modern artist Mike Winkelmann (aka Beeple) sold for 69($mil) at Christie's recently — an auction price beyond reaches for retail investors, admirers, and tiny collectors. Fractionalization also ensures a higher degree of variety. As a result, a piece of NFT can boost portfolio efficiency, or alpha, for a given level of threat.

Art creation can be called NFT, but once it has been divided into several parts, each of these parts may be represented by a fungible token, a token that can be used interchangeably with other parts of the same NFT. An NFT, on the other hand, can be fractionalized into several NFTs with different distinguishing properties and hence valuations while being non-fungible. A collector might be wanting to pay more for a shard of Mona Lisa's lips than for a fragment of the same painting's backdrop landscape. In any event, several different collectors can now own identical pieces of art, which has never happened before in history.

A further endowment of fractional NFT is possible. Owners of fractional NFTs could pool their assets to form a decentralized autonomous organization (DAO) and issue shares backed by that endowment. The example demonstrates that tokenizing unique assets open up a world of possibilities.

Nft Minting, Trading, And Auctioning

Artwork and in-game items are currently the most common use cases for NFT. It seems to be the case because NFT architecture eliminates the middleman between the artist and the audience, improving product reach, profit margins, and sales potential. It is commonly known that gatekeepers still exist in the art industry, limiting producers' access to the market. Exclusive locations, privileged organizations, and rent-collecting intermediaries are among them. The NFTs make it possible to bypass the art world's usual gatekeepers.

Notably, producers can use current online marketplaces (e.g., OpenSea, Rarible) or decentralized applications that directly connect them to the appropriate network to generate (mint) the NFT of their art piece or complete art collection on the blockchain. To mint, an NFT, a technique that reduces entrance barriers to the primary and secondary art markets, one does not need to be an expert. Further, it appears that minting an NFT is synonymous with marketing an NFT, whether at a fixed price or through various auction procedures.

A related problem is the rights sold in conjunction with the NFT. Existing standards are still adaptable. The present owner of the most expensive NFT to date, Beeple's "Everyday: The First 500 Days," which sold 69.3 million dollars, acquired the license to exhibit the NFT but not the copyrights. On the other hand, proprietors of the Hashmasks NFTs (16,384) get limitless rights to use, copy, and display the NFT. Surprisingly, the NFT of the tungsten cube sold on OpenSea only allows its owner "one visit to see/photograph/touch the cube each calendar year."

One may undertake systematic analysis and construct metrics that help determine how the wallets participating in this ecosystem interact by filtering publicly available information on the blockchain and organizing it in a graph model.

NFT AND BLOCKCHAIN

6 Key Properties

Blockchain-based NFTs allow users to own digital assets. However, this ownership of digital assets is different than physical ownership because these types of assets only exist within specific, purpose-built contexts, such as marketplaces, games, and whatnot, making them more challenging to move, at least for now. When blockchain technology comes into play, it can provide a layer of coordination for digital assets, granting users' ownership and permission to manage them and changing developers' relationships with their investments. All of this is possible thanks to 6 fundamental properties that set the rules for NFTs and represent the characteristics that make them unique.

Standardization

Standards serve to create a uniform set of rules that allow NFTs to integrate across platforms, be interoperable, and increase their utility value by extending their applicability.

As with all technologies, standards represent repeatable and shared ways of operating within a context. Standards arise from saving time and resources by eliminating unnecessary processes and are universally recognized within the community. A reference standard is always necessary to ensure that everyone operates compliantly.

When tokenization of a digital asset occurs within the blockchain, these tokens are enrolled through common, reusable, and inheritable standards. In other words, these are methods agreed upon and developed by developers that allow NFTs to operate in different ways. Each digital asset is represented differently—e.g., a game may represent its collection in an entirely different way than an event ticket. NFTs are based on a joint, public system whose standards include basic features such as ownership, transfer, and access control. That means that several purchased NFTs can interoperate within the same application if they are based on the same standard. Programmers can then create applications that use the same code to have all tokens within a decentralized platform, such as Ethereum's network. The three primary NFT tokenization standards on the Ethereum blockchain are:

- ERC721

- ERC998

- ERC1155

The acronym ERC stands for Ethereum Request for Comments. Anyone can create standards, but it is up to the author to explain them and promote support within the community. ERC was designed to provide information or introduce new features to the Ethereum network, so ERC is how programmers propose changes. Since Ethereum is based on blockchain technology, no one person can take over and make changes or adjustments to the protocols.

The numbers 721, 998, and 1155 represent the codes for those proposals. ERC721 in 2018 by Cryptokitties, where each cat to be adopted, nurtured, and raised was represented by an NFT. Before this standard, people could create fungible tokens such as Ether, but with ERC721, programmers can develop tokens with different properties, characteristics, and types, all from the same smart contract. ERC721 is the NFT standard that allows NFTs to be created and exchanged. While it is the most popular cross-platform, easy to integrate, and available NFT standard, it also has several inefficiencies depending on the use case.

ERC998 has a unique operation and was created to allow multiple ERC721 NFTs to be transferred within the network in a single bundle transaction instead of making several. With this standard, not only do you own an NFT but that NFT can also include your own NFTs, as in a sort of bundle. If an NFT is sold, all the tokens attached are sold. Thus, transferring the composition of the NFT means moving the entire hierarchy of associated elements. For example, a crypto kitty may own a scratching post and an eating dish that may contain fungible tokens, and in selling the crypto kitty, all of the items associated with it are also sold.

The ERC1155 token is a type of standard token that can store, within its authority, tokens that can act as if they were an ERC20 or ERC721 token, or both at the same time under the same address.

ERC1155 was created by Enjin, an Ethereum platform that allows non-fungible tokens and fungible tokens to be completed in the same contract. The standardization of NFT issuance makes possible a higher degree of interoperability, which benefits users. It means that unique assets can be transferred between different applications with relative ease.

The best example of ERC1155 can be found in blockchain games. Instead of requiring a new contract for each game item, multiple items can be created using the same agreement. Also, if, for example, both weapons and crypto coins are collectible in the game, you can write both with ERC1155, drastically reducing the resources needed to run blockchain-based games efficiently.

Interoperability

As we've already mentioned, all NFTs use the same standards to be on the same level and operate on the same Ethereum platform. That enables the transfer of NFTs across multiple ecosystems, immediately visible and tradable. Thus, based on the exact usage characteristics—

i.e., through standardization— interoperability allows NFTs to be freely tradable on open marketplaces.

Tradeability

That is the first time users worldwide can create NFTs that can be immediately available in marketplaces across the ecosystem. Here, people can buy, trade, sell, and auction NFTs. The extent of this property lies in the move from sales within closed marketplaces to the possibilities offered by a marketplace that has an open and accessible economy. The ease with which any user can create and trade NFTs worldwide through the blockchain is fantastic.

Liquidity

The speed and efficiency of blockchain-based marketplaces lead to a high level of liquidity, which describes how many people are making trades within the market and how often. This term is used to describe a group of activities within a market. High liquidity means that items are sold quickly and frequently. A marketplace based on blockchain technology allows for just such efficiency and speed in buying and exchanging, as is the case with bitcoins, which can, for example, be traded for real or fiat currency easily on Coinbase or Binance.

As with any other investment, anyone must sell and buy tokens quickly without lowering the price. To make this possible, the market you act in must be liquid. In other words, there must be a high level of trading activity, and the bid and ask prices must not be too far apart.

The NFT market must have high volume and good liquidity, especially for investors who buy NFTs, knowing that they have a large community of people to whom they can then sell them. For this cause, it is essential to keep an eye on the significant NFT projects to invest in. To understand if a market is liquid or illiquid, the best way is to look at three indicators: trading volume in a day, the depth of the order book, and the amount that separates the bid and ask price, which is known as the bid/ask spread.

With NFTs, it is also possible to develop real-world asset tokenization. These NFTs could represent fractions of physical assets stored and traded as tokens on a blockchain. That could introduce much-needed new liquidity into many markets that wouldn't otherwise have much, such as artwork, real estate, rare collectibles, and more.

Immutability and provable scarcity

Immutability, as the name implies, is the ability of a blockchain to remain unchanged so that it remains unaltered and indelible. To put it more simply, the data within the blockchain, as formerly mentioned, cannot be changed. In its technical nature, blockchain is configured as an immutable database, and it is not possible to manipulate the data already in the blockchain.

Each block consists of information, such as the transaction details, and uses a cryptographic principle called a hash value. That hash matter consists of an alphanumeric string developed by each block separately. Each block contains a hash referring to itself and incorporates the former one. That ensures that the blocks are paired retroactively. That is how this feature of blockchain technology ensures that no one can intrude into the system or alter the data stored in the league.

The most popular hash function is SHA256, or Secure Hash Algorithm 256. The hash value protects each block of code separately. The process of hashing generates a string of 64 characters. However, of the input size, the fixed length of the series, known as a digital signature, is always the same. That refers to the exact data entered, and the fundamental property of this hash value is that it cannot be decoded. The word immutable relates to something that can never be changed. Immutability is the key that imprints authenticity in digital assets and introduces scarcity. Immutability means that what belongs to a particular person in a game, for example, cannot be moved or changed.

Programmability

NFTs are fully programmable. They can, for example, be programmed to respond to triggers or actions taken by the owner. They can also react to external stimuli such as time or score. The programming possibilities of NFTs are endless.

TOOLS TO FIND UPCOMING PROJECTS FOR DIFFERENT BLOCKCHAINS

Platforms for NFT evaluation and Rarity can help you stay ahead of the game regarding NFT investing.

These are the shovels that will be used to locate the NFT gold nuggets. They will aid in the hunt for NFT rarities, the discovery of new NFT projects, the tracking of whale wallets, the making of wiser investment judgments and will undoubtedly be a part of your due diligence toolset.

Getting the appropriate information is crucial to the success of any crypto movement, as it is with any other. If you're a novice or a seasoned NFT collector, you'll need analytical tools to assist you in assessing the Rarity and availability of assets. Aren't you hoping to locate the next Bored Ape?

Fortunately, a few platforms have developed technologies that will undoubtedly assist you. While some are free to use, others require a subscription to access additional services. Here's a look at some of the best NFT analytical tools to help you along your way.

If you're a severe NFT investor, collector, or trader, you've probably used one, if not several, of the online NFT data analysis tools.

Rarity.tools

Rarity. When buying a non-fungible token, Rarity is one of the most important factors to consider. The best NFTs are extremely rare and highly sought after by collectors, which drives their price. Tools are an excellent NFT rarity tool for examining the NFT space.

Rarity. Tools is another website that collects real-time data on all NFT arts and collectibles—it's a popular choice among art collectors and artists (and one of mine), especially in the fertile art area.

Rarity collects and ranks NFT arts in order of Rarity, with a preference for new efforts. Unlike other tools structured primarily as charts and lists, the platform is developed with the aesthetics of an art-featured market in mind, and it has a charming appeal on the landing page.

Tools have a unique feature in that new projects can be listed in a few simple steps for 2ETH. The NFT collection list is also filtered on the free version by its unique traits, market volume, and sale prices. Users can click on any NFT to access additional information and pricing charts for Rarity's currency.

Rarity. Tools are also excellent for keeping track of upcoming NFT projects, allowing users to see them before going on public sale or mint.

On Rarity. tools, you may sort NFTs by their volume in ETH, average price, and market collections.

Each collection has its page, which lists all of the NFTs in that collection. Each item has its detailed card, on which you can view the asset's distinct characteristics. Rarity offers the added benefit of assigning a rarity score to each NFT.

The site charges a listing fee to creators. As a result, it's possible that it won't include all NFTs, as some may be unable or unable to pay the platform's cost.

Nft Calendar

NFTCalendar is the industry's first release and event calendar for Non-Fungible Tokens. It covers the most exciting events and NFT drops on various marketplaces and platforms.

NFT calendar is more than simply a calendar that copies information and data from the internet; it is a well-known platform that serves as an NFT calendar. It will be a complete marketplace containing information about NFT releases and reliable sites where traders may buy NFTs.

Whether you like to buy or sell NFTs, it will supply you with the necessary information. If you're looking to invest in new NFTs on any Blockchain, keep an eye on the NFT calendar for the most up-to-date information and details.

NFTCalendar is your companion in the world of Non-Fungible Tokens. It highlights crypto art and creators and reports on the latest news and events in Decentraland.

The purpose of the NFT calendar is to make the digital collectibles universe understandable and reachable to every NFT collector and movement follower. It lists all impending NFT (Non-Fungible Token) Drops and Auctions, ensuring that you do not miss out on anything significant.

Ethereum, Solana, Polygon, Cardano, Binance Smart Chain, WAX, FLOW, Cronos, Theta, Moonriver, Harmony, and EOSIO are among the blockchains on the NFT calendar.

Artists can include licenses when minting NFTs via secure channels provided by NFT marketplaces. The NFT calendar merely provides a medium for artists and collectors to communicate what they're selling and what they're going into.

Nft Scoring

All NFT initiatives are tracked and analyzed by NFT Scoring. It is a market research tool that aids in discovering exciting new projects.

NFT Scoring compiles all pertinent information regarding past and current NFT projects to assist you in identifying those with the most potential.

It keeps track of community size, growth, and engagement across all major platforms and provides a unique AI-driven rating system based on the most successful NFT initiatives. NFTScoring keeps track of social media and Discord activity to offer you a score for the best NFTs.

Twitter

The social media behemoth also changes the design of NFT profile photos, making illegitimate NFTs stand out if used as a profile image.

Tess Rinearson has been named as Twitter's new Crypto Engineering head, leading a new team focused on crypto, blockchains, and other decentralized technologies, including but not limited to cryptocurrency.

Twitter has unveiled a new crypto initiative that will allow NFT enthusiasts and creators to show off their ownership of the high-value virtual products as part of broader changes to the service that panders to the interests of its super-users. In keeping with its focus on crypto-communities, Twitter also announced that it would begin transacting in Bitcoin, allowing the service's top accounts to accept Bitcoin tips as part of a monetization initiative that started in 2021.

Icy.tools

Icy. Tools contain a plethora of knowledge that will put you ahead of the competition regarding NFT flipping. Icy allows you to spot trends early, such as the most popular NFTs in the last hour, the most famous NFT collections in the last hour, 6 hours, one day, and more. Based on the existing floor pricing, Icy also estimates the estimated value of all your NFTs in ETH.

Beginners love it because of its simple, transparent interface, ideal for a quick market survey. It offers a list of trending sales and projects, for example, ranked by volume and sale price.

The "Trending Collections" from the former day are the first thing you see on icy. Tools: If you have a wallet linked, you can narrow the ranking to the last three days or the last 15 or 30 minutes.

Each of the mentioned collections' floor price, average price, volume, and sales are displayed on the leaderboard.

The interface is simple, making NFT analysis simple even for inexperienced investors.

The top mints from the former day to the latest 15 minutes can be found on the "Discover" page. The wallet addresses of the top purchasers and sellers are also available.

The bonus version, on the other hand, has more features. Users can take advantage of transaction history on collections and balance searches on any wallet address. Users that want extensive research, available wallet tracking, in-depth market charts, and customized alerts should pay 0.03 ETH per month for the premium version.

Premium customers can also view the detailed pages for each NFT collection, including pricing charts and historical data for each NFT. Furthermore, premium accounts have access to each wallet address displayed under buyer and seller's trade history.

OpenSea

One of the most well-known platforms, OpenSea is home to coveted collections. This NFT platform can also function as an NFT tool for monitoring your future digital art investment, in addition to the remarkable digital art collection.

As a collector, you'll like OpenSea's comprehensive ecology, including the NFT shop and data. Having all the knowledge in one place makes deciding on the best NFT to purchase much more effortless.

OpenSea is the world's largest NFT marketplace, making it simple to track all activity and data for any NFT listed on the site.

Rankings and activity may be found under Stats on the main menu and provide real-time data about NFTs. The activity feed is convenient because it allows for a real-time feed of all activity on the OpenSea market.

OpenSea helps NFTs based on the Ethereum, Polygon, and Klaytn blockchains. Another benefit is that you can track NFTs on all three chains from a single platform. NFT can be filtered by nine different categories, including art, music, sports, and trading cards, in addition to blockchain.

Nansen

Many investors have long desired to identify opportunities in the NFT industry, and Nansen.ai was one of the first NFT platforms to do so.

This NFT analysis platform displays a leaderboard of NFT wallets ranked by total earnings. The analysis' findings can assist you in managing your assets and developing a strategy.

Nansen's analysis tool gives thorough information for each wallet on the leaderboard, including minting fees, secondary market fees, and all ERC-20 token details.

Nansen displays the leaderboard for each project, making it simple to identify and analyze owners. Furthermore, with this NFT application, you can track these wallets and their investments over time.

Nansen.ai is a must-have tool for anticipating trends and looking through the wallets of seasoned NFT collectors and traders with deep pockets, which are labeled. Nansen discusses the activities of over 90 million identified Ethereum wallets. So, you can tell the difference between the signal and the noise in blockchain data.

Nft Bank

NFTBank, a vital NFT instrument that can deliver rapid insights on investments, would delight NFT investors. The data presented include, among other things, ROI, activity, and spending. NFT Bank is one of the most excellent NFT portfolio management solutions available.

According to the company, investors that utilize NFTBank's platform uncover NFT investment opportunities ten times faster than others. Indeed, the user interface is simple and offers information that anyone can understand.

Users can track their portfolios and create a uniform profile that supports all NFT projects and blockchains using NFTBank.

Users can utilize the "Analytics and Signals" feature to locate new NFT investment opportunities because it gives indications to assist them in understanding the market and tracking other users' portfolios.

Nft Stats

NFT Stats is another simple-to-use and informative NFT utility. This NFT platform provides fundamental NFT collection insights. Trending collections, new collections, and the top collections in the last 30 days are all included in the NFT rankings.

The number of sales and total volume are used to rank the collections.

This NFT platform provides a quick snapshot of the most popular NFT collections sold in the former 24 hours, seven days, and 30 days. The NFT and the group it belongs to and when and how much it was sold for are all included in the data.

Each collection page includes information on recently sold NFTs as well as three-month pricing trends.

CryptoSlam

CryptoSlam is another excellent NFT tool for market analysis. Users can search for NFT collections based on a trading volume using this simple but powerful interface. Each NFT group has its complete website with live sales, marketplace, and minting information. You'll find a separate page for each NFT with all the information you'll need, including pricing, unique qualities, and rarity rankings.

Anyone may quickly locate and discover NFTs thanks to this all-time rating for all NFT collections.

NFT AS COLLECTIBLES AND DIGITAL ASSETS

What is an NFT, and why is it becoming such a big issue in the press these days? Cryptographic tokens, known as non-fungible tokens (also known as non-fungible tokens), enable someone to verify that an online asset is a genuine article. 2020 was a banner year for the cryptocurrency industry. The subject of decentralized finance has only gained prominence, with companies such as Tesla investing significant sums of money in cryptocurrencies and Bitcoin hitting all-time highs, among other things. Since the end of 2020, there has been a continuous increase in the popularity and usage of NFTs, which have sold for millions of dollars in some instances.

Cryptocurrencies such as Bitcoin are referred to be 'fungible' tokens since they are interchangeable and do not have a unique serial number. Therefore, if you were to trade one Bitcoin for another, you would be receiving the identical item. Each coin is similar to the others in terms of design. Non-fungible tokens, on the other hand, indicate something that is one-of-a-kind and cannot be replaced. An NFT may be stamped onto, for example, an original GIF or picture as evidence that the item being traded or sold is the genuine one. That is similar to trading or selling an original artwork that has been authenticated. Another way of putting it is that an NFT is a cryptographic token that enables someone to verify that an online asset is genuine. Because of this, resources are scarce, which in principle leads to the creation of value, even in the digital realm, where assets are not physically present.

You Are Maintaining The Security Of Your Nfts.

Given the potential worth of NFTs, it is only reasonable to consider the issue of protecting these digital assets from being compromised. Are they completely safe to use? In general, purchasing and holding non-fiat currencies (NFTs) is just as safe as buying and holding bitcoin. However, even though the technology that underpins NFTs is considered secure, there are certain precautions you should take to guarantee the safety of your investment. Here are some suggestions for keeping NFTs safe:

Select a safe and secure wallet. NFTs, like cryptocurrencies, is saved and utilized via a cryptocurrency wallet. The wallet you choose is critical since specific wallets are more trustworthy and safe than others. For example, a wallet that keeps your private key exclusively on your device needs strong passwords, supports two-factor authentication, encrypts your data, and requires you to set up a recovery passphrase are all desirable features. Hacken, a cybersecurity firm specializing in blockchain technology, conducted a case study examining nine non-custodial wallets. Based on different factors, including whether or not each wallet published its third-party audit results, whether or not each wallet requires strong passwords, and whether or not each wallet has a history of security breaches, they determined that Metamask and Enjin are the safest wallets available. For a more detailed description of the technique utilized and a list of wallets, please visit this page.

Make your password difficult to guess. You've probably noticed that you're using the same password for many different accounts. Please, don't do that! A long, one-of-a-kind, and complex password is required for your wallet. Pro tip: This recommendation should be followed for every account you have.

Enable two-factor authentication on your computer. Two-factor authentication, just like it does with your bitcoin wallet, is very beneficial. Due to the need for authentication before performing operations, the likelihood of an NFT being stolen or mistakenly given to someone decreases significantly.

Please make a note of your recovery phrase and keep it somewhere safe. If you forget your password, your passphrase will serve as a final option for regaining access to your account. If you are using a mnemonic phrase, be sure that your passphrase is not readily guessable and kept in a safe place. You will very certainly be unable to restore your account if you forget your recovery phrase.

Make frequent backups of your wallet. It is a good idea to keep many backups of your data. In the case of a system malfunction or the loss of a device, you can be sure that you will be capable of restoring your data.

Make sure to keep your software up to date. Security patches are included in software upgrades.

Make use of a protected internet connection. An attacker will have an easier time stealing your information if you use a public wifi network. If you must use public wifi, use a virtual private network (VPN) to protect your connection and turn off the Bluetooth connection on your device.

In addition to these measures, it is essential to be aware of your legal rights about your NFTs. Although NFTs demonstrate that a particular piece of data is one-of-a-kind, they do not prohibit someone from tokenizing anything that is not their own. Fortunately, there are legal safeguards in place that you may take advantage of. For example, NFTs may be subject to standard copyright legislation. Using the Digital Millennium Copyright Act (DCMA)*, you might, for example, submit a takedown request against the platform selling and the producers of these NFTs if you think your digital work is being stolen.

CoinDesk also advises that you specify what you offer to customers in your listing description. For example, what do you own if you hold the rights to a work you're selling? Do you own the underlying art (for example, an original GIF) or simply the digital representation of the work? Or, to put it another way, be precise on the front end by designing your smart contract to describe the rights that are being transferred when feasible or suitable.

WHAT GIVES THEM THEIR VALUE?

NFTs are created and issued using a variety of frameworks. ERC-721, a standard for printing and exchanging non-fungible assets on the Ethereum blockchain, is the most well-known of these frameworks. NFTs are built on Ethereum's permanent blockchain, suggesting they can't be changed. They're also "permissionless," which indicates that anyone can make, purchase, or sell an NFT without asking permission. Eventually, each NFT is one-of-a-kind and can be utilized by everyone. No one may take away the custody of an NFT or duplicate it.

Yes, it's like a one-of-a-kind collectible card shown in an always-open store window that everyone can value. Yet, only one individual (or cryptocurrency wallet, to be precise) may possess at any given time. A virtual artwork, such as a picture, will be used as a case in this book. In the NFTs platform, It's important to note, however, that it's not just about that picture (which can easily be replicated). The fact that it exists as a digital entity on the blockchain distinguishes it.

ERC-1155 is the latest and enhanced standard. It allows a specific contract to include both fungible and non-fungible tokens, which opens up a world of possibilities. The standardization of NFT issuance allows for greater interoperability that favors users in the long run. It essentially implies that specific assets can be easily shared among various applications. More will be explained on NFTs standardization later on in the book.

If you want to store and admire the elegance of your NFTs, Trust Wallet is the place to go. Your NFT will have an address, just like other blockchain tokens. It's worth remembering that NFTs can't be duplicated or exchanged without the owner's consent, including the NFT issuer. NFTs can be traded on open exchanges like OpenSea. These marketplaces bring buyers and sellers together, and each token has its meaning. NFTs, by their very nature, are subject to price fluctuations in response to market supply and demand.

But how can such items be considered valuable? Like any other useful item, the value of a functional object is assigned by people who think it is practical. Esteem is, at its heart, a common belief. You can do this in Trust Wallet with your NFTs. Your NFT will have an address, just like other blockchain tokens. It's worth remembering that NFTs can't be duplicated or exchanged without the owner's permission, including the NFT issuer.

NFTs can be exchanged on open exchanges like OpenSea. These marketplaces bring buyers and sellers together, and each token has its meaning. NFTs, by their very nature, are subject to price fluctuations concerning marketplace supply and demand. But how can such items be considered valuable? The value of a valuable commodity, similar to any other useful thing, is given by individuals who know it is functional. Value is, in essence, a common belief. It makes no difference if it's fiat currency, rare stones, or a car; they all have value, and people believe they do. Why not digital collectibles? This is how any valuable object becomes precious.

Characteristics Of Nfts:

Non-interoperable

CryptoPunks cannot be used as symbols in the CryptoKitties game, and vice versa. That also applies to collectibles like trading cards; a Blockchain Hero card will not work in the God's Unchained trading card game.

Indivisible

NFTs are inseparable, unlike bitcoin satoshis, and cannot be divided into smaller fractions. They only exist as a complete unit.

Indestructible

Each token cannot be lost, deleted, or reproduced since all NFT data is preserved on the blockchain through blockchain technology. The possession of these tokens is also unchangeable, implying that gamers and holders own their NFTs rather than the companies that make them. Regarding purchasing music from the iTunes store, consumers do not necessarily own the piece they are buying; instead, they are buying permission to listen to it.

Verifiable

Another advantage of storing past ownership data on the blockchain is that objects like digital art can be drafted back to the original maker, eliminating the need for third-party authentication.

Nfts Scarcity

The maker of an NFT is in charge of determining the asset's scarcity. Consider purchasing a ticket to a football match. The maker of an NFT may choose how many replicas there are, just like an event manager can decide the number of tickets to sell. 5000 General Admission tickets, for example, are often exact replicas. A ticket with an assigned seat, for example, can be issued in multiples that are very identical yet differs slightly. In another scenario, the creator may desire to make a one-of-a-kind NFT as a unique collectible.

Each NFT will also have a specific identifier (like a bar code on a standard "ticket") and only one holder in these scenarios. The NFTs' planned scarcity is essential, and it is up to the maker to decide. A maker may wish to make each NFT fully special to generate a lack or have good reason to make thousands of copies. Keep in mind that all of this material is available to the general public.

Nfts And Ethereum

Ethereum allows NFTs to work For a variety of purposes:

- It's easy to show ownership history because transaction records and token metadata are publicly verifiable.

- It's almost impossible to "steal" possession of a transaction after it's been verified.

- Trading NFTs can be done peer-to-peer without the need for sites that are willing to accept big commissions.

To put it another way, all Ethereum products can communicate with one another, making NFTs accessible through products. · The "backend" of all Ethereum items is the same. You can purchase an NFT on one asset and sell it on another. You can display your NFTs on several assets at once as a maker, and each asset will have the most recent ownership details.

- Since Ethereum is never down, your tokens will still be available to sell.

Fractional Ownership

Creators of NFTs may also create "shares" for their assets. That allows traders and fans to own a piece of an NFT without purchasing the entire investment. That expands the number of opportunities available to NFT minters and collectors. Fractionalized NFTs can be exchanged in NFT markets and even on DEXs such as Uniswap. That ensures there will be more buyers and sellers.

The price of an NFT's fractions may be used to determine its total cost. You have a more reasonable chance of owning and profiting from the things you care about. It's more challenging to be priced out of buying NFTs these days. You can learn more about Fractional NFT ownership om NIFTEX, NFTX.

It's possible that having a fraction of an NFT would entitle you to participate in a decentralized autonomous organization (DAO) for asset management in the not-too-distant future. In principle, this will allow people to do things like own a Picasso painting. You'd become a shareholder in a Picasso NFT, which means you'd be able to vote on issues like profit sharing.

Ethereum-based organizations enable strangers, such as global asset owners, to collaborate safely without trusting each other. That is because no money can be spent without the consent of the whole party. A developing market—NFTs, DAOs, and fractionalized tokens all progress at various rates. Nevertheless, since they all speak the same language: Ethereum, all their technology remains and can readily collaborate.

DIGITAL SCARCITY

The original creator determines the scarcity of an NFT.

An example below would give you more understanding regarding this topic. Suppose there is a sports event happening. It is only for the event organizer to determine how many tickets to sell for the event. Similarly, only the original asset creator has the right to decide how many copies he wants to create. Often the documents are a replica of the purchase. Other times a number of them are designed with a minute difference. In other cases, the creator may want to create an NFT where only one is minted, making it one unique and rare collectible.

Individually NFT would still have a unique identifier with a single one in the cases explained above. The creator decides to determine the scarcity of an NFT. It is something that matters. To maintain lack, the creator can create the NFTs entirely differently. If he wishes, he can also come up with many copies. All this is publically known.

Royalties

This concept is still under works, but it is one of the best. If your NFT has a royalty scheme programmed into it, you will receive your share automatically every time your art is sold. The ones who own EulerBeats Originals receive an 8% royalty whenever the NFT of their art is re-sold. Platforms such as Foundation and Zora back royalties for their artists.

The whole royalty process is automatic and stress-free. That is so that the artists who created the art don't have to go through a hassle and earn from their art every time it is sold again. Presently, there are a lot of issues in the whole royalties scheme as it is manual. Due to this explanation, a majority of the artists are not paid. If you pre-define that you will receive a percentage of money as royalties from the artwork in your NFT, you can keep earning from that art piece.

What Are Nfts Used For?

Below are a few more famous and widely known use-cases for the NFTs on the Ethereum blockchain network.

- Digital content
- Gaming items

- Domain names

- Physical items

- Investments and collateral

Maximizing Earnings For Creators

NFTs are widely used in the capacity of digital art. The reason for that is that the digital art industry has a lot of issues that need to be fixed. The platforms that they sold on would swallow their earning and profits generated, thus letting the artists suffer financially.

An artist puts up his work on a social network site and makes money for the platform that sells ads to the followers of the artists. That gives the artist publicity, but exposure and advertising don't make any money.

The NFTs power the new creator economy. In the creator economy, the original creators don't pass on the ownership of their content to the platforms.

Every time these artists make a sale, all the revenue generated goes to them directly. The one with whom he sells his art becomes the new owner. Whenever that owner would sell the art piece further, the artist would generate some revenue from the sale through the royalties' scheme.

The Copy/Paste Problem

Some people fail to understand the concept of NFTs and claim them to be of no use. The main statement that they pass over such a scenario is that if you can screengrab something and get it for free, why do you have to spend millions of dollars on it?

If you screenshot or google pictures of a painting by Picasso, it doesn't make you the owner of it.

If you own a real thing, that means that you won something valuable. The more an item becomes viral, the more in demand it is.

If you own verified something, it will have more value.

Boosting Gaming Potential

NFTs are commonly used in digital art, but they are also very applicable in the game development industry. The developers in the industry use the NFTs to claim ownership over the in-game items. It can help with the in-game economies and benefit the players in multiple ways.

You purchase items in almost every game that you play. If you buy an NFT, you can make money from it outside the game. It can also become a source of profit for you if the item is in demand.

The people who developed the game are the ones who issue the NFTs. That means that they have the right to generate revenue through royalty schemes every time an item is sold again. In such cases, there is a benefit for both the parties (i.e., the players and the developers.)

The items you have collected in the game are now yours, and that the developers no longer handle the game.

If there is no one to handle the game, the items would still be yours, and you will have complete control over them. Whatever you earn in the game can have a lot of worth and value outside of the game.

Decentraland is a VR game that allows you to purchase NFTs that symbolize the virtual parcels of land that you can use as per your liking.

Physical Items

If you compare the tokenization of digital assets and physical assets, you will realize that the tokenization of digital assets is more advanced. Several projects are working on tokenizing real estate, rare fashion items, etc.

Shortly, you will be able to purchase cars, houses, etc., all with the NFTs. That is because the NFTs are deeds, and you can buy a physical asset and then get an act as an NFT in return. With the advancements in technology, it will be real soon that your Ethereum wallet will become the key to your car or home. You will be able to unlock your door with cryptographic proof of ownership.

Nfts And Defi

The NFT space and the DeFi world are working together closely in several exciting ways.

Nft-Backed Loans

There are DeFi applications that allow you to borrow money using collateral. For instance, you collateralize 10 ETH so you can wring 5000 DAI. If the one who borrowed the money cannot pay back the DAI, the lender will be able to get his payment back. However, not everyone can afford to use crypto as collateral.

Presently, the projects have started exploring using the NFTs as collateral. Suppose you purchased a rare CryptoPunk NFT a while back with a present worth thousands of dollars. That means that if you put this up as collateral, you will access a loan with the same ruleset. If you cannot pay back the DAI, your CryptoPunk will be sent to the lender as collateral. Ultimately, you would see that it can work with anything you tokenize as an NFT.

It is not difficult on Ethereum. That is because both of these share the same underlying technology and infrastructure.

Fractional ownership

NFT creators can create "shares" for their NFT. Due to this, the investors and the fans have a chance to own a share of an NFT and not purchase it as a whole. That is an excellent way for the NFT creators and collectors to have more opportunities.

DEX's like Uniswap can help with the trade of fractionalized NFTs. The price of each fraction can define the total cost of the NFT.

Fractional NFTs are still a new concept, and people are still experimenting with them.

NIFTEX

NFTX

This means that you would be able to own a piece of a Picasso in theory. That is like you would become a shareholder in a Picasso NFT. You would be sharing revenue with every partner part of the NFT. Owning a fraction of an NFT will likely move you into a decentralized autonomous organization (DAO) for asset management.

The organizations powered and backed up by Ethereum permit strangers to become global shareholders of an asset. That would allow them to manage everything securely. They don't have to trust each other necessarily. In these systems, no one is allowed to spend a dime unless approved by every group member.

As we have been discussing, this is just the beginning. NFTs, DAOs, and fractionalized tokens are all developing at their own pace. However, their infrastructure has already been built, and all these technologies can work in close correspondence to each other as they are all backed up by Ethereum.

WHY YOU CAN MAKE MONEY WITH NFT

Nfts, Usability And Trends

The popularity of NFT has been increasing. From various trends to usability. The community has been innovative in providing a diverse range of NFTs and making them more approachable for newcomers to the Blockchain space. However, according to some statistics, only 47% of crypto users had learned of NFTs, and 57% had never used them. The most common NFTs were for collectibles (47 percent) and gaming (33 percent), according to a survey of nearly 30k people.

What do these stats tell us? Few people are comfortable engaging with NFTs, and that general knowledge about them is still restricted. The aim remains to bring more people into the space to understand Blockchain better and accelerate its development.

We must remain curious and pursue new projects to help space evolve and understand its functions to develop products for our users better.

A Little About Nfts

These are the most distinctive properties of NFTs, and it's important to remember them so we can understand what we can do with them and how they work:

Unique — Each NFT has its own set of properties, usually stored in the token's metadata.

Scarce is probably a small number of NFTs, with the most extreme example having just one copy, and the number of tokens can be verified on the Blockchain, hence its provability.

Indivisible — Most NFTs can't be divided into smaller denominations, so you won't be able to purchase or transfer a fraction of your NFT.

Like fungible tokens, NFTs ensure asset ownership, are easily transferable and are fraud-resistant.

The popularity of DeFi has recently aided the growth of the topic around NFTs.

How Can Nfts Be Used In Defi?

NFTs are considered the next big thing in the Decentralized finance universe. They can be used as collateral and represent other financial assets such as bonds, insurance, or options.

A DeFi borrowing and lending platform require collateral. That is where NFTs come into play to solve the problem. Yinsure uses NFTs in the insurance space; each contract is represented as an NFT, which can be traded on another platform (e.g., Rarible).

Another DeFi trend we have seen using NFTs is issuing governance tokens. Many sites and NFT marketplaces have begun to publish and distribute governance tokens.

How Brands Are Using Nfts

Technology has advanced in recent years.

Blockchain is one place that has seen some of the fastest advancements.

That does not mean cryptocurrencies like Ethereum, Bitcoin, and the slew of other cryptocurrencies own the crypto market solely.

Let's peek at non-fungible tokens (NFTs) and how labels can use them.

NFTs differ from cryptocurrencies because they have specific codes and metadata that indicate one NFT from another. Cryptocurrencies are fungible tokens because they stand all exact.

Because each NFT is unusual, it cannot be exchanged or traded for an equal NFT. As an outcome, each NFT is a digital collectible, an individual, non-replicable asset.

That's where the NFT craze originated. CryptoKitties, a combination of Tamagotchi and trading cards, burst onto the scene in 2017. Each kitten is unique and can be expanded, replicated, and sold for up to $140,000.

NFT mania was born, and interest in NFTs is increasing.

Why Are Non-Fungible Tokens (NFTs) Essential to Brands?

The ability to characterize digital files such as art, audio, and video is a critical reason NFTs are valuable to brands. They're so universal that they can be used to represent other forms of creative work like virtual worlds, virtual real estate, style, and much better.

What does this have to accomplish with your brand and marketing strategy?

NFTs have unlocked up new forms of brand storytelling and consumer interaction, which are the two critical pillars of a successful marketing campaign, thanks to the global interest they've created.

With NFTs, you can:

• Increase brand awareness

- Create unique brand experiences

- Encourage interaction

- Create interest in your product and brand

Finally, NFTs will assist you in increasing conversions and generating revenue.

Here are some examples of how companies use NFTs in their marketing activities.

Six Ways Brands Are Using NFTs

The concept of NFTs in marketing can be challenging to comprehend. The most effortless way to explain the most complex ideas is to look at examples.

Here are a few imaginative ways brands are utilizing NFTs. Hopefully, you will get some motivation from them.

Taco Bell GIFs

According to research, 83% of millennials choose to do business with companies that share their values. As a result, brands must publicly (and genuinely) endorse causes they believe in.

Taco Bell's basis has been doing this for years, but they obtained it to a whole new level by marketing taco-themed NFT GIFs to support the Live Más Scholarship.

All GIFs were reached within 30 minutes of setting their 25 NFTs (dubbed NFTacoBells) up for sale on Rarible. Each GIF had a starting proposal price of $1. However, they all marketed for thousands of dollars, with one going for $3,646.

Creating and selling NFTs was a wise move made by Taco Bell as it generated a lot of interest in mainstream and social media, which is always right for business.

Like Taco Bell, you can utilize NFTs to:

1. Drive brand awareness

2. Support a good cause

Both are potent factors that can aid in the growth of your business.

RTFKT Digital Sneakers

Looking for a way to make a reputation for yourself and disrupt the market?

NFTs can help you do that.

That's what happened when RTFKT, a relatively unrecognized Chinese virtual sneaker company, produced an NFT sneaker for the Chinese New Year and arranged it up for auction.

That's very special for a brand that's only been around for two years, especially given that they marketed a sneaker that can't even be handled, let alone worn. As impressive as this was, it was still way behind the $3 million they made from another NFT sneaker they designed with the 18-year-old artist, FEWOCiOUS.

While NFTs are still in their infancy, now is the most suitable time for marketers to get on board. It's a beautiful way to get people's attention and build a tribe of followers.

If you're a marketer examining new ways to use NFT technology, you can take a cue from RTFKT. Create restricted edition memorabilia to celebrate special occasions and holidays, and use them in your holiday marketing campaigns. You may give them away to the first X number of customers or sell them separately at an auction.

Grimes Videos

Six million dollars in twenty minutes.

Grimes made that much from a collection of ten NFTs auctioned on Nifty Gateway.

People are curious about NFTs, and brands can capitalize on that interest to sell their goods.

For example, you can:

- Partner with artists or auction sites to have your brand present at the auction.
- Conduct a contest (to generate leads) with NFTs as the prize.
- Make an NFT and auction it for charity.

Marketing is all about riding recent trends and using your imagination to capitalize on the buzz around them to attract attention to your brand.

The Launch of The Kings of Leon's Album "When You See Yourself."

The music industry has become highly competitive due to the many musicians and bands available building and maintaining a loyal fan base isn't as easy as it once was.

The Kings of Leon developed a strategy to get around that.

They unleashed their album "When You See Yourself" in the form of an NFT.

The Kings of Leon made history by becoming the first band to release an NFT version.

More importantly, it put them in the hearts of their fans by enabling them to own a digital collectible. That's a fantastic way to increase brand loyalty.

Kings of Leon have used three different types of tokens for this first-of-its-kind album launch. One type offered live show perks, the second featured exclusive audiovisual art, and the third featured a special album package.

The album is unrestricted on all music platforms, but the NFT edition was only available for $50 on YellowHeart.

The sale of the NFTs was only unlocked for two weeks, after which no more album tokens were produced. The tokens became a trade-able collectible as a result of this change.

Beeple Artwork

Mike Winkelmann, virtually unknown in mainstream art circles, has become a parable.

He marketed a JPG file for $69.3 million, making him the third most expensive living artist at the auction.

The file is a portion of art sold as a non-fungible token.

A flurry of bids came in as the auction was about to close, causing the two-week timed auction to be expanded by 90 seconds.

What lessons can brands learn from this?

Be swift to adopt new concepts and innovations. With the competition becoming more fierce by the day, you must be willing to take chances and be disruptive to outperform.

Nyan Cat GIF

A decade ago, the Nyan Cat GIF made a colorful impact on the digital scene. Developer Chris Torres created an NFT version of the GIF that sold over $500,000 on the crypto auction site foundation.

That's right! A vintage animated GIF sold for more than half a million dollars.

However, Chris didn't stop there. He organized an auction in which classic memes were marketed as NFTs. Bad Luck Brian, one of the memes, dealt for over $34,000 on the foundation.

What can brands learn from this?

The takeaway here is that consumers can pay for excellent service. Take benefit of this by converting some of your most successful ads into NFTs. Make an event where you auction them off and make sure it is well-publicized.

Not only would this increase brand recognition, but it will also help you reach out to new tech markets.

The Future Of Nfts

NFTs are still new, and their practical applications are still limited. However, people adore them and are willing to spend money on them. These are sure indicators that they are here to stay.

NFTs, including the blockchain technology that powers them, can play a significant part in the future digital world. Non-fungible tokens have opened up fresh ways to engage with your audience and create unforgettable adventures for them, which is particularly true for marketers.

Remember that most of the tools we use today (like social media) were once considered fads.

In today's world, we count on them for numerous things. NFTs can seem to be a fad right now, but they offer several benefits (such as clarity and security) that overcome the limitations of current technologies.

GROWTH OF NFTS

Nft Industry Growth And Cryptocurrency Markets

On-fungible tokens are gaining popularity in sports, events, and ID. Music, art, investors, and everyday use are examples of N management. New data has been discovered in many areas from a study that examined 20 million NFT trades. NFTs are still far behind other cryptocurrency cryptocurrencies and will need more attention from significant media outlets. While many mainstream media outlets monitor bitcoin rates, the large NFT transactions on OpenSea and WAX barely make the news.

NFT growth is hindered by public opinion. NFTs can only be traded privately, unlike crypto assets that are publicly traded. To put it another way: One market is open to all, while the other is hidden in the shadows. NonFungible is one example of an NFT aggregator platform that provides transparency in trading activity. Ironically, however, cryptocurrency and the blockchain technology underpinning them has paved the way to NFT growth. For various reasons, NFTs can raise funds much faster than cryptocurrencies. Let's look at three.

Affordability

The definition of meaning can be a bit fuzzy in theory. We believe something is essential because we think it is. Why is it that government-issued money has very little value? According to the system, that's why.

Money is an odd creature. Money is not just a promise wrapped in common metals, abundant (and renewable!) paper, and ink. Most people face financial challenges on both a macro and sometimes a fiscal level. The same applies to cryptocurrencies. Digitizing money can confuse people who have trouble understanding it.

What about tokens? Most people can grasp the idea of purchasing an item that has a specific and unique use. Anyone who has been to an arcade for video games will understand. That is the next step.

Gamification

Let's face facts; cash is boring. Indeed, some of the extravagant experiences and extravagances that money can buy can be pretty thrilling. But, looking at spreadsheets is not our idea of a good time. NFTs are, however, often associated with games and art. Their rarity and collectability are also boosting NFT awareness. NFTs are available to musicians, fans, players, and combinations thereof for many reasons.

OpenSea is the largest NFT marketplace in the world. NFTs allow gamers to take ownership of in-game items. As the public becomes more familiar with NFT, there are many new markets, including Nifty Gateway, owned by a billionaire. OpenSea, the most well-known group, is where we find the most data.

OpenSea users have increased from a few in mid-2018 to over 19,000 since then. Although this is a small number, it is a remarkable trend. Blockchain games and NFTs go hand-in-hand. NFTs are gaining popularity in tandem with videogames, which are experiencing a near never-ending rise in popularity.

Deeper Foundation

If you were alive before the Great Crypto Bullrun in 2017, you would be able to connect. Cryptocurrencies have been under the radar for almost a decade. The world began to notice bitcoin's rise in value, over $20k per coin. Coinbase accounts can be used for a variety of purposes. This massive increase in cryptocurrency wallets is a boon for the NFT industry. You are probably aware of the phrase "a rising tide lifts all boats."

As NFTs and crypto games often connect with crypto wallets, the number of users at 30 million is a good starting point. This number is only based on one transaction. NFTs have a home now, with hundreds of trades and wallet applications. NFTs don't have to start from scratch; they can build layers on a solid foundation. The creation of bitcoins and ethereum can be attributed to the growing popularity of non-fungible tokens.

Nft Use Case

It's more than a piece of art. Jehan Chu, the owner of the blockchain investment firm Kenetic, paid $84,000 for 680,000 HNS (HNS) NFTs. These NFTs give the bearer the ability to issue. The Handshake blockchain is used for NFT domain extension extensions. The Chu believes NFTs are the "real missing link" between offline and online items and that they can transform society, industry, and history. That is not a bold statement.

NFTs benefit from transparency because of their documentation on a publicly accessible ledger. That adds a layer of security for a collectible property that people tend to be attracted to. Rumors of NFTs playing a crucial role in decentralized finance (deFi) have led to proof of concept in Alpaca City's Ethereum based digital world. Alpaca's November tokens went on sale in less than 20 minutes and earned nearly 1,000 Ethereum. Alpaca NFTs won't be "bred" (remember CryptoKitties?). Their owners. NFT-collateralized loans and interest-bearing accounts could increase the tokens' value. NFT owners want to send and receive assets on different blockchains. This compatibility is crucial.

DeFi primitives can be found on many well-known blockchains like Ethereum and TRON. TRC-721 is the NFT standard of the latter, which allows users to track and transfer tokens on the high throughput platform. Individuals on both sides consider NFTs to be significant. Buyers want to play the game while firms offer safe and open NFT protocols. Many NFT projects are available on Ethereum, including CryptoPunks, Decentraland, Hashmasks, and CryptoPunks.

Why You Should Invest In Nfts

NFTs are a profitable venture for the following reasons:

Creates Value for the Tokenized Asset

NFTs allow tangible items like artworks to be tokenized. That prevents replication and gives exclusive ownership to the creator. That creates scarcity, which in turn generates demand for the painting.

It Increases Liquidity for Investors

Investors can leverage their assets more easily by tokenizing them. For example, a digital property owner might rent their digital property out to marketers or advertisers for a fee while still maintaining ownership. The owner still owns the digital property, but some have been rented out as rent.

Growth and development opportunities

NFTs can expand the land market. Virtual lands allow you to decide what you want to do with your property in real estate. Tying NFTs to the ground has allowed for tremendous growth and development. It can be rented out, used to advertise, or sold online.

NFT Projects with Increasing Growth

- Art Tokens

Boyart OpenSea has sold artworks worth over 400ETH and newer products fetching over 75ETH. Boyart is an artist with a lot of experience and has sold some of his art in tokenized form. The new mural paintings have been wrapped in NFTs and sold off.

Boyart has shown that crypto can create an art market in just a few months. That attracts investors who want to invest in assets of interest. The Digital Museum of Crypto Art also has Boyart's murals.

- Lil Moon Rockets

Lil Moon Rockets, a new NFT project, uses smart contracts to distribute unique works of art. The project uses vector art and computational genealogy to keep up with current trends. Every user will receive their own Moon Rocket picture right after the original artwork is sold. To prevent investors and first users from purchasing the best art, Lil Moon Rockets uses a "blind sale." All paintings will become public after the smart contract has ended. Unlike other NFT projects based on Ethereum blockchain, Lil Moon Rockets uses the Binance Chain for its NFTs and subsequent tokens.

While NFTs are a valuable source of revenue for Ethereum, Binance Chain allows easier transactions at lower fees.

- Cryptopunks

Crypto punks are one of the most standardized art forms for NFTs. They are a great example of the attraction to NFTs. Despite being standardized art, crypto punks rose in popularity and became one of the most loved collections.

After a specific social media campaign from prominent crypto personalities, Cryptopunks became the go-to place for risky investments and collections. Due to a combination of scarcity and growing popularity, the 10,000 characters of Punks are also enjoying a stable market for resale. The NFTs were modestly launched with an airdrop for anyone who has an Ethereum wallet. Prices climbed to $57,000. The market is highly active because of network effects of popularity, and the price does not matter how early tokens were distributed.

- Beeple's artwork

An artist known as Beeple is a member of the NFT global marketplace. He had been active on Instagram for many years and only recently gained recognition. Beeple's work has been compared to Pascal Boyart's. The market also values the more computational approach that combines art with technology.

- Hashmasks

Hashmasks is one of the most prominent projects in the NFT space. These collectibles feature alien or robotic backgrounds and are made postmodern. Over 16,000 images were assembled using computational combinations and artists' work. It is impossible to predict where these works of art will end. Hashmasks have become an identity mark in crypto-related social media.

They have been used in visual identities and social media games until now. The most expensive hashmask, which costs 420 ETH, has been until now. The most costly hashmask, which costs 420 ETH, has been 4 ETH.

ADVANTAGES AND DISADVANTAGES OF NON-FUNGIBLE TOKENS

Presently, NFTs have their advantages and disadvantages like any innovation, and in this segment, the accompanying can be featured.

Nfts Advantages

They permit us to address computerized and genuine items inside the blockchain in an exciting and unrepeatable manner. So we can utilize this innovation to deal with these articles securely and consistently. Would you like to tokenize your home or your vehicle using NFT? You can do it. Your creative mind is the cutoff.

The advancement prospects of NFTs are perpetual; anything that you can address carefully can turn into an NFT. For instance, space names (those used to distinguish website pages) can be addressed as an NFT inside a DNS on the BlockchainBlockchain. That is what occurs with the Namecoin project and the Ethereum Name Service.

The production of NFT can be adjusted to any blockchain, and it tends to be executed in a highly secure manner. A model is Bitcoin, which with its restricted programming limit, can address NFTs, keeping the security hazards for such resources for a base; it concludes out how to handle NFTs.

The presence of norms makes their creation, execution, and advancement simpler.

Opportunities for cross-chain interoperability with tasks like Polkadot or Cosmos.

Nfts Disadvantages

While there are norms for creating NFT, they are neither dependable nor complete as far as usefulness is concerned. The formerly mentioned is the primary motivation behind why, for instance, the ERC-721 badge of Ethereum (the most utilized for NFT in Ethereum) tries to be supplanted by the ERC-1155 token significantly more secure and has new capacities.

NFTs are overseen by complex shrewd agreements, making their tasks mind-blogging and weighty (as far as data). These two things raise the estimation of the commissions paid to complete exchanges. So, running NFT can be costly, mainly if the organization is blocked and commissions soar.

Like Defi, NFT stages are more defenseless to hacks since everything is taken care of by brilliant agreements and different interfaces to control them. This whole programming layer adds assault vectors that programmers can misuse for malignant increase.

Non-Fungible Tokens Value

NFTs derive their value from the same deflationary principles as bitcoin—the number of tokens is limited, and the articles cannot be replicated. Thus, owners of NFT tokens can fully own these individual digital assets knowing that they hold only such tokens. Authenticity also plays a role in verifying and can always be traced back to the original creator.

The value of NFTs is also based on the immutability of the product. NFTs cannot be destroyed, deleted, or duplicated. The token only exists on its native platform. It is stored on the blockchain items from one platform and cannot be moved to another.

The Nonfungible website found that NFT buyers increased by 66% in 2020, while the value of transactions rose from around $63 million to $250 million (52 to 207 million euros).

Non-fungible tokens are unified and extraordinary crypto resources that help make computerized shortages. NFTs have been made on the Ethereum (ETH) blockchain, as per the ERC-721 norm. Today, in any case, they are accessible on numerous other blockchains, similar to EOS, TRON, and NEO, and have many use cases. For example, NFTs can address advanced collectibles, craftsmanship, or in-game resources.

NFTs and their intelligent contracts contain distinguishing data, making each NFT special. Thus, no two NFTs are similar. For instance, you can trade one ticket for one more of a similar segment on account of banknotes. They have equal worth, so it doesn't make any difference which one you own.

Bitcoin (BTC) is a convertible token. However, its worth is as yet equivalent to one bitcoin. You can send 1 BTC to somebody; at that point, they can move it elsewhere. Since convertible digital currencies are separable, you can likewise send or get a more modest part of bitcoin-satoshi.

One of the primary NFT collectibles was Cryptokitties, an Ethereum blockchain-based game that permits clients to gather and raise virtual felines. Each blockchain-based talk is fascinating.

Most Expensive Non-Fungible Tokens Ever Sold

- Beeple, every day (The First 5000 Days, $69 million)

Beeple takes the top spot in our ranking, thanks to this period's most remarkable and surprising sale. Christie's closes his first online auction on March 11th, in which he has a work NFT that soars from an initial evaluation of $100 to a record of $69 million in a brief period. Beeple, therefore, found himself the third living artist most expensive in the world behind himself in Jeff Koons and David Hockney.

- Virtual Images of Rick and Morty ($2.3 million)

Another craftsman who has to conclude how to sell show-stoppers as NFT at an over-the-top cost is Justin Roiland, the maker of the famous energized arrangement "Rick and Morty." His assortment of 16 masterpieces was sold for 1,300 ETH, near $2.3 million.

A part of the closeout returns was dispensed to assisting the needy with peopling in Los Angeles, with Roiland saying it was an approach to test the restrictions of crypto artistry.

Strangely, a portion of Roiland's work of art has been delivered in numerous duplicates. Works named "It's Tree Guy" and "Qualified Bachelors" cost $10 and $100 for each piece, separately.

Show-stoppers made in a solitary duplicate were sold at higher costs because of their uniqueness and extraordinariness. The play called "The Simpsons" sold for $290,100. The closeout's beginning cost was $14,999, with its actual being sold for a similar sum.

- Land on Axie Infinity ($1.5 million)

In the first and second positions, we put computerized craftsmanship assortments sold through different exchanges. This time, nine land plots on the well-known blockchain game Axie Infinity were sold in a solitary NFT exchange. The client who made the buy paid 888.5 ETH, or $1.5 million, at that point.

Axie Infinity permits clients to construct a realm in which fabulous characteristics live. The existence where you can purchase virtual land is called Lunacia and has many spots. The entire plot is separated into 90,601 more modest plots, 19,601 more modest plots, 19% of which players possess.

Hawk called attention that the land he purchased is in a great area. Moreover, the pattern on Axie Infinity is consistently expanding, as confirmed by the developing number of dynamic clients. Later on, it will likewise be feasible to arrange occasions, like celebrations or shows, on "your territory" and accordingly bring in cash.

- Collectible character on CryptoPunks ($762,000)

Toward the finish of January, an NFT portraying a character from the CryptoPunks game was sold for 605 ETH, or $762,000, at that point. The universe of CryptoPunks is enlivened by crypto artistry development and comprises more than 10,000 extraordinary advanced characters.

Today, they can be purchased and sold in the committed CyberPunks market. It ought to be referenced that already the characters in the game were free, and you expected to have an ETH wallet to get them.

The NFT, initially founded in 2017 and sold at an exorbitant cost, is $2,890. It is a very uncommon 'punk.'

- A visit to the blockchain game CryptoKitties (600 ETH)

The most costly NFT in history is Dragon from the blockchain game CryptoKitties. This adorable advanced feline was sold for 600 ETH, or $200,000, at that point. Today, a similar measure of tokens costs around $1,000,000 million.

CryptoKitties is one of the primary endeavors to utilize blockchain innovation for diversion. The Axiom Zen studio created it. Like real felines, each virtual feline has a unique DNA and qualities called "credits," which can be given to posterity. Furthermore, each virtual feline is one of a kind and can't be repeated or moved without the proprietor's permission.

As a rule, past ages of virtual felines are viewed as more critical. Dragon uncommon—this is the 10th era of CrytoKitty.

- A Delta Time F1 vehicle ($110,000)

Another NFT is a Formula 1 vehicle on the F1 Delta Time game, explicitly the 1-1-1 model. An unknown gamer purchased this dashing virtual vehicle for a fantastic measure of 415.5 ETH. At the hour of procurement, it was more than $110,000. Until now, such a measure of ETH is worth around $665,000. This buy got the title of the most excellent NFT exchange in 2019.

- One F1 Delta Time track ($200,000)

This time, nonetheless, not a vehicle but rather part of a track. Toward the beginning of December 2020, a piece of the way on F1 Delta Time was sold for more than 9,000,000 REVV tokens, or $200,000, at that point. From that point forward, EVV has developed by 500%, and at the hour of composing this book, it would cost $1.2 million for a similar measure of REVV.

For F1 Delta Time, all significant game resources are addressed by NFTs. For example, the Circuit de Monaco's virtual track comprises 330 badges of this kind partitioned into four levels—from "Uncommon" to Summit." Each token addresses a virtual track share, giving its proprietor many advantages.

For this specific NFT, it was at the "Zenith" level. As a result, its purchaser will get 5% of all in-game income and 4.2% of first-class marking benefits from player stores. Both will be paid in REVV utility tokens.

- NFT Guarantee Money Insurance (350 ETH)

"5000.0 ETH-Cover-NFT" is a protection strategy dependent on insure. Money, an undertaking upheld by Yearn. Financial Because of an enthusiastic advanced approach, its proprietor profits by protection against mistakes in keen agreements on Curve.fi up to 5,000 ETH. NFT costs 350 ETH, which compares to more than $560,000 today.

Yinsure is otherwise called Cover, So, it is a consolidated protection inclusion ensured by Nexus Mutual and another sort of tokenized protection. Protection approaches are represented as NFT. Every one of them is a special NFT. Otherwise called NFT, and can be moved, purchased, or sold.

- 12,600 square meters of virtual land in Decentraland (514 ETH)

Somebody purchased 12,600 m2 for 514 ETH on the Decentraland blockchain game. The game is an Ethereum-based decentralized augmented experience stage. Its clients can make, analyze, and adapt their substance and applications.

Decentraland has a restricted 3D virtual space called LAND. It is a non-fungible computerized resource kept up by Ethereum shrewd agreements. The landowner has complete control of their virtual land.

- Land at 22.2 in Decentraland (345 ETH)

Here is Decentraland once more. This time, it's a land parcel in a "great area" at 22.2. In the realm of Decentraland, the size of the land is fixed. About 80% of its space is private, and the vast majority of the rest is sold and rented by Decentraland. Like streets and squares, the excess land doesn't have a place with anybody. Players can walk their characters on their territory and public land, so the situation is significant. Parts nearer to well-known regions will be more costly than those situated in more distant zones.

Taking a gander at how quickly the NFT markets are developing and what costs non-fungible tokens are sold, we can accept that this will be another gigantic pattern just after Defi. A significant quality of NFTs is that each has its own remarkable and exciting attributes.

PROBLEMS WITH NFTS

Risks Associated With Purchase And Sale On Nft

Like any new resource in the beginning phases of advancement and appropriation, NFTs convey some danger similar to far from mass acknowledgment. If a financial backer picks to purchase an NFT and interest in exchanging them slows down or even disappears, costs will fall, and the purchaser could be left with huge misfortunes.

NFTs are not absolved from misrepresentation. NFTs professing to be crafted by notable specialists have been sold for many dollars; however, they have been uncovered to be phony. Furthermore, similarly that digital forms of money can be taken, NFTs can depend on burglary, relying on how they are put away. Another danger to consider is that computerized content isn't altogether liberated from weakening in quality, record designs getting out of date, sites going disconnected briefly or even forever, or the deficiency of wallet passwords. For makers, printing NFTs to sell content doesn't ensure legitimate rights to responsibility for work, giving less assurance from burglary than they may anticipate. While NFTs and the commercial centers that sell them are decentralized, there can, in any case, be obstacles to acquiring segment and openness for their work.

Similarly, many stages are greeted as craftsmanship exhibitions, and other actual scenes select specialists address. Since NFTs can be created dependent on essentially anything computerized and advanced things can be effectively duplicated, there's the potential for misuse. In particular, there's nothing preventing anybody from making their own NFT dependent on computerized things created by others. In one model announced by Decrypt on March 13, craftsman "Odd Undead" has discovered individuals taking advanced works of art from their tweets. The pictures were utilized to create NFTs and were sold on an NFT commercial center, which the craftsman attempted to end. Bizarre Undead alludes to the training as "crazy and trivial copyright encroachment," which advantages the retail centers and individuals taking the pictures, not simply the craftsmen. The movement isn't restricted merely to fine arts. Likewise, there have been issues with individuals tokenizing tweets by others as NFTs and selling them. Once more, the training doesn't include the individual who composed the first tweet, who might eventually possess the copyright for the content. While it is conceivable for an artisan or the maker of media to sue under the existing brand name and intellectual property laws, the idea of how blockchain works can make it hard to discover who initially encroached to make the NFT. There's additionally the issue of which commercial center to trust in any case. Different blockchain administrations could each guarantee they have records that a particular NFT is interesting and the expert for the work. That is what might be compared to two closeout houses asserting they are the scene of an offer for an extraordinary piece of craftsmanship.

It seems to me that there is a level of participation between significant commercial centers regarding the matter. However, there has been no assurance that things will remain later on. Include that it is therefore workable for individuals to set up their commercial centers on blockchains. It gets more diligent to police the non-fungible tokens as being set available for purchase. These are issues that should be tended to eventually, both to make sure of specialists' occupation and to keep the deals of NFTs legitimate. For the occasion, these issues haven't blunted the craving for all-around obeyed purchasers. For Nadya Ivanova, COO of L'Atelier BNP Paribas, a developing statistical surveying firm that teamed up with Nonfungible on a report on non-fungible tokens in February, the innovation's most unique strength is additionally one of its significant shortcomings. Anybody on the web can make an NFT out of, in actual circumstances, anything, which implies there are a lot of "truly downright awful" out there, Ivanova reiterated in the meeting. It takes a prepared eye to remove what merits gathering or putting resources into. "That applies to the actual artistry market too — it's normally space for the educated. The same thing with NFT craftsmanship," Ivanova said. Also, despite the fact Ivanova views the NFT market as at last developing and proceeding with its course into the standard, she perceives a modest bunch of extra dangers and vulnerabilities new gatherers ought to consider about the maturing space.

The non-fungible token market experiences tremendous unpredictability, Ivanova said, to some degree because there aren't any instruments set up yet to help individuals value resources. Throughout 2020, the estimation of probably the most famous kinds of NFTs spiked by around 2,000%, L'Atelier's report found. On the Top Shot, a few features first traded for a couple of dollars are currently worth many thousands. Regarding liquidity — how promptly a resource can be sold for money —, NFTs are much more like baseball cards or art pieces than bitcoin or stocks; in cognizance of the circumstances, each merchant needs to discover a purchaser who will address a specific cost for a particular, unique thing. That can place authorities in a troublesome spot on the off chance that they, say, burned through $100,000 on a top-notch second the marketplaces start to tank, Ivanova said. Yet, illiquidity can likewise be something to be grateful for since it keeps individuals from settling on careless choices, Andrew Steinwold, a crypto-financial backer who began an NFT venture store in September 2019, told Insider. If individuals don't have the alternative to freeze and offload their NFTs, the market could keep off from the sort of falling qualities that would start such a selloff in any case, he said.

Most Popular Projects

It seems that hundreds of new projects are being created daily, even though millions of NFTs are available for purchase. How do you sort via all of the noise to determine which NFT efforts are the most promising and worthy of your time and attention, as well as your potential investment?

In the first instance, and depending on the amount of money you have available to spend, you may not want to consider NFTs as a potential investment choice at all. Existing assets on OpenSea (the most popular NFT marketplace) total 4 million, with potentially millions more on other exchanges, such as Bittrex and Coinbase (Rarible, Foundation, SuperRare, NBA Top Shot, and more). Because of the breadth and ongoing development of the NFT universe, it is reasonable to expect that not all of these assets will increase in value in the future.

If you're looking for traits in a project, you may be wondering what to look for. According to us, NFTs with practical applications (as mentioned below) is an ideal starting point for learning about NFTs and their potential future uses.

A utility NFT provides a practical use for a digital asset rather than just owning a piece of artwork. You can get a utility NFT if you purchase an NFT to utilize it later. A utility NFT might be anything from a genuine work of art that matches the NFT you purchased to exclusive access to an event, exclusive in-person memberships, or future use in the digital world (think to the game).

Remember that there is always the potential to come across a project that has a goal you can relate with and that will also benefit you. Because of this, you acquire more from your NFT purchase than only digital ownership of a tangible asset, which is a significant advantage (art, photo, video, audio, etc.).

Here are the most promising NFT projects for the year 2021.

Veefriends

One of the most successful serial entrepreneurs globally, Gary Vaynerchuk, founded VeeFriends in 2011. Gary operates in various capacities, including as Chairman of VaynerX, CEO of VaynerMedia, and owner/creator of VeeFriends, among other positions and duties.

Simply put, VeeFriends tokens are a ticket to Gary V's multi-day mega-conference, which is solely open to holders of VeeFriends tokens and is not available to the general public.

That is the world's first ticketed NFT conference, and it is also the first of its type in the globe. An event where token holders of VeeFriends tokens come together as a community to create long-lasting friendships, share ideas, and learn from one another is called a VenCon.

Crypto Baristas

The world's first NFT-funded café, among other things.

Season 1 of Crypto Barista will premiere with 60 caffeine-loving individuals whose ownership will aid in the conceptualization and opening of the World's First NFT-funded Café.

Caffeinated bonuses are available to Crypto Barista owners at all future cafe locations and websites for the rest of their lives. The "Barista Bank," a 15 percent fund put aside from the project's earnings for future use in the coffee industry, is likewise under the owners' authority. Some possible applications for the Barista Bank include supporting charitable organizations in the coffee industry, advancing the Crypto Barista initiative, and launching a new venture.

"The mission of Crypto Barista's is to create a community of like-minded people who share an appreciation for art, coffee, entrepreneurship, and innovation," says the company. The project aims to establish a physical venue in New York City where art and innovation will be at the heart of its processes. The destiny of Crypto Baristas will be determined by the holders and followers of our campaign beyond this point," says the founder.

Dan Hunnewell is the author of this piece (Owner, Coffee Bros.)

Aiming to address three issues in many NFT projects: governance, community, and ownership, the Coffee Bros. Crypto Barista project seeks to address these issues. Seasonal launches will be used to guide the project's development, with each season focusing on a different venture within the coffee area while also delivering benefits and governance to all holders.

Moon Boyz

Known as the Moon Boyz, they are a collective of 11,111 distinct individuals that live on the Ethereum Blockchain. Each NFT is one-of-a-kind and 3D created, and it includes unlimited membership to an ever-growing community and great utilities.

- Moon Boyz Party (the holders of the most irregular characters)
- Exclusive merch for holders
- Private club access
- And more

Mekaverse

In the MekaVerse, which has 8,888 generating Mekas that incorporate hundreds of components inspired by the Japan Mecha worlds, Mekas is created by the MekaVerse.

In the case of the MekaVerse project, Mattey and Matt B, two friends who are also 3D artists, came up with the concept and decided to go headlong into the NFT arena.

It is planned that high-quality 3D-printed toys will be accessible shortly to bring the Mekas to life as part of the MekaVerse project's implementation roadmap. The MekaVerse project is currently in its early phases, with the roadmap for the project being developed by the project's designers and the proprietors of the characters included in the project. Streetwear development, collaborations with well-known artists, and short films based on the characters are all planned for the project's future.

Creature Wor

Danny Cole, a 21-year-old graphic artist from New York City, is performing on a project called Creature World, in which he is aiming to bring the dream to reality.

In terms of the project itself, there has been a tremendous degree of curiosity among those in the NFT community, albeit it remains somewhat mysterious. An interactive segment where the animals join you on your virtual voyage may be found at the website www.creature.world. It is yet ambiguous whether or not your purchased characters will eventually emerge in the virtual world, as well as what the project's overall objective is. In any case, we're looking forward to seeing where this one goes, regardless of which direction it takes, since the mystery around the project is fascinating.

Adam Bomb Squad

If you are a lover of streetwear fashion, the Adam Bomb Squad project will be just up your streetwear fashion alley. This project, known as the Adam Bomb Squad, was devised by The Hundreds and financed by the National Science Foundation (a famous streetwear brand launched in 2003).

The project's three-fold premise is to instill a feeling of identity, community, and ownership in those who participate in non-formal education programs and activities. The "Adam Bomb" is the most well-known logo/character associated with The Hundreds, and the Adam Bomb Squad effort tries to record the character's 18-year history and widespread use.

As has been the subject in the past, we will continue to reward NFT members with incentives such as exclusive items and early access to drop dates. No matter how far ahead of the infrastructure our concepts are, a breakthrough with these NFTs will finally resolve the outstanding Ownership aspect in developing a brand. We are working on technology that will allow Adam Bomb Squad NFT holders to 1) buy The Hundreds gear that depicts their bomb and 2) get reimbursed for the clothing sales to others in return for their token (which is currently under development). There's no reason why our community shouldn't benefit from The Hundreds' win, and there's no reason why they shouldn't profit from The Hundreds' success."

The Hundreds are a group of individuals who reside in the Hundreds and are related.

Claylings

It is yet another highly sought-after project, and it is now ranked 5th in terms of total trending volume ($6.42 million as of the time of publishing of this article) in the world.

Known as Claylings, this project attempts to introduce clay animation to the blockchain to introduce 4,040 characters in the project's initial phase. To achieve one of the project's aims, a short 1laymation film starring at least one of the formerly developed characters will be produced (it would be cool to see your character in the movie).

Autograph.Io

Rather than a single effort, Autograph.io is more of a marketplace, with an intense concentration on sports, entertainment, culture, and one-of-a-kind digital experiences as its key focal areas.

In addition to Tom Brady's co-founding of the program, it received tremendous support from various advisors, including Naomi Osaka, Wayne Gretzky, Tiger Woods, and other noteworthy personalities.

Athletes are now driving the development of NFTs centered on Autograph.io, such as the actual signature of a professional athlete, access to future drops, and entry into a private Discord channel.

Because of the excitement and support displayed by everyone involved, it will be intriguing to observe how this effort develops in the coming months. Watch out for rapid development into entertainment and one-of-a-kind digital and in-person events, even though it is now primarily focused on sports.

Decentraland

Decentraland is a virtual environment with its own DAO (Decentralized Autonomous Organization), which decentralizes control of the virtual space and distributes it to the virtual space users.

The virtual in-game assets in Decentraland's environment, such as land, wearables (for your characters), and other objects, are driven by the marketplace for virtual in-game purchases on the Decentraland blockchain.

To be successful, all you need is a web browser and a cryptocurrency/digital asset wallet, such as MetaMask, to play the game. Even though it is not required, the wallet improves the entire game experience by protecting all of your digital assets, such as your names, valuables, and LANDS, from being stolen or otherwise lost.

ETHEREUM AND NFTS

How Is Ethereum Helping In Leading The Way For The Nfts In The Future?

D o you know what cryptocurrency is and what Bitcoin is? Here, in this case, we will be discussing and talking about Ethereum to divert the readers' focus towards this technology. Ethereum is important to understand if you are looking to invest n the NFTs. Ethereum blockchain is one of the essential parts affecting today's cryptocurrency markets. If you need to venture into this market, you know all the basics. It is something that you need to know at all costs because it is the future.

What Is Ethereum?

Ethereum originated in July 2015 as open-source blockchain technology. This technology came as a support to the decentralized applications and the functionality of the smart contracts. Ethereum came into existence to inflate and develop the abilities of Bitcoin by introducing the practice of intelligent contracts. It is a system of decentralized apps that are independent of each other. NFTs are influenced and controlled by the blockchain that uses the ERC-271 non-fungible Ethereum token standard.

What Is An Nft?

NFTs are non-fungible tokens that are in everyday use nowadays. They are used to display the copyrights of digital assets by any digital artist. That is an excellent practice for these artists to trade their work digitally worldwide without fearing their work being plagiarized. NFT is a token that is based on the Ethereum blockchain technology. All the transactions among the artists and the collectors are stored on a digital ledger over the blockchain network.

How Does Ethereum Play A Role?

Ethereum blockchain is used to distribute the ownership of these tokens. Using the Ethereum smart contracts, the man in the middle of all the transactions has been eliminated, and all the transactions are exclusive between the creator and the collector. The Ethereum blockchain technology used in these NFTs also enables people to see and track down the owners who formerly owned these NFTs. Ethereum blockchain networks make it easy to securely store this information on the digital ledger and record all the data using smart contracts.

Why Is This Intriguing?

What makes these NFTs special is their uniqueness. This uniqueness helps them provide solutions to all the problems that may come up due to the selling of fake and counterfeit products and goods. These tokens are legit and legal. They ensure the authenticity of the product. You cannot trade one ticket for another because they are non-fungible. Every key is unique from one other. Gaming and art industries have extensively utilized the NFTs.

Many gaming companies have tokenized avatars and add-ons that come built-in with the game for generating profit. For instance, a $270,000 digital cat was sold as an NFT by CryptoKitties' Dragon. The worth of certain digital assets such as Twitter handles domain names, merchandise, art, music, and more impel huge fiscal assistances that people often oversee. That is accredited to the scarcity of these assets and their failure to be copied. That is lacking in such industries. That is because people have access to all the information. The information that they have access to is not owners. Presently, they choose some people who agree to pay and can do so.

What Does This Mean For The Future?

The market has been growing consistently since the first NFT was launched in 2017. Currently, $207 million has been spent in the market, and this number is enough for people to see the future of this technology.

With the suggestion that Ethereum' layer 2' scaling will make its first appearance shortly, these transactions will be quicker and inexpensive. The majority of the creators have started to tip the iceberg into discovering the opportunities of NFTs worth in the music industry. Artists currently can monetize their work in the digital environment. As well as their merchandise, tickets, and much more drive up equitable worth and mention to a new individuality factor and standing from digital ownership. It is highly likely to see music festivals, where the ticket would look like an NFT that is unique and based on the QR code. That would prove the ticket's ownership and the validity of their acquisition during entry. As other creators realize the abilities these NFTs can provide their work and help them gain profits from the work they produce, they would likely choose NFTs over anything else.

OPENSEA

Opensea Market Place

OpenSea is a democratic and flexible marketplace for purchasing and sales of NFTs that is changing the game in the NFT industry. NFTs stand for Non-Fungible Tokens, which are distinct, collectible digital assets such as in-game assets, avatars, trading cards, and art.

There was a high level of NFT transactions on OpenSea in August 2021 only was well over $3.5 billion. Given that it only had $21 million in amount for the entire year of 2020, it's logical to conclude that the 12,000 percent increase in trading volumes is a clear positive indicator that OpenSea is experiencing growth in leaps and bounds.

The Bigest Nft Market

OpenSea prides itself as the first and biggest NFT marketplace in the globe. To put it another way, OpenSea can be likened to eBay for digital artifacts and collectibles. Going by its staggering quantity and achievement, that does not seem far from the truth.

Initially, the OpenSea group had a lot to prove to everyone. Besides initial sensations like Crypto Kitties, NFTs had failed to pick up on before 2021, which was quite disappointing. However, the team's prediction that people will cherish digital goods as highly as — if not more than — natural objects began to come true. Here are some background attributes to help you know what OpenSea is all about.

Cryptocurrency token buying and selling laid the groundwork for the present NFT craze. People are trading virtual money and utility tokens worldwide at all hours of the day and night. They're okay with owning things they can't see or touch virtually, signaling that the digitally savvy era has arrived.

As more and more people live their own lives digitally, interacting with digital items has become more common. Rather than bringing the physical into the digital in the early days of the internet, the present state is mostly about virtual inventions, such as good memes, games, and immersive experiences. All of these point out that humans have attained a digital era where digital items are now held in high esteem.

This is why users are ditching selfies in favor of personal pic caricatures on social networking platforms like Instagram, Twitter, and TikTok. Penguin avatars, pixelated punks, and jaded apes with laser eyes are taking over instead. And it is not just a fad anymore; it has come to stay.

In a larger perspective, every one of these signs speaks to the start of the Metaverse, a shared virtual realm that we all create and own collectively, or in which NFTs play a tremendous role. When considering or thinking of OpenSea, it's simple to conceive of it as the eBay of virtual things, but it's so much more.

When you purchase an NFT, it is akin to what foodstuffs do after purchase. But what if you want to switch it, sell it, or look for others similar to it? What if you're planning to purchase an NFT but want to check its possession background quickly?

Before now, there was no straightforward method to do any of these things before OpenSea.

Yes, OpenSea is a peer-to-peer NFT platform. Still, it's also the user experience layer that connects the network to ordinary people, making it easy to buy and utilize NFTs.

On OpenSea, you can do a lot of cool stuff. Trading, selling, and buying various types of NFTs are, obviously, the most popular actions. Furthermore, you can utilize the site to learn about the NFT business and novel initiatives. Again, with no former knowledge, OpenSea makes it possible to create your own NFTs. To begin, you must first create an NFT portfolio. After that, you can start submitting NFTs in the appropriate formats.

NFTs can symbolize any item on the chain, whether real or virtual. Isn't that a sweeping generalization? Thankfully, OpenSea has restricted the reach to a few valuable categories that capture the most prevalent NFTs today. Artwork, songs, web addresses, virtual communities, trading cards, collectibles, sports assets, and utility NFTs like membership passes are all available.

OpenSea has accumulated the most extensive stock of NFTs for sale on the planet. As a result, it has become the de facto marketplace for retail customers purchasing NFTs and an essential arena for innovators. On OpenSea, developers may quickly build specialized NFT marketplaces for selling in-game products, fundraising campaigns, and producing user airdrops, among other things.

For NFTs, Ethereum is the most essential and efficient blockchain on the planet. NFT artists, engineers, and enthusiasts have already given Ethereum the crown, much like decentralized financial projects.

Because of its weak scaling, the Ethereum service is not without its drawbacks, as so many people know. Due to high gas expenses, deals involving NFT sales and transfers are pretty pricey.

OpenSea's Polygon inclusion is particularly significant given Ethereum's existing flaws. Polygon is a chain that allows Ethereum tokens, such as NFTs, to be transferred quickly and cheaply. Indeed, Vitalik Buterin, the inventor of Ethereum, actually pushed NFT projects to move their tokens to Polygon.

On OpenSea, shifting between the Polygon and Ethereum networks is as easy as clicking – a good user-friendly feature that's simple for newbies.

Compared to distributed finance and other crypto industries, the NFT market is very young. Finding data and insights about single NFTs and many NFT indicators might be difficult if you don't know where to go. By basically gathering its market info for anybody to sort based on the most recent ranks (by overall sales) and activities, OpenSea has made this procedure a lot easier.

The idea is that OpenSea offers the NFT marketplace infrastructures for free, while customers pay a 2.5 percent fee on every NFT sale to finance the platform's maintenance. When you consider that eBay costs are about 10% for a start and go up from there, OpenSea's flat-rate sales fee is quite fair and decent. The charge given to OpenSea remains the same whether your NFT sells for $10 or $10,000,000.

When considering the number of various digital currencies available, purchasing NFTs can be difficult. The same NFT is likely to be valued in multiple currencies, including ETH, DAI, and USD, to make matters even more complicated. Ethereum is the most often utilized base currency for buying and trading NFTs. Is it also the most frequently used money on OpenSea? Although there's one thing, you must know: OpenSea adopts WETH, which is a rebranded version of ETH (wrapped ETH). Ensure you've switched some ETH to WETH before participating in an NFT auction. The most straightforward approach to convert is to use your OpenSea wallet. You can then choose a wrap for the fixed amount from the dropdown menu. You will also need some ETH to finish the work and pay for gas, but once that's done, you're ready to start bidding on OpenSea.

WALLET

Hold it right there. I can notice the twinkle in your eye. You want to dive headfirst into the NFT pool right now! Good for you. But before you start going fishing with hooks baited with diamonds, you're going to have to have a wallet for your NFTs and your profits to live in.

Not all crypto wallets are created equally. Just as there are a variety of blockchains, there are various wallets, and they aren't all compatible with each other or the marketplaces. Imagine the tragedy of minting an NFT that nets you several million dollars. Still, you don't have a digital wallet to receive the funds, or worse, you don't have a digital wallet that's compatible with the payment! Keep such nightmares from ever happening by doing your homework on wallets and matching your needs.

All About Crypto Wallets

So what exactly is a cryptocurrency wallet? Is it electronic? Is it a piece of hardware? The truth is it can be both. You cannot purchase and own Bitcoin or any other cryptocurrency, including NFTs, without a cryptocurrency wallet. And you better make sure that your wallet is compatible with your NFT and the cryptocurrency you want to deal in, or you'll have a payment that isn't collectible and essentially has given your NFT away. Whichever route you go, one thing is sure.

It's interesting how much a crypto wallet has in common with a physical wallet. Any paper money it contains in your physical wallet represents the value in storage at the United States Treasury. So a crypto wallet also holds proof of your digital cash. It has the public and private keys needed to buy any cryptocurrency, including Bitcoin. It also provides digital signatures that authorize each transaction like a blockchain. As mentioned before, these wallets can take the form of an online app, a website, or a physical device that you can carry around with you. You would want to protect your keys the same way you want to save a password since those keys allow you to trade or spend your cryptocurrency.

Before moving forward, we should mention that an Ethereum wallet doesn't work exactly like a conventional physical wallet. Your crypto wallet does not store ether. It's not stored anywhere. Ether doesn't exist in any definite shape or form. The only thing that exists are records on the blockchain, and your wallet contains the keys necessary to interact with the blockchain to enable transactions.

Let's suppose you decided to focus your NFT endeavors on where NFTs were born: the Ethereum blockchain. There are two primary flavors of wallets—hot storage and cold storage.

Hot Storage

A hot storage wallet maintains a constant connection to the internet. The excellent information about this arrangement is that you can easily access your funds from virtually anywhere in the world. But as history has demonstrated repeatedly, anything connected to the internet is vulnerable to theft. A determined hacker with no time limit can eventually find a way to steal your funds. Is it likely that this will happen? Who can say? But it is possible.

Cold Wallet

Therefore, cold storage wallets store your keys offline and only connect to the internet when you want to. That is a greater degree of security for your precious cryptocurrency.

Desktop Wallet

As the name implies, a desktop wallet is stored and runs on your desktop computer or a laptop. Depending on how much storage space you have on your machine, you have options. You can download a full client with the entire blockchain or use a light client. Light clients are easier to use and store, but a full client also has extra security since it doesn't rely on miners or nodes to pull accurate information. All the transactions are validated at the home base.

Desktop wallets aren't bad. They are convenient and relatively secure. You can only use them from the one computer where they were downloaded. But laptops and desktops are also connected to the internet, so it would be a good idea to spruce up on your cybersecurity measures. Ensure that the machine in question has not been hacked and is not infected by malware. And even more so, make sure that the computer in question is not at risk of being stolen.

Web Wallets

Web-based wallets have several things going for them. They're based on cloud storage technology which means that you can access them from pretty much anywhere in the world. They also clock a bit more speed than other kinds of crypto wallets. But in the eyes of many, a web wallet completely undermines the purpose of cryptocurrency. Since the wallet is stored online, your keys are also stored online.

Don't forget that the cloud is a third-party server, which means the security of that server is entirely out of your hands. The security of your funds and your keys rest squarely in the hands of whoever owns that server. That means that you are defenseless to take measures against hackers, cyber-attacks, malicious malware, phishing scams, etc.

Hardware Wallets

If you can't do without the familiarity of feeling a physical object in your pocket associated with your money, then there are hardware wallets. That is the ultimate cold storage method of cryptocurrency. They aren't unlike portable hard disks, except they are specifically made to work with cryptocurrency and blockchain technology. You can fill them into just about any computer when it's time to complete a transaction. Better yet, key generation takes place offline. No hacker alive is going to be able to get past that.

Aside from that simple feature of being completely isolated from the reach of cyber-attacks, many hardware wallets come with backup security options to ensure that you won't lose your cryptocurrency. Many also provide the opportunity of two-factor authentication and a password for an added level of security for your currency. There are now wallets on the market that also have a screen that allows you to sign for transactions on the device itself.

The extra security and peace of mind with the hardware wallet also comes at a price. You will lay down more money on a hardware wallet than you would on a software wallet. But if you're storing a large amount of cryptocurrency, then the investment will be more than worth it.

And like any device that was made for one singular function rather than a wide range of applications, hardware wallets weren't manufactured in massive quantities. So finding one for purchase might take a minute.

Custodial Wallets

Every so often, someone makes the news for losing their password or their security key to well over a billion dollars in cryptocurrency. The irony is almost too bitter about fathoming since the wealth exists in storage. Still, the means of accessing it has evaporated from existence, effectively separating its owner from the wealth.

A safeguard against this is utilizing a custodial wallet.

Again, some people see this as something that completely defeats the purpose of cryptocurrency. Since one of the whole points of crypto is to have complete control over your funds. A custodial wallet is third-party assistance that offers storage and protection of your digital assets. So, if, for some reason, you lost access to your funds because of some unforeseen loss with your keys or otherwise, you would be able to restore your ether from any other device.

Your security keys and your funds are both backed up by the provider's servers.

Minting Your Nfts

So it's time to bring a new NFT into the world. All of the marketplaces we just cited offer a page for minting a new NFT that is just as straightforward as uploading a picture to the internet and captioning it. The difference is that you're going to spend some crypto in the genesis of your new baby. But the actual creation of a new NFT is never rocket science. Whichever marketplace you do it in, you'll be walked through it step by step.

STRATEGIES TO MAKE MONEY

Tips And Secrets To Reach Huge Profit From Nft Investing

Many NFT creators, artists, and collectors are now clamoring to participate in this burgeoning trend. However, is there a lot of profit to be made from NFTs? In fact, how do you earn a profit on non-fungible token purchases? So, after accomplishing a lot of research on this topic, here's what I discovered.

You can profit from your NFT purchase in several ways:

- Flip Your NFT (Buy NFTs, then swiftly resell them for a profit.)
- Your NFT can be sold (When there is a sudden spike or steady climb in recent sales.)
- Hold Onto Your NFT (If your NFT has underlying value, it'll likely rise in value over time.)
- Unlockables (This is exclusives available to the NFT owner.)
- Purchase what you believe in (Buying an NFT you believe in can result in better-educated purchases.)

Now, let's take a tighter look at the many ways to profit from your NFT purchases.

Flip Your Nft

Flipping an NFT is one of the most typical ways to profit from purchasing. To convert your NFT, buy one and immediately put it back on the market for a higher price. The best part of restoring a non-fungible token vs. a traditional item like a house is that it doesn't require remodeling or updating. It's as simple as buying it and then selling it.

If you want to have the highest chance of flipping your NFT, look for one that has a constant upward sales trend. Furthermore, suppose you have the opportunity to purchase a low-cost NFT from a well-known developer. In that case, you may be able to immediately sell it for a significant return on investment (ROI).

Resell Your Nft

Rather than purchasing and immediately flipping your non-fungible token, you can buy one and hold onto it for a while until you witness a drastic increase in sales/sale prices or a constant and consistent growth over time. The secret to successfully reselling your NFT is to not keep it for too long.

It may be an excellent concept to sell your NFT shortly following a steady increase in sale prices or a sudden rise. If you wait too prolonged, you might not make any money or possibly lose money. Remember that you must ride the wave, but every wave will eventually end.

Hold Onto Your Nft

If you are in the NFT space for a long time and not simply looking to make a quick profit, investing in a long-term NFT could be a good idea. If you can find an NFT with underlying value for a low price now, it could be worth a fortune in the future. The most important aspect of this strategy is to ensure that the non-fungible token you buy has real value and is not just a quick fad.

Anything valuable, exclusive, or unique could be a wise long-term investment.

Unlockables

NFT Assets held on a decentralized storage network are known as unlockables. When someone buys a non-fungible token with these unlockables, they gain access to a variety of benefits, including:

- Merch Deals
- VIP access to live shows
- Monthly Meetings
- Exclusive Calls
- Physical Product
- Follows on social media

When it comes to NFT unlockables, the options are unlimited. I recommend purchasing NFTs with valuable unlockables if you can. You can take benefit of all the perks even if you don't resell it!

Buy What You Believe In

It's essential to purchase an NFT that you're passionate about. In general, if you are interested in a subject, you will better understand that subject. That means you have a better chance of buying something profitable because you know better.

It's just the right thing to do. You may either jump on the bandwagon and start buying trendy items you know nothing about, or you can make a more informed decision and support someone who makes something you genuinely enjoy. It's entirely up to you, but I only purchase items I like.

Overall, if your primary goal is to profit from NFTs, you must research to guarantee that you purchase an NFT that will deliver a return on investment.

Nft Categories With High Potential Profit

There are many different kinds of non-fungible tokens to choose from, and the list will only get longer. Here are some of the multiple famous NFT categories available to purchase and profit from:

- Art
- Gaming
- Photography

Art

Thousands of digital art NFTs are available for purchase. Look for one that has the potential to be valuable in the future. Also, anything you think would make beautiful memorabilia.

Digital art is fantastic because you can create it and transfer it to someone else right away. It is now possible to purchase a portion of digital artwork. That's exactly what the $69 million buyers of Beelple's piece did. He sold shares of the article to multiple people.

The good news is that if you are a creator, you can not only sell your work, but you can also set up NFTs so that you automatically receive a percentage of all secondary sales, which is known as a royalty. Formerly, as an artist, you could not receive any proceeds from secondary sales in the art world, but that is no longer the point.

NFTs can be utilized to make programmable art as well. Programmable art refers to artwork programmed to exhibit dynamic qualities based on how the code is implemented on the blockchain. A digital marketplace called ASYNC art is where you can make programmable art. You can not only make your master

copy there, but you can also add individual layers and change their attributes.

Individuals can contribute to the art, and different group members can control their activities. As a result, NFTs allow for collective art. Your art can be displayed on online marketplaces such as SuperRare and OpenSea, where it can be bought and sold once it has been created.

Music

NFTs have massive potential in the music industry! You can get lifetime VIP access to events, meetings, phone conversations, and more, but that's just the beginning. Consider this: music artists can suddenly use non-fungible tokens to fund their careers. That means that record label deals may no longer be necessary for musicians, and the artist may keep a more significant portion of the profit for themselves.

Furthermore, NFTs allow the artist and the audience to connect on a much deeper level than before. Musicians have so many customizable possibilities to include anything they want when it comes to minting tokens.

Gaming

With the purchase and sale of in-game items, money is made on popular video game platforms. Games like Dota 2 and Team

For example, fortress two on the Steam marketplace is extremely popular and sells quickly.

Crypto Kitties is another NFT phenomenon. Crypto Kitties are being purchased and bred to sell them. Another attractive niche to profit from is in-game items.

Furthermore, because it is decentralized, there is no limit to the types of game items that can be sold or the amounts that can be sold. Axie Infinity, one of the most popular games, has seen some high-ticket purchases. Other games, such as Skyview, Gods of Change, and others, can be swapped or sold for different cards.

Photography

Kate Woodman recently received $20,000 for a single NFT photograph. Photographs are ideal for NFTs because they are now digital.

Photographs capture moments, and some of these moments are significant to people. You can buy images or make your own NFTs and sell them on the various marketplaces.

The most promising part is that you don't have to give up your copyright or reproduction rights as a photographer. You are just selling the buyer the ownership of the NFT piece. You can keep showing that image or photograph, sell prints, or license it to companies.

Once you've determined whether you'll buy or create NFTs, you'll need to decide which type of NFTs you'll use. The next stage is to put them on the marketplaces for sale.

Best Tip To Sell Your Nfts For Profit.

Determine Which Marketplace you want to sell on

If you have NFTs that you purchased and want to sell, you can do so directly on the marketplaces. You can go to prominent market spaces like OpenSea, SuperRare, and Nifty Gateway once you have the digital asset you wish to sell. However, it would help if you inquired about the fees charged.

You have complete control over the number of editions you wish to sell. It does not have to be only one edition. You can have multiple editions of the same digital asset, and each will be distinct and have its token id. Please keep in mind, though, that having more can potentially lower the value of your asset.

Once you've done this, your digital item can't be duplicated or replaced in any way. As a result, no unique abilities or talents are required. You can benefit from locating or constructing an NFT that appeals to people in a specific niche.

Set a reserve bid, which is the lowest price you're willing to sell it for. That is similar to auction websites such as eBay. Don't overprice it or underprice it. Look for a reasonable profit margin, and it will sell.

Finding solid digital assets that have underlying value or that you believe will have value in the future is one method to profit from NFT. Invest in NFTs that you are confident will yield a profit when sold. Once you've purchased these, you can resell them for a considerably higher price on a marketplace. You can also utilize a variety of advertising methods to increase bids.

The value of NFTs is determined by two factors: novelty and scarcity. Focusing on these two aspects can result in high weight for your digital content. One of the secrets to profiting is acquiring appealing and unique creative art, music, and collectibles. Knowing the fees and transactions is vital to avoid losing money on your trades.

GAMING & NFTS

What Is Play To Earn Games?

The business standard known as Play-to-Earn is the most current innovation in the gaming industry. It is a business strategy that embraces the notion of an open economy and bonuses all players who supply value to the game environment via their contributions. It's likely to add new game concepts and retention models to current gaming that haven't been seen before.

As technology became more available to the general public, business models for video games developed. In the late 1970s and earlier 1980s, we recreated our games on arcade machines in neighborhood gaming centers. With only a quarter in their pocket, gamers would vie for the most elevated score.

Nowadays, we play matches on our smartphones when on public transportation or taking a break. We launch a game on our computer or home console when we desire a more immersive experience. However, each participant may find a business plan that works for the platform.

The foundation is free-to-play.

Consumers must acquire a license to access a premium game. They accomplish this by purchasing a request from a digital retailer or a physical copy from an online or brick-and-mortar retailer. Financial commitment is rather significant since paying $60 for a freshly launched game is not uncommon. While this is still a massive market, the free-to-play model has experienced the most growth in recent years.

The free-to-play business model enables gamers to obtain a game free of charge. Free-to-play or freemium games are constantly available for download and provide users with a confined/limited experience. Gamers will be required to pay to accelerate their progress or gain unique equipment. Users may be instructed to pay for in-game currency, more material, or specific cosmetics for their game symbols.

Several of the most famous games on the market are complimentary. Fortnite alone caused 1.8 billion dollars in deals last year, even though the battle royale game is free. Selling cosmetics to enable more personalization is a lucrative industry. Among the most famous games on the market are League of Legends and Hearthstone, which are almost entirely free. Each developer has its strategy for charging customers for more material or aesthetics.

These complimentary games have generated billions of dollars in revenue, and there is no reason to believe they will stop. That demonstrates that the free-to-play business model has developed and that developers have mastered the technique of monetizing free-to-play games.

The play-to-earn business model shares several characteristics with the free-to-play business model. Often, a play-to-earn game will incorporate mechanics from free-to-play games. However, play-to-earn games provide an opportunity for gamers to earn money or valuable digital goods.

Explanation of earn-while-you-play

Giving gamers the right of in-game assets and the ability to grow their worth via dynamic gameplay are essential components of the play-to-earn business model. By hiring in the in-game economy, players contribute to the game's development and benefit other players and the creators. They are rewarded in-game assets as a result. These digital assets might range from cryptocurrency to gaming assets tokenized on the blockchain. That is why the play-to-earn business model complements blockchain plays exceptionally well.

The play-to-earn business model rewards gamers for their time and effort invested in the game. For instance, participants in Axie Infinity win Small Love Potions (SLP). Players require these tokens to breed more Axies, but they may also sell them on the open marketplace to other players. Additional examples are the resources available in League of Kingdoms and the rewards available in the fantasy football game So rare.

Acquire worth to participate

In essence, a pay-to-win game should also be free to play. That is not always the case, though. At present, gamers must purchase three Axies before they may battle within Lunacia, Axie Infinity's universe. Additionally, So rare to ask users to spend money on player cards before earning cards through weekly tournaments. While games like Chainz Arena and League of Kingdoms are free to play, their idle gameplay mechanics and restrictions compel gamers to invest some money in the game. Thus, even if gamers gain anything, they must also pay.

It requires money to develop a video game, which firms generate. The virtue of the play-to-earn business model, on the other hand, is that a gamer will always generate something of value that can be sold. Even if a player must pay to begin, these obtained things may always be resold. Each card in So rare, as well as each Axie in your wallet, may be sold. Simultaneously, games like Fortnite and League of Legends generate billions of dollars. Players spend money and deposit their worth in an infinite pit. Their finances will be depleted when they quit playing these games.

That is altered by play-to-earn. Each thing collected has a monetary worth. That means players will always earn money even when not actively playing a game.

How Do Play-To-Earn Games Change The Economy?

When we hear the word "globalization," we instantly associate it with governmental policy, trade agreements, immigration, and large corporations. However, much of the globe's networking occurs outside of boardrooms, in virtual settings accessible from anywhere in the world. MMO (Massively Multiplayer Online) games have altered how we communicate, build friendships, and form communities by enabling individuals to connect and socialize without regard for geographical boundaries in virtual, fun spaces. One of the fascinating features of this fast globalization of communities is the economics that has developed duhow, how participants value and position digital products and services. Online games, mainly MMOs, have been at the forefront of creative economic techniques that allow for global involvement. That has included players seeking to sell their digital items in exchange for real-world cash, as well as giant corporations developing new business models.

Virtual Economies' Real-World Applications

While the practice of purchasing and selling digital items for real money is not new, it has become increasingly widespread as online communities have grown in size and become huge businesses. Venezuela gained international headlines when many residents switched to gold farming as their principal source of income, discovering that it offered greater financial security than traditional jobs. The practice has grown in popularity to the point where it now has its own Wikipedia and Encyclopedia Britannica entry.

Most game businesses have stringent Terms of Service (ToS) agreements that prohibit Gold Farming monetary exchange of in-game goods or account transfers. While these methods are intended to safeguard the community, they are more likely to establish control over the in-game economy, minimize exposure to KYC/AML regulations, and maximize revenues. These prohibitions preclude an individual player from realizing value from assets acquired or gained via games. By limiting trade, users cannot resell goods they have formerly received, highlighting that they do not purchase their purchased items. These methods have pushed some participants into the grey markets, where they face counterparty risks and account closures if caught.

Without a valid, transparent exchange of products, it becomes practically tricky for gamers to recoup some of the expenses associated with former purchases, much alone profit from their accounts and virtual goods gained while gaming. These closed systems may be restricting the economic possibilities of these gaming communities, as game companies own their growth.

Worldwide, new game economic models are as blockchain technology spreads worldwide emerging. In 2020, the Philippines witnessed a massive migration of non-traditional gamers to cryptocurrency-based video games to make money during the COVID-19 lockdowns. Grandparents, single moms, and taxi drivers turned to video games to supplement their incomes, creating, constructing, and exchanging digital commodities they could later sell on public blockchain markets for cash. What distinguishes these games from MMOs Gold Farming games are based on open economies, the elimination of restrictive Terms of Service, and innovative technology leveraging Non-Fungible Tokens (NFTs) that operate on the blockchain. These new models restore individuals' power by facilitating the ownership of their acquired and earned assets.

The System is Being Gamed

As early video games transitioned from boxed items to continuous-play online services, several facets of game design shifted accordingly. Online games built long-term relationships with their customers, necessitating the evolution of economic structures. Subscriptions and, eventually, microtransactions enabled incremental on-demand purchases. Regrettably, several areas of the game design remained incompatible with these new models. Randomized "Loot Boxes" offered motivation and reward in early video games but were not associated with commercialization in single-purchase, packaged goods game cartridges.

When marketed as microtransactions, certain publishers may monetize these randomized game components. When taken to its logical conclusion, this activity can be classified as gambling. More often than not, practical "Free to Play" games rely on retaining their most devoted players by granting them the ability to speed their game progress. Unfortunately, this might irritate some players, resulting in a lack of incentive to pay and placing the weight of income generation on a small percentage of the player population. A design that favors high rollers can irritate and stratify the playing base.

Thus, what do gamers enjoy? As it turns out, the virtual world closely resembles reality. Players enjoy amassing limited-edition digital items and expressing their social standing via the customization of their identity and virtual environment. The cosmetics sector alone is estimated to be worth $40 billion a year and continues to rise. The addition of blockchain to paid cosmetics and virtual goods has the potential to create new economic models for the gaming industry - models that are likely to be dominated by non-fungible tokens, which give players ownership over their purchases while sharing resale revenue with developers and adding economic value to the game community.

What Does This Mean for Investing Professionals?

While many investors look to major, publicly listed corporations for market direction, astute industry participants will monitor and wait to see how newer, more nimble companies perform before committing to these new ways to market. These investors are more inclined to adopt a wait-and-see attitude, allowing independents to take risks and evaluate proofs of ideas. Their tactic is frequently to enter after new models have been established and lucrative.

That is a unique chance for entrepreneurs, independent developers, and investors to get in on the first floor. While creator-based economies are not new, blockchain technology can expand existing economic models and propel growth to new heights. Cryptoeconomics offers gamer communities the opportunity to contribute to the success of the games they like.

The world closely monitors the present crypto and NFT excitement and anticipates what will transpire over the next 12 months. In truth, astute investors and developers will be looking at the next 3-5 years as the make or break moment for this technology and the associated new business models. If high-quality games are developed, blockchain-enabled open economies can become the fastest market segment of a market, reaching $200 billion.

TOP VIDEO GAMES THAT ARE AN OPPORTUNITY

The phenomena of video games that have incorporated NFT translate into a clear opportunity; the beginning has been Axie Infinity, and then more options have been developed within this industry, which has allowed the lovers of the gamer environment to receive a handsome percentage of profit.

The best NFT video games that yield substantial profits follow the dynamics and relevance of blockchain technology, all this has transformed into a path full of profitability, and you should know one by one to decide to invest in the one that best suits your aspirations within this field,

The Main Options Are As Follows:

- Axie Infinity.
- PVU.
- Wakana Farm.
- Crypto Cars World.
- Block Farm Club.
- Overlord.
- Binamon.
- MIR 4.
- CryptoZoo.
- Sorare.
- Alien Worlds.
- Dragonary.
- CryptoBlades.
- CryptoZoon.
- Splinterlands.
- Upland.

On the other hand within the NFT games sector, there are going to be essential releases such as the following:

- Battle Hero.
- Tethan Arena.
- Mist NFT.
- Block Monsters.

- Ember Sword.
- Illuvium.

The impact caused by each of these games ratifies the power that is being manifested on these investment options; they are also games that endorse the concept of "play-to-earn," that dynamic is the dream and goal of any lover of games, where the entry of some is free because the NFT is acquired according to your progress, or subsequent investment.

The blockchain ecosystem has included video games as one of the forms of investment, and even fluctuation; the success of Axie is the direct support, but so is the AXS that is presented as a governance token that is part of the game, i.e., it is a universe composed of cryptocurrencies, video games and NFT.

If you want to decide on one of the main games that you are betting on today, you should study the volume of each one, and especially from when it was launched to the acceptance of the same.

This game, frequently mentioned in most social platforms, is governed by the recognized token AXS, its capitalization has statistics of; $2,67,003,328 to this is added the participation of partners of the size of Ubisoft or Samsung, which follow the inspiration of Pokemon to carry out the creation of the game.

To start being part of this investment option, you must purchase three creatures with which you will battle and generate profits; that purchase is produced from its Marketplace, although there is the option to enter as a scholarship and play someone else's account, in general, the profits arise from battles, Axies broods, or investing for Lunacia resources.

Wakana Farm

In the middle of the video game, there is the opportunity to be a day laborer, that is the central role and within the game, where in addition to everything you can make purchases of items from the WanaShop, this fulfills the purpose of carrying out purchases and sales of items of collectible qualities.

The trading marketplace of this farm-style NFT trade is conducted using the WANA token, which makes it easy for users to buy items to keep their virtual lands in order.

Block Farm Club

Block Farm Club is presented as a game with a decentralized operation; that way, any user has the opportunity to earn tokens and NFT from the game farm; the profitability of the game has been positive during its first days, its operation has caused it to be compared to PVU.

The main distinction of this game lies in the other browser entertainment alternatives; it has innovative mechanics, it does not have a PAY TO WIN response, but you must buy tokens to start from the platform itself; that way, you can play and get tickets, energy, characters or others to exchange them.

Battle Hero

That is an NFT gambling project launching in 2021, during its operation, it has accrued striking fees that equal CryptoMines for example, it meets the earn to play mode, it has been strongly preferred in Spain and has not yet finished its development, but it is possible to make money from speculation.

The token cryptocurrency associated with this video game is BATH; it is generally a Battle Royale shooter genre. Also, the dominant mode is the free-to-earn, where you can earn money without investing, but rather that money you can spend on the purchase of unique items.

CryptoBlades

It is one of the free games that have the most significant number of users, under the token SKILL is managed by the company Riveted Technology, to offer a choice of entertainment and investment combat, operates under the Smart Chain network Binance, so it has become one of the most popular video games.

The attributes of the game are on the weapons and equipment; thus, the characters face each other; the outcome of such battles depends on a mathematical calculation that merits a considerable investment, thanks to the fact that a large diversity of SKILLs is generated from the exchange of weapons, with a high capacity of token generation.

Overlord

Overlord represents a copy of Mist, a play-to-earn mode is implemented, it has gameplay facilities to be available from a mobile version, the ecosystem is not promising but for the low entry fee is interesting, its launch has been rushed and therefore generates some doubts. Still, it is an alternative to follow closely.

Binamon

The inspiration of this project is to simulate and match what was generated by Axie; it presents a fusion between earn to play for profit without losing the quality of the game, surpassing the development of Alien Worlds or the intention that exists on CryptoBlades, thanks to bet on the theme of adventure, skill and an interface that fights monsters.

This approach is not new but seeks to compete from the similarity with Illuvium, Splinterlands, or Block Monsters; the fight against this type of creatures is one of the most fundamental concepts.

MIR4

MIR4 is not like other NFT games, as it has a high-level graphic design for an accessible mode, that's why the amount of interested users increases every day, it's a great option before the release of My Neighbor Alice and also Ember Sword; this happens through the user base, over the criticism it's a strong alternative.

Splinterlands

It is known as one of the most played NFT in the world, formerly known as Steem Monsters, where a dynamic of collectible cards is developed on Hive blockchains, a different type of battle is managed, and deck building is required to be carried out.

This game's preparation is strategic battles; unlike other NFT games such as Dragonary, this game takes strength thanks to its growing community.

Diversifying The Portfolio Of Video Game Nfts

Investment diversification is a guarantee to offset any risk; it is one of the principles that has ruled within cryptocurrencies and carries over to the NFT sector, especially when it is a market that frequents many video game projects from which it is possible to profit.

Putting together NFT investment diversification is possible, as long as you have different business models included to ensure that you follow the course of any winning dynamics or can amortize the lack of confidence that other paths may cause; for this, you should consult the following games that between them complement a good investment wallet.

The income value that is obtained utilizing this video game is striking, thanks to the point that the in-game currency can be obtained from internal battles that force you to have and use a good, competitive team that along with the gameplay is what creates an income that you can take advantage of.

Alien Worlds

As an investment, it is interesting because it follows a fantasy of creatures that have different races and qualities; as a result of these distinctions, you can use the cards to win most of the games within this game, on the side of the quotation of the virtual properties of the game, they depend directly on Trillium as its official cryptocurrency.

The community that defends the development of this game ratify the excellent decision to bet on cryptocurrencies, although it is best to evaluation its platform to consider the blockchain operations and base yourself on those numbers that are being generated as a result of the game, that is the ratification of how it works.

0x Universe

This NFT game maintains a wide availability from the Play Store for any Android user. Still, beforehand you should know that it is a game that pays off slowly, so it deserves patience and considers that you do not need to invest as a positive side of this option.

The game's main idea is to build ships, collect enough tokens to acquire planets, each of the properties you get to buy NFT; finally, the profits can be easily exchanged for Ethereum, the progress within the game is accelerated by investing in continuing accumulating more properties.

Sorare

If you are passionate about sports games, this option is to your liking because the primary motivation is fantasy football, which is fashionable in the gamer sphere, with the contribution of earning money for free, as long as it is possible to build teams, management, and other competitive football activities.

Like other NFT games, the start is framed by non-tokenized tokens; then there are internal gains in the game that make it possible to continue to invest; as you engage with the game, substantial gains will begin to occur, from the tokens or cards in the game a differential value emerges that you can trade with.

One of the NFT games that get a lot of attention is CryptoBlades, because it brings medieval role-playing to life, with the option to do battles against monsters and use weapons, all of which are easily converted into money.

The NFT within the game is on the weapons, that way is distributed up to 800 thousand tokens open to users, for that you must invest in weapons to raise the level of each of them, but the advantage lies on a free registration until you get the official currency of the game called as SKILL.

Gods Unchained

The popularity of God's Unchained causes must be about diversifying your NFTs through a card mechanic to earn rewards from digital tokens anchored in Ethereum; monetization is on the side of the coin that receives the designation as Flux.

The initial registration does not earn any token, but it is necessary to be part of an advance within the game until reaping the rewards, likewise, the funds are received in the same measure in which you play, it is essential to allocate time to play until you find the long-awaited gains you expect.

Snook

It is striking as a game as it is very similar to the typical Nokia entertainment, where users spend hours having fun controlling a snake that evolves as it feeds on the elements presented in the game. Still, this opportunity facilitates the generation of income.

When the snake goes eating everything you get in its path, it receives masks that increases the price quotation of the NFT thanks to that is evolving, in this case, the official currency is SNK that has presented good moves to motivate users to be part of this ecosystem, everything is measured according to the player's skills.

SMART CONTRACTS

We will take a more close look at some essential concepts to understand better NFTs and how to use them:

- Smart contracts are protocols that facilitate and verify the negotiation and subsequent execution of the contract. These are contracts in the form of programming language.

- Ethereum is the decentralized platform where smart contracts are created and executed.

- An API (application programming interface) refers to procedures aimed at solving a given task—in this case, the goal prescribed in the smart contract.

- The gas fee refers to a price or value required to successfully conduct a transaction or execute a contract on a blockchain. Gas in Ethereum is a division of measure for the work done by Ethereum to perform transactions or any interaction within the network. In Ethereum, the developers decided to attract constant values to the different operations performed in Ethereum. In this way, every activity in Ethereum has a defined gas value, which does not vary and is not altered by the increase or decrease in the value of Ether, Ethereum's native currency. The fact that this gas value is a constant response to the fact that although the price of Ether is volatile, the computational cost of operations always remains constant.

Now that you know these terms, we can delve into smart contracts.

Smart contracts are computer protocols that facilitate, verify, and enforce contract negotiation. They are programs executed on blockchain nodes and simulate the logic of contract clauses. The clauses and validating nodes represent a change of state of the blockchain itself; therefore, the transaction is created must find consensus through a community system. That is called "proof of work."

Any data can be recorded and inserted within the blockchain in a distributed, decentralized, and transparent chain. Data validation is done through peer-to-peer verification called "proof of work" or "PoW." None of the recorded information can be deleted or modified once encrypted. The nodes within the blockchain, as we have seen, exchange value in an entirely new trustless situation, which involves the absence of a third intermediary. Due to this nature, blockchain can hold and store all sorts of digital values and virtual assets.

The use of blockchain technology is limited to digital assets; dematerialized tangible assets can also be recorded within it. Smart contracts come into play when the data transferred on the blockchain platform must respond to predetermined conditions. Then, the platform is used to certify the transactions. Nick Szabo defined the concept of smart contracts in 1997, before blockchain. However, blockchain has played a vital role in ensuring the implementation of smart contracts by allowing information and transactions to be managed securely.

A smart contract is a computer protocol that facilitates and verifies the execution of a contract between two or more users. It automatically verifies the terms based on the clauses that have been agreed upon. It is called an intelligent contract precisely because of its ability to be brilliant in the sense of executing an agreement. It typically uses the "if/then" functions built into computer software and can only manage what has been predetermined in the programming phase.

The different stages of implementing a smart contract are as follows:

- Definition of the agreement between the parties involves the translation and registration of the details in a smart contract.

- Related verification and inscription of the smart contract in the blockchain is registered and made exclusive. The blockchain guarantees the automation of contractual obligations and their transparency in case of execution and the immutability of the collected data.

The smart contract then becomes an identified block simply by transforming into a hash value that allows for the maintenance, accessibility, and correct updating of a shared ledger or distributed ledger.

The proof of work (PoW) mining inside Ethereum occurs when the miner solves the cryptographic puzzle and sends it to the whole network. At this point, the contract applicant pays a fee, and the contract is registered.

The block is added to the immutable and certified chain. The whole operation has a public value and is entirely accessible. The hashes in the sequence are safe and cannot be counterfeited.

At this point, the smart contract can access third-party (external) applications to know the conditions of certain situations and occurrences for which it was programmed—for example, to know flight times to communicate delays. In practice, it queries the APIs to get the necessary information. This way saves a considerable number of resources in negotiation and execution, speeds up performance, and considerably decreases the chances of disputes between the parties.

Unlike a traditional contract, an innovative agreement is binding by its very nature—i.e., its particular technology. The blockchain node prevents pre-established conditions from being violated, and conditions related to the individual's conduct take a back seat. This irrevocability, which is triggered when the data is entered into the blockchain technology, leaves no room for exceptions.

Ethereum's virtual currency is Ether, which serves as the unit of measure and cryptocurrency. However, Ethereum, unlike Bitcoin, is not just a network for transferring value; it is a trustworthy platform for running smart contracts. Intelligent contracts can define rules as standard contracts and enforce them automatically through code. However, they are not controlled by a user. Instead, they are deployed on the network and executed as initially programmed. A smart contract on Ethereum uses the same operation as a vending machine: you receive the snack if you insert the coin and select the snack. The vending machine follows programmed logic in the same way as a smart contract. Any programmer can write a smart contract and deploy it on Ethereum's blockchain network. Deploying an intelligent agreement is technically a transaction, so you have Ether pay the gas fee just like a typical transaction. However, the costs of implementing the contract are much higher.

Since each Ethereum transaction requires computing resources to be executed, each trade requires a fee. Gas is the fee needed to successfully conduct a transaction on Ethereum. The ether and gas gee on Ethereum is essential to keep the network security to prevent any spam.

Ethereum has developer-friendly languages for writing smart contracts, such as Solidity and Vyper. Intelligent contracts are public on Ethereum and can be considered open APIs. That allows intelligent contracts to be composable. Moreover, you can start a smart contract on an existing one. It is also possible to enable a self-destruct option, which removes programs that are no longer used to improve effectiveness and performance.

With the help of smart contracts, digital assets can be programmed in such a way as to have additional functions compared to traditional modes. Digital assets based on a smart contract can execute clauses entirely autonomously, without the intermediation of third parties, thus increasing transparency and legal security.

For this reason, they have many possibilities within different areas and applications, such as the following:

- Cybersecurity: Although it is a system visible to everyone, everything in the blockchain is inscribed through encrypted keys that verify the data within it. The transmission of data is protected from interception and manipulation.

- Election systems: Blockchain enables voter identity authentication, secure record-keeping, and accurate and transparent counting.

- Internet of Things (IoT): When objects become intelligent and talk to each other, they can facilitate and verify the execution of operations within an enterprise. Smart contracts provide the backbone for the Internet of Things and allow for a ledger that can manage many devices.

- Public administration: Can offer monitoring to ensure secure and transparent governance.

- Crowdfunding: Enables campaigns where contributors can fully control the money invested. In this way, the donor is more secure, and the money is not spent on intermediary activities.

- Intellectual property: The very structure of blockchain allows you to keep track of everything, including transactions and ownership changes. That is why intelligent contracts find applications tracking individual properties with chronological accuracy.

START YOUR NFTS BUSINESS

Nfts Ownership

While FTs are a hot topic right now, buyers and sellers need to know the regulatory conditions that may apply to these properties. This is not an NFT, but you wouldn't be surprised to find it.

Nfts And Intellectual Property Law

NFTs are commonplace. How do they serve in with the existing laws and regulations? Does it matter?

NFTs are growing in popularity, but it is unclear how they will fit into the legal or regulatory structures regulating the technology, financial, and cryptocurrency industries. They cannot be considered a security because they are not the same as initial coin offerings. NFT operations are subject to laws, but customers must be aware of doing.

Breaking It Down

They are almost identical and live on a blockchain (such as Ethereum). Anyone can import and duplicate video clips and image files, but an NFT only has one owner. The image file in an NFT can still be downloaded. A tweet that you sell will remain available to all users on Twitter. You're purchasing a virtual note, not the actual tweet. These cards are very similar to autographed football cards. You can print as multiple cards as you want. You can print as numerous cards as you like, but it will most likely be the most valuable if a player signs only one card. For example, a Tom Brady autographed card sold recently for $1.32million.

Andrew Hinkes from Carlton Fields suggests that we may only be scratching the surface on what NFTs could do. An NFT can, at its most basic level, recognize a financial property that can lead to new efficiency in current transactions. An example of this is island ownership. Currently, people depend on land registries held by third parties such as a government department to prove they own a piece of land. Hinkes suggests that an NFT could be used to identify the property. That would allow a person to prove their ownership using a cryptographically secured and signed digital token.

Fabrica's Daniel Rollingher is a real-estate attorney who pointed out that NFTs in real estate may require consumers to borrow from lenders. NFT issuers must comply with consumer protection and disclosure regulations.

Holder Protection

Donna Redel, an associate professor at Fordham Law and a New York Angels panel member, says that NFTs can confuse customers. Besides that, NFTs pose additional concerns about who is conducting know your customer/anti-money laundering practices, documenting the selling of an NFT, and the rights buyers have.

She stated that she was not certain artists understood their rights and responsibilities under the contract and in the broader legal environment. "I expect to see more stuff such as [NBA] Top Shot," she said. Andrew Jacobson of Seward and Kissel says NFTs are particularly popular among a younger audience that is less educated.

Law

Jacobson suggests that NFTs could violate a nation's sanctions law. That prohibits residents from doing business or people with entities or

Individuals from sanctioned nations. There could be an exception for information or information content that allows citizens to interact with sanctioned nations' artwork. What would you do if an NFT was discovered in Iran, North Korea, or another sanctioned country?

He said that there is also the possibility of malicious actors using NFTs to raise or launder funds. He cited the Marine Chain ICO as one example of how a sanctioned organization has attempted to secure funding through cryptocurrencies in the past. Platforms that create, process, and offer NFTs must consider this. The media should also avoid being confused with money transfer companies.

You might argue that an NFT can be a valuable substitute because Financial rules regulate items that replace value. Financial regulations aren't concerned with the asset; they care about people and their conduct.

Intellectual Property and Copyright

It is essential to determine if buyers' expectations about what they bought match the legal reality. Sellers, mainly established businesses that jump on the bandwagon, face the same problem. Sellers should ensure that the NFTs they sell contain the material they want to sell. Unlike virtual files, NFTs cannot be edited once registered on a Blockchain.

"You can't undo anything; there's no turning around." While you can issue another token, the original NFT will still be in circulation. You must therefore understand and be aware of all possible risks. NFTs may also interact with existing copyright legislation. "There is no one serious about NFTs that entertains the idea that what you're selling might be the copyright or the master suggesting artists could sell some licensed material to buyers while maintaining the copyright.

Musicians and artists can make NFTs of their work, but anyone can make NFTs of jobs they didn't create. I am curious if the new NFT platforms can deal with this possibility. What if OpenSea began a few Mickey Mouse-related NFTs and Walt Disney lawyers contacted it?

Counterfeiting

NFTs often represent real-world objects. That increases the chance of a connection between real-world objects and NFTs that indicate it is damaged. You might sell something on a platform and claim it's an NFT.

That is residing on a blockchain. This is false. As they're not smart enough to verify, many users won't know if the NFT is true or false. The products could be an NFT or an excellent picture linked to another blockchain.

Securities and Taxation Rules

NFTs may be subject to securities laws. However, this seems less likely than many of the other regulatory regimes involved. A person who buys an NFT under the assumption that its value will rise will sue the NFT creator. It is comparable in that there is lots of public demand. However, traditional securities, sanctions, and commodity legislation would need to be adjusted.

NFT buyers may have to deal with different tax laws in other countries. NFTs tied to art usually require the buyer to address this issue. Who collects sales tax? When you buy art worth $4.6 million, sales tax must be paid. It's the responsibility of the buyer.

CREATE A BUSINESS PLAN FOR NFT

The following is all about creating a business plan for an NFT. That provides step-by-step instructions on determining what you should include and where to find what you need.

If you've always had great ideas but lacked the confidence or know-how in how to bring them into reality, it's time for a change! A business plan is critical. We'll discuss why it is important and guide you on how to write one for your idea for an NFT.

Why Is A Business Plan Important?

A business plan is often viewed as an essential aspect of a startup. Without one, you risk wasting time and money on dreams that never materialize. It provides a step-by-step process for turning an idea into a profitable reality. It will guide you through various tasks to help you create, develop, and market your new business venture.

How To Write A Business Plan For Nft?

Step 1 – Make Your Goal Clear and Attainable – Setting a goal makes it possible to determine what parts of the process are necessary.

Step 2 – Understand Your Competition – One must first understand the competition when writing a plan. While your idea may be unique, it will probably not be the first of its kind. Establish a clear understanding of what your competition is doing to identify points you can improve and those best suited for you. Also, learn about potential customers and their needs.

Step 3 – Determine Your Unique Selling Proposition (USP) – It is a product or service that will make it stand out from the rest of the industry and allow it to generate revenue in the beginning stages.

Step 4 – Create a Mission Statement – To maximize your success, you must develop a mission statement. That is essentially your purpose for existing in the business world.

Step 5 – Determine Your Strengths and Weaknesses – Analyze your skill set and determine which areas best suit you to market to customers. Write down all of these details.

What kind of people purchases products like yours or use services similar to their own?

Step 6 – Identify Your Target Market – While considering which markets will be the best for your business, you must identify who these consumers are. That will help the business plan show specific details about how it can satisfy customer demand in the future.

Step 7 – Assess the Competition – Understanding how your business will fair against the competition is essential. Not only does this provide information that you can use to your advantage, but it also helps you with marketing strategies and ways to promote your company.

Step 8 – Determine How You Will Market Your Business – Collect the necessary facts about what promotion methods will benefit the business most. Detail strategies that have been proven successful by competitors in the past.

Step 9 – Establish a Timeline – Just as with goals for the future, it is essential to create a timeline that details how the business will be operated. That should include what you will accomplish daily, weekly, and yearly.

Step 10 – Analyze Your Idea's Future Potential – Consider what might happen in the future if your idea quickly becomes successful. Provide details about how you will handle increased customer demand and other issues that might arise. Viable plans should be outlined in detail.

While it is essential to study the competition, it is equally necessary to create a product in demand by customers.

Step 11 – Assess the Potential Market – The next step is to get a rough estimate of how many customers could potentially purchase your product or receive your service. These potential consumers provide information that will help you with business planning.

Step 12 – Finance the Project – After creating your business plan, estimate how much money you will need to startup operations. That should include money for outlay costs, salaries/employees, and all other expenses that might arise.

Step 13 – Assess the Financial Status of Your Business – A business plan should detail the financial status of a company. That will assist you in explaining why you are planning to develop your particular product or service. In addition, it will help you to understand how much money your company will need to grow into significant profit for investors.

Step 14 – Draft the Business Plan – Once you have created an outline of your business plan, it is time for revisions and development. That allows for improvements in language regarding budgeting, timelines, and product development.

Step 15 – Send out Your Business Plan – Finally, send out your business plan along with a request for feedback.

Business Planning Basics Are For Startup In Nft

Of course, it is possible that while going through this process, you might find that your initial idea will not work as well as you had hoped. After all, if it isn't realistic or achievable, it will be a waste of time to move forward and lose cash on developing an idea that can't impact the market. In any case, the business planning basics supplied by the above guide should help create an outline for a solid and achievable plan for your business in NFT.

To make your business a natural and possible success, it is vital to start with the basics to know what to keep an eye on and what to discard altogether.

Before moving forward with business planning basics, it is essential to realize that starting a new business or developing one from scratch is not as simple as it might seem. It takes a great deal of time, effort, and money before even thinking about making any profit. Of course, this doesn't mean that you cannot succeed in NFT; however, you must be realistic about the benefits and possibilities available in this industry.

For that reason, it is essential to start with the business planning basics outlined above to ensure that you create a plan that is achievable by your company. A solid plan will mean that you will have some extra money and time to devote to developing your business idea.

Knowing a few business planning basics will make it easier for you to make critical decisions when developing your product and entering the NFT market. Do not be discouraged if your business doesn't get off on the right foot from the start; after all, many business owners are aware that their initial plans were not as good as they could have been. Keep in mind that you will make mistakes along the way, so it is best to prepare for them as best you can.

Using the business planning basics supplied by this guide will be much easier for you to put together a realistic plan. Keep in mind that this guide is intended for new business owners; however, those who have been involved in marketing businesses or are interested in entering the NFT market may also find it helpful. Many of these businesses begin with similar ideas and needs; however, there are often a few steps that will make things much easier overall.

Planning is essential for a few different reasons. Perhaps the most fundamental reason is that it will help you decide whether a particular business opportunity is worth pursuing. If you have decided to start an NFT business, this guide will help you determine how much time and money you ought to invest in your business before it starts making a profit. You can also use this guide as part of creating your NFT marketing plan.

Overall, there are many reasons why entrepreneurs get involved with NFT marketing. However, if you don't have a good idea of what you want to do or the best way to do it, there is a high probability that your business will not be successful.

And one of the most practical things you can do to make your NFT marketing plan more successful is to acquire all the information and resources you need for this purpose.

Create A Digital Wallet

To create a MetaMask digital wallet, go to the website and click on the blue 'Download' button in the top-right corner. We selected to install the browser extension because we're using a desktop computer, but there is also a mobile app.

When you first launch your wallet, it will prompt you to 'generate a new wallet and seed phrase.' It would benefit if you weren't concerned about what "seed phrase" means (simply a list of words that saves blockchain data). Say yes, then it's merely a case of agreeing to the conditions, creating a password, and going through some security checks to get your account up and running.

You'll need to add some ETH to your MetaMask wallet or any other digital wallet after you've created it. That's not difficult at all: click the 'Buy' button and pick Wyre as your payment method. You'll be carried to a screen where you can buy ETH with Apple Pay or a debit card. If you'd rather not spend any money yet, feel free to proceed; all you have to do is wait a little longer.)

Connect Your Wallet To An Nft Platform

Example for this purpose, but there are numerous other NFT platforms to explore.

In the right-hand corner of the screen, a button says 'Connect wallet.' Click here to connect your wallet with MetaMask. A popup will appear asking you whether you want to link your wallet with Rarable. Select "Yes," then "Connect," and agree to the terms of service before confirming your age.

GIFs can be used as NFTs; however, we advise you to create the file in an image editor like Photoshop or Paint because they give complete control over sizing and sharpness. To do this: Open your chosen software and create a new image of dimension 256 x 128 using black and white colors (if using Paint, make sure Advanced Mode is on). Paste your GIF into that new image, and scale it down to fit the whole picture.

You're ready to make your NFT now. The blue 'Create' control in the upper right should be clicked. After that, you may select a single one-off project or sell the same item several times. Choose 'Single' in this example. You must upload the digital file that you wish to convert into an NFT at this stage. Rarible takes PNG, GIF, WEBP, MP4, and MP3 files up to 30MB in size.

Upload your file; then, you'll see a glimpse of your NFT post on the right.

Put up an auction

In the next part of the form, you'll need to choose how you want to sell your NFT artwork. There are three options here. 'Fixed price' permits you to set a price and sell to someone instantly (like 'Buy it now on eBay'). 'Unlimited Auction' will enable people to carry on making bids until you accept one.

HOW TO MAKE YOUR NFT'S PROJECT

Should You Create Your Own Nft Artworks?

You probably doubt whether or not NFTs are worth a shot. When you think of the traditional art world, you see various art galleries, people spending hundreds of thousands or even millions on artworks. But then you get struck by the reality. Only a countable few people can make a living out of this. Even then, their revenues have to be shared with other parties involved in the sale.

However, the NFT world can be different. As the artist, you will control all strings of your artwork. Since NFTs' marketplaces are global, your artwork will be exposed to the whole world. There's no need to contact an agency or a gallery to sell your work. You also don't have to share your revenue with multiple parties or intermediaries. The NFTs' marketplaces will keep you in your artwork's sale loop all the time. You will be able to get a fair commission from every NFT artwork you sell. Besides, at any time, you are capable of proving the authenticity of your art, and there's only one person to be the valid owner of your artwork at a given time. The entire NFT artwork ecosystem provides a more democratic landscape for everybody to create, buy, and sell artwork.

Also, unlike in the traditional art world, where you get paid in weeks or months after selling the artworks, you will receive the money instantly into your crypto wallet as soon as you make the NFT artwork sale. That is real excitement and relief.

What makes it even better? If your initial collector gets an offer on the art and decides to sell it. Boom! Another 10% (for example) of the resale value will immediately appear in your crypto wallet in most services.

NFT makes it more convenient for those motion-based and 3D artworks. These kinds of art are hard to sell as physical pieces and shown best in digital form.

Your artworks will also be viewed from anywhere, and you can avoid shipping issues.

So, what are the downsides?

Your artwork will be tossed into a vast sea of art. Like other online businesses, you will still need to bring your work to the attention of potential buyers and collectors.

If you lose your crypto wallet login information, unlike the traditional banks that can help you reset your password, you will lose your artwork and money forever.

Another "gas fee" is associated with each transaction of Etherium that can quickly be added up. Although some companies are working hard on keeping down the price of the electricity used to create and track every crypto art piece, the cost is not ideal.

Tokenizing your artwork doesn't mean you lose your intellectual rights. You will always be able to sell your artworks traditionally — print them, show them, and sell them physically. The most you will lose is the gas fee and some time. On balance, it is still worth you dipping your toes in the crypto art pond.

Can Your Content Be An Nft?

Probably.

Almost anything in the NFT, like memes, songs, recipes, digital art, and even entire startups, is listed on the NFT marketplaces. There are very few restrictions regarding what types of content can be tokenized and turned into NFTs.

As digital art's demand continues to grow, it's a great time to experiment with this technology for your artwork. One rule that should be kept in mind is that avoid turning copyrighted assets or contents into NFTs.

What Is Needed To Start Creating Nfts? Step-By-Step Instructions

You won't need extensive crypto knowledge to create NFTs, while you do need several tools to get started. It's Okay if you are not acquainted with them yet. You will be able to get everything set up in only a few minutes from your phone. Let's get started.

Here you will learn to set up a crypto wallet, purchase ETH, and connect your crypto wallets to NFT marketplaces.

Step 1: Set Up Your Ethereum Wallet

What's your first step in your NFT journey? It's to create a digital wallet where you can securely store your cryptocurrency used to create, buy, and sell NFTs. This crypto wallet will also allow you to create accounts and safely sign in on NFT marketplaces.

Hundreds of platforms provide free wallets that can help you store cryptocurrencies.

Step 2: Buy A Small Piece of Ethereum (ETH)

There will be fees for turning your artwork into NFTs on most major digital art marketplaces. So, you will require to buy some ETH to cover the costs of making your first NFT.

Since the ETH's price fluctuates almost every second, it's challenging to track it. One more straightforward way to get started is by choosing your funds in dollars with the amount you are willing to purchase and invest exactly that much ETH. The Metamask introduced before allows you to buy crypto right inside your crypto wallet. In contrast, the Coinbase wallet needs you to purchase from another exchange platform and transfer it into your wallet.

Step 3: Connect the Crypto Wallet to NFT Marketplaces

After you set up your wallet and buy some ETH, it's time to choose a marketplace where you want to make NFTs and list your work. Rarible is an excellent choice for beginners who just started as they have the most straightforward and effortless setup.

To connect your crypto wallet to Rarible, go to their site and click the Connect button in the screen's top right corner.

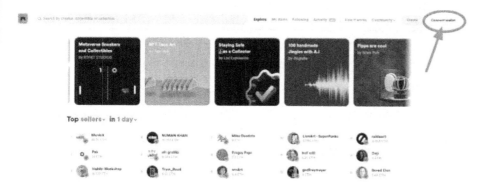

Connect Crypto Wallet To Rarible

On the next screen, choose the wallet you decided on in the preceding step.

Choose your wallet

The next step is almost the same, no matter which wallet you choose. A QR code will appear on the screen after selecting your connection wallet. Then, use your crypto wallet app to scan this code. After checking the code, confirm that you would like to connect your crypto wallet to Rarible.

That is a safe connection, and Rarible will always make you confirm purchases with your crypto wallet apps before moving forward with anything. Your Rarible account will be instantly generated once you connect to the wallet.

Now you have everything needed to create and sell your first NFT.

How To Create Nft Art With No Coding Experience

Step 1: Make a Digital Art File as NFTs

No standard technique exists to create a piece of art that can be used as NFTs. As long as the file you created is supported by the marketplace you are using to list it, it will work as NFTs.

There's an NFT. That contains lots of opportunities for the content you can monetize. On Rarible or Zora, the image as JPG, PNG, TXT, or GIF, and MP3 can be NFTs. A meme can be an NFT

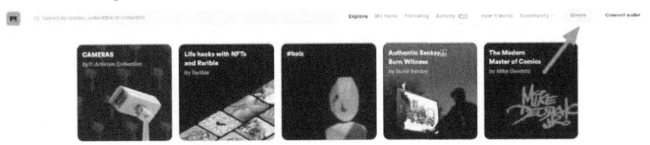

too. Construct a tasty recipe and have it saved as the TXT?

Here, we will use Rarible, with no coding experience needed.

First, click the "Create Collectibles" in the upper right corner.

Click "Create Collectibles" on Rarible

Then, we're going to see we can either create a single collectible or multiple. So, we can have one rare or make various collectibles. So, let's do various.

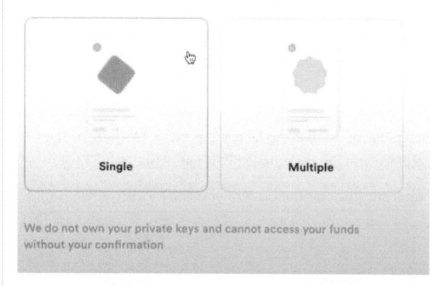

← Go back

Create collectible

Choose "Single" if you want your collectible to be one of a kind or "Multiple" if you want to sell one collectible multiple times

Single

Multiple

We do not own your private keys and cannot access your funds without your confirmation

Create Collectible

We're going to do multiple and start from scratch, and it's going to say select an image: jpg, png, or a gif. So, you can use any file as long as it is a jpeg, png, or gif. It could be a photo you took on your phone, and it can also be a picture you took several years ago that you uploaded onto your computer with a scanner; any file that meets these criteria.

If you already have a file or a picture you want to turn into an NFT, you can upload it right here, but let's say you have a file or an image that is not part of these formats. It's straightforward to convert them. You can go to onlineconvert.com, and you can convert an image to a png file or a jpeg file.

After you get the file in the acceptable format, you can upload it to Rarible.

You can take a png file or a jpeg file and compress it here. Please note that they recommend that the file is under 10 megabytes, so if you have a file above 10 megabytes and want to squeeze it, go to tinypng.com. Once we have those images, we can go back to Rarible and upload them.

But let's say you want to create an image from scratch. I prefer using Canva. It is where I do my work. Canva is a great software. There is a free version, and also there is the paid version which is about ten dollars per month.

Another helpful tool is Kapwing. It provides several well-suited tools to help you create and get more from your existing NFTs.

Here, let's make a short piece of NFT with Canva to upload to Rarible.

So, we're going to create a design. We'll do a logo here, but you can do any art, or you could do Instagram posts, Facebook posts, brochures, anything you can think of.

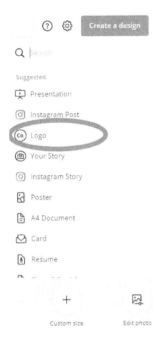

Create Deign

Let's make a crypto monkey. First, choose the monkey you like, and we can enlarge it. You can do whatever you want in Canva. It's straightforward to use.

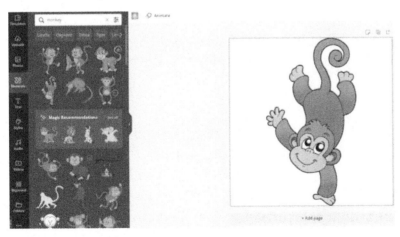

Create a monkey

We'll get an Ethereum logo. Now, this is our NFT.

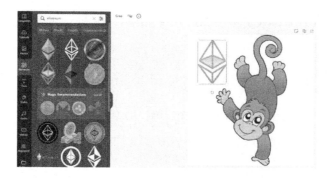

Add ETH logo

Next, let's save it and download it. We'll call it crypto monkey.

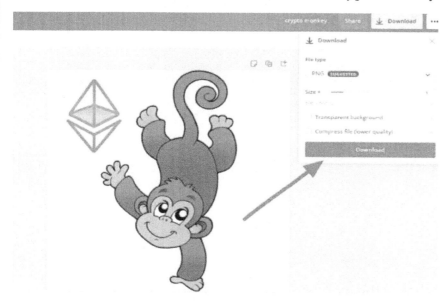

Save & download your work.

Step 2: Upload the Artwork to Rarible

We now have our png file. So, let's go back to Rarible and let's upload it. We're going to choose our image of the crypto monkey.

Create NFT on Rarible

We can also choose a collection on this page, or you can keep it on Rarible.

We can also provide it a title, calling it crypto monkey Super. Then, we can do an optional description: this is a crypto monkey Super, or whatever you want. Then, over here, we can choose how many copies we want. Since we did multiple collectibles, so we can do various compositions here.

Another thing we can set up here is royalties. That means that after you sell your NFT to someone, you will receive a royalty every time it is sold. They recommend or suggest 10, 20, or 30 percent.

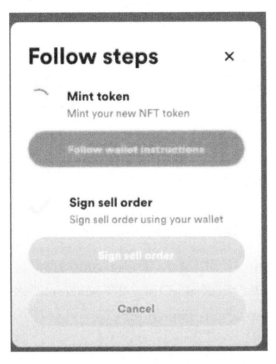

For properties, this will depend on what you're creating. For example, we'll do our property as the animal for our crypto monkey. You can go as heavy on this as you want, and you can create properties, or you can make no properties; that's up to you.

Then, we're going to set a price for it. Please note there's a service fee of 2.5 percent.

For unlock once purchase, don't touch that; leave that as it is.

After you check your pevaluation to make everything look correct, click Create.

Attention: this is where we run into the risk of creating NFTs.

Mint & Sell Nft On Rarible

You might have come to this, and you want to sell it at a high price. You may want to create a hundred of these NFTS, maybe a thousand, and think that one of them will eventually sell. However, the problem is every time you make an NFT, there is a transaction on the ETH blockchain, so you're going to pay a gas fee. Right now, the gas fee to mint this token is six dollars and twenty-one cents, which you might consider very low, but I've seen these gas fees for nine dollars, ten dollars, and even more.

FINDING PROFITABLE NON-FINANCIAL TECHNOLOGIES

You've reached the stage where you'll discover how to make money using non-traditional financial instruments (NFTs). Now that you understand how NFTs function, the many kinds of NFTs, how to mint your own NFT, and where you may purchase NFTs from other producers and resell them, it is time to learn how to correctly choose NFTs that will provide a significant return on your investment. The NFT market is still in its premature stages compared to other markets, but there is a lot of possible profit to be gained. In one case, a friend of mine realized a 7,400 per cent return on a single piece of NFT when he resold "Temporal Shark Dream," which was created by an NFT artist called Max Osiris had purchased from him.

This same friend has generated a total return on investment (ROI) of 2,005 per cent from 19 resales of multiple NFTs that he purchased on the cheap. His success in the NFT sales market has elevated him to the top three collectors on SuperRare regarding resale volume.

While you may not be able to achieve an ROI of 7,400 per cent on your first NFT investment, I can teach you the secrets that underpin the process of economically picking NFTs that can provide at least a 100 per cent return on your first capital investment. Keep in mind that the secrets I'm about to reveal to you are not hard and fast rules that will guarantee you a 100 per cent return on your NFT investments; instead, they are more like guidelines that can assist you in systematically investing in NFTs that have the potential to generate a 100 per cent return on your initial investment. In reality, it was via applying these concepts that I achieved an excellent 1,050 percent return on my NFT investments in a little over two years. If I can earn such a high return on investment using these ideas, I am confident that you will be able to do so as well. So, what exactly are these "hidden principles" that might assist you in making money off of your NFT investments? Consider the following examples.

The Untold Secrets Of Choosing Profitable Non-Firm Transactions

The Reputation of the Creator

Before buying any NFT collectible, the first thing to examine is the individual's reputation for creating the collectible. If you are purchasing a piece of art in the conventional sense, the importance of the artist who made it is usually considered before you make your final decision. The more well-known and intriguing an artist is, the more valuable their work is seen as being by others.

This behavior may be seen in the NFT space as well. This behavior was one of the elements that contributed to Beeple's NFT painting selling for as much as $69 million when it was auctioned off. When contemplating an NFT investment — particularly in the NFT arts — it is essential to ensure that the NFT you are considering was produced by a creator who has established a solid reputation in the industry.

Investing in such an NFT will make it much simpler for you to resale it at a much more significant price than you paid for it when you purchased it. The NFT environment, on the other hand, is not limited to just digital art and design. There are various NFT niches in which you may choose to invest, including gaming objects, player's cards, and other similar products. If you are contemplating acquiring such non-financial instruments, the following set of guidelines can assist you in selecting lucrative ones to put your money into.

Sufficiency is essential when investing in non-financial technologies (NFTs) to receive high returns. A shortage of a particular item in the traditional world leads to a demand for that specific item. This holds in the NFT world as well, assuming that the more rare an object is, the greater the perceived value it has. For example, a LeBron James slam from the NBA Top Shot moment sold for more than $200,000 since it was the only copy available at the time of the sale. In light of its rarity, other buyers on the marketplace bid more and higher on its price until it was ultimately sold for $208,000. Although the collector who purchased the artwork has not yet placed it for sale, you can imagine how much it would sell for if it were to be listed for sale on a secondary market when it does finally become available. In a similar vein, a player card showing Cristiano Ronaldo sold for $290,000 even though it was one of just a few available. Consider how much the card will sell for in the next two to three years as the NFT industry grows and develops. When looking for NFTs to invest in, it is typically more advantageous to invest in NFTs that are one-of-a-kind rather than NFTs that are duplicated in several locations. People are ready to pay more for an item that is one of a kind; but, when an NFT is available in several copies, people are less willing to pay due to the lack of distinctiveness.

The Amount Of Transactional Activity That Takes Place.

It would be best if you spent close awareness of the level of transactional activity associated with any NFT initiative in which you choose to invest. The greater the level of transactional activity around an NFT project, the greater the project's liquidity. When you decide to sell your NFT, you will have an easier time finding a buyer because of the high liquidity. You do not want to invest in an NFT project with low sales since this will make it more challenging for you to sell the project in the future.

Knowledge In A Specific Field

In the world of finance — particularly on Wall Street — there is a phrase that goes something like this: "invest in what you understand." This statement couldn't be more accurate when investing in non-financial companies (NFTs). There are a variety of sectors that are being transformed by NFTs, including gaming, art, virtual reality, and music, to mention a few. When contemplating whether or not to support a non-traditional investment, exploring NFTs that deal with topics you are familiar with is advisable. For example, if you are a severe gamer, your significant investing concentration should be on non-financial-transactions (NFTs) tied to gaming.

Similarly, if you are an art enthusiast, your significant investing concentration should be on non-financial-transactions (NFTs) tied to art. The ability to concentrate on and make investments in areas in which you are competent will enable you to find lucrative chances that other people may not be able to see until it is too late. For example, suppose you are a dedicated viewer of football matches. In that case, you will be able to quickly recognize individuals who have the potential to develop into great players in the future. As soon as you identify such players, you may select whether or not to purchase their player card and keep onto it until they begin to receive attention for their football abilities. More importantly, since you will be acquiring their player card when they are still relatively unknown, such cards will not be prohibitively expensive, with some player cards selling for as little as $20 on the secondary market. Consider the following scenario: you paid $50 for Cristiano Ronaldo's player card when Manchester United initially signed him. Consider how much a card like that would be valued now when he had successfully won five Ballon d'Ors.

Utility

The utility that an NFT gives may also assist you in determining if it will be a solid investment that generates a high return on your investment or not. How an NFT may be utilized determines its utility and is one of the critical categories of NFT that produces high-utility NFTs in the gaming category. A significant utility value may be derived from game-related NFTs, particularly if the game elements can be repurposed in a new application. To give you an example, a rare and powerful Crypto Space Commander Battleship was auctioned off for a little more than $45,000 in 2019. Consider the possibility that this identical gaming component may have been used in a different game or application, in which case the value would have been much more significant. Because of this, the greater the amount of utility that an NFT can supply, the greater its importance in the marketplace. Consider those NFTs that give more utility than others when considering whether to invest in them since these NFTs have the potential to provide a significant amount of return on investment.

Ownership History

The ownership history of an NFT is another useful statistic you may use to discover NFTs that have the potential to deliver a decent return on your investment. Consider the possibility of obtaining an NFT that an influential person formerly held. Reselling such non-financial-transactions (NFT) may provide a significant return on investment since consumers are fascinated by the idea of owning items that essential individuals once owned. The greater the influence or popularity of an NFT's prior owner, the higher the price at which you may resale that NFT — so making a decent return on your investment. However, the NFT sector is very speculative; the concepts outlined above are the keys to picking highly successful NFTs for investment. In time, as the NFT ecosystem matures, these ideas may be refined and refined into a more standardized and systematic way to identify viable NFTs that might provide significant returns for you.

THE CREATOR CLASS & NFTS

From a financial perspective, the pandemic hit the creator class hard. With the regular venues for live performances and shows closed, artists, musicians, singers, actors, and creators of every definition have been forced to fend for themselves. But something very new (and unique) happened. The outcome may be the emergence of a first-time-ever, self-sufficient, profitable designer class.

The stereotype of a starving artist is ancient and trite. Fine artists aren't assumed to care about things like food or shelter. They've been mourning for their art for centuries. Dancers aren't large eaters, so no one ever thinks about starving dancers. But musicians haven't managed much better. Papa Bach was a community organist and an organ repairman on the side. Mozart was always borrowing funds from his friends and families, although he did make some actual money now and again. Beethoven didn't die poor but lived from commission to commission. Before 2021, there was one thing that every artist has had in standard with every other artist who ever lived: they rehearsed their art at the pleasure of a patron.

Patrons

Whether it was a monarch, a rich person, a corporation, a media company, a label, a museum, a you-fill-in-the-blank, someone with money has funded practically every art project ever. Of course, there are a few notable exceptions, but they do not prove the direction. In modern history, the extensive majority of artists (no matter the art form) have both wanted and needed the match of a recording contract with a major label to eat and pay the rent while trying to accomplish their artistic goals.

The Mother Of Invention

The creator class has experienced one of the most prominent pandemic-accelerated digital modifications. See YouTube or TikTok, or Instagram, and you are sure to find a creator fully certified with direct-to-consumer (DTC) business tools. Everything a creator needs to get paid, from payment processing to analytics to production capabilities, is available with little or no investment. That is more than a digital version of passing the hat to support your busking. Massive tech infrastructure is emerging to power, help, and earnings symbiotically with the evolving developer class.

After its most current raise, Patreon (a platform that combines over 200,000 creators with about 7 million fans) valued $4 billion (triple its worth in September 2020). Cameo is a site that permits celebrities to send personalized videos straight to fans (for a fee, of course). OnlyFans is a favored app of sex workers and physical fitness experts.

What's essential to comprehend is that every social video post has become an opportunity to promote original content that fans can support.

Nfts, Crypto, And The Arts

Have you lately begun gathering NFT art? If so, you are at the forefront of the developing creator economy.

We are in the center of the NFT hype-cycle, so it's hard to divide the hucksters and charlatans from the real possibilities afforded by ERC721 and ERC1155 innovative agreements recorded on distributed ledgers. Due to the insane prices of some current NFT transactions, it seems like everyone who's anyone is bringing into the competition. Seven-time Super Bowl champion Tom Brady reported launching an NFT platform called Autograph in early 2021.

There are many excellent uses for NFTs, especially for the creator class. One of the most significant issues of our day is the ability for anyone to mash up anything and call it their own. Please take a few standards of music from one song, a beat from another, a good result from a favorite movie, a line of dialogue from a fantastic video, mash them up, and you've got a new (albeit derivative) job. Who gets settled, and how?

Our copyright and academic property laws afford security for creators, but enforcement is strict. It requires extensive, centralized organizations such as recorded music companies, publishers, performing liberties organizations, movie studios, media companies, and others to observe, manipulate, and control the granting of rights and the flow of money. NFTs can decentralize this entire ecosystem.

Said differently, as blockchain technology becomes, transaction speed increases and transaction fees decrease (all of which are slowly but surely happening). As more content becomes uniquely identifiable using NFTs, the need for central authorities (a.k.a. gatekeepers) will diminish and possibly disappear altogether, as the creator class will be able to do it by themselves. The idea of an open, honest, one-to-one relationship between creator and society isn't new, but the technology to do it at scale is.

HOW TO BUY NONFUNGIBLE TOKENS

NFTs are exchanged in cryptographic forms of money, so you first need to purchase digital currency and hold it in a wallet. You, at that point, need to set up an account with an NFT commercial center, like Nifty Gateway, OpenSea, or Rarible. Deals regularly appear as selloffs with a beginning NFT cost, so on the off chance that you enter a triumphant offer, you will take responsibility for NFT. On the off chance that the worth like this rises, you can set up your bartering on a commercial center to sell it for a benefit. While purchasing an NFT doesn't move the copyright for the work, it gives fundamental use rights like posting a picture on the web.

Nonfungible tokens can be bought on an assortment of stages, and whichever you pick will rely upon what it is you have to purchase (for instance, on the off chance that you have to buy baseball cards, you're best making a beeline for a site like digital trading cards, however different commercial centers sell more summed up pieces). You'll require a wallet explicit to the stage you're purchasing on, and you'll have to fill that wallet with cryptographic money. Nonfungible tokens can be bought on different online marketplaces such as Rarible, NFT Showroom, BakerySwap, VIV3, OpenSea, etc.

If you're not an artwork creator but are more interested in buying NFTs, how would you go about that? You'd have to do some marketplace research first. Once more, I'm not here to promote any marketplaces. I'm just giving you some ideas on where you can start to look.

Opensea is currently the largest NFT marketplace, according to their website. A beginner-friendly mint and market platform are Rarible. If you're more into auctioning collectibles, you may find Niftygateway a good choice or Makersplace. And art lovers may tend to go with KnownOrigin or Superrare.

Who Are The Stakeholders Of Nfts

1. Developers

The developer is the person or company that creates the game and owns the code. They are in charge of deploying the game to the blockchain, maintaining it, and adding new features.

The developer can be a centralized entity, such as a game studio or blockchain company. Or they can be a decentralized team, such as an open-source community of contributors. In most cases, developers will launch NFTs on top of an existing blockchain protocol (such as Ethereum). The developer then creates a smart contract to support their game. The rules of this intelligent contract determine how the NFTs are minted and transferred between players in the game. The developer also determines what happens when NFTs are destroyed or abandoned (later on).

2. Players

The player is any person who plays a game using NFTs and owns them during gameplay. There are many different types of players in any given NFT-based game:

- First-time users who want to learn how to play.

- Casual players who enjoy regular gameplay.

- Expert players who participate in high-stakes tournaments with prizes like cars or houses.

- A player may play just for fun but also for financial gain.

3. Collectors

The collector is any person who owns NFTs for investment purposes. The most common type of collector is an NFT investor or someone who purchases NFTs to sell them at a higher price in the future. There are many other types of collectors, including speculators and NFT traders. Collectors are interested in any game that uses NFTs, regardless of their popularity. Some collectors are highly selective about which games they support, while others collect as many different types of games as possible.

4. Traders

The trader is a player who specializes in buying and selling NFTs to make a profit. They can be players or collectors, but their primary goal is to buy low and sell high rather than play the game itself. Most traders are active on secondary markets such as centralized exchanges or decentralized exchanges (DEXes). A DEX is an online market where buyers and sellers can trade with each other directly without using a middleman (like an exchange). There are several ways that traders make money from NFTs: they can sell them at higher prices than they paid, short sell them, or trade them on margin.

5. Speculators

The speculator is a player who buys NFTs to sell them at a higher price in the future. Depending on their strategy, they may buy NFTs from other players or the developer. For example, they may purchase an NFT at a discount during its presale period and then sell it once it becomes more popular. Or they may buy an NFT that is highly sought after by collectors and hold onto it until it appreciates.

6. Investors

The investor is a player who purchases NFTs as part of a portfolio of assets (or with borrowed money). They expect to profit from their investment over time through price appreciation or dividends (more on this later). The most common type of investor is an asset manager or manages other people's money and uses investment strategies such as value investing, growth investing, or momentum investing. Investors can also be hedge funds, family offices, angel investors, venture capitalists, and others. They are interested in any game that uses NFTs regardless of their popularity. However, most of them are more selective about which games they support than collectors are.

Related Legal Issues Worth Your Attention

As we have noticed, anyone can make NFTs of anything worldwide, even if the contents don't belong to them. However, this brings the questions of copyright infringement and copyfraud to us.

Copyright Infringement

You may think creating NFTs from the public domain works interesting, while the issue that probably generates legal conflicts is doing the outcome from a person who is not its owner or the author. Another problematic phenomenon is that people began to create pieces that did not belong to them.

CorbinRanbolt has complained that some of his dinosaurs' artworks have been tokenized without his permission. Another artist, WerdUndead, had their works created and placed in OpenSea by someone else.

In both situations, the artworks have been removed from the NFT marketplaces, but it made us ask whether or not it is copyright infringement for the authorized creation of a work.

Creating and selling NFTs based on the artworks you don't own or hold the right to is an infringement. That is why the auction sites of NFT have rushed to create DMCA processes for removing those unauthorized ones. Some marketplaces only allow verified work, making it less problematic in this industry. However, it's not clear if this is enough that many sites are now actively encouraging the public to tokenize content that doesn't belong to them.

Artists can do derivative works based on their creations and sell them. As long as buyers are fully aware that NFTs are useless practically, there's not enough reason for the courts to get involved.

However, as we see the NFT industry boom, we are now seeing far more concerns regarding copyright infringement, and the system is getting abused.

What makes it more complicated is that even when the original artists don't care, you use their works first, but they can still see you at the end of the day Because the artwork owners can change their mind at any point in the future, and you are using their work in a way they're not happy about. A typical and exciting case example was that in 2019,

InfoWars paid Pepe the Frog creator Matt Furie $15,000 to settle the lawsuit against them. One of the critical lessons left for us is that creators should avoid making public statements saying they do not care about their copyrights or tolerance for unauthorized uses. The works' authorships are entitled to the same types of protections, no matter what form of service — online, print, social media, whatever it can be. So, if you sell other people's art for millions of dollars, they will certainly have the right to come after you. Another lesson is that virality or meme-ification will not decrease the copyright's strength. For example, if you see a meme going viral on social media, everybody is using it or joking about it, but this doesn't mean you are safe to transfer to your NFT and sell it.

Copyfraud

This term refers to making a dubious or false copyright claim over works in the public domain. Yes, public domain works can be used by anyone. However, sometimes an institution will claim the copyright over such works. The Global Art Museum (GAM) has tokenized some public domain works and listed them for sales on OpenSea. Now we know, if one person makes an NFT of a picture or image, they have to have the original file used to create the token. Although there might not be a legal issue with copyfraud, we need to ask if the GAM's tokenization of works can even be copyfraud. In GAM's case, they took artworks from the public domain's digital artwork collection at the Rijiksmeusm in Amsterdam. This collection is a celebrated and famous one that has gone entirely digital and is marked as being in the public domain.

Also, the Rijksmuseum encourages re-uses of their works, which is a strong political statement in the public domain's defense. At the same time, one should not enclose the public domain since it's for everyone. The Rijksmuseum has claimed ownership of all the photographs of their artworks. However, it doesn't seem to be interested in enforcing it.

GAM also stated clearly that all the works are from the Rijksmuseum and don't claim any of the institution's involvement. So, there're no ownership claims, only creating a unique version of the works that are not even a copy of the results themselves. This is not copyfraud.

The NFTs have a cryptographic sign to make the file unique, and this sign is not even from the author (since the artists of the public domain's works are no longer with us.) That is like you purchased something and tell others you own exclusive metadata, which others can reproduce. You may see it as pointless at best or slightly unethical at worst.

Could NFTs Help Rightsholders or Creators?

Put, yes. NFTs, give creators another innovative potential revenue stream by selling their works' unique copies and help keep track of ownership of copyrights.

In theory, creators can create the works, tokenize them, and keep the token both as proof of copyright ownership and creation. They can transfer this token as part of the copyright transfer. In reality, however, this is not how it's usually used. It's often used to create some "special" works' copies and sell those copies. Usually, it's not the creators who are reaping those rewards.

Currently, artists and creators need to explore this as potential piracy threats and business opportunities. If your NFT works need to capture the scarcity and uniqueness that this technology can bring to you, they need to be scarce and not just something anyone is capable of conjuring up.

HOW TO SELL THEM

How To Make And Sell An Nft

A step-by-step tutorial on creating and selling an NFT if you want to give it a go with your digital work.

Many artists are asking how to construct and market an NFT these days. non-fungible tokens continue to stir debate and elicit outrage due to the eye-watering prices that some pieces of NFT art have sold for. It's only natural that you'd be curious if NFTs provide a possibility to profit from your creative work if that's the case. This book will assist you in understanding how to make and sell an NFT if that is the case.

However, these are exceptional cases, and even if you manage to replicate their success, you'll generally discover that the bulk of the money won't flow to you. The firms that facilitate transactions and the platforms that generate and maintain NFTs charge various fees to NFT artists both up-front and after any sale, and they may even leave you out of pocket based on the price your work sells for.

There are several online platforms to create and sell NFTs right now. OpenSea, Rarible, SuperRare, Nifty Gateway, Foundation, VIV3, BakerySwap, Axie Marketplace, and NFT ShowRooom are examples of popular auction sites for buying and selling NFTs. Payment options include MetaMask, Torus, Portis, WalletConnec, Coinbase, MyEtherWallet, and Fortmatic.

Buy some cryptocurrency Ethereum cryptocurrency, ether is accepted by most platforms.

The first thing to note is that you'll have to pay a platform to "mint" (or generate) your piece. Most media want to cover the cost with ether, the cryptocurrency native to the open-source blockchain platform Ethereum, where NFTs first debuted.

Keep in mind that, like bitcoin and many other cryptocurrencies, the value of ether (abbreviated as ETH) is prone to huge fluctuations. From under $1,000 in 2021 to over $4,800 in 2021, with numerous peaks and valleys on the road, it's been known to swing by hundreds of dollars in a matter of hours.

To acquire Ethereum, you'll need to construct a "digital wallet" and link it to your NFT platform of choice. There are several digital wallet services available, but we'll use MetaMask, which is known as a browser plugin and as a mobile app for this purpose. If you'd instead utilize another provider or are familiar with digital wallets and have your own already, go straight to step 4.

When you first launch your wallet, it will prompt you to 'generate a new wallet and seed phrase.' It would be okay if you weren't concerned about what the "seed phrase" means (it's simply a list of words that saves blockchain data). Say yes, then it's merely a case of agreeing to the conditions, creating a password, and going through some security checks to get your account up and running.

Add money to your wallet.

You'll need to add some ETH to your MetaMask wallet or any other digital wallet after you've created it. That's not difficult at all: click the 'Buy' button and pick Wyre as your payment method. You'll be obtained to a screen where you can buy ETH with Apple Pay or a debit card. If you'd rather not spend any money yet, feel free to proceed; all you have to do is wait a little longer.)

Connect your wallet to an the NFT platform

The general workflow of setting up a digital wallet is similar across all platforms. Once you've got some ETH in your digital wallet available to spend, you may go to the NFT platform of your choice and start creating your NFT. We're using Rarable as an example for this purpose, but there are numerous other NFT platforms to explore.

Rarable is one of several digital collectible marketplaces.

To access Rarable, go to Rarable.com. In the right-hand corner of the screen, a button says 'Connect wallet.' Click here to connect your wallet with MetaMask. A popup will appear asking you whether you want to link your wallet with Rarable. Select "Yes," then "Connect," and agree to the terms of service before confirming your age.

Upload your file

GIFs can be used as NFTs; however, we recommend you create the file in an image editor like Photoshop or Paint because they give complete control over sizing and sharpness. To do this: Open your chosen software and create a new image of dimension 256 x 128 using black and white colors (if using Paint, make sure Advanced Mode is on). Paste your GIF into that new image, and scale it down to fit the whole picture.

You're ready to make your NFT now. The blue 'Create' switch in the upper right should be clicked. After that, you may select a single one-off project or sell the same item several times. Choose 'Single' in this example. You must upload the digital file that you wish to convert into an NFT at this stage. Rarable takes PNG, GIF, WEBP, MP4, and MP3 files up to 30MB in size.

Upload your file; then, on the right, you'll see a pevaluation of your NFT post.

Set up an auction

Choose the locations for your auction (Image credit: Rarible)

In the next part of the form, you'll need to decide how you want to sell your NFT artwork. There are three options here. 'Fixed price' allows you to put a price and sell to someone instantly (like 'Buy it now on eBay'). 'Unlimited Auction' will enable people to carry on making bids until you accept one. Finally, 'Timed auction' is an auction that only takes place for a specific time. That's the option we'll choose for our example.

The hard part now begins: establishing a minimum price. Set it too low, and you'll lose money on each sale because of the high costs. We'll set our price at 1 ETH and allow people seven days to make offers.

You'll be able to purchase it immediately after but, before you do, there's an option to "Unlock once purchased." That allows you to give your future buyer a complete, high-resolution copy of your work and other material via a hidden website or download link. The option labeled 'Choose Collection' is the most perplexing. That is a somewhat technical question regarding how the blockchain works. The default option is "Rarible," so we recommend leaving it that way.

Describe your NFT

You may now add a title and description to your item's listing. To increase the chances of selling your NFT, take some time to consider this. You'll be shown a questionnaire that asks you to choose what proportion of royalties you want to earn from any future resale of your work.

This time, there's a further balancing act: higher percentages will earn you more money over time, but they'll also deter people from reselling your work since they'll be less likely to make a profit for themselves. Finally, the file properties may be added as an optional field. You're almost done at this point.

Pay the fee

Click 'Create Item' to begin the listing procedure. You'll be prompted to connect your wallet if you don't have enough money in it. If you don't have enough money in your wallet, don't worry; you won't have to start over. Click on the wallet symbol in the top-right corner of the screen to add money directly within Rarable.

Just a comment of alert before you do so. The listing fee may appear to be relatively low, as it was in our case: $5.91. However, this is only the beginning of the costs you'll be subjected to. To indeed generate your NFT, you must first agree to a further charge of $42.99 before you can proceed any further in our situation. Aside from the fees for buying and selling NFTs, there will also be a commission payment when someone buys your asset and a transfer cost to execute the transaction. From our perspective, none of this was adequately clarified on Rarable's website when we tried it.

NFT SELLING PLATFORMS

NFTs can be purchased on a variety of outlets or platforms, and whichever you select will depend upon what it is you would like to shop (for example, if you would like to shop for baseball cards, you're the best heading to a site like digital trading cards, but other marketplaces sell more generalized pieces). You will require a wallet unique to that outlet you're buying on, and you will get to fill that wallet with cryptocurrency. Because the sale of Beeple's Everyday – the primary 5000 days at Christie's proved, some pieces are starting to hit more mainstream auction houses, too, so these are also worth watching out for. Just in case you missed it, that Beeple piece was the one that went for $69.3 million.

Because of the high demand for the many sorts of NFT, they're often published as 'drops' (like in exhibitions, when collections of tickets are always released several times). That suggests an intense rush of eager buyers when the drop starts, so you would need to be enrolled and have your wallet topped up before time. NFTs also is making waves as in-game purchases across different video games (much to the delight of oldsters everywhere). Players often buy and sell these assets and include playable assets like unique swords, skins, or avatars.

Also, due to the differing blockchain technology behind particular NFTs, not all NFT marketplaces buy and sell all kinds of NFT. Creators will often select an NFT marketplace supported whether that marketplace supports an established NFC token principle.

In recent years, more and more outlets dedicated to the sale of Crypto Art have emerged. Ethereum has published two standards now: ERC-721 and ERC-1155. Adversary, Binance, has since published standards BEP-721 and BEP-1155. The 2 "1155" standards differ from the first "721" standards because they permit multiple NFTs to be bunched and transacted together. Most NFT platforms require buyers to possess a digital wallet and use cryptocurrencies to buy. Today, because of the introduction of NFTs and Blockchain technology, digital artists and collectors can claim their place within the art market.

Here may be a list of websites that sell NFTs:

Opensea

OpenSea boldly describes itself as being the most critical NFT marketplace. It is a clearinghouse for nearly any sort of NFT like crypto-collectibles such as video games, apps. Digital artworks, making it be the "biggest marketplace for digital goods." Goods range from Rob Gronkowski's GRONK Championship Collection (the first pro-athlete to initiate NFTs) to Kings Of Leon's recent album (one of the significant primary records released as a set of digital NFTs). The album was published in three NFT formats constructed to unite "the strength of the band's music and their current album visuals to deconstruct, deteriorate, and warp iconic band symbols and photography." In February 2020, OpenSea registered a 400% increase in sales, from $8 million to $32 million.

Opensea offers a good range of non-fungible tokens, including art, censorship-resistant domain names, virtual worlds, trading cards, sports, and collectibles. It includes ERC721 and ERC1155 assets. You'll buy, sell, and find out exclusive digital assets like Axies, ENS names, CryptoKitties, Decentraland, and more. They feature over 700 projects, including digital art projects to collectible games, card games, and name systems like ENS (Ethereum Name Service). Creators can create their items on the blockchain using OpenSea's item minting tool. You'll use it to form a set and NFTs free of charge without needing one line of code. If you're developing your smart contract for a game, digital collectible, or another project with unique digital items on the blockchain, you'll quickly get added to OpenSea.

OpenSea is that the most democratic and easy-to-use platform of all. No verification is necessary; anyone can create an account and begin minting NFTs. You'll flick through countless collections to seek out particular artists or peruse rankings by sales volume to get fascinating pieces. OpenSea also makes delivering your art or digital collectibles simple. Just click on Create -> Submit NFTs then you'll be ready to create a replacement collection and begin adding new pieces. Even better, there's no coding needed; therefore, the barrier to access is low. It takes three minutes to accept your first part of digital art, and consequently, the whole process is free.

If you're selling items on OpenSea, you'll sell an item for a hard and fast price, create a decreasing price listing, or make a sales listing. If you want to sell your parts, you'll get to buy gas, which is the cost of discussing with the innovative agreement governing OpenSea, but you need to do ao just once. It costs around $50 to $100, counting on network traffic. Because it's so simple and the cost is so low, many collections on OpenSea tend to be composed of digital collectibles instead of individual artworks.

Rarible

Rarible is a decentralized marketplace that gives its users the ERC-20 token, the owner's token. Active users can earn RARI tokens by buying or selling NFTs on the platform. It distributes 75,000 RARI hebdomadally. The platform places a focus on art assets. It lets creators mint new NFTs by buying and selling their creations.

It allows users to create and sell their art assets, whether or not they are books, music albums, digital art, or movies. The creators can sell their work anonymously. They can also show a teaser of their creation to everybody who purchases NFTs from them. People can buy and sell NFTs in various categories like art, photography, games, metaverses, music, domains, memes, and more.

Rarible is analogous to OpenSea because it's democratic and open. Here, however, because you've got to buy each artwork you mint (i.e., create and place on a blockchain), there's excellent less noise and not many collectibles. Rarible has mainly been used to mint individual pieces. Its value is higher than getting your work seen here, as you'll be paying $40 to $80 for the minting of every job.

Established by Alex Salnikov and Alexei Falin in early 2020, it leverages the blockchain to connect digital artists and collectors. Rarible allows users to make, sell and buy artwork as non-fungible tokens (NFTs). What puts the platform apart is its decentralized independent organization (DAO). Through the RARI token, users can partake in protocol governance decisions through a voting mechanism.

Superrare

SuperRare was created in 2017 by Jonathan Perkins, John Crain, and Charles Crain. On the platform, digital artists can create artworks and tokenize them on the Ethereum blockchain, while collectors can buy the works securely and transparently via ETH. Users can see who the highest collectors and trending artists are on the platform, what percentage of jobs they need to be purchased or created, and how much they need to be spent or earned while checking subsequent trades on the second marketplace.

SuperRare features a strong focus on being a marketplace for people to shop for and sell rare single-edition digital artworks. Each of these artworks is genuinely created by an artist within the network and tokenized as a crypto-collectible digital object that you can own and transact. They portray themselves as Instagram's Christie, giving a new method to interact with art, culture, and collecting on the web.

Each artwork on SuperRare is a digital collectible, secured by cryptography and tracked by the blockchain. SuperRare is a digital collectible marketplace that features a social network. Due to their transparency, digital collectibles are very secure and easily accessed by anyone. All dealings are made using ether, the native cryptocurrency to the Ethereum network. At the instant, SuperRare works with a small number of hand-picked artists; however, you'll use a form to submit your artist profile to urge on their radar for their upcoming full launch.

Foundation

Foundation is an expert platform designed to attract digital creators, crypto natives, and collectors concurrently to manipulate culture forward. It calls itself the new creative economy. Its primary focus is on digital art.

In August 2020, in the first blog post on their website, they launched open participation for creators to explore crypto and manipulate the worth of their work. They asked them to "hack, subvert and manipulate the worth of their creative work." When artists sell their work on Foundation, they receive 10% of the sales value as a secondary transaction.

Foundation is that the most difficult to access of other marketplaces. You'll need a particular number of community upvotes from fellow artists to even post your first artwork. The simplest method to enter Foundation is via an immediate invitation from one among the artists already on the platform.

This way, you'll avoid the queue and jump straight into selling your art. The problem of getting into here and, therefore, the cost of gas for minting each NFT means you generally find better quality art going for higher sums of cash here. That is often definitely an honest place for already established artists and creators who have a massive following on other platforms and may bring them over.

Atomicmarket

AtomicMarket may be a shared liquidity NFT market smart contract employed by multiple websites. Shared liquidity means everything listed on one market also shows on all other markets. It's a marketplace for Atomic Assets, typically for non-fungible tokens on the Eosio blockchain technology.

Anyone can utilize the Atomic Asset criterion to tokenize and make digital assets and buy, sell and auction assets utilizing the Atomic Assets marketplace. You can record your own NFTs for purchase on the AtomicMarket, and you'll search occurring listings. NFTs of well-known collections get a confirmation checkmark, making it simpler to identify the important NFTs. Malicious assemblies are excluded.

Myth Market

Myth Market is a series of online marketplaces that support various digital card brands. At the instant, its featured markets are GPK. Market (where you'll buy digital Garbage Pail Kids cards), GoPepe.Market (for GoPepe trading cards), Heroes.Market (for Blockchain Heroes trading cards), KOGS.Market (for KOGS trading cards), and Shatner.Market (for William Shatner memorabilia.)

Bakeryswap

BakerySwap is an automatic market maker (AMM) and decentralized exchange (DEX) on Binance Smart Chain (BSC). It uses a native BakerySwap token (BAKE). BakerySwap may be a multi-functional crypto hub offering a variety of decentralized finance (DeFi) services and a crypto launching pad and NFT supermarket. Its NFT supermarket hosts digital art, meme tournaments, and NFT in games that users pay for in BAKE tokens. You'll use NFTs in 'combo meals' to receive bonus BAKE tokens. Also, creating and trading your artwork is a simple, precise process.

Knownorigin

KnownOrigin is a marketplace where you can locate and buy rare digital artwork. Every digital artwork on KnownOrigin is unique and authentic. It's a platform that enables creators to sell their work to collectors who care about authenticity. The Ethereum blockchain secures it. They can also submit digital artwork as a jpeg or gif to the KnownOrigin gallery, with all files on IPFS.

Enjin Marketplace

Enjin Marketplace is a tool by which you'll explore and trade blockchain assets. It's the official marketplace for Enjin based NFTs. To date, it's enabled $43.8 million of Enjin Coin to be spent on digital assets, involving 2.1 billion NFTs. 832.7K items are traded. You can use the Enjin Wallet to list and buy gaming gadgets and collectibles. Microsoft's Azure

FAMOUS EXAMPLES OF NFT

We like having things in our possession. We are particularly fond of possessing something that we consider value, whether emotional or financial. The desire to acquire tangible goods has existed throughout history; a particular allure is linked with the real-life features of our things that attract us.

NFTs, for example, is a phenomenon that has challenged our understanding of ownership (non-fungible tokens). Ownership and validity are proven via the use of distributed ledger technology. While they are not new ideas, they have only recently made their way into the public eye, as seen by the auctioning of totally digital artworks for astronomical prices.

Adopters and opponents are two sides of the same coin regarding innovation. Whatever your point of view, we feel that NFTs are an intriguing new mode of digital ownership. We should at the very least take inspiration, regardless of whether they gain widespread acceptance.

Let's take a deeper look at 21 instances of nonlinear functional transformations and what makes them unique.

Beeple's "Everyday: The First 5000 Days"

As the first entirely NFT digital artwork to be auctioned at a major auction house (for an eye-watering $69 million), this piece represents a watershed moment in the careers of visual artists throughout the globe.

William Shatner's Memorabilia

William Shatner is a well-known actor whose professional career has spanned more than 60 years. The year 2020 will see the publication of a series of his artifacts in the form of NFTs, including a diverse collection of images taken over his illustrious career. In only nine minutes, he sold 125,000 copies.

In his own words, "They're weird things - the trash of my existence, like leaving the dust of a comet in my wake," Shatner explains.

Grimes Releases Warnymph

In late February of this year, famous musician Grimes earned $5.8 million, selling her non-monetary tokens (NFTs) in a couple of minutes. Known as "WarNymph," a collection of ten digital assets created in conjunction with her brother, they resulted from their work.

In the decade of the 2010s, Nyan Cat was a spectacular relic of the internet. The video's author decided to transform it into an NFT and auction it off to commemorate the video's tenth anniversary. According to the current exchange rate, the video was sold for a stunning 300 ETH, which was around $852,300 at writing.

Jack Dorsey's First-Ever Tweet

Jack Dorsey, the originator and CEO of Twitter, sold the very first tweet ever sent on the network (on March 21, 2006) for roughly $3 million as a non-financial transaction (NFT).

In an interview with Fortune, Dorsey said that the money earned from the NFT sale would be converted to bitcoin and then given to a charity group called GiveDirectly, which provides cash to those experiencing hardship.

Sports Collectibles: Nba Shots

Top Shot is a non-profit marketplace where basketball fans may buy, sell, and exchange memorable moments from the National Basketball Association. As of right now, the most expensive collectible exchanged is a LeBron James slam against the Houston Rockets, which went for more than $387,000 when it was transferred in 2014.

Cryptokitties: Probably One Of The First Popular Nfts Created

CryptoKitties are similar to Pokemon cards, with one crucial difference: they are built on the Ethereum blockchain. That makes them one of the most widely used NFTs today. That is perhaps the first NFT project to receive widespread acceptance, and it occurred in the year 2017. In essence, it was the world's first blockchain-based video game.

Decentraland And Virtual Worlds

When users reported generating considerable gains from the purchase and sale of digital land, Decentraland gained widespread attention in the popular media.

That is the first multiplayer role-playing metaverse built on the Ethereum blockchain, and it is currently under development. That point should be stressed: unlike in a typical online role-playing game, there is no actual contact between players in a multiplayer game.

Cryptovoxels

Blockchain-based metaverse Cryptovoxels is a mash-up of social networking, gaming, and commerce powered by blockchain technology. In its own words, the platform is "a user-owned virtual world that runs on the Ethereum blockchain." Users may exchange land parcels, set up art galleries, and engage with other players on the game's server—something along the lines of Minecraft but with a greater emphasis on Bitcoin.

Andrés Reisinger's Virtual Design Objects

Andrés Reisinger, an Argentinian designer, has discovered a unique niche for his creative output: he offers non-functional furniture (NFTs). His most costly sculpture was sold for little about $70,000, which was a small profit. Even though they are not physically functional furniture, these things may be put in open worlds, such as Decentraland or Minecraft.

Rtfkt's Digital Sneakers

RTFKT is generating a lot of noise in the fashion world. Even though the customers who purchase his NFT sneakers will never be able to wear them, they are still prepared to spend upwards of $10,000 for a pair of his shoes.

In March of 2021, RTFKT launched a pair of shoes that he collaborated on with another artist named Fewocious, and they were able to gather $3,1 million in sales in a matter of minutes, according to reports.

Nike's Nft Sneakers

Nike Inc. sought for and was granted a patent in 2019 that will enable them to remain at the forefront of the NFT craze for the foreseeable future.

Nike's patent enables them to combine actual and virtual footwear, allowing them to monetize on both fronts simultaneously. Users of virtual shoes will have the option of being replicated and made in the real world.

Share Tokenized Tickets With Your Audience.

NFTs are more than just art treasures; the technology can represent any unique information, including event tickets, which is why they are becoming more popular.

NFT tickets may now be purchased at a special price via various sites, which event organizers can access. More crucially, this will allow them to gain from any potential resale of the event, as mentioned earlier.

Gary Vaynerchuk Is Launching Art Nfts Linked To Ethereum.

In recent months, serial entrepreneur Gary Vaynerchuk developed his NFT collection, dubbed "VeeFriends," which consists of a series of over 10,000 tokens and is available for purchase.

Even though these tokens do not possess any creative quality, Vaynerchuk's strategy relies on selling users' access to exclusive privileges. Following the scarcity of the ticket, the individuals who hold these tokens will be entitled to various advantages, services, gifts, and interactions with Vaynerchuk.

Nft For Good

This is another example of NFT technology being used for other than just acquiring ownership of the artwork. A charitable organization supported by Binance Charity and its partners that runs on the Binance Smart Chain is known as Binance Smart Chain. NFT for Good enables individuals to sell their artwork while raising awareness about humanitarian causes.

Taco Bell's Charitable Nfts

Recently, Taco Bell began experimenting with the NFT trend by commissioning a series of GIFs and pictures based on meals from their menu to be shared on social media. Their tokens were completely sold out within minutes on the debut day.

Their NFTs were reasonably priced—$1 apiece, to be exact. Even though they haven't earned a lot of income, they have attracted much interest on social media. More significantly, all of the proceeds were given to the Taco Bell Foundation, which is the charitable arm of the restaurant chain's parent company.

Unstoppable Domains

Unstoppable Domains' mission, a blockchain business, is to provide direct access to—crypto domains from all common browsers, a functionality that has formerly been inaccessible due to technical limitations. Once a part is claimed, it is minted as an NFT, giving the claimant complete ownership and control over the domain.

Real Estate Tokenization

Aside from the financial sector, blockchain is making its way into the real estate business, enabling investors to acquire property shares by tokenizing them. Asset owners benefit from tokenization since it allows them to sell their property more quickly and effectively, while investors benefit from increased transparency and liquidity.

The tokenization of an asset is breaking it into "shares" or "tokens" to make it more easily traded. In the case of an investment with a surface area of 1,000 square meters that costs around $1,000,000, you may split it into individual square meters and sell them separately for $1,000 per share, for example.

Licenses And Certifications

The paper certifications and licenses that we use to validate our skill sets are still in use today. Blockchain technology enables us to establish unquestionably reliable and unfalsifiable evidence of a degree or other certification acquired.

Businesses and organizations would stand to gain significantly from having access to licenses that include the functionality of NFTs. With this technique, there is less need for verification and record-keeping procedures.

Why Nfts Can Offer Marketing Opportunities For Fmcg Brands

It's hardly unexpected that the mania around NFTs has prompted many companies to try to cash in on the trend. To provide an example, Pringles has developed CryptoCrisp, which the company describes as their "newest virtual NFT flavor."

One such taste sold for a whopping $2,542 when offered for sale. Recently, the brand produced another 50 CryptoCrisp NFTs designed by artist Vasya Kolotusha and manufactured by the company.

The NFT toilet paper (yes, you read it correctly) produced by Procter & Gamble is another bizarre example. While these instances may seem silly to some, these are just a few of the companies that have received substantial media attention due to their decision to experiment with blockchain technology, which has undoubtedly increased their sales.

HOW TO LET THEM BE POPULAR

Direction To Becoming Successful In The Nft Market

Making digital art is not a new concept; it has been around since the early 1980s when computer developers created an art program utilized by the digital artist Harold Cohen. Nowadays, producing digital art is as simple as opening your paint program or taking a picture with your phone, adding a filter, and then uploading it for everyone to see.

You may already be a digital artist and be unaware of it. If you shoot images on your phone or draw on your paperwork, you need to polish your skills.

If you desire to become an NFT artist, you must follow some fundamental steps. Being an NFT artist is simpler than you think; but, building a following and being consistent may be difficult.

1. Choose the Kind of Art Work To Create

Before you begin your long and thrilling path of becoming an NFT artist, you need to pick out what type of artwork you will make. Having a constant specialization while making your digital art may help you develop your skills and enable your audience to realize what artwork you generate.

Suppose you are a digital artist who appreciates generating digital images of prominent sports levels, for example. In that case, your audience will recognize that you enjoy sports and develop work related to sports. However, if you decide to create a digital artwork of a unicorn one day, you risk confusing your viewers. That could be useful or bad, but it's essential to maintain consistency in your style so that people can learn to love or hate your work.

Choosing your art specialty should be very straightforward. Maybe you already have a thing you create for fun? It might be nature photos, cats, doodles - the sky is the limit when picking your specialization. My primary advice for developing your niche is to select a subject you like creating. Instead of choosing something hot or trendy, you may not experience the success you're searching for.

The fantastic thing about NFT art is that you can genuinely make anything into a one-of-a-kind masterpiece. You may produce music, videos, paintings, drawings, images, basically anything! So, be authentic to who you stand and your interests, then let your audience determine what they enjoy and what they don't like.

2. Choose How You Will Create Your Art

After determining your art niche, you must select how to create that art. For example, if you are a nature photographer, you may not need to purchase a picture editing application. However, if you are beginning from scratch or need to change your artwork, you will need to utilize editing software.

- Image editing software: There are a few standard solutions among NFT artists to generate or modify digital photos. Adobe Illustrator, Lightroom, and Photoshop are all solid options for picture editing.

- GIF and Pixel Image Creation Software: Adobe Photoshop (GIFs) and Piskel (animated sprites and pixel art)

There is, of course, other software available. But, finally, the sort of software you need is determined by your art style and personal goals for your art pieces.

3. Choose a Digital Art File Type

CATEGORY	FILE FORMAT
Video	MP4
Image	WEBP, PNG, JPG, GIF
Audio	WAV, MP3

Once you've decided what kind of NFT art you're going to make, you'll need to determine what file format you will use to create it. There are several file formats for each style of art.

Here is a list of possible digital art file formats for creating NFT art:

All you have to do is decide what kind of art you want to create and then proceed from there, making sure to choose the optimal file format for your purposes. Furthermore, you can always add unlocked content to your NFT art, which means they will have access to the best quality format you supply when someone buys it. That way, you won't have to produce the token as a big file, which may cause problems loading on specific markets.

4. Make Your Own Digital Artwork

Now that you've determined your art niche, how you will create your art, and the file format in which you'll save your craft, it is time to make your first piece of NFT art!

Keep in mind that your non-fungible artwork does not have to be perfect. Every day, the most important thing you can do is create art. Just because you develop new skills every day does not imply posting contemporary art every day. Instead, you should make new art every day for practice and get your creative juices flowing. Take, for example, the well-known NFT artist Beeple, who just sold a $69 million artwork featuring 5000 pieces of his art that he created every day for over 13 years!

Creating NFT art should be something you enjoy and are passionate about because becoming a successful NFT artist takes time and a lot of patience.

5. Market Your NFT Art

Things are starting to heat up now! When you're ready to sell your first part of NFT art, you'll need to decide which marketplace is best for your collection. There are several markets to select from, each with advantages and disadvantages. Furthermore, new markets will emerge as the world of NFTs and NFT art evolves.

You can sell your NFT art in the following marketplace: SuperRare.co, NiftyGateway, Rarible, and OpenSea.io.

When initially selling your NFT, I recommend making an account on all sites and publishing your work to more specific areas like OpenSea and Rarible. You would then apply to be an artist for the other sites needing application evaluation after some workup and a few pieces (SuperRare and NiftGateway).

Remember: When building your marketplace accounts, be sure to include all of your social media connections and personal websites in your profile. That enables individuals who find you to follow you on social media, increasing your following.

6. Build Your Following

Okay, this is the most crucial step. There are several methods to establish a following to aid in promoting your NFT art; but, what are the most excellent ways to build a following? It would help if you amassed a following or an audience.

To gain a following for your NFT artwork, you must create a brand around it or establish your brand while using your NFT artwork at every step of the way. In addition, participating in the NFT community via forums, podcasts, and blogs can help you create credibility and trust with your audience. Using social media is also an excellent idea.

This phase is vital since your brand's reputation is critical to your art's worth. The more individuals learn about you, the more they understand you and what you stand for. That makes purchasing a piece of your artwork easier for both sides. Consider this: would you instead buy something from someone you know and trust or from a random stranger you don't know anything about? The answer is straightforward.

You may use many approaches to establish a loyal following; let's go through some of the best ones.

Social Media

In my view, one of the simplest methods to begin building a following for your NFT art projects is via social media. To make the most of social media, be sure to join as many as you can and make a lot of noise. Once you're up and going, try to publish 1-2 times a day. You should be submitting your artwork and soliciting feedback, as well as providing input to other artists and assisting them whenever possible.

For six months, upload one piece of artwork every day across all of your social media platforms and watch what happens. Using appropriate hashtags to help your social media postings reach the right people can help you attract more followers who interact with your posts, which is precisely what you want.

Here are some trendy hashtags I've spotted on social media that are expected to acquire popularity in the next years. #NONFUNGIBLETOKENS, #DIGITALARTIST, #DIGITALART, #ETH, #ETHEREUM, #CRYPTOCURRENCY, #NFTCOLLECTOR, #NFTCOMMUNITY, #NFTARTIST, #NFTART, #NFTs, #NFT.

When creating your social media account, decide whether you want to use your account or create a separate account for your artwork. That is the scenario I mentioned earlier about personal branding vs. product branding. Whatever you decide, make sure to fill out your bios effectively, including details that describe you as an NFT artist, the type of art you create, and links to any other social media accounts or personal websites you may have.

Essentially, you want to build a webbed network to reach people across all platforms. As a result, try to keep your social media names consistent across all platforms; this aids in brand recognition.

Maintaining social media can be time-consuming. That is why it is best to start slowly and not get too caught up in how numerous supporters you have or how many likes your post receives. Instead, just be yourself and focus on providing the content. Growing your following takes time, patience, and consistency, but I know you can do it! Remember, we all started from scratch.

Websites

Aside from social media, you might take a more technical approach and build your website. However, even if you opt to make your website, it's still a good idea to be engaged on social media and utilize it to supplement traffic to your website, so people can see what you're giving.

If used correctly, a website may benefit your NFT art. For example, you may showcase your NFT art collection on your website by providing links to your art's marketplace, establishing a blog that attracts organic visitors, or even offering a service like making bespoke artwork for customers or teaching others how to produce their art. The possibilities are limitless.

Finally, if you are competent with computer technology, developing your website is viable for expanding your audience. You may also hire someone to create a website for you.

7. Engage in the NFT Community

It's time to tie everything together. It's time to get active now that you've set up your social media accounts and your website (if you have one). Spend time in your community answering questions, asking questions, and taking polls. For example, if you're a Rarible or OpenSea.io artist, go to their forums and start reading through the posts. Respond to any inquiries you feel comfortable answering, and if more information is needed, direct them to your blog or a YouTube video you created on the subject. Help others, and they will help you.

Never be afraid to seek clarification. If you're stuck, try to find an answer on your own or ask a member of the community for assistance. Indeed, if you're asking the question, it's very likely that someone else is as well.

Overall, gaining a following requires passion, patience, consistency, and selflessness. First, you must be passionate, patient while remaining consistent and selfless to assist others in solving their problems.

8. Maintain Consistency

The importance of consistency cannot be overstated. It makes no difference what you do in life; character is essential. If you intend to become a successful NFT artist overnight, I wish you the best of luck — you'll need it. Without consistency, you have little trust, and no one cares.

You must explain to others that you are serious about what you do and the NFT art you make. Beeple is a prime example. It took him almost 13 years to achieve significant success, but it was well worth the wait.

COMPARISON OF TRADITIONAL AND DIGITAL AREA INVESTMENT

We will compare digital land to traditional land investing in understanding better the opportunities of investing in digital land assets through NFT.

A key feature of blockchain innovation is eliminating intermediaries and the additional time and cost.

Digital land NFTs can be handled by smart contracts, which run on the blockchain to receive and send immutable transactions. A smart contract automatically runs and completes tasks within the pre-determined terms of the agreement.

Smart contracts offer ease of use. You can agree without trust and automatically release the NFT from the seller to the buyer after the funds have been deposited.

In comparison, traditional land requires a significant investment of time and effort, and multiple intermediaries typically sign contracts. With physical resources, specialists are usually needed to determine the asset's value, worth, and condition.

Digital assets can be purchased and sold quickly: no visits are required to investigate the quality and site of physical support. The acquisition cost is reduced to a small fraction of a conventional land investment.

The individuality of the digital asset is encoded in the NFT, and buyer/seller exchanges are handled automatically by a blockchain-based smart contract. Time-consuming title searches and property history checks are replaced with rapid trades.

Trading assets via smart contract-based NFTs offers so many benefits that the industry will likely evolve in the future to permit the purchase of physical land and real estate.

That would reduce costs and simplify the issuance of title insurance for banks and all parties entangled in the dealing. But for now, digital land investments stand uniquely arranged to benefit from the key advantages of investing and transacting on the blockchain.

Cash

Liquidity calculates how easy it is to transform an asset into cash.

Land and real estate are often big, illiquid investments. They require a significant amount of funds to purchase and are relatively illiquid.

You can't cash out your investment where and when you want. There are many restrictions, permits, and challenges you may face as you develop or sell the land, and it may take years to sell land or property.

Because they are digital assets, NFTs are much easier to trade and convert to cash than traditional land and real estate assets.

They can also be coined - created - on one outlet and traded on multiple markets. That makes more opportunities for potential buyers from all international markets than is feasible with traditional assets.

And as the NFT investment market matures and develops, opportunities to borrow against your digital terrestrial asset are likely to appear. Digital asset securities are in the early phases, but options exist to use them as collateral.

While initially, only cryptocurrencies like Ethereum could serve as collateral for a loan, digital assets, including NFTs for art, collectibles, and occupation names, are now contained as collateral-worthy assets.

The inclusion of digital assets as collateral indicates that as the NFT and DeFi sectors persist to evolve and mature, the liquidity of digital assets will expand over time.

No Maintenance Cost

Maintaining and maintaining traditional land and property can be expensive; you will be required to pay property taxes and other expenses.

You may have to pay to keep the land or property, such as regularly mowing the lawn or cleaning and repairing the property. If left undeveloped, the site's quality will deteriorate, wildlife will take over, and environmental problems such as flooding or leaks may occur.

In addition, land alone does not generate income. Developing the ground to a point where it generates income could be expensive and dangerous as an investment. For these explanations, it can be tough to get a loan on vacant land; there's a good chance you'll have to pay upfront, committing significant funds to the investment.

Digital assets, on the other hand, do not require maintenance and upkeep costs. You can choose to hold on to your purchase as its value increases over time as the digital platform grows or sell or develop your digital asset to develop revenue without extra charges.

Phergyson, an avid digital land dealer who proudly names herself a "faux real estate magnet," says owning digital land is "definitely" easier than possessing real estate. There are "no closing costs or regular costs for taxes and repairs. And, most importantly, no plumbing."

Traditional Land Use

The government can restrict the service of a land asset, with rules for the type of property or ways the land can be developed.

If you're buying land for residential or commercial development, you'll first need to ensure the ground has all the necessary permits and check the conversion regulations.

There may be instances where land-use restrictions may limit how the owner can use the land. Whether for horticulture, recreational purposes, or real estate development, obtaining permits and papers is often lengthy.

The availability of utilities could also influence expansion opportunities. How comfortable is setting up a sewer system, running water, electricity, gas, phone, cable, and internet?

Depending on the location of your land, access to necessary utilities could be expensive and limit potential development.

Digital Land Use

Digital land, however, offers multiple options to monetize the investment that are not present in traditional land; monetization also needs less investment and is potentially less restrictive.

As with customary land, the value of virtual land is based on where it is discovered, how much digital traffic it draws, and how owners choose to develop the land.

Let's take a look at the quickest growing NFT play in the current market, Decentraland, as an instance of the revenue-generating opportunities available to digital land investors.

According to Republic, famous expansions within Decentraland include:

- Art galleries where owners can sell their NFT digital art, Cryptokitties, and other NFT collectibles

- Casinos, where players can win MANA, the cryptocurrency that facilitates the purchase of digital land.

- Gaming sites

- Brand-sponsored content, such as the Atari arcade that features games that can be played in Decentraland

- Music venues where musicians can play and hold concerts

Digital land can also be leased, allowing owners to generate cash flow and income from tenants or other utilities.

For example, Alien Worlds, one of the most extensive digital land NFT games globally run in partnership with Binance, allows players to generate real income by permitting other players to come and mine from your plot.

These are just rare examples of the monetization possibilities of digital land. As more games and outlets emerge with digital land NFTs, the sky limits the type of virtual revenue landowners could pursue.

Virtual land allows the buyer to quickly develop and pursue multiple revenue generation opportunities they genuinely enjoy. The property can be made instantly in the virtual world, removing all the barriers associated with distance, time, and space in traditional investments.

Easy International And Borderless Entry

As in actual life, virtual real estate is about location, location, location. In traditional and digital real estate, value is heavily influenced by location and the amount of traffic the area attracts.

With physical assets, many aspects influence location and traffic entirely out of the buyer's control.

How distant or close an airport is, whether or not it has important landmarks that attract international users and visitors, reassurance of access, infrastructure, regulations for international travel, and unforeseen global events such as the Covid pandemic can all recreate a part.

In virtual platforms, people can visit immediately worldwide with their avatars. Virtual conventions, where parties can gather to watch a sporting event, network, or pitch ideas to investors in Crypto Valley, can draw a crowd and drive traffic to your location, increasing its value at no additional cost.

Annual Percentage Return And Roi

Revenue growth for video games is expected to increase from over $159.3 billion in 2020 to $189.3 billion in 2021. And from 2020 to 2027, the global enterprise is fixed for a compound annual growth rate (CAGR) of 12.9%.

And as more people and brands join the metaverse to enjoy a unique, borderless experience and broadcast to users, the value of digital land assets will continue to grow.

Compare that to the years spent obtaining planning permission and inventing traditional land investments, and it's obvious where the potential for higher annual percentage returns (APY) and ROI lies.

In 2018, Decentraland made headlines when digital land investors' returns soared 500%. Since then, the decentralized virtual world has continued to gain ground: digital land sold in early 2019 at Decentraland for $500 is now trading at over $7,860, with an ROI of 1,572%.

Decentraland's cryptocurrency, MANA, jumped in 2021 and has been in a bullish cycle for over a year. Decentraland is one of the world's most popular multiplayer games and the fastest growing blockchain, NFT, and digital terrestrial virtual world.

As more players succeed in the gaming ecosystem, the value of the digital asset increases. Low supply and exponentially increasing demand can drive up prices.

Youtuber LiteLiger shared a few examples of NFT investments in digital land that have increased significantly in value over a few months:

The Sandbox is an Ethereum-based game supported by institutional investors.

LiteLiger purchased a plot of Sandbox land for $100.

Eight months later, LiteLiger received offers to purchase $650 worth of its Sandbox land.

These phenomenal increases in digital land prices show the potential increase in valuation for digital land NFTs. The buyer purchases the ground in the early stages of game development and releases before gaining more significant traction in the marketplace.

Where you have a specified amount of land on one of these platforms, and it eventually attracts thousands if not millions of users, there is the potential for huge retrievals; the importance of your digital land assets can only rise as network effects, users, and brand dominance increase.

Tips For Investing In Digital Territory

The value of the games industry exceeds both music and movies combined. And with the most extensive application of NFTs in the gaming world, terrestrial digital NFTs offer a significant investment opportunity.

Early adopters will benefit from all the inbound trading in the metaverse. But as with any investment, there's no assurance that your digital asset will perform nicely and generate a sizable ROI.

So what are the critical properties of high-growth digital ground NFTs? And what stand the indicators that the virtual outlet is destined to grow? While there is a lot of money to be created in the NFT space, investors should comprehend the value drivers for an asset class before making an allocation.

NFT AND REAL ESTATE

There is nothing more fundamental in today's world than technology, and NFTs are proving it in a disruptive way. A universe is no longer a niche whose sales have exceeded 250 million dollars and continue to grow day by day.

Collecting, selling, investing, and earning are the keywords behind NFT. The capital is increasing more and more, and so is the interest in these products. How does an intangible asset that everyone can see achieve such value? How and who can create and sell their works in NFTs? What applications and results can they generate in the future? Is this a stable market in which to invest? Selling, collecting, investing, and earning, these and many others, are the possibilities that make non-fungible tokens a real technological bubble that is interesting and appealing to many. An interest that will not be extinguished will find more and more markets and uses. So many famous names have helped make NFTs even more popular. Non-fungible tokens are a unique resource of their kind. And in fact, everything about the interest and value of non-fungible tokens refers to uniqueness. What the non-fungible token creates is verifiable digital scarcity.

NFTs can be a revolution in terms of the many possibilities.

Nfts And Application Areas

Since Mike Winkelmann, aka Beeple, sold his digital work for just under $70 million, NFTs have become popular with the general public. More precisely, on March 11, 2021, at 4 p.m., what can now be called a true NFT mania exploded. NFT stands for Non-Fungible Token, a piece of digital information recorded on the blockchain. These tokens are called non-fungible precisely because they are not interchangeable; they are unique and cannot be divided. What is special about NFTs is their uniqueness and non-replicability, which makes non-fungible tokens appealing. These tokens are cryptographic, meaning they represent something unique, such as a work of art, music, or any other collectible, and digitally certify ownership. Before NFTs, it was nearly impossible to authenticate and own a digital asset.

Although it is a phenomenon that exploded recently, it is impossible to say that non-fungible-tokens have just been born as their origins are related to bitcoins and the projects delivered to manipulate them. The history of NFTs is recent, and with many branches, it is still being written, and it is continuously expanding with a considerable turnover. The decisive year for the rise of the first NFTs is 2017, when Ethereum begins to increase its importance by announcing its collection of Meme Pepe and then with the Cryptopunks project.

Non-fungible tokens today have branches in several areas, including:

- Sports. One of the first investors within the NFT world was Mark Cuban, owner of an NBA franchise. Since then, the world's top professional basketball league, several soccer clubs, and many other sports have realized the importance of NFTs. NBA Top Shot is designed for true fans and collectors and is one of the first and most critical NFT projects in sports. Owning an exclusive video of an action performed by your favorite player unmistakably is not a small thing. Sorare, on the other hand, empowers you to play fantasy soccer, having ownership of the purchased stickers and creating real teams. Sport with non-fungible-tokens opens to fans in a completely new and different way.

- Fashion. Digital fashion is today the vanguard of fashion, limited editions, and much more make possible unique fashion shows and collections and brings a high level of liquidity to a fast-growing sector. Digital objects, in the case of fashion, can be paired with NFTs, but that's just the first step. In the future, NFTs will make fashion.

- Collectibles. Collecting based on NFTs has its backbone economy. It opens up to digital media in a completely different way than before, coming to meet the generations of the future. Under the name of collecting, different visions are brought forward: the desire and pleasure of interacting and owning unique objects or the willingness to invest; collectors worldwide love to own works of art whose value, over time, can increase and generate capital.

- Art. Art has always generated interest and is fertile ground for investors. Now that NFTs have entered the market, there is no turning back. Collecting is no longer the preserve of a single privileged class, auction houses no longer hold a monopoly, and digital artists have found a way to profit from their creations. The NFT era is a new era for art.

- Gaming. One of the industries that first believed in non-fungible-tokens and received significant benefits is gaming. The market was ready; gamers have always been familiar with buying, selling, and exchanging digital assets. The problem was that they were buying something they couldn't claim ownership of until now. The non-fungible tokens purchased directly are verifiable and authentic. They create value for the players themselves and lead to new forms of collecting; in this sector, NFTs are not just a trend, a fad but something that is already revolutionizing the market.

- Real Estate. The digital real estate sector provides a cost of land production that borders on zero. Its actual value is connected to its uniqueness, to the fact of owning an asset or, better, an original and unique token. Here the convergence between real and digital has its highest expression. It becomes a thin line of demarcation, almost impossible to see. In places like

Decentraland, it is possible to have your store with digital assets linked to a clothing chain and much more. Several artists have created NFT villas and collections to visit and actual virtual events. On these marketplaces, the value of a property or a piece of land becomes much higher than the real one, and digital property is sold in a second without any need of a middleman.

- Music. The first great passage from physical to digital music has been a lost race for many entrepreneurial realities that don't seem to want to let this further innovation escape. From Mike Shinoda of Linkin Park to Kings of Leon up to Grimes, Elon Musk's partner, many artists are betting on NFT in a reliable and evident way.

Create an identity identifier. Digitizing documents of any kind while maintaining their uniqueness is a unique method of eliminating the possibility of fraud and creating a digital space where individual identity is recognized and protected.

These and many other undiscovered areas are the fertile ground where these tokens are exploding, generating a multi-million dollar business. If the classic economy has always been based on the concept of scarcity to define the at, the network has undermined this concept. The web market is overabundant and disintermediated. For this, the NFTs are born to bring back the value of the assets of the market inside the Internet. With their demonstrable uniqueness, NFTs are objects, works of art, music, and more that bring the concept of scarcity and perceived value of identity into a world like the hyper-productive web.

There are multiple marketplaces where you can trade or produce your tokens. Among the most popular and most used in different areas there are Opensea, SuperRare, Nifty Gateway, NBA Top Shot, Sorare, and Rarible are just some of the most famous. Specifically for Real Estate, everything revolves around platforms like Decentraland, Superworld, and The Sandbox. We are witnessing the convergence of natural and digital. That is because digital real estate has a cost of land production practically zero, and its value is linked to perceived scarcity precisely because it is NFT.

Today creating a store, a house, or any digital asset connected to Real Estate is possible and convenient. Thanks to smart contracts, it is, in fact, likely to acquire and establish ownership of different digital realities. Thanks to NFTs, it is possible to own a digital house to insert virtual works, always in ERC-20, or to proceed like the big brands, which open virtual stores where it is possible to buy tokens of everything displayed there. Virtual events within Decentraland, for example, can be much more profitable and require less effort than real ones. Because of this, many companies realize that having a virtual store allows for staggering sales. Overpricing is often questioned when in reality, the value of virtual land is potentially higher: a Decentraland store and storefront will enable you to reach many more people than the same store on a real street.

Demand and collective confidence in the value of virtual real estate is growing, and the change is happening fast. Another advantage of digital real estate is the ability to transfer ownership of the token and what is inside it in a practical and fast way. This transferability is much quicker and less expensive, and most importantly, does not require intermediaries. Transactions on Ethereum platforms are based on a transparent, unalterable, immutable, and unchangeable consensus mechanism.

It is the first time users worldwide can create NFTs that can be immediately available in marketplaces. Here people can buy, trade, sell and auction NFTs. The importance of these possessions lies in the reality that we are moving from sales within closed marketplaces to the possibilities offered by a marketplace with an open and accessible economy. The comfort with which users can create and trade NFTs worldwide through the blockchain is impressive and can bring many changes to the real estate industry. Transferability allows NFTs to be sold at a higher price than the real thing:

- Digital property can be sold in minutes without the need for a broker.

- Registration is self-contained.

- The property needs no maintenance.

Moreover, thanks to the smart contracts that regulate the transactions, each NFT provides a unique and non-falsifiable signature. The owners can then prove the provenance, making this purchase a more profitable and realistic investment. The virtual property built by contemporary artist Krista Kim is called "Mars House" and is a property that sold for $500,000. Mars House has a design conceived by rounded lines and edges and furnished with fine glass furniture. Kim collaborated with musician Jeff Schroeder of Smashing Pumpkins, who composed the ambient soundtrack introducing the virtual property.

The owner of this virtual home receives the individual file of the project that can be uploaded to three-dimensional worlds like Decentraland and experience its augmented reality. An artist like Kim believes that the NFT real estate market can parallel the real one. Also, the home's furniture can be built in real-life replication by select Italian glass furniture manufacturers.

Real estate is notoriously slow to adopt new technologies. However, the very nature of real estate makes it ideal for blockchain applications: it is immobile and readily available to third parties with blockchain-based claims on it, such as collateral. The world of digital assets is expanding, and we are only now starting to see every part of daily life and business activities converted into a computer-readable format. Money is already digital; think that only 8% of the world's currency materializes in the form of cash. Through blockchain, exchanges, transactions, and sales will begin to have fewer problems. Through these digitized platforms, key stakeholders will see increased speed and lower transaction costs, along with an increase in available data. Transaction transparency and privacy protection are essential when it comes to creating a healthy environment for buyers, sellers, and real estate agents.

NFTS IN SPORTS

Collectibles have long piqued the interest of the sports industry. Whether it's assets from sports video games, sports cards, or a famous player's jersey, NFTs can represent them all on the blockchain.

The following is a list of NFTs that have made their way into the sports world:

- The NBA with NBA Top Shot is number one.

- .Football (soccer in the United States) with Sorare

- Formula 1 with F1 Delta Time is number three.

- Rob Gronkowski's Championship Series NFTs in American Football

- Baseball with the World Series Champions of Major League Baseball Virtual Worlds of NFTs

As the globe gets increasingly digital, some people aren't frightened to start a new life in a digital cosmos. Many games exist as digital replicas of the natural world to fill these voids.

Then, as these simulations get more popular, the value players assign to their assets in these worlds rises. What better way to own those in-game assets but with NFTs!

A list of Virtual Worlds with NFTs:

- Somnium Space

- Axie Infinity

- DecentraLand

These platforms can have millions of dollars in monthly trade volumes for their in-game assets thanks to the creation of NFTs. These NFTs can be used in various ways inside the open-world gameplay that many of these worlds provide.

Why Are Celebrities Embracing Nfts?

NFTs can be utilized as ownership certificates for one-of-a-kind assets with psychological worth.

Given fans' devotion to their favorite celebrities, it's easy to see how digital products created and published by them could be considered valuable.

It's more like a chain reaction as more celebrities realize how easy it is to make money in the NFT industry and seize this current opportunity.

Nba Top Shot

NBA Top Shot is now the largest NFT marketplace, with sales exceeding $500 million since its launch.

NBA Top Shot sells 'moments,' which are similar to trading cards. A moment is a digital collectible in an NFT that contains a video of a particular basketball highlight.

Each moment includes:

- The Highlights video
- The player's and team's artwork
- Statistics about the game and the players
- The description of the highlight
- A unique serial number.

The popularity of the highlight determines the worth of the moment. Some moments are commonplace, while others are rare and valuable.

Several moments have sold for thousands of dollars, the most costly being $208,000.

Some players collect to connect with NBA icons, while others collect to sell and profit.

What Do You Get When You Purchase An Nft?

Since an NFT can have just a single owner at any one time, when you purchase an NFT, you buy the exclusive ownership of a particular digital asset. Nonetheless, this doesn't mean that you own the exclusive rights to who gets access to look at or share that specific artwork.

Take, for instance, the most expensive NFT sold to date: Beeple's Everyday: The First five thousand Days, a 5,000-piece digital collage. Vignesh Sundaresan is the owner of this NFT, the founder of the Metapurse NFT project, and the bitcoin ATM provider, Bitaccess.

While Sundaresan is the legal official owner of this NFT, the image has been shared, copied, and seen by millions of potential buyers around the world, and that's fair game! Therefore, when you buy an NFT, it's a little like purchasing an autographed print. The NFT is usually signed exclusively to you, but anyone can view the work.

An NFT can be any digital asset. So far, they have included:

1. Artworks

2. GIFs

3. In-game purchases

4. Tweets

5. Songs

6. Domain names

7. Essays

Why Would Anybody Buy A Non-Fungible Token?

The more you try to understand the weird and magical world of non-fungible tokens, the more you ask yourself why anybody would buy an NFT. In any case, there are a few reasons why those who have spare cash are opting to invest.

There is nothing like a perceived sense of rarity to increase the value of a particular item. Since NFTs can only have one proprietor, they create this impression of scarcity by the bucketload. That will encourage potential buyers to fixate on a particular piece, and they would begin to worry that another person may become the exclusive owner of an NFT they want.

You may think of it like when you find a pair of sneakers you want to buy and the website tells you that there's only 'one pair left.' For most of us, this increases your sense of scarcity, and it will make you want to purchase it before it runs out of stock

Collectability

Like swapping baseball cards on the playground, NFTs primarily trade cards for the super-rich. While these cards have no inherent value other than what the market assigns them, their unstable worth makes their collectability and trading value like a high-risk gambling game. Therefore, it's easy to compare the NFT and the art market.

Unlike the art market, NFTs give artists more autonomy as they no longer rely on auction houses or galleries to sell their work. By removing the middle-man from the picture, artists can sell their artworks directly to end-users and rake in more profits by doing so.

Why Art Nfts Are Growing

Many people have been perplexed as to why NFT art has been flourishing at such a rapid pace recently. Some people are starting to realize that NFTs help further democratize the art market by allowing upcoming artists and artists with Internet access in any country in the world to get their art creations to the market and enable other non-artists to support artists directly.

Nfts As A Vehicle For Positive Change

We must understand that nothing is more valuable than human inventiveness. While there have been continuous disputes concerning the energy usage of NFTs and cryptocurrencies in general, the economic benefit of funding artists' creative work across genres is apparent. I haven't heard many people discuss how much help there is in removing barriers between creativity and commercialization. Many people also don't talk about how many artists and creatives can now do a job doing what they love.

No one has done the study or done the math yet. Still, I'd want to see a comparison of the resources required by the global centralized banking system and electricity against decentralized finance and blockchains. When we consider that there are no actual bank branches constructed of steel, concrete, electricity, or building machinery, I assume that the blockchain network consumes far less energy.

Should You Buy Nfts?

Since you can buy NFTs, does that mean you should? It depends on your own choices.

"NFTs are risky because their future value is uncertain, and we don't yet have a lot of history to judge their performance. Since NFTs are still evolving, investing amounts you can spare is wise.

In other words, investing in NFTs is essentially a personal decision. It may be worth buying some if you have some spare money, especially if a piece holds meaning for you.

But note that an NFT's value is based entirely on what someone else is willing to pay for it. Hence, demand will drive the price rather than technical, fundamental, or economic indicators, which typically influence stock prices and generally form the basis for investor demand.

That implies that an NFT may resale for less than the price you paid for it. Or you may not see a buyer resell it at all if no one wants to pay for it.

Also, know that NFTs are subject to capital gains taxes—like when you sell stocks at a profit. Since they are considered collectibles, they may not receive the preferential long-term capital gains rates that stores do and may even be taxed at a higher collectibles tax rate. However, the

IRS has not yet ruled on the types of NFTs considered for tax purposes. Know that the cryptocurrencies used to purchase the NFT may also be taxed if they have increased in value since you bought them; this implies that you may want to consult a tax professional when considering adding NFTs to your portfolio.

Approach Nfts Like You Would Make Any Investment:

Make sure you carry out proper research.

Understand the risks—including that you might lose all of your investing dollars—and if you decide to take the bold step.

Proceed with a healthy dose of caution.

Are Nfts The Same As Crypto?

NFTs have been present in the bitcoin world since their creation. But don't be fooled: they're not the same thing.

NFTs are not interchangeable (i.e., non-fungible) like Bitcoin or Ethereum, even though they both contain a digital certificate of authenticity recorded in a blockchain.

Cryptocurrencies like Ethereum, on the other hand, can earn interest and be borrowed, lent, and sold in any number of brick-and-mortar institutions across the United States. That is referred to as DeFi in its broadest sense (or decentralized finance). Anyone can participate in DeFi by using what is known as "dapps" (or decentralized apps). Coinbase, for example, is one of the most popular cryptocurrency trading platforms, with crypto investors at the helm (Except for Hawaii, it serves 49 states.)

So, where do NFTs fall into all of this? At least one DeFi platform plans to accept NFTs as loan collateral due to their value in the cryptocurrency industry.

How Is An Nft Different From Cryptocurrency?

We know by now that NFT stands for non-fungible token. We also know that it's generally built using a similar kind of programming as cryptocurrency, like Ethereum or Bitcoin, but that's where the similarity ends.

Cryptocurrencies and physical money are "fungible," which implies that they can be traded or exchanged for one another. They are also equal in value—one dollar is always worth another dollar, so one Bitcoin is always similar. The fungibility of cryptos makes it a trusted channel for conducting transactions on the blockchain.

But NFTs are different. Each artwork has a digital signature that makes it impossible for NFTs to be exchanged for or equal to one another (hence, non-fungible). One NBA Top Shot clip, for example, is not similar to EVERYDAYS simply because they're both NFTs. (One NBA Top Shot clip isn't even necessarily equal to another NBA Top Shot clip, for that matter.)

Pros And Cons Of Nfts

The worth of some NFTs has skyrocketed in the past year and captured a lot of attention from the investment community. There are some advantages to consider when buying and using NFTs:

- Smart contracts. That implies that a set of coded commands built into the blockchain can guarantee that creators and artists get paid based on the use and resale of their artwork in the future.
- It makes some physical collectibles (such as art) with a long track record of gaining value, and digital art could showcase the same price appreciation.
- Selling and Buying digital assets as NFTs yields access to potentially far more buyers and sellers than in the past.
- However, there exist some other reasons why you may not invest in and use NFTs:
- Since most NFTs stand for static assets that don't generate any income on their own, they are generally valued by subjective metrics such as buyer demand. Therefore, sky-high prices may not last forever, and the NFT could lose considerable value.
- Creating and selling NFTs is not free, and the fees can skyrocket to more than an NFT valued by other users on a marketplace.

NFTS AND THE MUSIC INDUSTRY

Non-Fungible-Tokens (NFTs) have had the music world quiet. Well, let's say "excited" in recent days. The numbers were staggering, and the headlines were breathless. In only 20 minutes, Grimes could sell $5.8 million in NFTs. For $11.6 million, 3lau sold 33 NFTs! T-former Mobile's CEO paid Steve Aoki $888,888.88 for an NFT titled "Hairy"! PERFECT! The rumor mill is accurate. The clubhouse is home to many NFT and crypto-art clubs, with several Twitter threads of people shouting at each other about the actual existence of NFTs.

Experienced thought-leaders in the music industry believe NFTs are crucial. Speaking at the NY: LON Connect conference in January, Shara Senderoff, president of music/tech investment firm Raised In Space, accurately guessed that NFTS would "explode" owing to the "willingness for a fan to buy a product that is scarce, limited, and has prospective offerings attached to it that make them as a dedicated fan feel special and compensated."

On the Pro-NFT side presently, there are a considerable buzz, cash, and opinions to be heard, and we're covering those perspectives. What, on the other hand, is the alternative viewpoint? Is there a possibility that this will become another ICO (initial coin offering) bubble like the one in 2017? What if people are dipping their toes into a technology they are unfamiliar with? WTF NFTs?

We asked two people who work closely with entertainment and blockchain technology a fundamental question: what's the other end of all this buzz?

Their responses weren't entirely critical, but they provided an alternate, stunning viewpoint on the ongoing frenzy of exaggerations and multimillion-dollar total. When blockchain technology is hyped up like this, their general message is to be cautious.

Nfts To Music Industry

Simply put, you can release your music as an NFT in addition to existing platforms such as Spotify, Bandcamp, and anywhere else. Another advantage of NFTs is that they can take multiple forms and do not have to be entirely owned by a single person.

Let's pretend you're a rising star who's about to release your first album. You may make a one-of-a-kind NFT that reflects the entire album and thus becomes a collectible object. Now, the album will have unique content that is only available to one valid owner. For instance, they might receive a percentage of all album sales in perpetuity, a hidden single, or exclusive backstage access to your shows. You get to choose which features to contain, and it's simple to set up.

Benefits To The Artist

You start by hosting an album sale on sites like Foundation or OpenSea or whichever marketplace you so desire, where your fans can bid on your collectible. Suppose the song becomes a smash, and one lucky fan that purchased the collectible and backed you gets to share in your success and all the rewards that follow.

You may also profit from reselling by including a percentage in the contract for any reselling of your collectible. So, if your NFT, which reflects your album, becomes a major success and is sold for vast amounts of money, later on, the artist will continue to be rewarded every time these transactions occur. Advantages to the Collector

By taking out the middleman, they can help their favorite artists in a more significant, more intimate, and powerful way than they do through other services like Patreon. They will also be able to invest in the artwork. As a result, if the artist's career takes off, so does their collection. It turns into both a fascinating investment option and a show of support.

How To Get Started

It's now relatively simple to have your music minted and stored on the blockchain. In reality, when you have enough ether, you can tokenize and transform your music into a collectible NFT in a matter of a few minutes.

Setting Up Your Nfts Album, Ep, Or Track

The first step is to obtain a free and stable cryptocurrency wallet. This digital wallet is where you can store your ethereum if you get compensated for your work and then convert it back to hard currency (such as USD, Euro, or Pounds) whenever you need it.

After you've set up your wallet, go to any open marketplace that provides free service in your areas, such as Binance, Gemini, or Kraken, and buy some there.

Once you've completed your setup and purchased some ether, move it back to your wallet, and you're done. You're now able to get your music distributed across the chain!

From here, you can go to one of the more common sites, such as

Opensea or KnownOrigin, where you can sell your art and set the terms and conditions, price, excellent content, and all of that. Set up your account on these sites according to the guidelines and create your first NFT.

Why It Matter

The music industry requires a better and stronger future economy, and decentralized NFTs are the answer. While streaming platforms and artist

support services have made a big difference in spreading artists' work around the globe and providing avenues for fans worldwide to support their favorite artists; these services often struggle to provide an acceptable return on investment for the art itself.

To make a better environment for our future ravers, shower singers, subway riders, and fans worldwide, we should strive to promote and encourage quality work. NFTs contribute to coming up with a solution to this current problem. They can readjust the value return gap by prioritizing quality of work over the illusion of who an individual is via social networks or streaming algorithms.

NFT FOR VIDEO MAKER

Joseph Niepce was the foremost person to take a black-and-white picture in 1826. Joseph Plateau, a rare years after (1832), became the first to manufacture motion images in his creation named phenakistoscope ("spindle viewer").

Video production has constantly evolved from the earliest days of "emotional pictures" more than a century ago in reaction to new technology. As long as new instruments, formats, and platforms are widely acknowledged, every creative working with video must adjust.

While the way we see videos has altered permanently with technological innovation, distribution techniques and the creation of videos also need to continue to stay at pace with these fast-changing circumstances. Over time, new video technology, job positions, and the primary way businesses integrate video into their more comprehensive plan for commercial success has affected presentation processes. The digital video did not prevent the change of television broadcasting, the video did not kill the radio star, and TV did not quit the invention of films.

On the opposite, the more than one century of film and video composition that before it applied the way for today's video environment is feasible. It has always been vital to adjust to new technologies, whether the future of video, watch a video with a growing digit of technology and media, and many new tools and platforms to produce and distribute it.

How Can A Video Creator Use Or Create Nfts?

The globe judges like it's rapidly switching during the pandemic period, and Non Fungible tokens have come on the radar lately, with Digital Artists such as Beeple producing as much as $69 million for an image file. Now appears to be the most suitable time to understand some essential knowledge about making an NFT as a Video Maker. As a Video Maker, there are potentially multiple advantages if you can mint and offer your artwork for sale. Cryptocurrency technology will affirm you as the original owner on the blockchain and continue to pay you some royalties (Just as considered in the case of photography).

Making your video content can be done using any video-creating software. Anything in the help file formats under a 100MB JPG, SVG, PNG, GLTF, GIF, MP4, WAV, WEBM, GLB, MP3, OGG can be created. As a Video Maker, you can develop a good video below 100MB. The last step is to mint the footage with a platform available and put it up for sale. You have the chance to give unlockable content when someone purchases the NFT through an external link to another platform.

What Can You Sell?

You can sell anything digital from tweets, contracts, images, video skits, an album, any audio, 3d model, e.t.c. Some platforms accept file designs: JPG, SVG, PNG, GLTF, GIF, MP4, WAV, WEBM, GLB, MP3, OGG. With a full file size of 100 MB

Platforms To Sell Your Nft

Presently, there are many outlets on the Internet, and they all have their advantages and disadvantages, depending on what you are selling. Some venues are SuperRare, Foundation, VIV3, OpenSea, Axie Marketplace, Rarible, BakerySwap, Nifty Gateway, and NFT ShowRoom.

OpenSea seems to be more reasonable in terms of file size because they accept files up to 100MB, unlike Rarible where the maximum file size that can be uploaded is 30MB. Another advantage is that they seem to be more significant NFT marketplaces that don't demand an invite, unlike other platforms like Niftygateway and Superrare. They also offer some great free details on using their platform.

Related Nft Video Sales

NFT has been very famous that everyone wants to mint their artwork (Image, Music, or Video) on supported platforms to get some returns. NFT created from an image seems to be the most popular, and other digital arts are getting some attention from creators.

One of the most popular NFT video clips is a 10-second video that sold for a whopping $6.6 million at the NFT auction. Pablo Rodriguez-Fraile, a Miami-based art collector, spent over USD 67,000 on a 10-second video in October 2020. The video could have been watched online without cost because we live in a technologically sophisticated age where everything is now available on the Internet. Still, he chose to spend USD 67,000 to obtain the video for his collection rather than do so. In February 2021, he sold the property for a total of 6.6 million dollars.

As considered in NFT by photographer, the blockchain was used to authenticate the video created by a digital artist known as Beeple, whose real name is Mike Winkelmann, "the blockchain is a trustless platform that serves as a digital signature to verify and certify who owns it and that it is the original work."

Another popular NFT video that got people's attention is the LeBron James slam dunk sold for $208,000.

The launch of the U.S. NBA's Top Shot website has been said to be the start of the rush for NFTs, and it is possible to trade, sell or buy NFTs in the condition of video highlights from games on the website open anybody interested.

The platform says it has hit over 10,000 users buying NFT with nearly $250 million of sales. The NBA is also said to receive royalties on every sale on the marketplace. And February 2021 is said to be the highest sales on the platform so far, with a total sales of over $198 million, which multiplies January's sales of $44 million.

The most significant transaction on February 22 on the platform was when a user paid $208,000 for LeBron James slam dunk video.

During an interview with one prominent NFT investor, known as "Pranks," he stated that he had put USD 600 in an early NFT project in 2017. His portfolio of NFTs and cryptocurrencies is now worth a total of seven digits to him. Pranks claim to have spent more than a million dollars on Top Shot and made approximately 4.7 million dollars from the resale of his various game collections.

You must be wondering this is it; NFT has nothing to offer another industry except an industry that involves graphics like image or video, but NFT has not stopped there; it is available for anything digital technology, even music. How can the piece be displayed as an NFT? Well, it is like owning an album of music as one of your collections.

UNDERSTANDING NFT STOCKS

When you consider Art's resale value, NFTs become a compelling investment opportunity. It's close to purchasing physical works of Art. If you want to keep the Art, possessing it will not benefit you.

Of course, staring at the work of Art can provide you with a sense of fulfillment. However, big money comes from selling art pieces to the most elevated bidder. To put it another method, if you can buy a one-of-a-kind NFT and then sell it for more additional than you paid for it, you will benefit handsomely.

The strength of blockchain is that it eliminates the possibility of fraud and theft. There will be codes and authentication to confirm and validate the authenticity of the work of art you own. Others can also create copies of an original digital art piece, but only one original remain. The original belongs to the person who owns the NFT for that art piece.

If anyone asked you in January what NFT stocks were, you'd probably stare at them blankly. This week, the enthusiasm has sparked Wall Street rallies in a slew of tech stocks. As I formerly said, some of these have little to do with the NFT niche. However, based on speculation, investors believe these companies will gain exposure to NFTs.

It's difficult to tell if NFT stocks will take off in the long run at this stage. Examine cannabis stocks and cryptocurrencies from 2017 to 2019. If history is any guide, the excitement surrounding NFT stocks will likely fade away soon.

With all of the hype, it's easy to ignore it as science fiction that will never come to pass. However, if we look near, we can see that something is going on behind the scenes, and why am I saying this?

Last year, according to Nonfungible, the overall volume of NFT transactions increased to $250 million. NFT transactions totaled more than $220 million last month alone. It seems that we are experiencing something that is rising at an unprecedented rate.

Traditionally, any digital art shared, saved, or downloaded on the internet can be easily shared, saved, and downloaded. However, there isn't a clear sense of ownership since anybody can use it. Assume you're an artist, an exceptionally talented one.

You also create some of the most stunning works of art, but what about putting your imagination to good use?

You seem to have had little success with it so far, at least with most citizens. However, there is a way to give digital art a sense of individuality using NFTs. It also provides an opportunity for sound artists to continue doing innovative works.

The art industry has many scopes for NFTs. However, first and foremost, the market must be regulated. There is currently no law dictating who can build NFTs and who is not. Before then, I wouldn't invest in NFT stocks without first waiting for the dust to settle but, don't get me wrong: I adore Art.

I genuinely believe that this can change how art is perceived in our culture. Maybe it's just me, but before investing in NFT stocks, I'd like to see more concrete developments. However, this is merely my opinion; the final decision is yours to make. Make sure you do your homework and study.

Crypto-assets are starting to stir up mainstream knowledge is behind the interest in NFT stocks. The hunt for stores linked to non-fungible tokens (is heating up, and investors are frantically looking for opportunities. Celebrities such as Jack Dorsey and Elon Musk have experimented with offerings, and brands follow suit.

Are you the sort of investor who is willing to take on a high level of risk in trade for the possibility of a high return?

NFT stocks can be erratic. As you'll see below, many businesses are experimenting with NFT offerings. Others use a mix of online sleuthing and social media gossip to reach new heights. As a result, the early-stage trend is scorching but extremely risky.

When evaluating these businesses, make sure to weigh the risks and research what makes them unique.

Do you think it's great that they're associated with NFT targets or blockchain technology?

Are their companies ripe for potential cryptocurrency deals?

Do they have any NFT services that produce revenue?

There is money to be made in the room as digital artist Beeple made nearly $70 million for a single piece, but money is also lost.

With that in mind, here are the top ten NFT stocks that InvestorPlace is currently tracking.

- Takung Art is a form of martial art (NYSEMKT: TKAT)

- Jiayin Group is a Chinese conglomerate (NASDAQ: JFIN)

- Group of Oriental Culture (NASDAQ: OCG)

- Media in Liquid Form (NASDAQ: YVR)

- Hall of Fame Resort & Entertainment is a resort and entertainment complex located in Las Vegas, Nevada (NASDAQ: HOFV)

- Funko Pop! (NASDAQ: FNKO)

- Cinedigm is a film production company that specializes in (NASDAQ: CIDM)

- Color Star Technology is a technology that allows you to see colors (NASDAQ: CSCW)

- WiseKey is a program that will enable you to create a (NASDAQ: WKEY)

- KBS Fashion Group is a fashion company based in Korea (NASDAQ: KBSF)

SUCCESS & FAILURES

Nfts Help Artists Solve Vital Problem

Kevin Abosch, a New York-based artist, has sold a $1.5 million painting of a potato, created a neon artwork inspired by cryptocurrencies, and even auctioned his blood on the blockchain network.

In several respects, the 51-year-old Irish artist's entry into the non-fungible tokens (NFTs) space was the natural next step for his work, which investigates digital currency and value themes. Non-fungible tokens (NFTs) are digital tokens that prove a digital collectible's authenticity and ownership. The technology has been present since at least 2017 and is a spinoff of the cryptocurrency industry that uses the blockchain.

Is It Possible For Anyone To Become An Nft Collector?

However, in March, the NFT frenzy reached new heights when Christie's, the famed art auction house, sold off a digital collage by an artist known as Beeple for about $70 million, instantly making him the of the most expensive living artist ever.

Many people are perplexed as to why someone would like to acquire an NFT. What does it imply to own art in the first place? For artists like Abosch, NFTs assist in resolving a long-standing dilemma in digital art: how can you take possession of something that can be readily and continuously reproduced?

Abosch started working on a series of images in 2020 that dealt with encryption and alphanumeric codes. Following the cancellation of many of his in-person presentations due to the Covid-19 outbreak, Abosch felt that now was the ideal time to sell his work as NFTs. He planned to sell them on OpenSea, the world's leading token market, that receives 1.5 million weekly visits and triggered $95 million in sales in February 2021 alone.

He made a $2 million gain from the collection, including all work that can't be physically moved to a gallery or put on display. He became the most popular NFT artist on the OpenSea marketplace due to it. On the eve of the auction in March 2021, he told the Guardian that the notion that art should be a tangible product that can be exhibited is soon becoming obsolete.

"Some individuals are troubled by this concept since they wish to know what you genuinely own," he explained. "However, persons of a younger generation do not have this problem.

"Wanting to grasp something in your hand is a very outdated tradition as if the ethereal or immaterial has no value."

An NFT auction functions similarly to an online auction on sites like eBay. Every work is shown as an image file with metadata – that means "data about data" – including the title, number, and who owns it.

Abosch's 1111 series debuted on OpenSea at 11:11 a.m. EST, where he posted 111 works for a limited time. Following the beginning of the auction, prospective purchasers visit the Abosch sale page to bid on specific art jobs - in this case, using the crypto Ethereum.

While the NFTs were traded on Opensea, the actual sequence of characters that links the owner to their new NFT is saved on Arweave. This program acts as a form of permanent internet by storing files in perpetuity over a decentralized network of systems, preventing them from being erased or damaged in the future.

To put it another way, a buyer will pay for an image on the NFT trading site OpenSea with an Ethereum token and receive an Arweave address certifying the acquisition and ownership of the image file in exchange. In the end, 53 different collectors bought 106 of the 111 works, with the most costly selling for $21,242.

Some artists, including Abosch, are attracted to the NFT tech because of its democratizing nature: anybody can connect and buy the items, and the work comes with a publicly available ledger of its entire history - when it was minted, who possessed it, who bought it, and for how much. This, according to Abosch, is a break from former art purchases, wherein investors put special art in-store to hold it for a period when it will be more expensive.

The prominence of cryptocurrencies and the increase of art market speculation have been proliferating for some time. However, the coronavirus outbreak has further positioned the sector for the triumph of tech like NFTs, according to Andrei Pesic, an art history professor at Stanford.

"As we've had to transfer so much of our life online in the years 2020 and 2021, it has opened or hastened the idea of pricing digital products in the same manner that we value physical products," he said. Abosch, who has been utilizing blockchain technology to mint art since 2013, says the NFT mania was sparked by two factors: the tech is intriguing and practical, and any new bright thing that promises to make people rich will quickly readily attract attention.

"We are in a significant evolutionary time – it's like we're in the middle of the biggest storm, except instead of everything being damaged, we'll see new constructions that are quite fascinating," he explained. "However, there will be some rubble."

The Old Art World's Problem

- The Power of Gatekeepers

The Problem In The Old Art World:

In a fundamentally hierarchical structure, individuals and organizations with lengthy histories, huge money, and pre-existing business connections exert significant power over who gets to participate.

- The NFT Difference

New, decentralized markets can accept artists and participants without sanctioning the art establishment. While some NFT marketplaces (like SuperRare and Nifty Gateway) will only welcome artists by invite or registration, for the time being, others (such as Rarible) will enable any enthusiastic artist to begin trading in their market.

Ameer Suhayb Carter, an expert cryptocurrency designer and advisor preparing to launch the Well Protocol, an NFT network, archive, and support system with a particular emphasis on BIPOC and LGBTQIA artists, exemplifies the blockchain art world's most transformative power.

"In many situations, these are folks that can't even find a job in their home country. Carter, who also operates as an artist under the nickname Sirsu, told Artnet News, "We're giving voice to the voiceless."

"The idea is for them to be able to establish the communities they want in their way. I supply them with the devices they need to take control of their lives. I'm not going to build for you; I'm going to build with you."

The Collectors' Values

- The Problem in the Old Art World:

The changing structure of upper-echelon art acquisition is part of what makes existing gatekeepers so strong. Investors fight to represent the same types of artists that buyers crave: artists who look like them, that is, primarily white and male persons who have contacts within the high-art society.

- The NFT Difference:

Until now, many, if not all, NFT purchasers have come from outside the conventional art business circles, and they have shown minimal concern in recognized investors', advisers', and collectors' ideas on what is worth collecting—and at what price.

According to Kevin McCoy, the artist who built the first NFT as part of Rhizome's Seven on Seven conferences in 2014, "the cash flowing into the NFTs space is cash that was already in the space." "Cryptocurrency investors are buying NFTs. I've constantly believed that fresh makers and collectors, not the old art world, are the source of power."

Wealth Redistribution

- The Problem in the Old Art World:

When it comes to profiting from art, practically all of the significant benefits go to the collector on resale. Even the most successful artists are usually only paid a pittance in resale royalties. The UK, for instance, has a resale royalty maximum of €12,500 (about $17,300) for its inhabitants, regardless of how much a work sells for when it is resold; the US, on the other hand, has no resale royalty at all—at least, not outside of revenue generated in California during a one-year time in the late 1970s.

- The NFT Difference:

Since percentage-based resale royalties may be built into the conditions of each NFT sale, creatives can profit appropriately and indefinitely as their pieces travel through the market.

Most importantly, this redistributive mechanism can be completely automated. What is the reason for this? Because the "smart contract," a collection of instructions that operates on the blockchain network without human involvement if independently verifiable conditions are satisfied, is the primary mechanism of NFT exchanges. (For example, "ownership of this asset goes to the sender as soon as the sales price enters the present owner's account," state hypothetically.)

According to Amy Whitaker, a professor of visual arts administration at New York University that began exploring blockchain in 2014, the potential get much more exciting when NFT artists utilize intelligent contracts to redistribute assets to more than just themselves.

For any prospective NFT pieces, artist Sara Ludy reportedly arranged a new sales share with her New York gallery, bitforms: 50% for Ludy, 15% for the NFT network, and 35% for bitforms—with the latter amount equally distributed in 7% increments between the gallery's founder and four employees.

Whitaker compared the move to a tip jar for restaurant employees. It's a way of "collectivizing economics," as well as "trying to combine for-profit and nonprofit frameworks so individuals can route some of the earnings towards grantmaking or charity" without having to fill out extra tax forms if the creators so desire.

Preservation And Ownership

- The Problem in the Old Art World:

Possession of (and copyright) works like installation, performance, and video sometimes devolves into a quagmire of misunderstanding outside traditional physical media.

Investors and creators must create term sheets from the start for every piece, with the final papers typically veering between unnecessarily plain and frustratingly complicated. All for the collector to regularly misinterpret or ignore their responsibilities, particularly when it comes to the long-term care of the piece.

- The NFT Difference:

The blockchain network stores the work's full provenance and copyright information and the possibility to add a wealth of additional data that would be useful to historians and archivists. Standard contracts, such as ERC-721, are widely used by artists unsure about establishing their agreements. Should a disagreement over intellectual property emerge, an NFT's whole transaction history may be audited back to its creation, providing irrefutable "on-chain" evidence of which party's rights are valid?

GAMING, DIGITAL IDENTITY, LICENSING, CERTIFICATES, & FINE ART OF NFTS

Collectibles, art, games, and virtual worlds are the key categories of existing NFT use cases. However, other categories, such as sports, fashion, and real-world properties, are increasingly growing.

Terra Virtua is one of the world's first immersive digital collectible networks, with some of Hollywood's biggest names, including Topgun, The Godfather series, Pacific Rim, Sunset Boulevard Lost in Space. It also has a relationship with Paramount Pictures.

Antiques and collectibles

Collectibles are currently one of the most common applications of NFTs in terms of sales volume, accounting for about 23.6 percent of all sales in the former month. CryptoPunks, which debuted in June 2017 and has since sold for thousands of dollars, is one of the first collectible NFTs on Ethereum.

They were created before ERC-721 was launched, and a wrapper had to be designed to be traded on exchanges such as Opensea. CryptoKitties have become well-known collectibles, with sales reaching more than $38 million since their launch in November 2017,

Playing Video Games

Gamers, as formerly said, are an ideal target market for NFTs since they are already acquainted with virtual worlds and currencies. The gaming industry is booming thanks to NFTs, which enable in-game objects to be tokenized and easily transferred or traded using peer-to-peer trading and marketplaces.

On the other hand, traditional games forbid the selling or transferring in-game objects such as uncommon weapons and skins.

Since players have complete control of their digital properties, NFTs make the gaming experience more tangible and satisfying. They're also spawning a new economy, as players can now benefit from their in-game properties by constructing and improving them.

Artpiece

One of the most challenging problems for digital artists is copyright infringement, but NFTs are a remedy because they provide evidence of ownership, authenticity and eliminate counterfeiting and fraud concerns.

As museums and galleries close due to COVID-19, many artists have switched to NFTs and online showrooms, according to a Coindesk post, and "just as Bitcoin paved the way for peer-to-peer transactions by establishing a public events ledger, cryptoart has provenance built-in."

In July, "Picasso's Bull" set a new record for the NFT highest-valued art auction sale, selling for more than $55,000. "These ventures can also boost and streamline artists' income by linking them directly to customers via blockchain-based payment and exchange solutions," according to Cointelegraph.

Interactive Universes

Digital worlds are another application for NFTs. Users can build, own and monetize virtual land parcels and other in-game NFT products on decentralized virtual reality platforms, including Decentraland, The Sandbox, and Cryptovoxels.

Decentraland's LAND is permanently owned by the group, giving players complete ownership of their virtual properties and creations. Given Gen Z's experience with virtual worlds and how their understanding of valuable assets varies from that of former generations, virtual world assets provide them with the versatility and option that they value: "

Properties And Documentation From The Real World

Real-world properties such as property and bonds, and documents such as credentials, licenses, medical records, birth and death certificates, can be tokenized.

However, this category is still in its early stages of growth, with few applications. As the crypto world and NFTs grow and expand, who's to say you won't be able to own a vineyard in another country thousands of miles away one day (perhaps soon)? Your digital wallet can soon contain proof of every certificate, license, and asset you own, for all we know.

PROJECTS CONSTRUCTING A STRONG FOUNDATION BENEATH THE MARRIAGE OF DEFI AND NFTS

Digital collectibles on blockchains are operating the retail mania for crypto higher right now because they are calm and in part. After all, the market seems to have finally reached this consensus: Provable ownership of digital items can accrue real value.

When there is actual worth, there is finance. These collectibles also comprehended as non-fungible tokens (NFTs), have been verified recently to have very high importance. "NFTs are a foundational structure block of the emerging virtual economy," Stephen Young, the creator, and CEO of NFTfi, stated in a press release.

The most delinquent data point in the continuing story of the union of NFTs and decentralized finance (DeFi) is the latest funding for NFTfi. This project allows borrowers to post-digital items as collateral. NFTfi announced an $890,000 investment round from backers including CoinFund, 1kx, The LAO, and Dapper Labs CEO Roham Gharegozlou, among others.

NFT is one of several companies making it a lot easier to get money in, earn yield and bring it back out of the digital collectible space.

How It Operates

NFTfi is primarily like DeFi giants Compound and Aave, both money markets, but those two use fungible collateral, like ETH or various stable coins. NFTs are non-fungible, and they are demands with less liquidity, making price discovery more challenging.

That's transforming fast with more and more products coming onto the market, making it more manageable for liquidity to flow through the many outcomes. And recall, this is crypto: Switching fast means a wildly diverse thing in this enterprise than in the pokey ancient world of mobile phones and social networks. "As NFTs re-imagined how we create and define the right of digital content online, we'll also, in turn, start to re-imagine a whole new category of financial services established on these new building alliances," Lasse Clausen, a partner at the experience firm 1kx, said in a press release.

Beyond NFTfi, here are ten more projects that are making the NFT market almost as complex, flexible, and liquid as the remainder of crypto:

NIFTEX

The startup, whose outlet makes fractional ownership of NFTs possible, is working on a new version with many new features. For example, it will allow creators to earn royalties on trades of fractions, governance over the underlying NFTs for holders of a bit, and other tools that permit more fine-grained ownership. Also, a decentralized independent organization (DAO) is coming to manage the whole application. "Fractional ownership of songs, books, other scope is a no-brainer. One edition, lots of proprietors, individuality is king," co-founder Joel Hubert told CoinDesk in an email.

Ark Gallery

This company made a DAO that built wrapped CryptoPunks, making Larva Labs' pioneering NFTs more fungible. Ark has afterward created additional tools to enhance liquidity for the original non-fungible token, and probably merits some recognition for today's white-hot CryptoPunks market. It is presently working on Blank. Art. "We will launch NFT projects that are commandeering financial ideas and themes for artistic purposes," Ark's Roberto Ceresia told CoinDesk in an email.

Mintbase

Mintbase is an outlet that makes it leisurely to mint non-fungible tokens. It had an investment round lately led by Sino Global. It mainly enables users to mint on Ethereum, but the NEAR blockchain has gone out of its way to be consistent with the original smart-contract chain. Right now, Mintbase is establishing a characteristic on NEAR that allows royalties on sales to be shared with up to 1,000 people. "That is the fractional ownership part evis talking about," COO Carolin Wend told CoinDesk.

NFTX

This one allows community-owned index funds so that one token defines right in many NFTs. It has tokens for specific varieties of NFTs and others representing a scope of the market. "There are, however, numerous people out there that don't have the time or understanding to sell individual NFTs but would like disclosure to NFT markets. These are the NFTX mark users," the firm composed in January.

Charged Particles

This protocol aims to help any NFT encode or embed with an ERC-20 token. So just in point, there was any doubt an NFT had value, a user could cover it with interest-earning tokens, and it would contain been worth it beyond any doubt. That is the same as what the upcoming

Aavegotchi game is doing. What will it mean for non-fungible and fungible assets to become roommates? Time will tell.

Zora Protocol

According to its white paper, "Zora provides a cryptographically enforced registry of media independent of any platform." One of Zora's creators, Jacob Horne, told CoinDesk in an email, "We've directly built the market into the NFT, and we've created a net new auction model specific to NFTs. Zora auctions are perpetual; anyone can bid in any currency, the owner can accept any bid." If that sounds head-scratching, check out this new genre of poetry built with the help of the Zora team.

Unifty

"Unifty is an NFT management system. Think of it as 'the WordPress of NFTs,'" Markus Medinger of the Unifty team told CoinDesk in an email. Unifty has a marketplace with new features around copyright management and value drops, among others. The platform is somewhat unique in that it essentially performs off Ethereum. "We already help xDai, BSC [Binance Smart Chain], Polygon [née Matic], Celo, and Moonbeam Alpha. Multi-chain aid is one of our expertise," Medinger added.

Upshot

That is an as-yet-unrroject for crowdsourcing NFT appraisals. "The next step for financialization is cracking the NFT price discovery problem in a capital-efficient way," CoinFund's Jake Brukhman told CoinDesk.

NFT Trader

A peer-to-peer trading task for NFTs, still in beta. Be alert!

Polyient Games

This company is all over NFT financialization, from investing in the sector to more robust construction tools. It operates a decentralized exchange for NFTs, has its approach to fractional ownership, and has products built for NFT protection. The company is mocking a game now that vows to make DeFi more game-like. "Polyient Games is our decentralized ecosystem created to drive forward NFT invention, both internally and through third-party participation," Craig Russo, the co-founders, informed CoinDesk in an email.

State Of The Market

The initial DeFi players have not instantly made a lot of noise around NFTs yet. Scott Lewis of DeFi Pulse is entangled with NFTX and Aave supported in the video game that uses its tokens, Aavegotchi. "Aave community has an enormous interest," Stani Kulechov, CEO of the money market Aave, told CoinDesk in an email.

Usually, this is the portion of the post where we'd tell readers just learning about NFTs and DeFi that they should take a minimal amount of ETH or stable coins and buy some little things and play around. None of this stuff makes sense until a person tries it. Unfortunately, right now, most people can't spend a negligible amount of money on DeFi because transaction fees ("gas," in Ethereum parlance) make everything costly.

Layer 2 platforms are those that pose atop Ethereum and other blockchains, taking benefit of the underlying blockchain's protection while also allowing cheaper, faster transactions. NIFTEX's Huber told CoinDesk he foresees layer two solutions fundamental to this sector. Still, too little liquidity has moved onto anyone layer 2 to make it worthwhile for an app like his to move there yet. As made it hard to enjoy the DeFi playground on ETH mainnet," Marguerite deCourcelle of Blockade Games told CoinDesk. The blockade is in the middle of moving its users to layer 2, now comprehended as Polygon. "I think we're about to witness a lot of additional users and developers on L2," she said.

Nfts & Defi: A Good Combination?

If you want to understand what non-fungible tokens (NFT) are, why they are evolving increasingly famous in the crypto scene. What they have to accomplish with decentralized finance (DeFi), we must first dig the idea of "value" in depth.

What Is Value?

Value is the natural quality of a thing that makes it desirable to a certain extent. This value can be related to several tangible and intangible characteristics, mainly rarity.

Therefore, the economic value of something depends on its quality and scarcity.

Why Is Value So Significant To Nfts?

Non-fungible tokens (NFTs) are cryptographic tokens that are not backed by a traditional asset and instead are representative of something else, such as an artwork, an event, or a digital item. Thus, many people mistakenly jump to the conclusion that NFTs do not have value.

However, non-fungible tokens are indeed valuable. NFTs represent unique assets and are rare and cryptographically secure. They are not interchangeable and thus introduce scarcity to the digital world. Each of these tokens acquires value due to this scarcity. That occurs following the customary law of supply and demand — partakers are willing to pay more for a specific and rare NFT.

NFTs are thus optimally fitted for decentralized applications (dApps) to create and own special digital items and collectibles.

NFTs can be traded at businesses that connect buyers with sellers. In these exchanges, every NFT is individual and therefore gets its worth.

What Accomplish Nfts Have To Do With Blockchain?

It all began in 2016 when Bitcoin-based trading cards were issued as some of the first NFTs. In 2017, these early NFTs were printed on the Ethereum blockchain using CryptoPunks, a platform offering NFTs describing the artwork. However, the natural buildup started in December 2017 with the deployment of the blockchain-based game CryptoKitties, which uses NFTs to convey ownership of digital cats on its platform. Today, more than 131 million USD is wrapped in these two projects in Ether.

In the years since this initial NFT advertisement, hundreds of other NFT iterations have become known on the market.

Since the origins of using NFTs on the blockchain, various standards have been created to promote the issuance of NFTs. The most popular of these is ERC-721, a standard for the distribution and trading of non-fungible assets on the Ethereum blockchain. A more recent, improved average is ERC-1155, enabling a single contract to contain fungible and non-fungible tokens.

This standardization of NFTs allows a more high degree of interoperability, suggesting that unique assets can be transmitted between applications with relative ease, ushering in additional use cases.

What Are The Potential Areas Of Application?

It is clear that NFTs offer an increased status of interoperability and act as terms of non-traditional assets.

That means that NFTs can be used in many areas. That includes video games, digital originality, licensing, certificates, or fine arts. These tokens can and even allow for the fractional right of objects.

That is precisely where DeFi comes into play.

In all fields they are applied to, NFTs represent some worth. These values can be managed entirely in the blockchain via smart contracts. That perfectly fits the definition of a DeFi project: a financial tool operating along with the blockchain.

Present Defi Nft Offerings:

Current developments in this area are already diverse.

For example, DeFi projects represent themselves as a decentralized trade for NFTs. One of the best comprehended in this area is Rarible.

Another instance of NFTs and DeFi is Aavegotchi, an entirely decentralized collection game.

Likewise, Tinlake combines NFTs and Defi by offering a service that forms a bridge between real-world assets and DeFi. Its goal is to access bankless liquidity.

POTENTIAL CONCERNS OVER INTELLECTUAL PROPERTY

The controversies that surround this issue revolve around the definition of ownership and copyright. While NFTs are generally considered a strong representation of ownership over the digital art that it is linked to, there are some concerns regarding the ownership and copyrights associated with NFTs that will be addressed. Does owning an NFT mean that you own its copyright as well? The responses to these questions will have to be clearly defined within the budding NFT scene so as allow all stakeholders to grasp the legalities they are dealing with.

What Does Digital Ownership Truly Mean?

When you own an NFT, what does it indeed mean? There is a common misconception that when NFTs are minted, the digital files linked to them are also stored on the blockchain. Unfortunately, this is not the case. Digital media are often too large to be held on the blockchain. Instead, these digital files will be stored somewhere else on the web. When NFTs are created, the token will then be permanently linked cryptographically to the location of the digital file. The information stored on the blockchain is thus equivalent to directions that will point you towards the establishment at which the file is stored.

Files stored online are always at risk of being deleted or being moved. That means that NFTs may become worthless if the digital file it points to gets removed. To protect NFT owners from losing ownership of their digital assets, the Interplanetary File System (IPFS) was created. IPFS is a decentralized digital file storage solution whereby storage capabilities are distributed globally across multiple networks. The files uploaded and stored on the IPFS are permanent, and the location of files on the system will be suitable for being linked to an NFT.

In a nutshell, the purchase of an NFT represents your ownership of a digital file stored in a location recorded on the blockchain. That is the extent to which digital license means, which has thus far proven to be a sufficient representation of ownership.

Copyright Conundrum

Traditionally, there were only two forms of media. They had clear property distinctions, which led to different copyright laws imposed on physical and digital media.

The First Sale Doctrine Of Physical Items

The "first sale" doctrine was introduced to cover all physical items. The principle states that all material items bought can be then resold in a secondary market without the original creator having any control over the terms of the secondary sales. Royalties cannot be imposed on physical items, which is why we have items such as paintings, trading cards, and vinyl records being resold between individuals where the seller can keep the total proceeds from the transaction. The first sale doctrine was introduced because owners of a physical item cannot derive value from the work's copyright. It would thus be unfeasible to protect the physical object from any copyright law.

Rejection Of A "Digital First Sale" Doctrine

As the world became increasingly digitalized, it soon became apparent that a digital-first sale doctrine would be disastrous for digital content distribution. That is because digital files can be easily reproduced and copied. It is not easy to replicate a physical item completely, so the first sale doctrine makes sense. Under the original first sale doctrine, purchasers of digital files can make unlimited copies of the file and distribute it at a profit. That would be unjust to the creators of that file as the sellers would benefit directly from the work's copyright. For this reason, American legislators blocked the first sale doctrine from applying to digital files under copyright laws.

Differences Between Nfts And Traditional Digital Files

Up till the time before NFTs were created, all digital files could effectively be considered to be fungible since copied files are essentially the same, and none of them can be regarded as a unique digital asset. The non-fungibility of tokenized assets parallels physical items because no two material things can be identical. Two bicycles of the same model produced by the same company may have minor differences, no matter how small. This non-fungible quality of physical items has allowed the first sale doctrine to work out so well for physical works.

The advent of NFT technology then challenged the fungibility of traditional digital files. To take the example of Cryptopunks, they were algorithmically produced back in 2017. Its current value can be attributed to its legacy status and history. Another NFT linked to a copy of an image of a Cryptopunk would not be valued anywhere near what the original versions would be worth today. While the copied NFT may be linked to an identical piece of artwork, the apparent differences in their unique identifiers recorded on the blockchain have created a massive distinction between the copied NFT and the original Cryptopunk NFT. The success of NFT is primarily attributed to how it was able to assign a non-fungible attribute onto digital files effectively. That is where the problem comes in. NFTs are digital assets while also being non-fungible. Which copyright law shall it be covered under then? It becomes clear that none of the existing laws can be applied to NFTs, and a new set of rules will be needed to define the legal boundaries of NFTs.

Relationship Between Copyrights And Nft Ownership

What exactly does ownership of an NFT entail in terms of copyrights? When you purchase an NFT, you are not purchasing the copyright for that work. Copyrights for the job will still belong to the creator of the work. Distribution or printing the digital files without getting permission from its copyright owners can thus be considered to be copyright infringement. In this case, the rightsholder will be entitled to sell and distribute copies of the original NFT to the public. That can be seen in how NFT minting services allow for the creation of multiple NFTs that are linked to the same digital file. In summary, purchasing an NFT from the marketplace does not come with the copyrights associated with the work. Buyers should be made fully aware of this information to understand the full scope of what they are paying for.

However, there are cases where the copyrights to a digital file can be sold alongside its ownership. That can be facilitated by creating a smart contract that transfers the associated rights along with the digital asset to the new owner during a transaction. To illustrate how the smart contract can be used to generate specific terms involving the rights of a digital file, we can take a look at the $69 million Beeple NFT as a case study. The artist who created the artwork has included certain display rights in the image, enforced through a smart contract. However, the original artist retained the copyrights to the idea. In the case of NBA's Top Shot collectibles program, purchasers of the NFTs that the organization issued obtained a limited license that allows them to use, copy, and display the digital files for non-commercial and personal usage. Through these examples, we can see how artists can selectively confer rights to buyers to fit the desired terms of their NFT transaction. Creators may thus also choose to add full rights to their work to enhance the value delivered to the buyer of the NFT.

Controversies Surrounding Nft Creation

The default case for all digital works is that no NFTs exist before an entity chooses to mint that NFT. That creates a huge problem surrounding how copyrights can be proven before an NFT is minted. Unfortunately, anyone can take a screenshot or upload a digital file to mint an NFT. That means that while you may have created an art piece, someone else can take the file that you have uploaded and mint an NFT linked to it. In this case, even when you are the rightful owner and creator of the work, it appears as if another person owns your digital file and may even profit from the sale of that NFT.

The unauthorized creation of NFTs based on another person's work is evil and is an apparent infringement of copyrights. However, there is still a high risk of it happening to your work, and it essentially becomes a race for creators to "register" their work before anyone else steals the opportunity to do so. In some ways, it is equivalent to how patents work. The reason why the unauthorized minting of NFTs is occurring on a large scale is simply that it is too lucrative. Infringers are taking advantage of the information asymmetry to make a profit, and this occurrence has necessitated the creation of protocols designed to protect creators from copyright infringement.

To prevent unauthorized NFTs from being created and sold, marketplaces have instituted DMCA processes to identify and remove NFTs created from stolen content. Some of these marketplaces have also taken a stronger stance against copyright infringement and thus only allow verified works to be put up for sale. As the NFT market continues to grow and mature, we can expect stricter legislation to be imposed on the scene in a continued effort to protect stakeholders.

Technical Challenges Of Transacting Nfts

With the long list of legal obligations that may be tied to the smart contract of each NFT, there is the consideration of what level of liability sellers will have to hold in terms of fully representing the terms of rights to the buyer. It can be argued that all times of the sale are listed in the smart contract on the blockchain, and all of this information is fully accessible by the buyer. The seller would then not be responsible for clearly representing the information to the buyer before the transaction as the responsibility falls to the buyer. On the other hand, given the technical complexity of how the blockchain and smart contracts work, buyers may not get a complete picture of the terms of the sale, even after evaluationing the intelligent contract. In this case, it can also be argued that the seller should be responsible for explaining the full details of the upcoming transaction.

In cases where NFTs have royalty-based smart contracts encoded into them, the legality of how each NFT is represented also comes into play. For instance, the creator of a digital piece of art may sell the NFT linked to it to a seller while clearly stating that the creator retains all copyrights. The buyer may then inaccurately represent this information during a resale, where the buyer promises to provide all copyrights related to the work. That would naturally increase the valuation of the NFT. During the transaction, the owner of the NFT may then take a 10% cut as part of the intelligent royalty contract. There are grounds for the secondary seller to be accused of fraud in this case. As the original creator benefits from this instance of deceptiveness, to what extent would he be held responsible?

The technical challenges involved with understanding the terms of a sale will have to be overcome by creating strong guidelines regarding the sale of NFTs. In the most optimal scenario, each NFT transaction that takes place should have to be done with the provision of a comprehensive and straightforward description of its smart contract and sale terms.

AVOIDING SCAMS AND HOW TO SPOT THEM

Here are some of the most prevailing scams that occur in NFT, as well as tips on how to prevent them:

Nofraud.Org

In this case, the site utilizes catchy names and perks to get visitors to sign up for free trials, which ultimately results in them having to pay money.

Email

The con artists will provide them with a link to a website that seems genuine (but is not), or they will lead them to sign up for something on an actual website by transferring their email address to the con artists. Threats of legal action generally follow that if they do not sign up right away.

Nigerian Money Scam

That is the point at which you'll be requested for your bank account information so that they may transfer monies into your account, but this never occurs, resulting in you losing all of the money you've supplied them with and having no method of recovering it.

Phishing

In phishing, you are urged to do something by clicking on an email, a website, or even a phone call, and in exchange, you get something in return. Following that, you'll most likely be taken to another page or invited to download a file to your computer. This attachment may contain malicious software.

Surveys

Some websites may ask you to participate in a survey before allowing you to proceed with your purchase – but be aware that these surveys are paid by the company itself, which then uses the information to enhance their goods and services to meet your requirements better.

Fake Evaluations

Fake evaluations may be very damaging to brands and businesses developing new goods and services. If someone lures you in by writing a positive evaluation about a product, it would be easy to believe that the product will live up to those expectations, and even if that were to occur, they would introduce more competition to the market, which would be detrimental to the brand's business or product (as well as yours)

No Shipping Charges

When you purchase goods, you may be charged a delivery cost or be required to pay extra shipping charges that were not disclosed before buying the product.

Lack Of Trust

You're often urged to believe what others say about a product on the internet, but it's essential to read between the lines and understand that not every evaluation you read will be candid! One of the most productive ways to stop falling victim to this scam is to thoroughly study the critiques and ensure that they are authentic!

Refunds

If you are ever requested a refund, don't comply. There might be various reasons you need a refund, such as the product not lasting long enough or the product's appearance on your body not being what you expected it to be.

Fake Shipping Charges

That occurs when you are charged more for shipping than what was stated or when there is no tracking information provided for any products being shipped to your home - both of these are scams that can cause significant problems if they are not discovered until after the packages have been sent to the destination address.

Sales

Certain websites are quite deceptive in the manner they conduct sales. After purchasing a product at a low price, you'll see that the price has been raised later on. However, you won't be capable of withdrawing your purchase since it has already been sent.

Catch Up Scams

These are situations where you are offered membership or a subscription for a certain amount of money. They are required to pay them again every month if you want to continue using the service - this might wind up being far more costly than if you had paid once!

A LIST OF NFT PROJECTS I'M GOING TO INVEST IN 2022

N FTs—an emerging technology that uses crypto platforms to authenticate ownership of digital files. During the final crypto boom, the region—home to some of the most affordable power in the U.S.—was beset with a new energy-hungry home industry: basements and sheds loaded with racks of computers churning through advanced mathematical calculations to "mine" valuable crypto coins like Bitcoin and Ethereum. But even small crypto mines can overload local grids, making them a problem for energy companies. Far larger cryptocurrency mines have been set up from Texas to Iran to China's Inner Mongolia.

That may surprise artists and other NFT fans who are far removed from the technology's environmental toll. "You don't see your money is moving to a miner who's going to pay for fossil-fuel-based energy with it," says Alex de Vries, a financial economist.

Some in the crypto world are operating on solutions. Ethereum's developers promise to launch a less energy-intensive approach by 2022. But cryptocurrencies are popular partly because they're decentralized, attracting people who distrust governments. That means there's no single leader who could force a change.

Nft Topmost Projects

NFT-focused projects and products have improved in tandem with the rapid development of the NFT subspace. The top four NFT projects are listed below.

- OpenSea: This is the best place to buy and sell NFT collectibles and art. The marketplace accepts a variety of virtual currencies, including ETH. Virtual pets, ENS, and land plots are among the items listed. Notably, the marketplace agrees with various virtual currencies, including DAI and ETH.
- Async.Art: Async is another marketplace for non-fungible tokens where you can purchase, sell, and create non-fungible tokens. The platform has several programming features that will enable artists to define the appearance and actions of their work quickly. It also allows customers to buy and change "layers" of an artwork. In reality, it will enable customers to customize parts or "layers" of a piece of artwork that they bought.
- CryptoKitties: This project deserves to be at the top of the list of NFT projects because it brought the NFT game to the forefront. Even though we've already covered this project, it

still needs to be included in our top NFT projects list since it launched the entire NFT industry.

- The Ethereum Name Service (ENS): This is a design for a domain name service released in mid-2017. ETH domain names are non-fungible tokens (NFTs) that use Ethereum's ERC-721 formats and can be traded in the NFT market. The . ETH domain names are non-fungible tokens (NFTs) that follow Ethereum's ERC-721 specifications and can be sold on NFT exchanges.
- Decentraland: is a top NFT project that focuses on a distributed virtual environment. Participants can purchase virtual land here. In addition, each "inhabitant" has a unique digital passport that identifies them.

What Is Causing The Current Rise In Nfts?

The recent explosion of blockchain-based collectibles, particularly on the Ethereum blockchain, has created a new class of assets that anyone can own in the world and which has been dubbed Crypto Collectibles.

While this sounds exciting to many people, there is still a lot of confusion about what a crypto collectible is and how it differs from other crypto assets such as cryptocurrencies.

Is There A Market Bubble For Nfts?

Going back to the basics of a bubble, there is an extreme spike in the value of non-fungible tokens. But, how long will this bubble last? That is an inquiry that only time can answer. It is possible that NFTs are in a drop and that the bubble will pop, but we won't know for sure until the market adjusts to a new price.

Speculation

The crypto market is full of speculators and people who believe that they can predict the future. These people have been buying NFTs, hoping that the value will continue to rise. This type of behavior isn't necessarily a bad thing, but it can create a bit of volatility. Some people get hurt when the market fluctuates, and others make money. The goal is to make money, but many people cannot predict how high or low the price will go.

Media Attention

Many of the top NFTs are being used in games and virtual worlds. Some crypto art projects are making it big in the media and social circles. When something gets this much attention, it is easy for speculators to jump on board and buy NFTs at a higher price. When there is more demand for NFTs, the price will increase.

Limited Supply

A limited number of NFTs are being created each year for each project. The amount of tokens available at any given time is being reduced because of the projects creating new tokens. Some people believe that this reduction in supply will lead to a higher price, but it isn't necessarily true. A higher price will only happen if there is more demand for the tokens.

The Rise In Popularity Of Decentralized Games And Virtual Worlds

The popularity of decentralized games and virtual worlds is on the rise. Many projects are creating new games and virtual worlds that will utilize NFTs. Some of these projects have been victorious, while others have failed. When a project fails, it could mean that the value of the NFTs associated with that project will decrease.

Before launching yourself head-first into the world of NFTs, there are some common mistakes that you really must avoid. Although the creation and selling of NFTs have not been going on for too long, it is noticeable that some people are making the same mistakes repeatedly.

These mistakes can be catastrophic for your success in the NFT world. You will probably make other small mistakes when you are just starting, and that's OK. As long as you learn from these, it is OK. It would help if you avoided these vast mistakes that can mean the difference between success and failure.

NFT MISTAKES THAT YOU MUST AVOID

Thinking Too Short-Term

Yes, some NFTs have sold for millions over the last year. But that doesn't mean that you can create NFTs or invest in them and make a substantial amount of money the first time around. If you try to make too much money too fast with NFTs, then it is very likely that you will fail and give up on the whole idea.

There is no doubt that the NFT journey can be an exciting one. This doesn't mean that you will be a millionaire by this time next week, though. You are highly likely to fail if you go into NFTs with a "get rich quick" attitude.

The best way to succeed with NFTs is to provide value. You will also need a reasonable degree of patience as you may not sell your NFTs right away. Be consistent with your marketing efforts and take the time to form collaborations and partnerships that will serve you well in the future. If you are serious about the NFT game, then commit to it for the longer term.

You Are Not Promoting Your Nfts Enough.

It is just not enough to create your NFTs and list them on OpenSea, and expect the money to start rolling in. There are already millions of NFTs listening on OpenSea, and most of these are struggling to find buyers.

Forget about the "build it, and they will come" concept. It is not going to happen. You need to create a marketing plan and then stick to it. Identify your target audience and then find out where they hang out.

Use social platforms to leverage your NFT promotions. Use Discord forums, Clubhouse and Reddit to your advantage as well. Do whatever you can to obtain the word out about your NFTs and the talents that you have.

Some people might get lucky with their NFTs. They may list them on OpenSea, sell them quickly, and have people begging for more. Instances like this are sporadic. You cannot count on this kind of luck, so be sure to have a promotional plan and follow through with it.

Choosing The Wrong Marketplace For Your Nfts

This is another classic mistake that we see over and over again. NFT creators cannot do the necessary research, and they opt for OpenSea because it is the biggest platform. Yes, OpenSea does get a lot of visitors (nearly 40 million a month and growing), but this does not indicate that it is the best platform for your NFTs.

It would be best to find out several things about an NFT marketplace before you use it. The essential thing is knowing whether your target audience uses the marketplace or not. You need to consider if the NFTs you want to create are a good fit for the ethos of the market.

With several new NFT marketplaces emerging all of the time, you need to ascertain whether the market you are considering using is safe. The size of the community in the market is essential, but more important is whether the community is responsive and helpful.

Unfortunately, there are scam NFT websites already in existence. For example, these people will collect fees from you to pay Ethereum, and you will never sell anything. To avoid these scam NFT websites, use the Dapp Radar website to check for legitimacy.

I Am Doing Nfts On The Cheap.

The more that you can invest in your NFT venture, the better. Many people make the mistake of thinking that the world of NFTs is a free one and that they can do everything on the cheap. While platforms do not have fees for listings, most of the best quality ones do, so you need to factor this into your NFT budget.

In this guide, we have told you several times that the Ethereum blockchain network is by far and away from the most popular for NFTs. If you want to use the Ethereum network, you will have to pay gas fees.

You need to put some money after your NFT marketing as well. Unless you have a massive following on social media, you will need to use social media ads to showcase your NFTs. That is a reasonably inexpensive way to achieve results pretty fast.

While gas fees and listing fees may come down as NFTs become even more popular, this cannot be guaranteed, and you cannot rely on this happening. If costs come down in price, use the money you saved for more marketing. You need to take your NFT journey seriously and be prepared to invest in it for the maximum chance of success.

It does not understand how NFTs work.

We have seen so many people make costly mistakes because they didn't understand the basics of blockchain and crypto.

It would be best to have a good overview of how NFTs work and blockchain.

INVESTING AND FLIPPING OF NFT'S

If you are not aware of the term "flipping," you buy something at a low price and then sell it at a more elevated price. There are many examples of this in life, such as purchasing a real estate property for a low price and trading it for a higher price. You can apply flipping to things like comic books, services, and much more.

Investing in NFTs and flipping them for profits is something you can do. Not everyone is artistic and cut out for creating and selling their own NFTs. NFT trading is growing considerably, and investing in NFTs right now can be a brilliant move.

Benefits Of Flipping Nfts

Today, the NFT market is relatively new, and the competition is not that great. There is a lot of room for growth in this market. People are already making profits from flipping NFTs, and there are a lot of opportunities to do this if you know what you are looking for.

As an example of the profit potential in buying and selling NFTs, a token was sold in 2017 called CryptoPunks. This NFT sold for $456, worth around $26,000. There are a growing number of NFT collectors, so you should see these opportunities available for quite some time.

The people involved in NFT flipping right now realize profits from 10% to 50% in just a few days. They are building NFT portfolios, and some of the investors hang on to their investors longer-term to make even greater profits.

People Are Buying Nfts

You know from reading this guide and external sources that NFTs are very popular today. There is no doubt that blockchain technology is here to stay. Many businesses and organizations worldwide are looking at how blockchain technology can improve what they do, and some have implemented it already.

When you have major blockchain networks such as Ethereum allowing the tokenization of digital art, video clips, music, in-game items, and more, there is a massive appeal for owning NFTs.

The central selling point for an NFT is uniqueness and provenance. Many things are copied in the digital world, but there can only be one proven owner of an NFT. People are interested in purchasing different NFTs, and they vary in value.

Nft Flipping Opportunities

No form of investing is guaranteed, and this applies to NFTs. There are certainly opportunities for NFT flipping profits, but you have to know how to spot the best options. Flipping NFTs has already been confirmed to be a simple and relatively quick way to make good money.

There are no hidden secrets for finding NFTs that are good flipping opportunities. It comes down to 2 things:

The Nft Is Currently Undervalued

The NFT is expected to increase in value

Because there are NFTs in many different niches, it can be tempting to try and find opportunities in all of these. But this is not the best approach to use. You need to find a profitable NFT niche and learn everything about it. It is not likely to be an expert in every NFT niche. The more you know about an NFT niche, the higher the chances of good flipping projects.

We recommend that you do not go for more than 2 NFT niches. Start with one and then really dig into the community around it. Find forums and subreddits around this NFT niche, watch YouTube videos about it, listen to podcasts, and chat with people in the community.

It will take time for you to become knowledgeable about an NFT niche, so you need to be committed to this. You can never do enough research, so commit to learning about your chosen NFT niche(s) every day.

An NFT niche could be a popular game. The Decentraland game has a virtual real estate theme. An NFT investor made a profit of over $83,000 in just one year with this game. He purchased parcels of land from the game at a low price and sold them for a higher price. This guy knew the market and was able to capitalize on his knowledge.

Find Nft Flipping Opportunities On Marketplaces

You can go to popular NFT marketplaces such as OpenSea and Rarible to find flipping opportunities. We would liken these sites to garage sales, where you can find undervalued items. OpenSea, in particular, is a great marketplace to find hidden gems because there are a lot of crypto artists finding their way with the platform.

There are NFT flipping opportunities in the collectibles market as well. Here we are talking about niche opportunities at sites like NBA Top Shot, CryptoKitties, Atomic Assets, and Decentraland.

If you have some experience buying and selling trading cards for a profit, the Atomic Assets marketplace is ideal for you to start. This site keeps up with trends, and many collectors use it to find the NFTs that they want.

There is considerable interest in the NBA, and the Top Shot marketplace has NFTs available valued at more than $600 million. Creators drop new NFTs all the time on this outlet, and it is a very active marketplace. If sports memorabilia appeals to you, this is a great place to start. The bottom line is that you need to know and follow your niche.

For crypto art, the best sites are Nifty Gateway and Known Origin. The best way to profit from these marketplaces is to look for emerging artists and any high-quality art that you believe to be undervalued. Finally, you will see the entire market at SuperRare and Christies.

Use Nft Buying Strategies

Several successful NFT investors seek out bulk buys. That is one of the best ways to make a healthy profit from NFT flipping. Bulk buys are more common in the collectible and trading cards markets. Some of these bulk buys can be on a large scale, as many NFT sellers are happy to sell in a bundle because they do not want the hassle of trading individual tokens.

You can haggle the price on an NFT with sellers. The best way to do this is to connect with NFT sellers in the communities for your niche using private communication methods (instant messaging etc.). A lot of NFT investors make their most considerable profits through haggling.

Be prepared to network within the communities of your NFT niche. Constantly maintain an eye on the market and look for different trends. The more you are on top of your NFT niche, the more profit you are likely to make.

FUTURE OF NON-FUNGIBLE TOKENS

Since the beginning of NFT, the favor of NFT games has skyrocketed. NFT projects have been created by several prominent organizations, including the video game producer NBA and Ubisoft. As of January 2019, Dapper Labs, the organization that made CryptoKitties, has started collaborating with other NFT providers to facilitate interoperability between game platforms. That means that a native NFT can now be used on another platform without modification.

In current years, the potential for NFTs has expanded dramatically beyond the gaming industry. Organizations and organizations are investigating the possibility of non-fungible tokens as a means of establishing identity and certification, ticketing, and fractional right of both digital and physical assets. Any condition in which there is a requirement for traceability and explicit license falls under the purview of NFT use issues.

The fate of NFTs will heavily depend on the progress of the Ethereum network and broader blockchain technology.

It's secure to assume that as blockchain technology persists to grow, NFTs will mind – whether it's on the Ethereum blockchain, another broad network, or a remote web.

Crowdfunding A Non-Fungible Token

Non-fungible tokens are still moderately new, and most game developers have had to find out how they can be made as they go. Many NFTs are built using living smart contracts or making their protocol. In some circumstances, the founders of an NFT will also create a game to showcase its features and utility. That allows users to purchase the game and give it a level of credibility.

The Nft Approach To Crowdfunding

Allocation for a new company by using crowdfunding is a moderately new idea. NFTs (Non-Fungible Tokens) have been available on the Ethereum network since 2015. But they are still somewhat obscure among game creators and a broader audience. That means that many developers may not have the tools or resources to create an NFT. That is one of the reasons that the NFT Approach to Crowdfunding was made. This approach allows NFTs to be designed, hosted, and spread on any outlet (including mobile gadgets and web browsers). In expansion, game developers can also build crowdfunding campaigns using the "NFT-Crowdfund" standard. It supplies developers with the tools and resources they need to create their own NFT. That allows them to make their ERC-721 token; an NFT used as a crowdfunding campaign.

Constructing Nft-Crowdfund

Here is how you can potentially construct your NFT-Crowdfund:

- Make your colored token for crowdfunding on a platform (Ethereum Wallet, Metamask, etc.) or via a command-line interface (console).

- Use the NFT-Crowdfund protocol for creating and distributing the NFT.

- Use ERC 721 to convey your game items.

- Use ERC – 684 for constructing pre-order items with a deal. These will not be fungible behind the Crowdfund ends. Unsold pre-order things are burned.

- Rename your NFT if required to remember the marketplace name.

- Document your rare item(s) on a marketplace for selling post-crowdfunding using the NFT registry, or create your marketplace. All pre-order items must be re-categorized to fit your new marketplace category.

Buildup Art Nft Marketplace

Finally, I wanted to present you with this revolutionary project named Hype Art. I am creating with a team of art and cryptocurrency lovers.

Non-For-Profit (NFP) projects started to gain widespread notice. Although crypto was going through a downturn, the industry saw significant growth.

The most accustomed marketplaces for NFT (Superrare, Niftigataway, Rarible) present their platforms more to Amazon and eBay than to a craftwork gallery: collectors don't feel any creative venture when scanning these outlets.

The Artist is not in the middle of the discussion. No space is given to the idea and the thought behind its work.

What Do We Desire To Create?

We think the creative vision of the NFT creator needs to be placed at the center of the narrative. Each Artist will share the creative idea behind their work through a live interview (hosted by Koinsquare) jointly with a curated definition of the work presented.

We strive to create a 3d virtual gallery that allows the collector to repeat the same feeling of visiting works displayed in a real gallery.

We want to encourage the community of our collectors by using gamification; therefore, auctions will be completed in parallel to airdrops to our followers.

Where?

Hype. Art will utilize Opensea (ETH blockchain) and FAN (Tron blockchain) as venues where the Auction will carry place to access a bigger market.

Hype. Art will instead promote the community's artistic promotion and a structured team to allow artists to customize their "online exhibitions."

Key Players

There are three key players: the Zulu Republic, Koinsquare, and Satoshygallery.

The Zulu Republic is a location on the blockchain where people, businesses, and organizations can thrive on their representations. Our objective is to help promote the development of decentralized technology, which is likely to have an enormous effect on the advancement of human rights and empowerment throughout the world and mitigate the digital gap.

Koinsquare is a project that strives to promote and disseminate knowledge and knowledge in blockchain and cryptocurrency technology.

With our commitment, passion, and professional approach, we present and analyze different topics such as Cryptocurrencies, Smart Contracts, centralized/decentralized Exchanges, ICOs, the Fintech Industry, Market values of the significant crypto assets, Mining systems, and much more.

Satoshi Gallery was born in a very early stage of cryptocurrency history. Since 2013, it has been using iconography and art to fill the opening between technology developers and the general public and spread the crypto culture to a larger audience. Satoshigallery has provided art paintings to various private collectors worldwide, illustrated books for Andreas Antonopoulos, and drew some of the most iconic logos in the crypto space (Bitfinex, Tether, etc.).

When Will The Project Launch?

- March 2021: Hype. art was born

- April 2021: Platform and artistic development

- May 2021: Marketing development

- September 2021: Launch of platform for public

Do You Want To Participate In Airdrop?

Art. The art exhibition will include thousands of Airdrops and a premium Auction, ready to scream out the first Artist with the launch of Hype. You have been one of the first to get an invitation to view the Exhibition and bid in the Auction. We will be providing a date announcement to the subscriber as soon as possible.

HAS THE BUBBLE ALREADY BURST?

Even as some people remain optimistic about the future of non-fungible tokens, others believe that the bubble has indeed burst, and the statistics are there to prove it. Ethers, for example, lost over 50 percent of their value between the spring and fall of 2021, including a five-day, $1,000 devaluation in September. That was accompanied by an almost $10,000 drop-in Bitcoin, leading many to believe it was more of a market correction for cryptocurrencies. Still, other statistics show that adjustments are happening in the non-fungible token world.

At its peak, collectibles like CryptoPunks were leading the way to total sales. Their grasp on the market was staggering, outselling all other forms of non-fungible tokens by a wide margin. In August of 2021, total collectibles sales reached almost USD 165 million over seven days. Within a month, that had dropped to a mere $9 million. Similar drops were seen in art, gaming, sports, utility, metaverse, and Defi purchases.

Most charts showed a roller coaster-like rise and fall while others, namely sports, flatlined. Much of the buzz around sports non-fungible tokens is tempered by the fact that, unlike collectibles and art, they are limited as to which wallet can hold them and how they are sold. Dapper Labs has its wallet for non-fungible tokens traded on the NBA's Top Shot marketplace, which some collectors do not like. Major League Baseball's Champions series, non-fungible receipts of baseball players in the bobblehead style, are rising in price, mainly because the world's biggest baseball league ended their partnership with creators Lucid Sight, making the non-fungible tokens rare commodities.

But others believe the most robust future lies with businesses like NBA's Top Shot and other sports-related digital memorabilia, at least from a collectible point of view. The cartoonish CryptoKitties and CryptoPunks may have set the bar, but in a sports-obsessed world, non-fungible tokens of real-world athletes and sports teams could take things to the next level. Ethernity Chain, armed with its own crypto Erns, is banking on just this. They have entered into exclusive non-fungible token production of current athletes like Dallas Cowboys running back Ezekiel Elliot, former athletes like soccer's Péle, and athletes who have passed on, such as boxing icon Muhammed Ali.

"With the non-fungible token boom we have seen in recent months, it is clear in my mind that authenticated non-fungible tokens from actual real-world sports and entertainment statistics are the only real future for non-fungible token collectibles," said Ethernity CEO Nick Rose Ntertsas.

"When we launch a drop with Tony Hawk, Muhammad Ali, or the legendary footballer Pelé, these are all authentic, endorsed, and backed by these people, thus creating an actual underlying value for them."

Ethernity has taken collectibles to another level, adding a particular twist to their NFTs featuring Dallas Cowboys quarterback Dak Prescott. His digital collectible cards will change their look depending on how Prescott performs during the football season. They are linked to his quarterback rating, a mathematical formula that rates a player's performance based on his game statistics. A bad game and the card goes grey, with lightning strikes in the background; a good game, he's blue, and excellent performance will see him red, as in red hot, hoisted on the shoulders of his teammates.

Looking further down the road, Althea Artificial Intelligence has developed what they are calling intelligent non-fungible tokens. Through their technology, non-fungible tokens will become animated, allowing owners to interact and even converse with their digital art. In doing so, they have created a sub-category for non-fungible tokens, intelligent-non-fungible tokens (NFTs). Still, in the developmental stages, the company raised $16 million in capital through a private token sale in August 2021. They see iNFTs as the cornerstone of future, interactive metaverse technology.

As exciting as this is, it is still all speculation.

The Tulip Lesson

History is rife with economic bubble bursts, and the one drawing a lot of comparisons to the non-fungible token market is the Tulip Bubble of the mid-1600 in Holland. Economics moved a lot slower in those days, so it took longer to play out, but the similarities are glaring. Early in the Century, tulips arrived from Asia, brought by traders along what was known as the Silk Road. Europeans loved the unusual-looking flower, and it soon became a luxury item for the rich to have in their gardens. Like so many fads, people looked down on people who did not have tulips in their garden.

Unlike modern tulips, many of which can handle the harshest winters only to pop up in the spring, the tulips of the 17th Century were fragile and needed extra care and cultivation. That further elevated their status as a sign of prosperity. While tulip seeds could take over ten years to start flowering, the bulbs would bloom annually, so people scrambled to get the bulbs. When a mutant strain created striped tulips as opposed to those with a single color, an even greater status symbol was born; and the wealthy were willing to pay whatever it took to get the flowers into their gardens.

Like the non-fungible token market, people looked for ways to get in on the tulip action. Farms outside of the cities went from food production to tulip production, and the price of a bulb rose to the modern equivalent of $10,000 to USD 50,000. By 1636 tulips were being traded in the Dutch stock exchanges. It seemed nobody wanted to miss out, so people began borrowing against equity to buy bulbs. At one point, a tulip bulb cost more than a house along Amsterdam's Grand canal. Much of the cause of the price rise was that producers could not keep up with the demand due to the long time it takes for a tulip seed to reach maturity.

With so many bulbs bought on credit, panic set in when the price began to drop. Not wanting to be stuck with debt, buyers became sellers, and the price plummeted. By 1638 tulip bulbs were back at their regular prices. Stories emerged of investors who lost everything and were forced to eat the tulip bulbs they once prized. It is questionable whether "tulip mania" devastated the economy as much as history likes to believe, but it did explain why investing is risky.

With the significant drop in price and sales, it is not hard to see why some financial analysts believe there has indeed been a burst. That is not to say that non-fungible tokens are going away. Their usage is becoming more streamlined, but making a quick profit through buying or selling might not be as leisurely as it existed in early 2021. While the collectible market may be down, other markets like sports are up. Still, others believe that the gaming industry is the most bankable future for non-fungible tokens.

Already a 100 billion-dollar-a-year industry, the next step could be the convergence of non-fungible tokens and DeFi in gaming. The idea is somewhere along the lines of a rental shop for gamers. Investors could buy game pieces like a specialized weapon or armor, then rent them to a gamer for a small fee. This way, a gamer could profit from the game as they play. Swedish game developers Vorto are going hard at this concept with their game Hash Rush. Even in 2021, with the game not set to debut until 2022, Vorto is selling game pieces, and eager gamers are already scooping them up.

Fraud

For all the exciting and sometimes baffling news surrounding non-fungible tokens, there is an equally ugly side that could scare a lot of people away if it does not get better. If one thing can bring down a market, it is bad press. Even as marketplaces scramble for better security procedures, stories keep emerging about scams and hustles designed to exploit the unprepared.

Earlier, we consider the Russian men posing as women selling the Famed Lady Squad non-fungible tokens and an employee at OpenSea engaging in insider trading. Are there other scams or manipulations you should be concerned with? The answer is yes. Crooks are descending on the non-fungible token world, knowing there are a bunch of unsavvy buyers and sellers ripe for the picking. The one item they desire more than anything is your passkey.

If you recall, the key is the set of 12 words that secure your wallet. Scammers have become very creative in their attempts to get your key, including setting up fake sites that look and feel like a popular non-fungible token marketplace but with a subtle difference; they are listed as not .oi. The unsuspecting victim logs on but has problems accessing their wallet, usually connected to the site. They try and try, but the problem continues. The scammers hope that eventually, they will access tech support. When they do, the scam begins.

It usually starts; they ask the usual questions to make the victim feel at ease. The scammers can work in pairs, bringing in a second "technician" to help fix the problem. That can go on for hours, and it usually does by design. They are trying to wear you down so that eventually, you slip up. You reveal your keycode or the QR code that allows access to your wallet. Once they have that, everything ends. When the victim goes back and checks their wallet, everything, non-fungible tokens, and crypto alike, is gone.

Because the technology is so fresh and it draws in so many buyers unfamiliar with how things work, there are plenty of easy victims for the scammers to attack. But these guys are so good that collectors well versed in the non-fungible token community are also falling victim. To alleviate the problem, OpenSea closed their customer service segment of their website and moved it to Discord, a Voice Over Internet Protocol, instant messaging, and digital distribution application that has become the central hub for the non-fungible token community. Even then, the scammers followed (author's note: After purchasing some non-fungible tokens and joining Discord, I was asked about my wallet within two posts). So bold are these scammers that they even pretended to be OpenSea's customer support lead and their head of product by using their names. In one instance, respected digital artist Jeff Nicholas lost USD 480,000.

Impersonators

Scammers have also taken to impersonating artists and selling bogus non-fungible tokens. This sucker job is pulled by setting up a marketplace page that looks exactly like the actual artist's page but with subtle differences. The YouTube site Non-fungible Token Times illustrated these differences with a Bored Ape scam page listed as the "official" BAYC page. What was missing, and it is easy to forget, was that the page was not verified even though it had the verification checkmark next to the page's profile picture. Everything else looked legitimate, including links to the BAYC webpage and different social media accounts. The scammers hope that you miss the small details and take their bait.

HOW TO DISCOVER AND ANALYZE PROJECTS

At the outset of my foray into the world of non-fungible tokens (also known as digital assets), I had no clue where to begin or figure out which of the projects would be the best fit for my particular situation. After spending over a year in space and gathering a large number of NFTs, I think I have established a reliable method for selecting the most appropriate project for you and your long-term financial objectives.

The following three basic guidelines must be followed when selecting the finest NFT to purchase for yourself and retain for the long term:

Invest In Non-Financial Companies That You Are Interested In.

First and foremost, you should only invest in non-financial companies that pique your interest. After all, what's the purpose of spending money on something you're not going to use or enjoy? Consider looking for the "next greatest" NFT rather than the "next best" NFT corresponding to your specific interests.

There is no way for everyone to have the same interests and no way for everyone to make the same informed decision about anyone NFT project since we all have different degrees of comprehension of the category we have chosen to invest in.

For example, suppose you truly appreciate soccer and know a lot about the players and teams. In that case, it's fair to assume that a soccer NFT project would be an excellent topic to start your study on while developing your NFT project. Alternatively, if you are a true admirer of modern art, you should be delving further into the works of contemporary artists and their NFTs.

Carry Out Your Investigation

Who doesn't like a good bit of research? Once you've identified an NFT that you're interested in, it's time to get your hands dirty and understand all you can about that particular NFT. The process of researching NFTs isn't quite as simple as browsing the "evaluations" area of a website and reading all that other customers have to say, but it's close.

When you sit down to investigate any NFT, the following are the topics I urge you to attempt to collect as much information on as you possibly can:

- The creator(s)

- The community
- The project (brand)

The creator(s)

In my opinion, it is critical to identify that when you buy in a non-fungible token, you are genuinely investing in the person who is driving the project forward. As with betting on your favorite sports team, you place your wager on the player's ability to perform rather than on a random group of individuals.

When evaluating a project's originator, there are a few aspects that I look for, including their prior success and ability to execute, their social position, and their capacity to develop brand recognition within their target audience.

The community

Don't forget about the people in your community! A successful NFT initiative will have a thriving community due to their efforts. The presence of a generally pleasant attitude, helpful individuals, and a high level of communication from the project manager are all indicators of a thriving community. It is expected that this communication will include project updates, notifications and help with any difficulties that community members may be experiencing.

Okay, so now you're likely wondering where you can learn more about a project's community; the answer is simple: everywhere you go online and look for it.

The project (brand)

Finally, we get to the most critical component of the puzzle: the actual project. In my opinion, the projector, as I like to refer to it, the brand—is unquestionably one of the most significant parts of the NFT jigsaw. The brand attracts customers and maintains a high demand for its assets.

Don't Fund More Money Than You Can Afford To Lose.

The last piece of the puzzle in determining the ideal NFT for your position and goals should not just be regarded as a rule but an essential must! Do not put more money into an investment than you can afford to lose. There should, in my view, be no exceptions to this general norm.

Putting all of your funds into a project with no money to fall back on may place yourself and your family in a difficult financial situation. It's awful if you wind up losing all of your hard-earned cash on an NFT project that finally turns out to be of less value than you had anticipated.

I try to get into any endeavor with the mindset that the project might fail and be refunded. I understand that no one likes to consider the possibility that the initiative they have invested in may fail, but that is just the reality of the market.

NFTS AND DEFI

Both the NFT and DeFi (Decentralized Finance) ecosystems have collaborated in a variety of ways, including the following:

Nft-Backed Loans:

Some DeFi apps are available that allow you to borrow money by pledging collateral.

When a person wants one bitcoin, they must first provide 25 or 26 ETH as collateral. A person can acquire the loan he needs, and the lender can take the collateral if the borrower defaults on the loan. However, not everyone would have the necessary quantity of cryptocurrencies on hand to obtain the loan they require.

Some prospective projects are beginning to investigate the strategies for employing NFTs as collateral to assist such persons. As an example, suppose you purchased a rare NFT a few days ago that is now worth $63,000 at today's pricing. You can get a loan for 26 ETH if you hold this as collateral. If you can't pay back the ETH, the lender will take your rare NFT as collateral. Anything that can be tokenized as an NFT could be used in this way.

Because both the DeFi and NFT worlds employ Ethereum's blockchain technology, this will be a simple operation.

<u>Fractional Ownership:</u> In addition, creators can create shares for their specific NFT. That allows investors and fans to own a portion of an NFT without purchasing the entire asset. Miners and collectors of NFTs will have access to an increasing number of chances due to this.

The NFT marketplace and Decentralized Exchanges (DEXs) like Uniswap would be used to trade such fractions of NFTs.

There would be significant growth in the number of buyers and sellers.

The fractions of an NFT can be used to calculate its overall price. You will have a window of opportunity to possess and earn from goods that are important to you. It would be terrible if you desperately desired something but couldn't afford it.

To put it another way, this would be like owning a piece of Picasso art. You'd own a bit of a Picasso NFT, which means you'd also be a part-owner and have to say over things like income sharing. It's likely that having a piece of an NFT will enable you to form a decentralized autonomous organization (DAO) to administer that asset shortly.

DAOs are Ethereum-based institutions that allow anonymous people, such as global asset shareholders, to interact securely without trusting the rest of the globe. Even a single cent cannot be spent without the consent of all of the group's members.

As formerly stated, the space of NFTs, DAOs, and fractional tokens are all evolving at different rates.

Nonetheless, because they are all part of the same network, Ethereum, all their infrastructures may exist and work together.

Nfts And Ethereum

Ethereum enables NFTs to work smoothly in various ways, some of which are listed below: Token transaction history and information are open to the public and may be verified by anybody. As a result, proving ownership with the use of NFTs is simple.

It is impossible to change existing data after successfully verifying a transaction, which means the ownership status cannot be stolen.

NFT trades might be made directly, eliminating the need for platforms that often take a percentage of the money as compensation.

The technology used in Ethereum's goods is the same as that used in Bitcoin. As a result, even if you have an NFT on one platform, you can sell it on another as long as it is Ethereum.

Creators can list several properties simultaneously, and all of those items will have the most up-to-date information.

Because Ethereum is available 24 hours a day, 7 days a week, you can sell your NFTs whenever you choose.

Minting An Nft

The following steps are taken to create an NFT.

- The existence of the NFT as a blockchain asset should be proven.

- The creator's account balance should be adjusted to reflect the asset's inclusion. It can be ensured that the person owns the help in this way.

- The transactions, as mentioned earlier, will be confirmed and appended to a block on the blockchain, making them permanent (immortalized).

- It should be verified as valid by others in the network before recognizing that the NFT is on the web and belongs to the originator.

Anyone can check it because it is recorded on the public ledger. Finally, the creators' income potential would be raised due to this.

The duties, as mentioned earlier, are typically carried out with the assistance of miners. Miners inform other network members about these NFTs and who owns them. If the process isn't demanding enough, anyone can claim the NFT by claiming bogus ownership. There are numerous incentives in place to encourage miners to work honestly.

While data blocks are being added to the Ethereum blockchain, they must be created consistently. As a result, a data block will be added to the blockchain every 12 seconds. Nobody, however, will be able to change the data that is being uploaded to the blockchain. For example, suppose a hacker attempts to change the data of an NFT in block #200. When he tries to do so, the data on the other blocks will alter, and any Ethereum blockchain miner will be able to spot it and prevent it from happening.

Every day and NFT transactions are both added to the blockchain in the same way, so a block with no NFT transactions is the same as a block with NFT transactions. As a result, the computational power needed is the same. As a result, rather than being caused by NFTs, the environmental damage is caused by the blockchain or Ethereum.

Drawbacks

We've gone over most of the benefits and characteristics of NFTs, and a few things stand out. However, NFTs have some disadvantages listed below: Is it a bubble?

Ethereum, like the majority of other profitable cryptocurrencies, may be subject to additional scrutiny. If all governments agree to prohibit cryptos and everything linked with them, you will lose all of your priceless NFTs. As a result, the future implementation of cryptocurrencies is unknown.

Cryptocurrencies and related activities have been outlawed in Bolivia, China, Algeria, and Morocco. Furthermore, governments like India are attempting to enforce a ban on cryptocurrencies, and progress is being made.

So, if something seems too fine to be true, it probably is, and the same may be said of cryptocurrencies and NFTs.

Theft:

Assume someone put forth a lot of effort and created digital art. Someone else could steal it and make it his NFT before he could mint it as an NFT. There is no precise regulation in place to restrict such behavior.

Partiality:

People who have become renowned and have established a reputation may amass a large fan following and earn a lot of money, whether from music sales, art sales, or other means. So, what about up-and-coming musicians who are seeking to build a fan base? They are unlikely to make much money because most people prefer to buy anything from celebrities. As a result, it may benefit aspiring artists and innovators at the start of their careers.

Environmental Damage:

The most significant downside of NFTs is that they are based on Ethereum, which requires mining to add data blocks to its blockchain.

That is true not only for Ethereum but for most cryptos, particularly 'Bitcoin.' Using a Proof-of-Work (PoW) consensus mechanism to mine would necessitate a massive amount of computing power. High-tech computers and a lot of electricity would be required. The amount of energy consumed for Bitcoin mining is more significant than Argentina's total energy consumption. That would be harmful to the environment, and the carbon emissions might be substantial.

NFTs got a lot of publicity and popularity after Bitcoin, and there will be a rise in activity relating to them. As an outcome, there is a probability that NFTs may become the second most significant source of carbon emissions and environmental damage among all cryptos in the cryptocurrency ecosystem.

Data Hosting:

The digital asset and NFT are maintained separately, which means the NFT is on the blockchain while also containing the digital asset's location. A link is frequently used to connect the digital asset to the NFT. The association would stop working if the digital asset was destroyed from where it was stored or if the server that hosts the NFT encountered any technical difficulties.

As a result, the NFT will lose its value. If such a circumstance arises, there is no way to restore the NFT.

However, as formerly stated, Ethereum intends to migrate to Proof-of-Stake (PoS) from Proof-of-Work (PoW) (PoW). They can increase significantly less environmental damage because they will not require highly advanced computers or a significant quantity of electricity.

THE MOST FAMOUS TYPE OF SMART CONTRACT IS NFTS

In principle, an NFT is precisely the opposite of a cryptocurrency. By definition, all cryptocurrencies are fungible. Said differently, your bitcoin and my bitcoin are worth the same amount of fiat currency, which means we can easily trade one for another. NFTs are non-fungible. In principle, each NFT is unique, so you cannot change one for another as each has a market value of its own. In the physical world, most of the things we own are non-fungible. Your car and my car are both cars, but they cannot be exchanged for one another. That is also true of houses, most clothing, and most jewelry.

The two most widely-used NFT standards are smart contracts written and stored on the Ethereum blockchain:

ERC-721: A standard interface for non-fungible tokens, also known as deeds.

ERC-1155: A standard interface for contracts that manage multiple token types. A single deployed contract may include any combination of fungible tokens, non-fungible tokens, or other configurations (e.g., semi-fungible tokens).

NFTs are made ("minted") when a unique, standardized token and associated smart contract are registered on a blockchain. In theory, NFTs are non-fungible. Said differently, the NFT of Nyan Cat (sold at auction for roughly $560,000) is special and not interchangeable with other versions of the same file. Find a list of popular sites where you can mint your own NFTs here.

Using Nfts For Fan Or Audience Development

People have begun using the term "NFT" interchangeably with "digital collectible." That is unfortunate because while most of the digital collectibles in the news are NFTs, the technology can create value in many additional ways. When thinking about fan or audience development, which we define as a collection of purpose-built tools designed to grow communities of interest, perhaps the most obvious use for an NFT is a ticket to an event. Let's evaluation some of the benefits you might expect from combining a ticket, some unique digital assets, and a smart contract.

Nfts Are Smart Contracts

All NFTs are smart contracts. A smart contract is like an old-fashioned verbal or paper contract, except with a smart contract, the contract executes automatically when the conditions are met (digitally). Immutable, self-executing agreements coupled with the automatic exchange of funds (or tokens) open up a world of possibilities for ticketing.

The Elimination Of Duplicate Or Fraudulent Tickets

Every NFT is unique, and ownership is written on a public distributed ledger (blockchain) which anyone can read. If your request for an NFT has been validated, a quick matching of public and private keys (using something as familiar as a barcode reader) would instantly verify that the person with the NFT in their digital wallet was the authentic owner of the ticket.

Revenue From Secondary Markets

If someone sells their NFT ticket, that transaction can trigger royalty payments to the issuer as well as any other stakeholder â€ "artists, sports leagues, athletes, sponsors, promoters, a charity, or anyone with a digital wallet. These business rules can be hard-coded into each NFT, and like all smart contracts, when a transaction occurs, and the conditions are met, funds automatically change hands.

Visibility Into Transactions

Bots, scalpers, bad actors, criminals, and 2nd-party sales on eBay or other auction sites. NFT tickets offer an easy way to gather actionable business intelligence about how and where your tickets are being sold and resold. You can find the exact moment of the transaction, the same address of the digital wallets in use, the amount of the transaction, and much, much more. Contrary to popular mythology, NFT transactions are not anonymous. Several commercial firms such as Chainalysis and CipherTrace offer blockchain BI tools.

Reduced Ticketing Costs

NFTs are not mined; they are minted. That is a non-trivial technical distinction. Today, you can coin NFT tickets for less than 10 cents apiece ", and the price of NFT ticket production will continue to drop.

New Revenue

You can, of course, mint NFT tickets as stand-alone digital collectibles. But you can also use NFT keys to allow fans access to an auction where they might bid on NFTs containing more valuable exclusive content. Because of the NFT's ability to collect 1st party data, they can also augment loyalty programs. The marketing techniques will need to be tested, but the technology is built-in.

Data-Driven Marketing Opportunities

Today, if you purchase six tickets to a sporting event and bring five family members or friends, the ticket seller has a business relationship with you but has no information about the other five people in your party. NFTs have the power to change that. If each attendee were required to present an NFT for entrance, the NFT would need to be transferred to their digital wallets. Depending upon how you wrote the business logic and what data you asked for as a condition of the ticket sale, the NFTs could collect a wealth of actionable first-party data.

Defi Opportunities

NFTs can be bought, sold, traded, swapped, or used as collateral, borrowed, or lent. In other words, your ability to financially engineer to create additional value is only limited by your creativity and your audience's willingness to participate. The blockchain's ability to democratize finance is part of what makes the technology super-exciting, super-dangerous, super-volatile, and fabulous! It is also why the world of crypto and DeFi (decentralized finance), writ large, has the attention of governments and regulators worldwide.

Next-Level Marketing

Whether your audience is a community of interest, a community of practice, or a community of passion, next-level marketers will have the opportunity to let their imaginations run free. What does your audience value the most? How can you empower them to participate? What additional value can you help them obtain? What is the next generation of loyalty programs? How much "access" to the star attraction can they achieve? Smart contracts will give smart marketers the tools they need to design new kinds of marketing programs with ongoing, automated value-creation components built-in.

What's Next

Traditional ticketing software has been a race to the bottom. Most of the systems are old and tired. Not surprisingly, almost every major ticketing company has announced that they are planning or already working on or about to launch a new NFT ticketing product. This is great. While there will be way too many different approaches, some will emerge as better than others. Consumers will vote with their wallets (as they always do), and this new tech will evolve.

Notably, some of the most exciting blockchain projects are poly chains or multichain, built to aggregate disparate blockchains. These new blockchains will empower Web 3.0 and certainly play some role in the evolution of NFT ticketing. In the meantime, I hope some of these ideas resonate with you and get you thinking about new ways to create value for your business.

SOME BRANDS ARE ALREADY INTO NFTS

Nike

Nike is now including a digital version of your next pair of kicks in the box.

Nike is a household name, and the legendary shoe and sportswear brand has begun to use NFTs to guarantee the authenticity of a pair of sneakers. Under the Crypto kick project, purchasing a couple of the brand's sneakers will now upload a digital merchandise replica to your 'virtual locker.' Given the burgeoning youth culture of acquiring, selling, and reselling shoes, adding a digital stamp of legitimacy to the token's physical counterpart elevates it to new heights and levels. Given that this is a digital collectible related to a tangible item, it is a unique method for NFTs. Still, it can also be utilized for cartoon characters or online sneaker communities, demonstrating that digital fashion is a purpose for NFTs far beyond more "traditional" aesthetic use as presumed by many.

Team Gb Nfts For 2021 Olympics Games

The NFT project initiated by Team GB after this summer's very unique Olympic Games, which will go down in the history books for its lack of worldwide fans and supporters, is another excellent example of NFT. The British Olympic Committee formed an NFT shop where fans could buy NFTs for restricted collectibles like murals by artist Ben Mosley or one-on-one encounters with Team GB gold medalists. It was a fantastic project to assist and compensate supporters who could not go to stadiums to cheer on their national side while recognizing their accomplishments and raising donations for the British Olympic Association.

The Nba And 'Digitally Owning' Moments

The NBA has designed a method that may very well be the game-changer of this field. The National Basketball Association (BNA) has launched 'NBA Top Shot,' a novel online marketplace of registered digital collectibles where enthusiasts can buy moments from their favorite sports teams, players, or games and obtain a certificate as well as an original clip, to broaden its attractiveness to Western audiences and switch its attention to more virtual and efficient service delivery. Buying and selling collectible cards is one of the sports' earliest extra revenue schemes, and the NBA has developed a system that could very well be the future of this field. With NFTs, the future is bright for NBA.

Taco Bell

Yum Brands, the parent firm of some of the world's largest most well-known fast-food franchises like Pizza Hut, KFC, and Taco Bell, has also developed an NFT approach. Taco Bell made and sold a set of NFT gifs on the specialist online market Rarible in February 2021, with all of them sold out in less than 30 minutes. The ad demonstrates that NFTs are not just suitable for artworks worth hundreds of thousands of dollars but also for $1 gag buys to fundraise for a Taco Bell-affiliated scholarship scheme. Some of these pieces have a resale value of $3,000 or more.

Coca-Cola Participates In The Nft Movement By Holding A Nonprofit Auction.

For International Friendship Day in 2021, the Coca-Cola Company held an NFT bidding, releasing the first-ever variety of electronic collectibles that "re-imagine a few of Coca-famous Cola's trademarks for the metaverse, with each NFT driven by shared experiences of friendship. A future recreation of the legendary Coca-Cola delivery jacket, virtually usable on Centralland, a distributed 3D virtual reality environment, was among the one-of-a-kind objects up for auction. Special Olympics International, the world's most prominent institution for impaired athletes, received 100% of the funds from this promotion.

Asics: Sunrise Red

Asics was one of the first to jump on the NFT bandwagon, releasing its debut collection in August 2021. It was a test for the brand and the recreational vertical as a whole to bridge the print and virtual divide for brands.

Asics, Joe Pace, leader of business development, stated that Digital experiences are part of the daily routine; he said he finds it difficult to envision a tomorrow without digital items prevalent in most people's lives. He explained that Asics decision to be part of it was part of being inventive, ahead, and having an idea for what the tomorrow might seem like from a business development perspective, or more importantly, from an invention development one. The sportswear company is establishing an artist-in-residence program, with earnings from the NFT auction supporting digital artists.

WHAT ARE NFTS ROYALTY SHARES?

Even after selling their NFTs, artists and content creators find that these tokens can be very advantageous since NFTs are in the glare of publicity. This feature is principally thought-provoking; they're called NFT royalties. You may want to know what NFT royalties are if you are new to this field. Let's find out!

What Are Nft Royalties?

All those times when you can sell your NFT creations on a marketplace, you will get a portion of the sale price; this is due to NFT royalties. Smart contracts automatically execute ongoing royalty NFT payments. You can choose your royalty percentage in most marketplaces. A standard royalty is about 5-10%.

There are numerous differences between NFTs and other traditional royalty payments.

When an author makes resales, some incentive is given back, known as the royalty payout. Royalty payouts are recorded into the smart contract on a blockchain. Whenever a resale happens, the smart contract ensures that the NFT set terms are achieved. In royalty specifications, a certain amount of money is sent over to the original artist from the revenue generated from the resale.

Every NFT does not yield royalties; this should be kept in mind. If you wish to receive royalties from your NFTs, you have to mention that in the terms and conditions. Those terms and conditions are recorded in the Ethereum blockchain network, and the rest of the process is all done automatically. It is not necessary to have intermediaries, and also it does not depend upon the wishes and demands of the person who is transacting. That is great for digital content, gaming accessories, physical items, etc. NFT royalties are a never-before-opportunity to increase the revenue generated by the artists and content creators. That is a benefit for the artists they get from these NFTs after creating or repeatedly producing something. As more and more these artists become popular, they may increase the returns that they receive from their work.

That is an excellent scheme that the NFTs offer. That makes the artists and digital content creators work with more motivation and enthusiasm. This is also motivating them to become a part of the NFT industry. The system of royalties may be different for each of the marketplaces. Many new marketplaces are developing other techniques and ways to help artists receive enough money for their production.

The artists would not be paid enough before the royalties' concept began on the NFT marketplaces. They would only be paid for the time they sold their work as an NFT on the marketplaces. After selling their work online, the artists would not track other subsequent transactions that occurred after that. The only time they made a profit was for selling it the first time, and then the buyer would gain profit after reselling. That was not something that motivated and inspired these artists and digital creators.

The people who would buy their work would wait for the right time and then sell that at excellent prices. This system only benefitted the buyer and not the artist who created the art initially. The artist got no penny from his artwork, and all that profit would go to the pockets of those who bought. Hence the familiar concept of artists as penurious or the starving artist.

NFTs have changed this whole concept from the grass-root level. Artists will be given a justified share every time their creations are sold. This will be forever.

How Do Nft Royalties Work?

Here, the question arises that how does the royalty system work? So basically, what happens is that at the time of minting the NFT for an original piece of artwork, the artist can decide over a certain amount that he would get after any other subsequent sales made by the buyer. Whenever the buyer sold an artist's painting, he would get the pre-determined amount of money from the revenue the buyer would generate from the sales. All the marketplaces do not allow you to have royalties claimed while minting the NFT However, Rarible does give you the option of royalties at the time of minting the NFT.

For example, you have an NFT artwork created on Rarible. Somebody buys that NFT for, let supposes, 8 ETH. That means that you have earned 8 ETH from your artwork. While minting your NFT, you have clearly stated that you would get a 10% revenue generated anytime this artwork is sold again. That means whenever the buyer sells that painting, you will get 10% of the money generated.

Now let suppose the buyer waits for the right time for a resale. Your popularity has grown by now, and the buyer sells your artwork for guessing 200 ETH. But as you have stated in the terms and conditions already, you would get a 10%incentive, which means you would get 20 ETH from the sale that was just made. That means that the buyer made a lot of money, whereas you, the original creator, could not earn that much.

Now let's imagine that the new owner might also sell your artwork; you would get 10% proceeds from that sale. That means that every time your painting is sold, you will get some revenue out of it. You will repeatedly be paid for your sold artwork. With the NFT royalties, you are at an advantage. That is an excellent way for the authors and original creators of the art to get paid for as long as their artwork is sold.

That means that no artist will have to suffer now. No content creator will struggle financially. There will be no fake or counterfeit products available in the market. Even if they are, they would not be worth the original product—identification of what is authentic and what is not has undoubtedly become easy.

All these great things are a result of blockchain technology. Blockchain technology works on a distributed ledger that records all the transactions that happen over the blockchain network. That makes the whole transaction process transparent and decentralized.

This digital ledger which records the data of transactions, makes the work more authentic. Whatever conditions are set in the smart contract are to be fulfilled at all costs, and that is possible due to the automated protocols of the network. You do not need an intermediary to process any transaction or dealing. All that is done automatically with excellent transparency.

Who Gains From An Nft Royalty?

Musicians creators, content creators, and artists gain from NFTs royalties. That is not again for the artists only but also the buyer. The buyer cannot be cheated as he would know what is authentic and what a replica is. He would not be fooled to buy something that is not original. That lets the buyers show off their digital collectibles and purchased assets and can resell them at higher prices. It's a win-win situation for both parties!

NON-FUNGIBLE TOKENS – RISKS AND CHALLENGES

In 2021, NFTs have made quite a stir, especially following the $69.3 million in March NFT sales. Many people are wondering how long the NFT trend will continue. As a result, it's critical to consider the most significant NFT risks and problems. Non-fungible tokens, or NFTs, are one-of-a-kind digital assets. They have specific qualities, and exchanging them for other assets is difficult.

Non-fungible tokens have found their way into various industries, including music, domain names, art, and real estate. While NFTs have the potential to increase in the future, it is prudent to consider the potential NFT hazards. The next meeting will provide you with a thorough overview of the risks and issues associated with NFT so that you can better understand them.

Challenges And Risks With Nfts

Non-fungible tokens, or NFTs, are an entirely new sort of digital asset, meaning that the NFT ecosystem is prone to extreme swings and unpredictability.

The following are examples of frequent NFT challenges:

- Legal and regulatory challenges

- Evaluation challenges

- Intellectual Property or IP rights

- Cybersecurity and fraud risks

- Anti-money laundering (AML) and CFT challenges

- Smart contract risks and NFT maintenance

- Consideration of NFTs as securities

- Environmental Social Governance (ESG) challenges

Let's look at these NFT dangers and obstacles to see how they affect NFTs.

1. Legal and Regulatory Challenges

NFT lacks a clear definition and may be used to describe a wide range of assets, relying solely on specific characteristics. NFTs, for example, are one-of-a-kind, not interchangeable, and not fungible. However, there are several regulatory approaches to NFTs that are worth mentioning. In Europe, the proposed Markets in Crypto-assets (MICA) Regulation by the European Commission might establish a regulatory framework for NFTs.

Existing legislative suggestions suggest that the management of NFTs in the EU and the UK regulatory regimes may differ in the future. The European Union's proposal for Markets in Crypto Assets Regulation, released in September 2020, can serve as a platform for regulating specific NFT-related market activity. The current regulatory precedents in the UK, on the other hand, are most likely to exclude NFTs. However, a case-by-case analysis of how to sell or market NFTs and derive value from them might aid in deciding if NFTs would be subject to regulatory precedents. Surprisingly, NFTs are included in MICA's definition of "crypto-assets." Furthermore, the current draft of MICA's description of "crypto-assets" does not indicate that NFT issuers must publish a whitepaper.

According to the FCA rules, NFTs might be exempted from the UK promotion regime due to the idea of qualified crypto assets. NFTs may qualify as e-money, security, or unregulated tokens in these regulatory settings, depending on their qualities.

In Singapore, NFTs do not qualify as legal tender. NFTs are excluded primarily because they are non-fungible and may only be exchanged for particular items. Additionally, they might fall under the category of "limited purpose digital payment tokens," which would exclude them from PSA restrictions.

For the Payment Services Act of Japan, NFTs in Japan are classified according to their ability to fulfill an economic function, such as functioning as a payment method or being exchanged for cryptocurrencies. The Payment Services Act does not apply to NFTs with restricted activities, such as in-game products or trading cards, and no engagement in economic operations, such as payment instruments. Such NFTs should be thoroughly examined and evaluated in line with the functions and specifications of the NFT in question. In addition, the structure of the NFT platform or application and how the NFT is used should be taken into account.

The technical improvement in NFTs demonstrates the significance of considering legal and regulatory NFT issues. As NFTs continue to grow and extend into new use cases, laws and regulations should adjust. Many of the existing legislation relating to NFTs are now stalled on determining the best definition for NFTs. It's becoming more challenging to develop a strong foundation for NFT compliance as the type and quantity of NFTs grows.

2. Evaluation Challenges

The ambiguity in calculating the value of non-fungible tokens is another significant addition to the list of non-fungible token dangers and issues. The scarcity of NFTs, the perceptions of owners and purchasers, and the availability of distribution channels all have a role in their worth. It's incredibly impossible to predict who will be the next buyer of an NFT or what variables would influence their decision. As a result, the value of NFTs is primarily determined by how the buyer perceives their price, resulting in volatility.

3. Intellectual Property Rights

Intellectual property concerns are the following significant element in NFT risks and obstacles. It's crucial to evaluate an individual's rights to a certain NFT. It's critical to determine whether the vendor genuinely possesses the NFT before purchasing. There have been instances of someone photographing NFTs or minting reproductions of NFTs. As a result, when buying an NFT, you acquire the right to utilize it, not intellectual property rights. The metadata of the underlying smart contract contains the terms and conditions for owning an NFT.

However, all illusions about traditional law not applying to decentralized blockchain technology must be dispelled. The intellectual property risks and constraints associated with NFTs imply that buyers only have the right to exhibit NFTs and are the sole proprietors. The limitations on NFTs are also visible in the service standards that customers should adhere to when utilizing NFT markets. As a result, it's critical to examine fundamental IP rights such as copyrights, trademarks, patents, moral rights, and the right of publicity.

4. Cyber Security and Fraud Risks

The exponential surge in popularity of NFTs, along with the digital world's expansion, has resulted in significant cybersecurity and fraud issues. NFT is concerned about imitation stores that seem identical to legitimate NFT stores and use the same logo and content. Fake NFT stores are another significant difficulty linked with the hazards and challenges involved with NFTs in cybersecurity. Fake NFT retailers may sell NFTs that were never there in the first place. Buyers must also be aware of the risks associated with artist impersonation and counterfeit NFTs.

You should also be aware of the dangers of social media frauds that advertise NFTs. Some shady characters can mimic well-known NFT artists and sell counterfeit NFTs in their names. Copyright theft, copying of popular NFTs or false airdrops, and NFT giveaways are other major non-fungible tokens threats and issues regarding cybersecurity and fraud.

For example, some companies created NFTs from artworks in the digital collection of public domain paintings on exhibit at the Rijksmuseum in Amsterdam without the museum's permission. The instance of hackers taking NFTs from Nifty Gateway customers is one of the most recent examples of the NFT cybersecurity concern.

5. Smart Contract Risks and NFT Maintenance

One of the most significant worries in the NFT ecosystem is smart contract risk and NFT maintenance problems. Hackers recently targeted the renowned Defi protocol Poly Network, which features cross-chain interoperability. The NFT heist, which resulted in a loss of over $600 million, focuses on severe flaws in smart contract security.

For such large-scale assaults, hackers could take advantage of Poly Network's smart contract vulnerability. The poly network allows users to transfer tokens across multiple blockchain networks while collaborating. The hackers have returned about $300 million to the Poly Network as of writing.

6. Consideration of NFTs as Securities

One of the most significant non-fungible token dangers and concerns is the treatment of NFTs as securities. According to the Securities & Exchange Commission Chairman, most NFTs on the market are sold as securities. In contrast, the Supreme Court has linked NFTs to the idea of an investment contract. As a result, to demonstrate their eligibility as securities, NFTs must meet the Howey Test's unique requirements.

The following are some of the critical concepts of the Howey Test:

- determining whether or not the NFT is a security

- If the NFT is security, look to see if it was registered under the Securities Act of 1993.

- Check if participants are registered as securities broker-dealers if the NFT is about securities.

- Verify if platforms for security-like NFT transactions are registered as securities exchanges.

- Take into account the potential exposure for security NFT sellers under SEC Rule 10b-5 for the Use of Manipulative and Deceptive Practices.

7. AML and CFT Challenges

In July, the FATF published a study stating that distributed ledger technology poses risks. The paper focuses on NFT risks and problems, with a specific emphasis on AML/CFT. AML and CFT issues might arise due to decentralized blockchain transactions and allow for non-intermediary peer-to-peer transactions without any supervision. Furthermore, because there is no clear precedence for regulating NFTs, they are connected with jurisdictional problems.

As a result, it might put the traditional FATF rules, which focused on the regulation or oversight of intermediaries, to the test. In October 2020, the Office of Foreign Asset Control (OFAC) issued an advisory warning, identifying high-value artwork as the source of restricted people's access to the US market and financial system.

Bottom Line

The field of NFTs certainly faces a broad spectrum of dangers and problems. Because it is a new area, resolving non-fungible token risks and issues will aid its development. Identifying many dangers and problems with real-world consequences emphasizes the seriousness of each case.

Learn more about NFTs and how to deal with the problems and hazards they pose. As the globe becomes more accessible to NFTs, it's critical to have a consistent regulatory architecture, tailored AML and CFT norms, and safe platforms for NFT development and exchange. Furthermore, having a clear picture of the consequences of each risk and issue might aid in the discovery of alternative solutions.

BECOMING PART OF THE NFT COMMUNITY

The entire concept of decentralized finance, which includes cryptocurrency and NFTs, is a concept that came into public consciousness a little more than ten years ago. NFTs, in particular, have been around for less time than that. Thus, the field is still malleable and fluid, with everyone coming up with many different concepts and ideas. As an outcome, some of these ideas will fall by the wayside, and some of them will define the future of NFTs in both particular and decentralized finance.

A few early adopters and far-seekers are already seeing the potential in NFTs. They are preparing to be at the forefront of the evolution by seeking like-minded individuals to form a community, given that communities have a farther reach than an individual can ever have—even if the individual has the most modern gadgets or is the most experienced trader or businessperson.

There is a common misconception that creators and traders will shape the NFT space. While those people are undoubtedly crucial to developing the NFT space, they are not the only people who have significant roles to play. So, if you are a newbie coming into the NFT space, I'll advise you on finding a community to join. Once you have entered that community, you can then find other ways to contribute to the growth of your NFT community.

Blogging (Includes Podcasts, Youtube, Vlogs)

It is usually misconstrued that most of the jobs available for people in the NFTs world are for "artists" or "graphic designers" since NFTs are "artsy"; however, many people entering these fields are looking for information and regular updates along with guidance. This need is where sites and blogs come into the equation. There are now tons of people who don't even trade in NFTs and have never created a single NFT artwork, but who have made huge money by aggregating ideas from different people into helpful information newbies can use, along with more experienced creators and traders.

My point? Bloggers make tons of money from explicitly blogging about NFTs. If there are millions of people trading and performing different operations on NFT platforms, millions of people seek to acquire more knowledge about them. The truth is that most people in NFTs either have no time to do exhausting research of subjects in the field or are overwhelmed by the fluidity of the space. So, if you can harmonize seemingly disparate ideas, and break complex notions or ideas into more straightforward concepts, then blogging about NFTs might be helpful for you to break into the NFT space.

Community Managers

The ultimate determinant of whether a field will grow is the creation of communities. And the people who will be at the forefront of those communities and who will shape their futures are not just good at the technicalities of NFTs but are also good at bringing people together—not only across different spheres, but also across different states, countries, or even continents.

A space where community managers will prove crucial is in areas at a disadvantage because of their location—for example, people in technologically less-developed rooms like in sub-Saharan Africa, Asia, parts of Latin America, or even within the United States itself.

Thus, if you can bring people together and have the ability or the time to moderate a forum where everyone—regardless of race, gender, or location—can express their ideas without being intimidated or silenced, you can be part of the NFT community.

Researchers

Researchers collate data and process it to become information. A researcher aims to provide valuable details about improving a product or service. People and companies are beginning to get honest about the fact that not only have NFTs come to stay, but they are also the future. Therefore, researchers are constantly working on improving the platforms to improve blockchain's security. Researchers also conduct in-depth analyses about the NFT industry.

Most traders and creators have day jobs that might not do much research. Thus, researchers need to understand and predict the volatility of the NFTs market since it's all a business of risk. Researchers who can make a difference in volatility prediction have a front-row seat in the NFT world.

Web Developers

While it may sound like web developers do the same work as software engineers, they don't. Software engineers build and maintain NFT platforms and applications while web developers write and maintain code. With the plethora of NFT platforms and applications available now, there is no denying that web developers will look for jobs in that space. Usually, being qualified gets you a job, and in the NFT market, there seems to be a lot of emphasis on qualification and expertise. Therefore, web developers must have Python, Solidity, React, and JavaScript skills.

Writers

There is a need for writers who are not just bloggers but skilled at technical and academic writing. If history serves well, the first Bitcoin white paper was written by Satoshi Nakamoto.

Although Bitcoin did not boom upon its creation, Nakamoto's white paper kept hope alive for his dream. The white paper gave investors something to believe in, and they invested in it well enough to make it become the current boss of all NFTs platforms. As a result, the development of NFTs is moving beyond hobbyists and enthusiasts to include academic studies, so writers must document this development.

Without a doubt, the rapid expansion of NFTs will lead to more forms of NFTs aside from the ones we know now. Hence, there will be a need to write white papers for these NFT start-ups. Most founders do not do this job alone; they try to see who can help convey the purpose of their platforms in more readable terms as this will help fetch investors. And as we all know, investors make companies grow.

Business Representatives

In every company, there is a group of people whose sole job is to represent their interests wherever they find themselves, or more specifically, wherever the company sends them. For most of these business representatives, what works for them is conducting analytical research on the company they wish to work for. Thus, these employers are satisfied they don't have to worry about bringing them up to speed about the mission and vision of the company.

This situation also occurs for NFTs. With the pool of competition, there is a need for experienced people who can adeptly communicate the company's strengths and benefits to investors and the public. It is no longer news that today's world is becoming a world of propaganda where people believe what they are told to think, regardless of the source. Therefore, it is better to have people who communicate "the real thing" to the public. For NFT platforms, traders are willing to use which serves their interests most.

Many "big leagues" on Bitcoin discourage people from making Bitcoin their number-one choice. Business representatives can meet the need for other platforms that serve their interests.

Strategists

This list is incomplete without these people. As most people call them, strategists or financial analysts help people and companies make the right decisions when it comes to trading or investing in NFT platforms. In addition, these people constantly conduct analyses of NFT platforms, which gives them the authority to advise people on the market's volatility.

Strategists help tell traders and investors when it is wise to go long or short, when to trade, and when to retain. In addition, they enlighten their clients through online chain tool accounts and explain how to expand their trading ledgers realistically.

Much emphasis has been placed on the necessity of communities being incorporated into NFTs due to the latter's expansion. Software engineers are needed to build reliable NFT platforms and applications. AI engineers are required to program good algorithms for blockchain. Bloggers are required to offer up-to-date information and resources to people invested in NFTs. Researchers are needed to collate information and conduct an in-depth analysis of NFT growth for predictions. Writers are required to write white papers to woo investors and categorically state the mission of emerging NFT platforms. Yet, you should know these occupations are only a few of the roles available in the booming NFT world.

There is no doubt there will always be a place for human communities in NFTs. The NFT community has come to stay and will continue to grow. One should not misconstrue this situation as humans being a means to an end, but rather, the key to continuing forging the expected future for NFTs. It is also essential to cite that you do not have to be restricted to a single role; you can be fluid and perform different functions, just like NFTs. The most important thing is to continue growing and learning about the NFT space.

TOKENIZING

The concept of tokenizing is taking an object and assigning a digital token. That has always been done by attaching the token to the physical object itself in the past. Think of it as a coupon or a gift card. You can't take the value with you when you go, but you can use it in that store or restaurant. That works great for physical items, but what about digital?

NFTs allow us to attach that "coupon" to something digital. Your item is then represented on the blockchain and can be used by others as they see fit. That opens up a lot of potential in the digital world. We wouldn't usually take or store many items digitally, but now we can.

That is a new frontier for the digital world, and there is still much to learn and discover.

What Is Tokenization

Tokenization is the process of taking a digital object and turning it into a digital token. That is commonly done with collectibles. For example, if you have a rare item, like a Pikachu card or a pack of cards with one valuable card in it, you can tokenize it and take that value and turn it into something else. You can then sell the digital token to anyone in the world with crypto. In other words, Tokenization will allow you to take your items and make money out of them if you don't want them or need them anymore.

Minting An Nft

Minting is the process of taking an NFT and making it available to be sold. When a token is minted, it is created out of thin air, and you own that token. The token will show up in your wallet as a new asset when this happens. That can be done with any NFT with metadata attached to it.

There are two of the most common ways to mint an NFT. The first way is to take your item and scan it into a mobile application like Decentraland or CryptoKitties. Then you can send that item into their system, where they track all of the things in their ecosystem and assign them an ID number.

The second way is to upload the image file of your item into an online platform like Rare Bits or OPSkins. Once this has stood accomplished, you can go on either app and search or buy your item from yourself.

You will need to research which one is right for you. Rare Bits and OPSkins have both been around for a while and have done well, but Decentraland and CryptoKitties are sometimes considered up-and-comers. Decentraland, in particular, has a lot of hype around it, so it is worth looking into when you are researching Tokenization.

The Process Of Tokenizing

The process of tokenizing can be broken down into four steps: creating a token, the initial offering, the trading/trading pairing, and the final exchange.

Token Creation

The first step is creating a token. That is a way of assigning value to an item or object. You can do this by creating a new token with a fixed value. Then you can use that item or object as collateral for the token's value. That is the same concept as a gift card because it was created after it was bought.

Initial Offering

The next step is to offer that token for sale. That is done through an Initial Offering (IO). The IO involves creating a smart contract that will allow people to buy and sell your token on an exchange. When you conduct this sale, you take the value of your physical object and turn it into a digital deal. If you were to sell your physical object, you would be selling its monetary value and not its actual object. That's why this process is called Tokenization.

Trading Pairing/Listing

This part of the process involves pairing your new token with another crypto asset so people can buy it on an exchange. That is the process of pairing your token with tokens already on sale, so people can buy it using an existing crypto asset. For example, if you wanted to sell your Pikachu Pokeball token, you would need to pair it with BTC, ETH, or any other token already on an exchange. This pairing is done using the smart contract you created in the IO.

Final Exchange

This part of the process is to list your token on an exchange. Once your token has been paired with another crypto asset, you can list it on a deal for people to buy and sell it. That will give your new token an accurate market value that anyone in the world can take advantage of.

Tokenizing Guidelines

Now that you have a fundamental idea of Tokenization, here are some guidelines to consider. That will help you when it comes time to tokenize your items.

Value

First of all, the item should be valuable to a broad audience. That is a safety precaution and will ensure that your item will always have value. Think of a rare piece of art or a one-of-a-kind item from the past. Those are perfect uses for Tokenization. Digital collectibles are also a great idea since they can be created and destroyed at any time by the creator.

Authenticity

The digital token you create should be linked to a physical item or object. That can be a simple serial number or an item ID tied to the original piece. That will ensure that no one can fake your item and sell it as the real thing. It will also allow people to track the history of your item, ensuring that they can trust the history and value of your token.

Liquidity To Fiat Currency

Once you have created your token, make sure you know how to liquidate it back into fiat currency. That is important for two reasons:

You can get your money when you are finished with the item.

You can sell it to someone else and allow them to continue the life cycle of your item. If you are tokenizing a vintage baseball card, for example, the token should be sold back into fiat currency.

It should be able to be sold again as an NFT.

Trustless

Your NFT should also be trustless. That means that you don't have to trust the issuer to hold on to them to retain their value. That makes them much easier for people who are collecting or looking at items as investments since they don't have to worry about the issuer backing out on them or not being able to liquidate their tokens back into fiat currency.

Should Be A Digital Asset

The token created should be a digital asset. That means it will be stored on the Ethereum blockchain and won't have any value outside the blockchain. That will ensure that no one can do anything with the token that you wouldn't like, like sending it to an address they control or creating replicas of your item and selling it as accurate.

Transparency

You also want to ensure transparency about how your tokens work. Explain what they are for the public in a way that makes sense and how they can use them. Also, make sure you provide information on how to access them, who owns them, and what the contract is storing them on the blockchain if someone wants to get into your NFT details more deeply. Transparency will help create trust in your NFTs from your supporters and users across the industry. That will also ensure that people are confident in selling goods in the future that may be tokenized.

Have A Blockchain Labeled For Your Token

It would help to create a blockchain specifically designed for your token. You can do this by making your blockchain or using an existing one like Ethereum. That will ensure that your NFTs are easy to find and accessible across the internet in the future. It will also allow you to have specific functions written into the smart contracts that tokenize your item, so people can access only certain things about it, like how much it is worth or when it was created. You can even create a marketplace on your blockchain to sell items and offer rewards for doing so in exchange for tokens on your chain.

The Importance Of Certificates And The Basics Of Issuing A Tokenization Certificate

Tokenization Certificates are the first step to turning your physical item into a digital token. The Certificate is a document issued by a trustworthy third party that tells you that your own thing is now tokenized. This Certificate will contain information on what item it is, the date of issuance, an ID number for the tokenized asset, and your ownership. The Certificate will also have details on when you can sell your tokenized asset or whether you can only trade it with other people who have issued certificates, or if it can be switched on a digital exchange.

For example, let's say that you collect baseball cards and have 30 valuable baseball cards in your collection. To protect these cards from being lost or damaged, you decide to have them protected digitally through Tokenization. You go to an NFT Certifier and submit 60 baseball card cards to get them all tokenized at once. After some time has passed, you receive your Certificate, and now your baseball cards are officially tokenized.

The issuer of the Certificate may charge you for this service. That can be in the form of cash or NFTs that they own. For example, if you were to take your baseball cards to a certification agency like NFT Certifiers, they would issue you a Certificate for each card worth USD 0.25 Each. You can then take these certificates to another third party and exchange them for other NFTs on their platform or sell them on an exchange.

How To Issue Your Tokens/Certificates

There are different ways to issue your tokens/certificates depending on what asset you want to tokenize and how much trust you want in your business or brand.

One way is using a platform like NFT Certifiers, a neutral third-party forum that issues certificates for physical items and digital assets/NFTs. You could also set up your certificate issuer and have it act as a broker between you and the customer. You would have to make sure that the assets you issue are secure and cannot be copied or forged.

You can also issue your certificates through your digital wallets. That can be done by taking pictures of the physical objects you want to tokenize or scanning them with a camera, then adding them into an excel document with their names, descriptions, images, and ID numbers. You can then check this document into your digital wallet. Then when someone wants to buy one of these tokens, you will send them the token directly from your wallet, just like any other digital asset or NFT.

IS NFTS REALLY REVOLUTIONARY?

In many ways, NFTs have the potential to be revolutionary. They are an asset class that has formerly been nonexistent, and they have already shown themselves to be a significant disruptor in the world of gaming.

However, NFTs are not perfect. There are many challenges that developers will need to overcome if they want to make NFTs a reality for everyone. That is where things get tricky.

NFTs, by their very nature, cannot function without some form of blockchain technology or another similar technology. That presents a significant problem for most developers because the current blockchain space is relatively inaccessible for developers who don't have the proper technical knowledge or resources at their disposal. For this cause, there is a strong need for better developer tools and a more robust blockchain infrastructure if NFTs are going to achieve mainstream adoption anytime soon.

In addition to these challenges, it will take some time before players get used to having digital assets that can be traded freely on secondary markets and even longer before people start spending money on digital assets instead of spending money on traditional video games themselves. That being said, as long as progress is made on both of these fronts (developer tools and more robust infrastructure), it won't be long before NFTs become a reality for everyone.

NFTs are still in their infancy, but there is no denying that they have the potential to be revolutionary. They have already shown themselves to be major disruptors in the world of gaming. If developers continue to push forward with them, it won't be long before the mainstream population uses them. However, there are still many challenges that developers will need to overcome if they want to make NFTs a reality for everyone.

What Makes Nfts So Unique:

NFTs are a particular type of digital asset that has never existed before. These assets are very similar to traditional digital ones, but they can be far more valuable and exciting than conventional ones.

Traditional digital assets have existed for many years now, but they haven't changed much over the years. With NFTs, however, there is a possibility that they will change a lot in the coming years. They can vary by becoming more secure, getting more adoption from developers and gamers alike, and getting more widespread support from exchanges and other organizations.

Because of this, NFTs could become far more valuable than traditional digital assets. That is because of their potential to create actual ownership over in-game items and even other things such as land or even tangible goods such as cars or houses in the future.

Another reason why NFTs are so special is because they are genuinely open source for anyone who desires to use them in their games or on their platforms. Everything is already built into the NFT protocol, and everything is open source. Because of this, developers can create unique games and applications without worrying about copyright infringement or other legal issues that may arise when using NFTs with other technologies like blockchain technology or smart contracts.

However, there are still some challenges that developers will need to overcome if they want to make NFTs a reality for everyone. These challenges include that NFTs can only function with blockchain technology or another similar technology. That means that most developers don't have the proper technical knowledge or resources at their disposal to create NFTs for their games. That is why there is an emotional need for better developer tools and a more robust blockchain infrastructure if NFTs will achieve mainstream adoption anytime soon.

What Are The Conditions For Nfts To Go Mainstream?

It's an excellent question, but one that is difficult to answer. Theoretically, NFTs could be used in various applications and even have their currency that can be used to buy/sell items or pay for services.

However, the actual execution of this is not so simple. NFTs need to solve two main problems: scalability and interoperability. Let's research each of these in more detail.

Scalability

The NFT ecosystem has two problems that prevent it from being genuinely scalable: blockchain bloat and slow transactions.

To understand blockchain bloat, we must first understand the difference between State Channels and Off-Chain Transactions (OCT). A State Channel is a communication channel between parties in which transactions are conducted off-chain instead of on-chain (which most blockchains do). That means that transactions do not need to be broadcast across the entire network but only between the parties involved in the transaction itself. That saves time and computational power and reduces blockchain bloat by limiting transactions to just those relevant to a specific contract or innovative contract operation (in our case, an NFT transaction). To learn more about State Channels, click here.

OCT refers to transactions being conducted off-chain (in a State Channel) or on-chain. For example, Ethereum currently uses on-chain transactions, meaning that every transaction has to be processed by the entire network.

NFTs have their unique scalability issues due to the nature of NFTs themselves. The Ethereum blockchain is currently incapable of processing all on-chain transactions needed for an NFT ecosystem (e.g., all transactions related to auctions, commerce, and transfers). That is because it takes an extremely long time for Ethereum's Proof of Work (PoW) algorithm to process a transaction. And even then, it's not guaranteed that your transaction will be included in the next block (it could take hours or even days). That means that users are limited in how much they can transact within a certain period — if you try to transact too much at once, your transaction may never go through. It's just not scalable enough for mass adoption yet.

The solution? State Channels! Using State Channels can eliminate some of these issues by allowing users to conduct NFT transactions off-chain and limiting the number of transactions to only those relevant to the contract or intelligent contract operation. That permits quicker and more efficient transactions that don't have to be processed by the entire network.

But how can we do this with NFTs? Currently, State Channels are not compatible with NFTs. That is because an NFT transaction is essentially a simple "message" between two parties, meaning that it doesn't include any vital information about the transaction itself (e.g., "the sender transferred X amount of tokens to the receiver at address Y"). So how can we create a State Channel that works with NFTs?

We need a protocol that allows us to use State Channels with an NFT — one which gives us:

Privacy: State Channels allow users to conduct transactions off-chain without broadcasting them on-chain. That means that they are not visible to other users on the blockchain (or other blockchains). But for this to work, all parties involved in a transaction must see the details of the transaction. So how can we ensure privacy while using State Channels?

Fungibility: As mentioned above, a significant issue with NFTs is that each token has a unique identifier, meaning that each token is not interchangeable. That means that if I were to send you a token with an identifier that you don't recognize, you would reject it. That is because it is essentially useless to you — there's no way for you to determine whether or not the token was sent to me by mistake or if I am trying to scam you by sending you an unusable token. But what if we could eliminate this problem?

Uniqueness: State Channels only allow us to broadcast transactions on-chain in the case of an error or dispute (i.e., a conflict arises when the two parties involved in the transaction disagree on what happened).

State Channels are an excellent solution for scalability issues, but they cannot be used for NFTs without these three requirements above. So how can we solve these problems? Well, let's take a look at some solutions and their limitations:

Solution 1: NFTs Without State Channels (on-chain)

This possibility does not require any protocol changes. It simply requires that users use the Ethereum blockchain directly to conduct NFT transactions. In this case, all transactions are visible to everyone on the blockchain. That means that there is no privacy or fungibility issue. Still, it also means that the network would have to process many on-chain transactions (e.g., every transaction between every NFT owner).

Solution 2: Non-fungible Tokens (NFTs) With State Channels (off-chain)

This option requires protocol changes that allow for privacy and fungibility of NFTs while using State Channels. This solution is theoretically possible but difficult to implement. It would require some anonymization layer for each token so that two tokens with different identifiers can be used interchangeably within a single transaction (i.e., it allows you to send me an NFT even if I don't recognize its identifier). That can only be done if all NFTs are stored in a single address, meaning that all tokens are fungible and there is no privacy issue.

The problem with this solution is that it requires each NFT to be stored in a single address, meaning they are not genuinely non-fungible. For instance, let's say that you created a CryptoKitty and want to sell it for some ETH. If all NFTs are stored in a single address, then anyone can easily see the value of your CryptoKitty and buy it from you (or copy your CryptoKitty's identifier and make their copy). That means that you would lose ownership of your CryptoKitty without getting paid.

For this solution to work, we need to come up with some way to hide the value of each token while still allowing for privacy (so that no one can see which tokens are owned by which users). The most helpful way to do this would be through Ring Signatures — an advanced cryptographic method used for ring signatures (and often used in cryptocurrencies) that allows users to conceal their identities while sending transactions. But even then, there is still a risk of loss because if someone could copy your NFT's identifier, they could still copy your token. That is because Ring Signatures only allow you to conceal the transaction sender's identity, not the sender's address.

Solution 3: Non-fungible Tokens (NFTs) With State Channels (off-chain) and Protocol Changes

This option requires protocol changes that allow for privacy and fungibility of NFTs while using State Channels. The protocol changes necessary for this solution are similar to those needed for Solution 2 above, but with one significant difference: they require that all NFTs be stored in a single address — meaning that all tokens are fungible and there is no privacy issue.

But what if we could eliminate the possibility of copying an NFT's identifier? Well, we can! But first, we need to understand how Ethereum works with smart contracts. Currently, all smart contracts in Ethereum are stored on the blockchain. That means that any information within a smart contract is visible to everyone on the blockchain (i.e., all smart contracts are public). So how can we solve this problem? We need to store only an encrypted version of our smart contract on the blockchain instead of the entire agreement.

HOW IS A PIECE OF DIGITAL ART ONE OF A KIND THROUGH AN NFT?

When it comes to online copyrights, digital artists - or those who digitize their works - have had a hard time in history. It's easier to use non-fungible tokens with smart contracts to protect copyrights. That is because non-fungible tokens enable you to have detailed attributes like owner identity, metadata, and a safe connection.

Let's face it: paying for an abstract property of digital content hosted on the internet goes against the well-known mode of operation, in which you can download absolutely anything for free with just one click. And this essentially means the original copyright for a piece of work cannot be easily verified after many different copies go into circulation. The amount of art then loses its value, and there is no compensation for the original author of such art.

NFT experts agree that this technology can solve exactly that dilemma: the near-impossibility of leveraging digital works of art and assigning a monetary value to them. Since we know that "NFT is an individual digital asset passport that records the ownership," it makes sense that it can be leveraged. That can be done by simply attaching a unique identity to an original copy of digital art and its subsequent digitalized copies.

For example, you bought yourself a seat on the train. It is characterized by a unique combination of carriage and number. Even if you print out a thousand tickets and distribute them to everyone around you, the seat is yours only. Also, anyone can download a digital asset for themselves. Nevertheless, it is allocated to the owner in the same way as the seat on the train endorsed by the ticket. It turns out that NFTs are tokens that give rights to unique items.

Tokens can only have one official owner. A decentralized blockchain protects them - information is stored by thousands of nodes worldwide. Since they write every operation to the registry, it is nearly impossible to change or tamper with it. Moreover, the details about the owner are easy to verify. Also, NFTs can be easily bought, sold, or created, which is also a convenient way to transfer ownership.

Let's take this step by step. First,

What Is Cryptoart?

Any artwork tokenized using blockchain technology is referred to as crypto art. These are limited-edition multimedia artworks in pictures, videos, or GIFs with unique tokens. That enables collectors, artists, and enthusiasts to purchase, sell, and exchange digital goods as if they were physical goods. The certainty that a limited number of artist-authorized 'pieces' of the artwork encourages 'tradability' of the artwork at a value. As a result of stable blockchain technology, the digital signature on the file is indelible and non-fungible.

In simple language, crypto art is a digital art prized as physical since its ownership can be proved.

The authenticity of IK Aivazovsky's original work "The Ninth Wave" from the Russian Museum is checked by his signature on the raft, art critics' opinions, and scientific knowledge. Using NFT (Non-Fungible Token) technology, the cryptographic image's validity is checked in probably even more secure ways.

The ease of copying and redistributing digital art is a significant and ongoing problem. When something is freely reproduced and distributed, its value plummets, and the whole market perspective disintegrates. An object or service must be in short supply to be valuable.

By implementing the blockchain, digital artists can solve this dilemma. Simply put, blockchain has come as a solution to the long-standing problem of digital artists, and this is just by introducing the concept of "digital scarcity"; this means that the artist has only a limited copy of his art in the digital world, and each of this copies is linked to a unique propriety token.

The token is a digital certificate stored in the blockchain, a stable and decentralized ledger. It validates your right to anything unique. It can be attached to any image, including JPEG, GIF, MP4 files, and music. The blockchain stores this token, proving ownership of the "original" file.

"NFT is a type of intellectual property whose ownership is publicly verified on the blockchain."

Anyone can download and exchange your painting and even print and display it on their wall, but only you can own it. And you stand the only one who can sell this work of art. To put it another way, in the crypto world, the blockchain will be the "expert" verifying the validity or the originality of IK Aivazovsky's paintings.

A New Direction In Art

Digital art is part of our trendy culture and is something from our current cultural graphics. Technology is now allowing us to address authenticity in digital art, making digital art as it stands a potentially colossal investment. The advancement of blockchain technology and the concept of digital property have given artists the most significant technology recognition.

Digital art products offered through digital galleries like Superrare have grown significantly over the past few months. Most importantly, the stakes on these digital artworks have also increased considerably.

It is entirely unclear whether the value of these works will increase or decrease over time. In retrospect, we can only determine the actual value of each piece of art or the entire amount of skill.

One of the current problems with digital art is that it is difficult to display. A virtual reality world like Cryptovoxels can provide a way to present digital art to viewers. But there is also the requirement for a physical way to showcase digital art. Maybe a particular screen will be introduced. These unique displays will allow the owners/creators to display their favorite pieces stored on the blockchain in their digital currency package. Digital art can also have moving images, highlighting the importance of using a screen instead of a canvas.

Art's direction now follows a mode of operation that deviates from the conventional norm. Soon, it can almost be concluded with certainty that NFT will verify the identity of most artworks (even physical art). That then raises the question of how. How can NFT be used to confirm a piece of digital art or any other form of digital asset?

Confirming The Authenticity Of Digital Art

The record of transactions that indicates how an artwork passed from one owner to another, linking it back to the actual owner — the artist — is known as provenance. Many art galleries and auction houses use origin to determine the authenticity of a piece of art. To trace an artwork's history to its creator and show that it is authentic, auction records, exhibition records, gallery bills, shipping labels, or dealer stamps are commonly used. Sadly, provenance records are often forged or counterfeited despite all precautions, and fake artworks are sold as originals.

NFTs provide enhanced security and also the unique authentication of valuable assets. In doing business, one essential attribute is trust, and blockchain can defeat this trust and encourage trade and more commercial activity in markets that are deemed risky. Distributed Ledger Technology (DLT) (the blockchain network in this case) helps build trust in industries concerned with non-fungible assets where counterfeiting and tampering are common, such as art and memorabilia. According to a study carried out by Havocvscope, approximately about $480 million worth of art or even more is stolen annually in the UK. Technology can always recognize the originality and authenticity of the collectible (maybe a digital art); track it; create a legal and operational supply chain; and set documents on the ownership, control, and transfer of that collectible.

For example, artists are given a token after submitting a picture of the artwork or a URL of digital painting. They also offer a few basic details to companies that provide tokens, including title, measurements (size and dimension), and date. When the token is provided, the artwork will be added to the blockchain simultaneously. If an artist sells an artwork, the artist passes the token to the new owner along with the artwork, and this token exchange is digitally registered on the blockchain. When an artwork is sold, the change of ownership is written on the blockchain by generating a new block with the deal's data and a time stamp. Any sale is then added to the permanent transaction record.

Therefore, the owner of a piece of art will always remain as long as the blockchain network exists or the ownership token is not transferred to another address. That is very similar to how Bitcoin is monitored and tracked when a transaction takes place. The token is exchanged between two addresses. Depending on how innovators design the application for their intended use, this technology will also record the history of non-fungible assets; add timestamps of critical events, and provide auction prices and other confirmed information.

The blockchain, like provenance, is a ledger, a collection of transactions linked together by cryptography. However, unlike provenance, blockchain is a decentralized technology. A vast network of computers confirms and records transaction data any time a change of possession is recorded on the blockchain by solving complex mathematical algorithms. This history of transactions is nearly impossible to falsify.

Suppose one machine attempts to tamper with these documents. In that case, the rest of the network will notice and reject the modification, making the records nearly impossible to forge.

By tracking the artwork's blockchain URL, you can see how many times an artwork has changed hands since it was created and easily trace it back to the creator. Suppose the token for the artwork you want to purchase comes from the artist's wallet. In that case, you have irrefutable evidence that the artwork is genuine.

Additionally, blockchain technology and NFT are ideal for selling digital art multiples. Creators can sell limited edition digital art to several collectors by simply sending one token to each collector. An artist may authorize an entire series of works by obtaining 50 or 100 tokens as certificates of authenticity.

CRYPTO

CRYPTOCURRENCY

Definition

A cryptocurrency is a currency present in a digital form that does not have a physical presence. Cryptocurrencies make use of the cryptography method secure from being double-spent and work based on blockchain technology.

In simple terminology, a cryptocurrency is a type of digital money dependent on a blockchain network, distributed across many computers, and maintains a public ledger of all the information. Blockchain technology is a decentralized system, which means that they exist so that the governments and central authorities are not involved.

The term 'cryptocurrency' is broken into 'crypto' and 'currency,' which means encrypted money based on encryption techniques used to secure the network. Blockchains, which we have considered already, are the organizational methods for ensuring that the transactional history is valid and the crucial component of most cryptocurrencies.

According to the banking and finance sector experts, it is believed that blockchain and the technology related to it will create many hassles in various industries, including finance and law.

However, Cryptocurrencies are being criticized for various reasons, such as their use for illegal activities, volatility, and the network's vulnerabilities. Nonetheless, they have been appreciated for their portability, divisibility, resistance to inflation, transparency, among many other aspects.

Cryptocurrencies are the type of money that grants access to make secure payments online, present in virtual 'tokens' (literally meaning that they don't exist) represented with the ledger entries made internally into the network. Here, 'Crypto' points out the various encryption methods and cryptographic techniques that oversee such ledger entries, including elliptical curve encryption, public-private key pairs, hashing functions.

Cryptocurrencies like Bitcoin are not physical money, yet they have strived to become a financial breakthrough. Here is your comprehensive overview for understanding cryptocurrency and all other relevant aspects. Are you thinking about knowing whether it's the right time to become a part of the cryptocurrency market? That is good, and most people are thinking of doing the same. If you want to go with crypto mining and earn money, you can refer to the information mentioned earlier in this e-book. However, some other methods help you make money with the help of cryptocurrencies, which we will discuss below. Not only that, but the information that we are about to provide will be helpful to you in knowing extensively about cryptocurrencies.

The financial journey of cryptocurrency owners (especially when it comes to specific ones such as Bitcoin) has been volatile since the beginning. Glancing at Bitcoin, we can see that It started as a typical worthless investment, yet it went on and became an asset with a price of $64,500 by the time of writing this e-book. This price has seen many ups and downs, and by downs, we mean drastic drops that would make any investor panic.

There are even some banks that are interested in the application of blockchain technology in their business activities. Yet, cryptocurrencies such as Bitcoin were developed to avoid the use of banks altogether. Developers of cryptocurrencies and their fan communities like the ideology of a decentralized network that will not require any other parties to process a transaction. Even with a centralized network, a bank would still be a third-party that wants to access the information and is nowhere near cryptocurrency. Therefore, Crypto owners usually tend to go with their money.

History: How did it start? To answer that, we might have to look at the past as far as 1983. During that year, an American cryptographer named 'David Chaum' came out with an idea for cryptographic electronic money known by ecash, which was known for maintaining its anonymity. After some time passed by, in 1995, he implemented his idea through Digicash, the first type of electronic payment. That makes use of cryptography and requires user software to make payments similarly. We usually withdraw notes from a bank and designate specific encrypted keys before that very payment can be sent to another recipient. This feature allows digital currency to be anonymous and untraceable by a bank, the government, monetary authority, or any third party, for that matter.

In 1996, a paper was published by the National Security Agency, namely 'How to Create a Mint: The Cryptography Anonymous Electronic Cash,' which explains the procedure and working of a Cryptocurrency system, which was first published in an MIT mailing list. Later in 1997, it was also published in 'The American Law Evaluation.'

After that, in 1998, Wei Dai published an illustration of 'b-money,' which is distinguished as an anonymous, allowed electronic cash system. After that, Nick Szabo stated it as bit gold within a short time. Like bitcoin and other cryptocurrencies that would pursue it, bit gold was described as an electronic currency system. It required users to complete a consensus algorithm (Proof of

Work) function with cryptographically put solutions together and published. People should confuse it with BitGold, a gold-based exchange that came into existence later.

However, the first decentralized cryptocurrency that came into existence was Bitcoin, created in 2009, presumably by a person or a set of people known by the pseudonym developer Satoshi Nakamoto. It used SHA-256, a cryptographic hash function, and implemented a proof-of-work consensus protocol. We will discuss more on Bitcoin in a few more moments. In April 2011, a cryptocurrency named Namecoin, which happens to be the first attempt at creating a decentralized DNS (Domain Name System), made internet censorship to become quite tricky. Within a short time after that, Litecoin was released in October 2011. Instead of using SHA-256, it uses the script as a hash function.

Why was it invented? – What was the actual reason that a person had to go and invent some digital currency such as a cryptocurrency? Why wasn't everyone happy with the paper currency most used by the people of the nations in the world?

Paper currency was not the first currency that people have used to purchase things or make transactions. First, the evolution of money went from seashells, wheat bags, and other not-so-traditional forms of money. Then, people started using more valuable things and could be easily stored or managed.

To understand the evolution process of money, we might have to look at some of its characteristics, making it the best to use.

As we all know, money is used to maintain some value to get other objects. That was the primary objective of money when there were no other obligations, such as transactions and forex trading.

When a person wants to buy bread, gas, or anything else, they might have to pay money (of the equivalent value) in exchange for those objects. Here, the person compensates the seller of those objects with cash for what they acquired. In this manner, money keeps revolving from one person to another while helping them gain the things they want.

As considered before, paper currency was not available, and people opted for a wide variety of things. However, back in the early ages, a system in implementation known as the 'Barter System' roughly translates to an exchange system.

Here is a brief description of how the barter system works. Suppose there were two people, where one person had a wheat bag, and the other had some fruits and veggies. Then, the first person wanted to have what the second person had and vice versa. Now, they exchange their things between them, resulting in mutual satisfaction. It sounds like a good system. Well, we are coming to that part.

When the barter system was in effect and a few centuries after that, the most common things that people used for money were stones, seashells, wheat, salt, and gold.

Ideal Characteristics: Money would be considered superior when it has some characteristics, which we will discuss below.

- Long-Lasting:

One of the primary features of money is that it should be long-lasting. Who would want to have money if it is not durable and perish within a specific period? Nobody! That is the problem of using salt or wheat because eventually, they expire and cannot be held for a long time without being harmed.

However, some other forms of money used in the old days would last long. Yes, we are talking about precious metals like gold and silver. That is among the reasons why precious metals still have a great deal of popularity among people.

- Divisibility:

If you wanted a bag of wheat and you have a stone to offer in exchange for that (yes! Stones were used at a particular time for sale), the load of grain is only worth half the stone. How are you going to accomplish what you desire?

Therefore, money should have divisibility, which is especially important to make transactions of an exact value. Like when you buy something worth $2.50 and give $3 to the seller, the seller returns $0.50.

- Convenience:

Imagine that you were in one of those ages mentioned, and you were throwing a massive party to all your friends, relatives, and family members. For this, you need many objects such as fruits, vegetables, meat, wheat, and many other things. Let us assume that, by that time, the only thing that money was was salt. Now let us say that ten bags of salt get you one bag of wheat, and you need ten bags of grain. How are you going to transport 100 loads of salt? Even if you do so, how could you have stored them?

Nowadays, if you like to purchase something, you could pay in cash or even make a card transaction or transfer money online. In such a way, money should be very convenient to use, whether for carrying or storing.

- Constant value:

Money must constantly maintain its value because when it is volatile, people will not have money worth the weight they acquired earlier. Moreover, people will face many difficulties if the funds cannot consistently maintain their value.

- Intrinsic Value:

Intrinsic value is nothing but the underlying value of the asset. So, for example, cash worth $100 is not worth $100 as it doesn't have that much value (since it is nothing but paper). However, gold can fulfill this obligation as gold has the underlying value/intrinsic value. That means that $1,000 worth of gold has an actual value of $1,000.

- Rarity:

Money should be rare. If it were available everywhere, it would not have that much value, which means people cannot use it to get what they want.

- Acceptance:

Another significant characteristic of money is that it is accepted anywhere. Unless it is accepted everywhere, it defeats the primary purpose of being used by people to get what they want.

Depending on these characteristics, precious metals and cryptocurrencies are the only types of money considered flawless and an ideal form of money.

Cryptography: Cryptography is making something secure and confidential, which is the most relevant term for information/data. Cryptography is achieved by creating code, which makes the respective data invisible. Why does anybody want some data to be hidden? People generally have some confidential data, which must be made invisible. Otherwise, people who are not authorized to access that data will get their hands on it. Hence, that very data is made secure with the help of cryptography, which makes it available for the people for whom that data is intended.

WHAT ARE THE CRYPTOCURRENCIES?

Different Types Of Cryptocurrencies To Invest In

Bitcoin (BTC)

New Bitcoins are formed as a reward for mining, which keeps the Bitcoin protocol running. The Bitcoin protocol is configured to control the production rate of new Bitcoins around a certain average. Suppose some processing power is taken from the network, the difficulty of mining further Bitcoins decreases. Mining becomes harder if more processing power is deployed to mine for new Bitcoins. The protocol was developed with a limit of 21 million Bitcoins, after which no more Bitcoins will be released.

Bitcoin can be split into smaller units, MilliBitcoins, MicroBitcoins, and Satoshis. The shortest team of Bitcoin is the Satoshi (0.00000001), which was named after the mysterious inventor of Bitcoin. Bitcoin is the easiest to get as the first-ever current cryptocurrency and enjoys the widest acceptance.

Ethereum (ETH)

In the long run, Ethereum has much more security than Bitcoin. While the two competing cryptocurrencies depend on blockchain technology, they have significant differences in purpose and ability. Bitcoin is rigidly a payment system, which is only one application of blockchain technology. Somewhat of concentrating on one use as Bitcoin did, Ethereum allows developers to build all kinds of decentralized apps. That means that Ethereum has the capability of revolutionizing all services and sectors that are currently centralized. There are two similar Ethereum blockchains, Ethereum (ETH) and Ethereum Classic (ETC). Ethereum Classic was presented after a split following the hacking of the Ethereum-based DAO project in September of 2016, where about $50 million Ether was stolen.

Litecoin (LTC)

One of Lee's significant changes was the cryptographic 'hash' operation used by Litecoin. Unlike Bitcoin, which operates the SHA256 hash, Lee introduced 'scrypt' in Litecoin—switching to scrypt permitted Litecoin to process and verify transactions faster. Litecoin trades are confirmed in about two minutes, while Bitcoin might take 10 minutes to verify transactions. Another benefit of using 'scrypt' is that it allows users with consumer-grade CPUs to mine for coins, unlike Bitcoin, which demands miners to have CPUs specialized for mining.

By doing so, Lee handed Litecoin more liquidity since there are more coins obtainable for purchase, stopping the hoarding that has become so common with Bitcoin buyers. Another significant distinction between Litecoin and Bitcoin is that Litecoin uses a slightly different mining protocol, which allows a fairer allocation of mined coins. Litecoin also allows for more rapid testing and execution of new technology. For instance, Litecoin pioneered and enforced SegWit (Segregated Witness) technology way before Bitcoin. All in all, Litecoin is a practical cryptocurrency with a good reputation and solid economic principles.

IOTA (IOT)

IOTA includes things like internet-enabled cars, computers, kitchen appliances, microchips, home automation devices, hospital devices, and so on. By being the spine of IOT, IOTA strives to fulfill its call of being the 'Ledger of Everything.'

Apart from being the backbone of IOT, IOTA was also created to solve some of the challenges encountered by Bitcoin, including issues of scalability, speed, and transaction fees. IOTA has one key difference from other cryptocurrencies like Bitcoin. With blockchain-based cryptocurrencies, the network of computers ought to confirm a transaction before it is finished. With the Tangle, proof does not depend on the web. Instead, the Tangle counts on a system that needs the sender to prove work before making their transaction. By doing so, the sender agrees to two transactions, thereby connecting the trade and its guarantee.

This has two advantages. First, by stopping miners, the Tangle makes IOTA fully decentralized. Instead of having players who affect the network without using it (miners enable the web, but they do not use it), the IOTA network is maintained solely by the 'users' making trades. Second, by having the sender support two transactions before they can complete their transaction, this system makes the IOTA protocol faster. It also means that increasing users leads to a faster validation speed, unlike what happens typically with other cryptocurrencies like Bitcoin; expanding the number of users delays the guaranteed term. Since there exist no miners, users do not have to settle any expenses for sustaining the network.

Ripple (XRP)

Unlike many cryptocurrencies, Ripple was not created as a variant of Bitcoin. Instead, its creators built it from scratch and incorporated some significant changes in its architecture. Unlike most cryptocurrencies that use a proof-of-stake or proof-of-work system to verify transactions, Ripple uses a unique consensus system. The computers in the network keep watching any changes. Once most of the computers in the network monitor a transaction, it is added to the public ledger. The consensus system has several advantages over the proof-of-work or proof-of-stake methods. Transactions confirmed under the consensus system are validated quickly and require less processing power. While it might seem likely for hackers to compromise the consensus system, it is designed so that the network rejects any unreliable results.

Since the Ripple network encourages cross-currency conversions, Ripples can be traded for a wide range of fiat currencies and altcoins. Some businesses also allow customers to swap Ripples for air miles and reward points. Unlike altcoins, like Ether and Litecoin, sold on cryptocurrency exchanges, you have to go through Ripple Gateways to buy Ripples. The Gateways operate in the same way PayPal works.

Dash (Dash)

Dash is a cryptocurrency that Evan Duffield and Kyle Hagan developed. Launched in 2014, it was initially known as Darkcoin. After a year in presence, it rebranded to Dash, the abbreviated understanding of 'digital cash.' Kyle and Evan wanted to create a secret and anonymous cryptocurrency by designing Dash. Most cryptocurrencies are not thoroughly anonymous. Though talks are not linked to personally identifiable information, the network knows the digit of coins within each lesson. Anyone can keep track of cash as they move from one address to another. That makes it possible for someone to independently know the identity of those users who do not take measures to protect their identity. Dash uses a decentralized master code network to keep users anonymous, making Dash trades practically impossible to trace.

The high level of anonymity presented by Dash is enabled by a system known as Darksend. With this system, specialized computers known as master codes collect several trades and execute them simultaneously, maintaining the transaction untraceable. It becomes unthinkable to follow the source and destination of the coins. To make your dealings even more anonymous, you can choose to have the master codes mix your transaction for numerous rounds before completing the transaction. To keep this anonymity, the Dash ledger is not publicly available. The high level of anonymity has also stopped wide approval by businesses.

Another distinctive part of Dash is its hashing algorithm. Rather than using the SHA256 or scrypt hash, Dash uses a unique X11 hash which demands less processing power, letting users with consumer-grade CPUs mine for Dash coins. Dash's other notable advantages include its speedy transaction verification (4 seconds) and low transaction fees. However, the prices will probably increase once more people join the network. Dash also has a voting system to implement significant changes quickly.

Monero (XMR)

Monero is another cryptocurrency that focuses on privacy and anonymity, just like Dash. Monero was launched in 2014 by seven programmers, five of whom chose to stay anonymous. Due to its anonymity attributes, it quickly gained popularity with cryptocurrency enthusiasts. Like most other cryptocurrencies, Monero is entirely open-source. The community and donations drive the development of the platform. This design is a digital version of group autographs. A group of cryptographic signatures enshrouds each transaction on the Monero network. This way, it is inconceivable to identify the actual sender or recipient in the trade. Even with someone's wallet address, it is unbelievable to see the number of coins in the wallet or keep track of their spending. That suggests that Monero coins can't become tainted due to former dubious transactions.

Monero transactions are verified using the same proof-of-work system that Bitcoin uses. However, a significant difference between Bitcoin and Monero is that while Bitcoin block sizes are restricted at 2MB, there is no boundary on Monero block sizes. The absence of limited block sizes presents the risk of malicious miners using huge blocks to clog the system.

Neo (NEO)

NEO is a Chinese cryptocurrency founded by Erik Zhang and Da Hongfei. NEO is designed to be an intelligent economy platform, much like Ethereum. It has even been directed to as 'China's Ethereum.' NEO was first established under the title Antshares. In August 2017, it was renamed to NEO Smart Contract Organization. NEO's intent is identical to that of Ethereum. NEO supplies a platform where developers can create decentralized applications and deploy smart contracts. Unlike Ethereum, which only sustains its Solidity programming language, NEO can be used with common programming languages like C#, Python, and Java.

Since agreement under the dBFT system only needs to be completed by a subset of the network, this system demands less processing power and allows the network to handle a higher transaction volume. NEO claims it can take over 1000 trades per second, whereas Ethereum only handles 15 transactions per second. The dBFT system also eradicates the possibility of a hard fork, which makes NEO an excellent option for digitizing real-world financial assets.

OmiseGO (OMG)

OmiseGO is a cryptocurrency that has gained popularity from cryptocurrency enthusiasts lately. Launched in 2013, it is an exciting yet very ambitious project which aims to use Ethereum-based financial technology to un-bank the banked. OmiseGO is presently built on the Ethereum outlet as an ERC20-token, though it will eventually launch its blockchain. OmiseGO's vision is to evolve the leading P2P cryptocurrency trade platform. Instead of being just an altcoin, OmiseGO is built to act as a financial platform to disrupt the financial sector as we currently know it.

OmiseGO intends to solve a challenge that most cryptocurrency trades have failed to address. To buy a cryptocurrency in most cryptocurrency exchanges, you have to start with a fiat currency. To swap one altcoin for another, you have to convert the altcoins to fiat currency or Bitcoin and convert the fiat currency/Bitcoin to your preferred altcoins. Throughout this procedure, the exchange charges fees for each transaction. That means that you will pay fees to convert altcoins to fiat currency/Bitcoin and then pay fees again to restore the fiat currency/Bitcoin to other altcoins.

OmiseGO plans to decipher this problem by linking all current cryptocurrency wallets to a central OmiseGO Blockchain. This way, users can smoothly exchange altcoins for other altcoins without converting them to fiat currency or Bitcoin. That means that instead of multiple fees, users will pay a one-time price.

OmiseGO also strives to bring decentralization to cryptocurrency exchanges. Currently, most dealings are centralized operations. The records of all transactions and data about different users are stored in databases reserved on the company's servers. OmiseGO aims to decentralize the trading functionality by keeping all the blockchain's transaction info and user data. This way, the data is more assured since a hacker would need to execute a 51% attack (gaining authority over 51% of the computers in the network) to breach the blockchain, which is virtually impossible.

WHY SHOULD YOU TRADE CRYPTOS?

According to the description of the World Bank, the number of people who live their lives under the poverty line is incredibly high. That shows that the welfare and aids that help the economy grow are distributed disproportionately among different regions and countries. These economic chaos, civil war, governmental collapse, and plague are developing in areas (Prahalad & Hammond, 2002). Besides, poverty is primarily caused by economic factors, including the restricted key to financial services (Beck & Demirguc-Kunt, 2006) and increased inflation rates (Aisen & Veiga, 2006). Moreover, analyses have argued that a low level of trust (Barham, Boadway, Marchand, & Pestieau, 1995) and corrupt government institutions harm economic development (Olken, 2006).

Cryptocurrencies could provide a substantial advantage by overcoming the lack of social trust and by raising the entry to financial services (Nakamoto, 2008) as they can be considered as a medium to sustain the development process in developing countries by expanding financial inclusion, delivering better traceability of funds, and to enable people to escape poverty (Ammous, 2015).

Before we move on to an overview of the cryptocurrencies and their usage in developing countries, we must understand the advantages and disadvantages of the cryptocurrencies delivered for users compared to the central bank-issued fiat currencies, identical to the Euro or the US dollar. Not just that, but also their deliberate emergence from the fundamental technology. The majority of the cryptocurrencies function using blockchain technology. Blockchain is distributed on different nodes that are a part of the network. The entries of the blockchain are stored in the form of blocks.

The first digital currency that was ever invented is bitcoin. Bitcoin is the first-ever digital currency that works on an algorithm. The transactions on a decentralized peer-to-peer network are recorded and kept track of. All the participants of the network can see and monitor these transactions. The market cap of bitcoin is over $189 billion.

Satoshi Nakamoto is the inventor of bitcoin. He invented bitcoin in the year 2008 when he published his white paper "Bitcoin: A Peer-to-Peer Electronic Cash System" (Nakamoto, 2008).

Ethereum is an open-source and decentralized platform. Ethereum is based on a blockchain network. It is also a computing platform for smart contracts. Additionally, it backs the improved version of Satoshi Nakamoto's consensus mechanism. Ether is the cryptocurrency that gives energy to the Ethereum blockchain network. Ether is the second-best and popular currency, the first being bitcoin. It has a market cap of $18 billion.

Opportunities Through Cryptocurrencies In Developing Countries

As per the investigation of the economic complications faced by the developing countries, cryptocurrencies can hasten the development of several fields. It holds that innovations are strategic solutions for the catch-up process of developing countries, as explained by Chudnovsky and Lopez (2006).

To benefit from the advancements offered by crypto, people need to have the internet. It means that those who have the internet can do trading of cryptocurrencies, whereas those who would not be able to do so. Aiming at this reason, it has been seen that the practice of the internet in developing countries has improved intensely over the past decade (Aker & Mbiti, 2010; Tapscott & Tapscott, 2016).

With no cryptocurrencies, the fiat currency needs to be exchanged to those widely used currencies like the US Dollar or the Euro. Then it has to be re-converted into the economy which is being used. Subsequently, most of the time, there is no liquid market that could be used to exchange the fiat or local currency to the target fiat currency. Optimization of this could be done using crypto- currencies. It would make the process faster and cheaper (Ammous, 2015).

Let's consider an example of an Indian worker based in Chicago. This worker can use a local service provider that exchanges US Dollars into Bitcoins to transfer money to his family living in India. The family can deduct Rupees at a local service provider that would change Bitcoins back to Rupees. This process results in making companies like Western Union indisposed. It is still essential to have a liquid market that could interchange the Bitcoin with US Dollar and to Rupee to maximize its proficiency. A few startups were founded for the sole purpose of creating a liquid market for Bitcoins. For instance, BitPesa was launched in Kenya. BitPesa provides liquid markets for some specific currency passageways, e.g., for the direct exchange of Kenyan Shilling to the US Dollar.

Cryptocurrencies can help get involved in trading internationally without a bank account. Bitcoin is a cryptocurrency that can help facilitate businesses and individuals to get involved in international trade on a smaller level. These businesses and individuals can use Bitcoins in exchange for trading goods. That helps in evading traditional e-commerce systems (Scott, 2016), which requires creating a bank account.

The financial situation of the developing countries can be improved by using crypto-currencies, which means that cryptocurrencies can help the developing countries to serve as a quasi-bank accounts. That is because everyone who has access to the internet can download a Bitcoin wallet (Honohan, 2008). Bitcoin wallet can be used as a quasi-bank account. That is where people can conduct savings and daily transactions (Scott, 2016).

The high costs faced by the transactions can help increase the odds for microcredits. That comes at the expense of reducing the transaction costs. If these costs are eradicated, there are high chances that international financing could bloom. People from developed countries can send money to people in developing countries; all this is possible due to cryptocurrencies. As these are small transactions, they would be of less money, but that could have a lot of impact on a person's life in a developing country.

At this point, microfinance transactions like such can cost a ton of cash due to the borrowing and then repaying of transactions, which face high trade fees. This transaction fee is sometimes as much as the money being transferred. However, when transaction costs are enormously minimized or disregarded completely, it can make loans more popular, and such loans could become more widespread (Ammous, 2015).

Additionally, an amalgamation of cryptocurrencies and smart contracts can prove to be a defining factor for the solidification of social trust as well as battling corruption via a more transparent system. It would become possible for ordinary citizens to use the data of the cryptocurrencies available publicly in the blockchain to observe how the funds from the state are utilized. The governments could also benefit from this as they would be able to track and monitor the total expenditure of their money and in what ways they can improve their budget provision. (Schmidt Kai Uwe, 2017).

Based on the literature analysis, here we shall focus on the qualitative research centered around the interviews of experts. Social sites such as Xing and LinkedIn were used to choose an interview partner. The experts that are a part of this differ hugely, considering the information and knowledge. They may be representatives of some startup, a lecturer, or an ambassador at consultancy companies. Another reason that makes them different from one another is their geographical location. As per the region they live and work in, they differ considerably. An overview of this is provided in Appendix B.

Cryptocurrencies And Local Fiat Currencies

Money has three main functions.

- Money has to be acknowledged and recognized as a medium that can be used in exchange for trading goods and services.

- Money essentially needs to be appropriate as a medium that can store value for saving wealth.

- Money must perform as a unit of account. It can be used to measure and compare the value of goods (Ammous, 2018).

Gold is considered to be the oldest form of money. Cryptocurrencies are matched to the fiat currencies that are issued by the Central Bank as well as gold.

It is of notice that the conventional types of money considered gold and fiat money achieve all characteristics of money. Cryptocurrencies are more appropriate as the exchange medium. That is because cryptocurrencies are divisible and can be transferred globally.

(Ammous, 2018).

One of gold's essential benefits is the best-collateralized form of money. That is because the medium of exchange has value in contrast to the notes issued by the bank or digital money. Cryptocurrencies are a decentralized form of currency, whereas the fiat currency is issued by the Central Bank under the government's rules, thus making it completely centralized. That is a fundamental difference between fiat currencies and cryptocurrencies.

The reason which can be regarded for the cryptocurrency's high instability is its decentralization for crypto and the lack of security. So, it destructs the store of the value function and the unit of account function.

One of the significant issues with crypto-currencies is the instability in their price. Due to this reason, during the value transfer, no considerable fluctuations in the financial aspect can be seen (Expert 1, 2018). To attain a more stable price and fluctuate less, the majority of the cryptocurrencies progress toward a regulated currency (Expert 5, 2018). Furthermore, a trend in most cryptocurrencies is observed to vary from a complete decentralized system to a more centralized approach. In this centralized system, the players can maximize any possibilities of development. Most of the cryptocurrencies in use transition from a decentralized system to a centralized system. They do so despite all the odds. This transitioning may lead to a decrease in value. There can be a reduction in its price stability through centralization and support provided by economic policy decisions. Cryptocurrencies can develop significantly (Aisen & Veiga, 2006).

Cryptocurrencies have to be restricted to national boundaries to attain political support. This way, the governments will have the power and will be able to control the economic parameters to retain financial dominion (Expert 6, 2018). However, this would be a way that would ultimately reduce the pros of the cryptocurrencies and would result in a system that would be centralized.

We cannot say that cryptocurrencies are not a replacement for the currencies that the government issues. Additionally, this has given the national authorities a reason to describe cryptocurrencies as digital assets and not cash. This way, it makes it similar to gold. It is also undecided as it needs to be regarded as an asset or as a form of money. It is safe to say that

- Bitcoin is a digital token that two parties can exchange in a transaction.
- If you compare this token to fiat or national currencies, you will see its worth.
- You can use it to exchange for something tangible. It is used occasionally in trivial amounts.

Improvement Of Financial Inclusion In Developing Countries

A significant advantage of cryptocurrencies is the betterment of financial inclusion for the people living in developing countries (Darlington, 2014). Crypto-currencies can reduce the time and cost of transactions. It will act as a bank account that permits people to make their daily transactions and save. (Honohan, 2008; Scott, 2016).

Cryptocurrencies can help make fast and less expensive transactions compared to conventional money transfers through bank accounts like the SWIFT process. It can be achieved by eliminating third parties involved, thus resulting in cost reduction and increased speed of transactions (Tapscott & Tapscott, 2016).

THE MOST POPULAR CRYPTOS

Different types of cryptocurrencies can be classified into the following two groups: Coins are designed to be used as a currency and created on their blockchain. For example, Ether is a cryptocurrency established on the Ethereum blockchain.

"Altcoin" directs to any blockchain-based cryptocurrency that isn't Bitcoin. The word "altcoin" was coined as a shorthand for "alternative to Bitcoin," Most altcoins were created to improve Bitcoin somehow. Namecoin, Peercoin, Litecoin (LTC), Ethereum, and USD Coin (USDC) are instances of altcoins.

Some cryptocurrencies, like Bitcoin, have a limited number of coins that help develop demand and reinforce their sensed worth. For example, the total supply of Bitcoin is checked at 21 million, as defined by Bitcoin's creator(s).

Tokens are made on a recent blockchain but are programmable assets that enable the formulation and execution of unique intelligent contracts. The exterior of the blockchain network, these contracts can be used to confirm ownership of assets. Tokens can represent units of value such as money, coins, digital assets, and electricity and can also be sent and received.

Stablecoins peg their values to various currencies or assets, such as gold. Most often pegged one-to-one with the U.S. dollar, stablecoins give users a way to sell into a help carrying the same value as a national currency but one that can still be transacted and stored in a crypto-Esque fashion within the ecosystem.

Nonfungible tokens, or NFTs, are yet another type of cryptocurrency, denoting that it is a one-of-a-kind asset and cannot be replaced. A Bitcoin, for instance, is fungible, meaning you can swap one for another and get exactly the identical thing. However, a one-of-a-kind trade card, on the other hand, cannot be repeated. You'd get something altogether separate if you changed it for a different card.

Before interacting with any given asset, it may be essential to look up its type and function depending on your goals. Not all digital assets were created for investment purposes.

Today, while many users of crypto comprehend and appreciate these distinctions, traders and lay investors may not see the difference, as all types of token tend to trade in the same way on crypto exchanges,

Bitcoins

Bitcoin, often defined as a cryptocurrency, a virtual currency, or a digital currency, is an entirely virtual type of money.

It's like an online interpretation of cash. You can utilize it to buy products and services, but few shops have accepted Bitcoin yet, and some countries have prohibited it altogether.

However, some companies are starting to buy into its growing impact.

In October last year, for instance, the online expense service, PayPal, informed that it would be letting its customers buy and sell Bitcoin.

Ethereum (Eth)

The first Bitcoin alternative on our checklist, Ethereum, is a decentralized software platform that allows smart contracts and decentralized applications (dapps) to be made and run without downtime, fraud, control, or interference from a third party. The purpose behind Ethereum is to make a decentralized suite of financial products that anyone in the world can willingly access, however of nationality, ethnicity, or faith.[2] This aspect makes the importance for those in some countries more compelling, as those without state infrastructure and state designations can access bank accounts, loans, insurance, or a combination of other financial products.

The applications on Ethereum are executed on Ether, its platform-specific cryptographic token. Ether is like a vehicle for driving about on the Ethereum platform and is aimed mainly by designers looking to create and run applications inside Ethereum, or now, by investors examining to make buys of other digital currencies utilizing Ether. Ether, launched in 2015, is presently the second-largest digital currency by market capitalization after Bitcoin, although it lags after the dominant cryptocurrency by a substantial margin.[3] Trading at about $4,000 per ETH as of November 2021, Ether's demand cap is less than half that of Bitcoin's.[4]

In 2014, Ethereum established a presale for Ether, which received an overwhelming reaction; this helped usher in the initial coin offering (ICO) age. According to Ethereum, it can be operated to "codify, decentralize, protected and trade just about anything."[5] Following the raid on the decentralized autonomous community (DAO) in 2016, Ethereum was split into Ethereum (ETH) and Ethereum Classic (ETC).

In 2021, Ethereum transitioned its agreement algorithm from proof-of-work (PoW) to proof-of-stake (PoS).[6] This move is planned to allow Ethereum's network to run itself with far less energy and improved transaction speed and make for a more deflationary economic environment. Proof-of-stake enables network parties to "stake" their Ether to the network.

Those who do this are awarded Ether, similar to an exciting account. This approach helps to ensure the network and process the trades that occur. That is an alternative to Bitcoin's proof-of-work mechanism, where miners are rewarded more Bitcoin for processing transactions.

Litecoin (Ltc)

Litecoin, established in 2011, was among the first cryptocurrencies to observe in the footsteps of Bitcoin and has often been directed to as "silver to Bitcoin's gold."7 It was designed by Charlie Lee, an MIT graduate and former Google engineer.

Litecoin is founded on an open-source global settlement network that is not maintained by any central authority and uses "scrypt" as proof of work, which can be decoded with the help of consumer-grade CPUs. Although Litecoin is like Bitcoin in many forms, it has a faster block generation rate and offers a quicker trade verification time. Other than designers, there is a growing digit of retailers that acknowledge Litecoin. As of November 2021, Litecoin has a demand capitalization of $14 billion and a per token value of around $200, causing it the seventeenth-largest cryptocurrency globally.

Cardano (Ada)

Cardano is an "Ouroboros proof-of-stake" cryptocurrency designed with a research-based practice by engineers, mathematicians, and cryptography experts.

The job was co-founded by Charles Hoskinson, one of the five initial founding partners of Ethereum. After having some conflicts with the direction Ethereum was taking, he left and later helped create Cardano.

The team behind Cardano made its blockchain through extensive experimentation and peer-evaluationed research. The investigators behind the project have written over 90 papers on blockchain technology across various topics.

This study is the backbone of Cardano.

Due to this strict process, Cardano seems to stand out among its proof-of-stake peers and other major cryptocurrencies. Cardano has also been anointed the "Ethereum killer," as its blockchain is said to be qualified for more.

That said, Cardano is still in its before stages. While it has whipped Ethereum to the proof-of-stake consensus model, it still has a long way to run in decentralized financial applications.

Cardano strives to be the world's financial operating system by launching decentralized financial products similar to Ethereum and supplying solutions for chain interoperability, voter fraud, and legal contract illustration, among other items. November 2021, Cardano has the sixth-largest earner in market capitalization at $57 billion and one ADA deal for approximately $1.79.

Polkadot (Dot)

Polkadot is a unique proof-of-stake cryptocurrency desired to deliver interoperability among other blockchains. Its protocol is created to secure permission and permissionless blockchains and oracles to permit systems to work jointly under one roof. Polkadot's core feature is its relay chain that enables the interoperability of varying networks. It also provides for "parachains," or parallel blockchains with their native tokens for specific-use cases.12

Polkadot differs from Ethereum in that rather than creating just decentralized applications on Polkadot, developers can create their blockchain while also utilizing the security that Polkadot's chain already has. With Ethereum, designers can create new blockchains but need to create security measures, leaving new and smaller projects open to attack. The more extensive a blockchain, the more security it has. This idea in Polkadot is comprehended as shared security.

Polkadot was developed by Gavin Wood, another member of the core founders of the Ethereum project who had differing views on the project's tomorrow. As of November 2021, Polkadot has a demand capitalization of roughly $41 billion and one DOT deal for $39.13

Bitcoin Cash (Bch)

Bitcoin Cash (BCH) holds a strong place in the history of altcoins because it is one of the earliest and most prosperous complex divisions of the actual Bitcoin. In the cryptocurrency world, a fork handles place due to debates and discussions between developers and miners. Due to the decentralized character of digital currencies, wholesale modifications to the code underlying the token or coin at writing must be made due to consensus; the mechanism for this procedure varies according to the particular cryptocurrency.

When different factions can't agree, the digital currency is sometimes divided. The actual chain remains true to its original code, and the new chain begins life as a new version of the last coin, complete with changes to its code.

BCH began its life in August 2017 due to one of these divisions. The argument that led to the creation of BCH had to do with the problem of scalability; the Bitcoin network has a boundary on the size of blocks: one megabyte (MB). BCH raises the block size from one MB to eight MBs, with the theory being that more giant blocks can hold more trades within them, and the transaction speed would therefore be increased.14 It also makes other changes, including removing the Segregated Witness protocol that influences union space. As of November 2021, BCH has a demand capitalization of about $10.5 billion and a matter per token of $555.15

Stellar (Xlm)

Stellar is an open blockchain network that links financial institutions for large transactions and provides enterprise solutions. Huge trades between banks and investment firms—generally taking several days, involving several intermediaries, and commanding a good deal of money—can now be done almost instantaneously with no mediators and control little to nothing for those making the trade.

While Stellar has set itself as an enterprise blockchain for institutional trades, it is still an open blockchain that anyone can use. The design allows for cross-border transactions among any currency. Stellar's aboriginal currency is Lumens (XLM).16 The network needs users to hold Lumens to transact on the web.

Stellar was established by Jed McCaleb, a founding member of Ripple Labs and developer of the Ripple protocol. He eventually quit his position with Ripple and co-founded the Stellar Development Foundation.

Stellar Lumens have a demand capitalization of $8 billion and are esteemed at $0.33 as of November 2021.18

Dogecoin (Doge)

Dogecoin, seen by some as the original "meme coin," caused a stir in 2021 as the coin price skyrocketed. The coin, which uses a picture of the shiba inu as its avatar, is taken as a form of payment by some prominent companies, including the Dallas Mavericks, Kronos, and, perhaps most notably, SpaceX, an American aerospace manufacturer possessed by Elon Musk.

Dogecoin was created by two software engineers, Billy Markus and Jackson Palmer, in 2013. Markus and Palmer reportedly made the coin as a joke, remarking on the wild speculation of the cryptocurrency market.

The price of DOGE hit an all-time high of $0.71 during the week Elon Musk was scheduled to emerge on Saturday Night Live. As of November 2021, Dogecoin's market capitalization is $29.2 billion, and one DOGE is valued at around $0.22, making it the tenth-largest cryptocurrency.

THE CRYPTO MARKET

Understanding Cryptocurrency

In a nutshell, bitcoin is a new type of digital money. You can digitally transmit traditional, non-crypto currency money such as the US dollar, but this is not the same as how cryptocurrencies work. When cryptocurrencies become more widely accepted, you may use them to make electronic payments the same way you can with traditional currencies.

What distinguishes cryptocurrencies, though, is the technology that powers them. "Who cares about the technology underlying my money?" you may ask. I'm solely concerned about how much of it is in my wallet!" The difficulty is that the world's present money systems are riddled with flaws. Following are some examples:

- Credit cards and wire transfers are antiquated payment methods.
- In most cases, a slew of intermediaries, such as banks and brokers, take a piece of the action, making transactions expensive and time-consuming.
- The global financial disparity is increasing.
- Approximately 3 billion individuals are unbanked or underbanked and have no access to financial services. That equates to around half of the world's population!

Cryptocurrencies hope to solve some of these issues, if not all of them.

Understanding The Basics

You know that your regular, government-issued cash is kept in banks. And that you must have an ATM or a bank connection to receive more of it or transfer it to others. Well, with cryptocurrency, you might be able to do away with banks and other centralized intermediaries entirely. That is because cryptocurrencies rely on a decentralized technology known as blockchain (meaning no single entity is in charge of it). Instead, each computer in the network verifies the transactions.

Cryptocurrency History

Bitcoin was the first cryptocurrency ever created! You've undoubtedly heard of Bitcoin more than anything else in the crypto business. Bitcoin was the first blockchain product made by an unnamed individual named Satoshi Nakamoto. Satoshi Nakamoto proposed Bitcoin in 2008, describing it as a "purely peer-to-peer version" of electronic money.

Although Bitcoin was the first official cryptocurrency, numerous attempts to create digital currencies years before Bitcoin was formally released.

Mining is the method through which Bitcoin and other cryptocurrencies are produced. Mining bitcoins, unlike mining ore, requires powerful computers to solve complex issues.

Until 2011, Bitcoin was the only cryptocurrency. Then, as Bitcoin enthusiasts began to notice its weaknesses, they decided to build alternative coins, commonly known as altcoins, to improve Bitcoin's design in areas such as speed, security, privacy, and others. Litecoin was one of the most earlier altcoins, striving to be the silver to Bitcoin's gold. However, there are over 1,600 cryptocurrencies accessible at the time of writing, with the number projected to grow in the future.

Some Advantages Of Cryptocurrency

Still not convinced that cryptocurrencies (or any additional form of decentralized money) are preferable to conventional government-issued currency? Here are a few solutions that cryptocurrencies, because of their decentralized nature, may be able to provide:

Reducing corruption

When you have a lot of power, you also have a lot of responsibility. When you give a lot of energy to just one person or entity, the odds of that person or thing misusing that authority grow. According to Lord Acton, a 19th-century British statesman, "Power corrupts, and absolute power corrupts absolutely." Cryptocurrencies seek to address the issue of absolute power by sharing authority among many persons or, better yet, among all network participants. That is, after all, the basic concept of blockchain technology.

Eliminating extreme money printing

Governments have central banks, and when faced with a significant economic situation, central banks can print money. That is also known as quantitative easing. By printing additional money, a government may pay off debt or depreciate its currency. This method, however, is like putting a bandage on a broken leg. It rarely solves the problem, but the harmful side effects can sometimes outweigh the initial issue.

When a country, such as Iran or Venezuela, issues too much money, the value of its currency plummets, causing inflation to spike and citizens to be unable to afford essential goods and services. Their money is worth about as much as a roll of toilet paper. In addition, most cryptocurrencies have a fixed number of coins accessible. When all those currencies are in circulation, there is no straightforward method for a central entity or the firm behind the blockchain to generate more coins or add to its supply.

Giving people charge of their own money

You essentially hand over complete authority to central banks and the government with traditional cash. If you count your government, that's fantastic, but keep in mind that your government can quickly freeze your bank account and refuse you access to your funds at any time. For instance, in the United States, if you die without a valid will and own a company, the government inherits all of your assets. Some governments may even discontinue issuing banknotes as India did in 2016. As a result, you and only you have access to your funds when using cryptocurrency. (Unless someone snatches them from you.)

Cutting out the middleman

When you transfer traditional money, an intermediary, your bank, or a digital payment firm, gets a percentage. With cryptocurrencies, all network members in the blockchain serve as the middleman; their compensation is structured differently from that of fiat money intermediaries, and so is minor in contrast.

Serving the unbanked

Many of the world's citizens have no or limited access to payment systems such as banks. Cryptocurrencies hope to alleviate this problem by extending digital commerce worldwide, allowing anyone with a mobile phone to make payments. And, yes, mobile phones are more widely available than banks. More people own smartphones than toilets, but blockchain technology may not solve the latter issue at this time.

Various Myths About Cryptos And Blockchains

During the 2017 Bitcoin frenzy, several misconceptions about the entire sector increased. These fallacies could have contributed to the bitcoin fall that followed the spike. It's crucial to remember that blockchain technology and its consequence, the cryptocurrency market, are still in their infancy, and things are moving quickly. Let me clear up some of the most common misunderstandings:

Cryptocurrencies Are Suitable Only For Criminals.

Anonymity is one of the critical features of some cryptocurrencies. That is, your identity is not revealed when you conduct transactions. In addition, other cryptocurrencies are based on a decentralized blockchain, which means a central government does not solely control them.

These characteristics make such cryptocurrencies appealing to criminals; nevertheless, law-abiding residents in corrupt countries can also gain from them. For instance, if you don't trust your local bank or nation due to corruption or political instability, blockchain and cryptocurrency assets may be the best way to keep your money safe.

All Cryptocurrencies Allow For Anonymous Transactions.

Many people, for whatever reason, associate Bitcoin with anonymity. However, like many other cryptocurrencies, Bitcoin does not have any form of anonymity. All transactions involving these cryptocurrencies are recorded on the public blockchain. Some cryptocurrencies, such as Monero, value anonymity, which means that no one outside of the transaction can determine the source, amount, or destination. Most other cryptocurrencies, including Bitcoin, do not work in this manner.

Bitcoin Is The Sole Application Of Blockchain Technology.

Bitcoin and other cryptocurrencies are a minor side effect of the blockchain revolution. Many people believe Satoshi built Bitcoin solely to demonstrate how blockchain technology can operate. That couldn't be further from the truth. However, practically every industry and business in the world may benefit from blockchain technology.

Every Transaction On The Blockchain Is Private.

Many individuals mistakenly believe that blockchain technology is not available to the general public and is only available to its network of everyday users. Although some businesses construct their private blockchains for usage only by staff and business partners, the bulk of blockchains underlying popular cryptocurrencies such as Bitcoin is open to the public. As a result, anyone with a computer can view the transactions in real-time.

Risks

Like anything else in life, Cryptocurrencies arrive with their own set of risks. Whether you trade cryptocurrency, invest in it, or keep it for the future, you must first evaluate and understand the dangers. Volatility and a lack of regulation are two of the most considered bitcoin hazards. Volatility reached an all-time high in 2017, when the prices of most major cryptocurrencies, including Bitcoin, surged beyond 1,000 percent before plummeting. However, as the cryptocurrency craze has subsided, price fluctuations have grown more predictable, mirroring the patterns of stocks and other financial assets.

Another key concern in the industry is regulations. The irony is that both a lack of regulation and exposure to rules can become risk events for bitcoin investors.

Some Crypto Essentials To Know Before Jumping To Make Transactions

Cryptocurrencies exist to make transactions more straightforward and faster. But, before you can reap these advantages, you'll need to arm yourself with crypto devices, find out where you can get your hands on various cryptocurrencies, and get to know the cryptocurrency community. Cryptocurrency wallets and exchanges are among the essentials.

Some cryptocurrency wallets, which store your acquired cryptocurrencies, are similar to digital payment services such as Apple Pay and PayPal. However, they differ from ordinary wallets in that they come in various formats and levels of protection.

Exchanges

After you've obtained a cryptocurrency wallet (see the last segment), you're ready to go crypto shopping, and one of the most incredible places to go is a cryptocurrency exchange. These online web services allow you to use the traditional currency to purchase cryptocurrencies, exchange different types of cryptocurrencies, and even store your cryptocurrency.

Note: Storing your cryptocurrency on an exchange is considered high risk because many businesses have formerly been subjected to cyber-attacks and scams. When you're finished with your transactions, the most significant thing you can do is transfer your new digital support to your personal, secure wallet.

Exchanges come in a range of forms and sizes. Some function as a middleman, similar to traditional stock exchanges, which crypto specialists say is a slap at the start of the cryptocurrency market, eliminating a centralized intermediary. Others are decentralized and provide a service that connects buyers and sellers where they deal on a peer-to-peer basis, but they have their own set of issues, such as the risk of locking you out. The third sort of crypto exchange is called a hybrid, and it combines the features of the former two types to provide users with a better, more secure experience.

Before You Jump In, Make A Plan.

You might want to acquire some bitcoins and keep them for future growth. Alternatively, you may like to become a more active investor, buying and selling cryptocurrencies regularly to optimize profit and revenue. Regardless, you must have a strategy and a plan. Even if your transaction is one-time and you don't want to listen to anything regarding your crypto assets for the following ten years, you still need to learn how to identify things like the following:

- What to Buy
- When should you buy it?
- How much should I spend?
- When is it OK to sell?

The following segments provide a high-level overview of the procedures you must complete before purchasing your first crypto.

BITCOIN THE PROGENITOR

Understanding Bitcoin

So, to gain a good grasp of cryptocurrency, what better way than to look at its history? And what better way to look at its history than to look at the very first and original cryptocurrency. You probably know it: Bitcoin.

Bitcoin was the first cryptocurrency launched and run. It sparked much controversy and debate but is still one of the leading cryptocurrencies today and is highly unlikely to lose its first place anytime soon. A beginner needs to know the history of Bitcoin and its rise in popularity. Without Bitcoin, cryptocurrency would likely still be a digital dream.

History Of Bitcoin

Bitcoin was registered in 2008 through a paper written under the name of Satoshi Nakamoto. Nakamoto implemented the source code and launched Bitcoin in 2009. However, Satoshi Nakamoto is probably a pseudonym. No one knows who the designer of Bitcoin is (although a lot of work has been done to try and discover their identity).

Bitcoin started the moment Nakamoto mined the first blockchain in January 2009. That was called the Genesis block, as it was the beginning of thousands more to come. And it has had its reasonable share of bumpy roads throughout the years.

Hal Finney was the first receiver of a Bitcoin transaction. He had downloaded the software on the day of its release. He was then awarded 10 Bitcoins from Nakamoto. Many analysts believe that Nakamoto had mined an approximation of 1 million Bitcoins before disappearing from the game. The alert key and control codes were passed onto Gavin Andreson, who became the lead developer in the Bitcoin Foundation. Andreson worked hard for decentralized control, and the path of Bitcoin started to grow at a rapid pace.

Timeline Of Bitcoin

From 2011 to 2012, the first major users of Bitcoin were that of the black market. In February 2011, the value of Bitcoin started to rise by $0.30 per Bitcoin. However, on June 8, 2011, it spiked to $31.50. The weight dropped to $11.00 within the month. As you can see from the timeline that follows, the currency is very volatile, with currency prices swinging wildly.

- In the year 2012, it started at $5.27 per Bitcoin.
- In 2013, it started trading at $13.40

- April 2013, it shot up to $220
- Mid-April 2013, it dropped to $70
- October 2013, it traded at $123.20
- December 2013, it traded at $1,156.10-three days later dropped to $760.00
- January 2015, it traded at $315
- January 2017, it traded close to $1,000.00
- March 2017, it traded at $975.70
- December 2017, it traded at $20,089.00
- 2017 to 2019, Bitcoin's value dropped below $10,000
- June 2019, the price of Bitcoin reached above $10,000
- January 2020, it traded at $7,100.00
- November 2020, it traded at $18, 353.00
- As of 31 July 2021, it traded at $41,936.26
- Advantages and Disadvantages of Bitcoin

So, with it being the original cryptocurrency, you might naturally ask whether you should consider investing in Bitcoin? There is no transparent black and white answer. You will have to see the advantages and disadvantages and assess whether it is worth the risk.

First of all, Bitcoin is the world's largest cryptocurrency at this point, and if Bitcoin were to fail, it could cripple the entirety of the cryptocurrency community. Whether or not you want to fund in Bitcoin entirely depends on your risk tolerance, as well as the objectives you have in mind,

The first advantage tagged to Bitcoin is that it is indeed a fast and very affordable service. Anyone knows the time and costs of sending money overseas can be staggeringly high, often discouraging people from even considering such payments. However, when you make the transfer via Bitcoin, the cost is minimal, if at all existent, as the middleman is removed. Also, there is no limit as to where you can send Bitcoin. Considering it works within the digital realm, there are no rules in that specific manner. The world of internal payments and receiving payments is far less regulated.

Because Bitcoin is decentralized, it doesn't have the regulations that exist with every legal tender. It means it cannot be created by the government nor distributed by any means in the central bank. Decentralization removes the big power fiat money (regulated-legal tender, such as dollars, rupees, euros) tends to have over people, and no authority can freeze, charge, or remove the coins from your ownership.

When it comes to Bitcoin itself, there are reduced risks of fraud at play, as well as higher levels of transparency. You can complete any transactions without giving away any of your information to the seller, allowing you to remain anonymous. So the openness will enable you to work on the transactions at any time of day freely. In contrast, anonymity allows your personal and private information to be protected from anyone who might try and exploit your data.

Nevertheless, there is a flip side to this story, where Bitcoin's risk of loss. If any wallet files or hardware files crash and get corrupted, then you would have officially lost your Bitcoin. There is genuinely nobody that can be done to retrieve the information, so the loss is genuine. That means you have to be forever cautious of viruses, which can play the same role as a hardware crash and cause the loss of your money.

Economy and customer protection may also work as a hindrance towards Bitcoin. That is because there are likely to be a lot of hidden frameworks or loopholes in the design yet to be exploited. That means that Bitcoin is quite a risky choice, regardless of how you reduce the risk.

Furthermore, like any other form of cryptocurrency, Bitcoin is volatile and unpredictable (as proved in the timeline above). That suggests that there will always be a level of uncertainty despite any analyses and predictions. So keep in mind, if anyone tells you they can guarantee results in cryptocurrency, they are either a desperate and lying advertiser, or they are a scammer because anyone with the proper and thorough knowledge and crypto will tell you that in this market, including Bitcoin, nothing is guaranteed.

The Future Of Bitcoin

That may make you consider why people even try to predict the direction in which Bitcoin will go. Despite the level of unpredictability, people still try to forecast the weather. Forecasting occurs to be best prepared for what is to come, especially when people risk money in investing. It's only fair to get some idea of what could happen and whether or not they should continue with a particular investment over a certain period. With Bitcoin, there are two opposite ideas of what people believe will happen. One sways to the negative, while the other sways to the positive. It is up to you to determine which one you think is more likely to occur and make your choices accordingly.

Ever since the COVID-19 pandemic, more people have been reverting to the digital form of money out of fear of recession and potential market crashes. That means that the popularity of cryptocurrency has been on a rapid rise as more and more people accept and use it.

First, let's look at why people believe Bitcoin will fail, while others seem to think it will succeed in the decades to come. There is no real value when it comes to Bitcoin. The only value that exists is what people perceive it to be. That means the market can swing around like a crazed pendulum, where the volatility adds to the risk. It does not carry the same amount of confidence and certainty which a fiat contains.

Second, there is no force out there to stabilize Bitcoin. Fiat currencies have a government to back them up and defend them if push comes to shove (this does not mean that a legal tender will never fail, because they have before). Still, it does mean that if there is a force or pressure on a particular currency, it has protection. Bitcoin does not have this, and in some countries, they have even made the use of Bitcoin and other cryptos illegal. Therefore, there is no considerable power or power to back this cryptocurrency.

Third, Bitcoin is actually in competition with national currencies. Many people are claiming the value of Bitcoin, trying to have it replace the traditional monetary system. That links it back to the reality that a governmental system is not backing up Bitcoin, but if Bitcoin poses too large of a threat to the country, it could just as quickly be banned and left for scrap in the long term. That is fatal for specific financial systems, meaning the government will eliminate the threat.

Finally, investing in Bitcoin is not the same as investing in blockchain technology itself, which is the driving point of value in cryptocurrency. Keep in mind; it is pretty easy to separate the two, using the blockchain for other purposes, such as other forms of digital money or even anonymous voting. Blockchain is likely also to be used when fiat currency becomes fully digital, thus kicking out the value Bitcoin has had from the start.

All these reasons are massive and overwhelming, making you believe in Bitcoin's destruction. Yet again, there is a flipside to this. Here are the reasons people believe that Bitcoin will never fail in the future.

First, a tight-knit community has ensured Bitcoin's survival from the beginning. Even though Bitcoin had had its fair share of crashes and issues, it never seemed to drop to the point of no return. Bitcoin has always been able to make a comeback because of the community supporting it, alongside many technology developers working to advance the features of Bitcoin and developers focusing on improving the design. The district also tends to be active on social media, using telegram to communicate the latest updates, news, and information about Bitcoin. There are many people focused on Bitcoin's overall well-being, which is a massive benefit: knowing people are looking out for this cryptocurrency, especially considering its value is based on the opinion of people and not as a legal tender (fiat money).

Second, Bitcoin is, for the most part, transparent. That is always ideal for any group, making it very easy to see how Bitcoin is mined and how people can indeed evaluate a transaction. The created innovations work as they should, and the blockchain's integrity's commerce is confirmed.

Third, Bitcoin also passes the test of real-world usage. That is when people can use Bitcoin for various reasons around the globe. Bitcoin is also used as a template for other cryptocurrencies, where the vast majority of crypto's original ideas start with Bitcoin itself. That means Bitcoin's design and the idea remain one of the most popular ones to this day.

More and more people, as well as businesses, are accepting Bitcoin's nature, especially merchants. El Salvodor was the first country to adopt Bitcoin as a legal tender. That means more and more people are starting to trust the nature of Bitcoin despite the risk, and its popularity keeps on growing. Bitcoin users can even use payment cards these days, and Bitcoin ATMs are even available for use. That shows the reality that some countries are accepting Bitcoin instead of fearing it, as some other countries do.

WHY BITCOIN AND CRYPTO STAND GENERATING NEW WEALTH EVEN TODAY

Is It Also Late To Invest?

As a newbie, there is something you need to know before you dive into investing in cryptocurrency so that you can get off to a good start, you can sleep well at night, and you can manage your crypto assets like a boss!

Before getting into cryptocurrencies, you need to know that you are your bank. You and only you control your money, and no one else controls it for you, so you are also solely responsible for it. Unlike the standard banking system, which prevents you in every way by offering you an entire system that handles your money and your many transactions, you don't have this privilege with cryptocurrencies. Because of this, you might feel a bit scared, but I can assure you that your bank has its benefits, one of them being that you are not ridiculously charged for every transaction you make on your account. You can also choose to create a wallet from anywhere in the world and send and receive without going into any buildings to fill out forms or wait in long lines! Especially since you are your bank, you must keep your currencies safe and your device. I have tried to synthesize and simplify this as much as possible this aspect to give you a clear overview and so that you can draw your conclusions. Many investors believe that the value of a single Bitcoin to $500,000 in the next five years.

Since its beginnings, bitcoin has had growth to date of + 2.628.458% and has an average increase of 200% per year, and Ethereum has grown by +1.359.126% has an average growth of 250% per year despite ups and downs.

We can see that even if you were to keep your cryptocurrencies in a hardware portfolio (without trading), they would be able to generate substantial gains and revolutionize your finances, unlike stocks, bonds, or precious metals.

Despite the deliberate misinformation of the mass media, it is absurd that even today, some people do not realize the real earning potential in both the short and long term and the value they represent.

Only an insane person with a DeLorean from Back to the Future would travel back in time and wouldn't buy the shares of Cocacola!!!!

Perhaps the lack of a clear overview hinders the minds of those who think they can enter the market today with 100$ and exit tomorrow with a million dollars without even contemplating the fact that Bitcoin represents above all the decentralized alternative to the central bank and the blockchain will eliminate all those institutional amount and costs of intermediaries that until today have kept us in check.

The massive investments by institutions directed towards Bitcoin are further confirmation.

Wall Street, billionaires, and even blue-chip companies are heavily getting in on the action.

Another opportunity to multiply your Bitcoins and your cryptocurrencies are trading. Still, to teach you this, I would need another book where, in addition to illustrating my / our method, we should address the critical point or manage the various emotional aspects that determine the 87% of trader's losses. In comparison, the other 10% of failures are caused by "whales" who deliberately blow all the stop loss and then buy. However, I want to show you the three bots (DCA bot and grid bot) that I usually use with great satisfaction with 30% of my capital that I hold on the exchange so that you can, if you want, start to understand how they work.

Bots for cryptocurrency are robots used in the investment of digital assets. A crypto Bot or Robot for cryptocurrency works through algorithms to automate certain functions and procedures, replacing a human person. The fundamental aspect of each bot is the setting of its parameters that, if done correctly, 'art allows you to make considerable gains without having to stay attached hours and hours to the computer.

Here they are:

- 3 Commas (free)
- Tradesanta
- Bitsgap
- Trading and Investing in Bitcoin

If you like to understand how to trade and invest in bitcoins, BTC is the symbol used to represent a cryptocurrency.

To achieve a high claim on your crypto assets, you can begin with a savings account. This type of accounts can pay you up to twelve percent. However, you can experience some risks with this type of account.

Despite the volatility of the Bitcoin market, you invest in Bitcoin the way you do stocks.

Here are the processes to follow:

- Sign up for a brokerage account at an organization that allows investment in bitcoins.
- Transfer funds from your bank to a brokerage account.
- Use those deposited funds (cash balance) to buy cryptocurrencies or, precisely, bitcoin.

- Sell your stocks when you feel you can get some profits.
- After the sales, funds are retransferred into your account and added to the cash balance.

These procedures could vary with each trading platform. Also, you can acquire Bitcoins using your credit cards. Another way is to transfer funds directly from your account to the bank. Other platforms accept a direct transfer of Bitcoins into their exchanges.

Here are some areas where you can trade and invest in bitcoin:

- BlockFi: Enables you to lend and earn interest on your assets. You can also borrow in addition to your help.
- Gemini: Focuses on the protection of investors' assets.
- Binance: A cryptocurrency platform for trading
- Robinhood: Provides free crypto trade on the platform. Invest in Robinhood, and you get a free share of stocks.
- Coinbase: You invest with U.S. dollars and buy Ethereum, Litecoin, bitcoin, and others.
- Bitcoin IRA: Here, you exchange currency, but your profits are taxed accordingly.
- Fundamental Analysis of Bitcoin

When you do a significant investigation of Bitcoin, with the end goal of putting resources into it, you should utilize various measurements to what you would use for a bond or stock.

It is, in any case, a significant advance to take before you bounce in and toss your cash at it. In the first place, you need a comprehension of Bitcoin, and once you have that, you can proceed with your examination of it as a sound venture.

Find out about the job that Bitcoin plays as a cash frame and assess things like the all-out inventory.

Likewise, you can follow all Bitcoin exchanges, and you can get a gander at the creation details. Make yourself mindful of the number of wallets, both existing and recently made. That will give you a smart thought of the information and the patterns you need to consider.

Technical Analysis Of Bitcoin

One of the primary considerations that feature venture development and give you a reason for exchanging is when the interest is referred to can be assessed.

Bitcoin has been at present for a very long time, and there has been adequate exchanging on Bitcoin trades that make a specialized investigation suitable.

When it was first presented and was daintily fanned out, it was powerless against wide swings in cost, and when a venture resembles that, it is hard to apply the specialized investigation rules.

So, Should I Invest In Bitcoin?

Incredible growth. Even though Mt. Gox caused a genuine misfortune, Bitcoin has recuperated monstrously and is currently on the way to fast development. Only a few months prior, the estimation of Bitcoin shot past one official ounce of gold worth and is presently encountering much greater edges over the cost of gold. If you had contributed years prior, say $100 in 2011, your venture would now be worth around $600,000.

Fixed supply. The authority Bitcoin site says, "Bitcoin is expected to blow up in its initial years and become stable in its later years... With a stable money-related base and a steady economy, the estimation of the cash ought to continue as before." Although quite possibly a lower supply of cash will bring about individuals storing it and subsequently causing collapse, this isn't probably going to happen to Bitcoin because we realize that the stock is fixed.

Effective diversification. Bitcoin is quickly beginning to be observed more truly by financial backers. It was scarcely known about; presently, it's all over. There are Bitcoin-explicit booths now for exchanging, and the money is being used practically consistently for exchanges, interchange, and venture. Appropriation rates are up, and trust has been reinforced altogether.

Coinbase, Binance, Cash App, Paypal, And Other Answers For Trading Cryptocurrency

Coinbase has restricted "altcoins" (Bitcoin options like Ethereum, Ripple, and Litecoin). Accordingly, numerous brokers utilize famous crypto-to-crypto-centered trades like Binance, Bittrex, and Kraken to get to a more extensive cluster of crypto resources.

To achieve admittance to a more extensive scope of coins, a broker or speculator may utilize more than one trade, accomplishing something like purchasing Bitcoin on Coinbase utilizing USD, and afterward sending their Bitcoin to Binance to exchange Bitcoin for other cryptos (changing over back to Bitcoin to sell on Coinbase when they are finished).

With the above covered, few out of every odd dealer/financial specialist will need to or have the option to manage cryptographic forms of money straightforwardly. Fortunately, there are some circuitous choices also. These include:

An application like Square's Cash App, PayPal, or Robinhood (TIP: For the individuals who would prefer not to go the Coinbase course, Square's Cash App is an incredibly decent beginning stage for newcomers who need to purchase/sell Bitcoin and in any case keep things basic).

A digital money IRA (these have downsides like charges, yet they can be essential decisions for long-haul contributing).

A stock identified with digital money such as MicroStrategy, Bakkt, Coinbase, or Riot Blockchain (these offer circuitous openness to digital currency).

Presently, a few merchants will be acquainted with more specialized exchanges and won't be US-based. These brokers might need to take a stab at utilizing influence, for instance, on Coinbase Pro or Kraken, or may even consider crypto "subordinates" like prospects and alternatives offered by stages like Bakkt, CME, FTX, or BitMEX. Influence and subsidiaries aren't novice benevolent; however, they can bode well for prepared merchants new to crypto. Every option has its advantages and disadvantages, yet prominently, just a trade agent wallet crossover like Coinbase/Coinbase Pro permits one to exchange, contribute, store, send, and get coins straightforwardly utilizing a solitary stage. Use Cash App if you need to maintain things straightforward and purchase Bitcoin, use PayPal or Robinhood on the off chance that you need a more extensive yet restricted determination, use Coinbase on the off possibility that you are organized for genuine digital money contributing and exchanging, and ultimately whenever you have dominated Coinbase move onto Coinbase Pro, Binance, and Bittrex to get a more extensive choice of crypto resources. Binance is an Exchange used worldwide and is undoubtedly the most famous, reliable, and suitable for beginners and experienced users who want advanced features. In a short time, Binance has surpassed all the competition because the platform is studied in detail. Binance is used to exchange Digital Assets, namely cryptocurrencies, and in 2019 it was awarded as the best Exchange site. One of the essential advantages of Binance is the meager commissions, and also, the customer service is always on 24 hours a day to support users.

DECENTRALIZED FINANCE

DeFi is short for Decentralized Finance. But, in essence, DeFi refers to the use of cryptocurrency or blockchain technology to disrupt the usual financial models run by intermediaries. Bain Capital Venture's partner states that people like DeFi because "they have a libertarian streak."

While Ethereum uses blockchain technology to create smart contracts for various applications.

The one application of DeFi – cryptocurrency – has already rattled the world. The idea behind cryptocurrency was also to take money out of the government's clutches. Fiat currencies are heavily influenced by government policy. Wall Street can halt trading and get bailed out if the market does not behave well. Centralized banks can make bad decisions, push economies into recession, and still get stimulus packages from Federal reserves to bounce back. DeFi is the ultimate financial equalizer that takes power out of the hands of a few and places it in the hands of the many. DeFi is controlled by vast computer networks, investors, traders, and miners. Its movement lies entirely outside the jurisdiction of governments or any other central authority. Along with privacy and anonymity, DeFi promises newfound levels of freedom.

DeFi is a giant step towards this freedom. It promises an ecosystem where people can use the existing and familiar financial instruments without working under the shadow of a central authority. Managing Partners of the $100 million crypto fund, Dragonfly Capital, puts it succinctly, "The goal of DeFi is to rebuild the banking system for the whole world in this open, permissionless way. You only get that shot every 50 years."

Many examples around the world highlight the need to replace current financial institutions with decentralized finance. But none illustrate that need more tragically than the failed state of Venezuela.

Venezuela is a resource-rich country. With plentiful oil reserves, it had become one of the wealthiest countries in South America. A steep drop in international crude oil prices and poor governance leads to financial ruin despite its natural wealth. Incredibly, the country went from being among the wealthiest to becoming one of the poorest countries in the region. At its worst, the annual inflation rate in Venezuela was 350,000% in 2019. While the drop in crude oil prices was a setback, the government and the federal banks created the calamity.

This failure at the very top makes a case for DeFi even stronger. With DeFi, people no longer have to worry about their life savings being destroyed by the somewhat subjective factor of political will. With DeFi the national Flag flying over your head becomes irrelevant to your financial life. People will be empowered to conduct business from anywhere in the world. So, they can move funds, invest in different asset classes, and enjoy greater control over their financial future.

While the Venezuelan economy offers a compelling case study, the more recent upheaval in the financial markets has again shed light on the necessity of going the DeFi route. If there is a time for DeFi to make a grand entrance, the GameStop fiasco was it.

If you are not aware, here is a little background for you – GameStop is a chain of retail stores standard fixture across malls in the United States. For a long time, the company's fundamentals had been poor. Why would a computer-savvy gamer visit a physical store instead of downloading the game online? Their sales had been dropping consistently, and in 2019 they touched a new low of $1.8billion. With no rebound plan, the company was doomed. Undoubtedly, it was a bad investment. Big Wall Street hedge funds like Melvin Securities and Citadel Securities thought likewise. Citadel Securities is the biggest customer of Robinhood. Both these hedge funds held millions of Gamestop shares. Their strategy was to short the Gamestop shares, push the company to its end, and get out with a profit of millions of dollars.

But a subreddit had other plans. A small group of investors contributing to the Reddit thread called WallStreetBets saw the goal of the Wall Street elite. They wanted to put the power back in the hands of GameStop's unsuspecting small retail investors and give the black suits a taste of their own medicine. And boy, they did. The market capitalization of GameStop went from $650 million in the latter half of 2020 to $28billion on January 28.

But what happened next hammered home the need for a DeFi system. Robinhood stepped in. The ironically existing platform to "democratize finance for all" prevented retail customers from buying and selling the GameStop stock. Reportedly, this was done under pressure from the significant hedge funds. Other similar platforms like E-Trade and Ameritrade mirrored the move. But Robinhood took the heat from the investors. A Twitter storm ensued that resonated the need for a system without censorship.

Cryptoexhchange Gemini's President said, "The pandemic made people appreciate #Bitcoin as an inflation hedge. The de-platforming of Wall Street Bets is making everyone appreciate its censorship resistance." (honestly, this event is what caused us to want to complete this book so quickly, Defi is my personal 1776, my 4th of July, my Declaration of Independence ~Shawn)

Blockchain's founder also chimed in, "A shot across the bow for institutional investors everywhere, there's incredible power in decentralized groups of individuals, and the future of finance will be built less like Wall Street and more like the internet: by a decentralized group of individuals. My thoughts and prayers are with the many institutions that will learn this lesson the hard way."

Many other financial experts and gurus joined Blockchain and Cryptoexchange in condemning the heavy-handed censorship that was on display during the GameStop incident.

Unlike Wall Street, a cryptoexchange makes it impossible for such events to occur in the first place. Even if the promoter of a cryptoexchange is influenced, they have no control over the flow of its funds which is ensured by its distributed nature and democratic functioning.

DeFi is of the people, for the people, and by the people. That's by immutable design.

MINIMIZING LOSSES AND MAXIMIZING GAINS

Trading in crypto with an understanding of the market is either a very lucrative or costly venture. Most common crypto traders will probably lose money, but experienced investors can profit and, more importantly, protect themselves against massive losses.

To understand how a loss is inevitable, let us consider that the price of a currency can change in two ways: up or down.

If we buy coins when the market is up, we will probably benefit from this increase. But if we buy coins when the market is down, we will probably lose money.

Some trading techniques can help us trade effectively, minimizing losses and maximizing gains. But there is no way to turn a loss into a profit or vice-versa.

Losses Are Inevitable In Crypto Trading

To begin with, let us consider that it is not a good idea to trade on margin; margin trading provides unlimited leverage and, therefore, more potential profits and more significant losses.

If you trade on margin, you will have to pay interest daily. And there is the risk of being liquidated if your trading balance falls below a certain percentage of your total deposit (25%). That means that your broker will start selling parts of your portfolio to reduce the amount you owe.

For this reason, we can say that losses are inevitable in crypto trading.

Our goal should be to minimize losses and maximize gains by employing various strategies. Here are some guidelines:

As we know, buying low and selling high is a good rule for any trading strategy, but it is essential when the market moves up or down very fast. The market may be going up or down very fast but, in a short period, the price usually crosses the critical resistance/support levels, and that can make a solid upward movement (bull move) or a solid downward movement (bear activity). To maximize gains, we should always buy low and sell high. We should believe when the price is below the critical support level and sell it above significant resistance for a bullish move. For a bearish move, we should sell when the price is above necessary support and buy below this level. All the time doing this, we are maximizing our gains. The same strategy can be used in a sideways market, and it will always give us a significant positive return.

Never Stick To One Trading System.

Being too optimistic or pessimistic about the market can destroy any trading strategy. In case of an upward trend, traders will usually buy high and sell low; in a downward trend, they will usually buy low and sell high. Both strategies are wrong and should be avoided. So we must keep in mind that it is better to buy low and sell high, but we must also protect ourselves against massive losses. The best way to do this is to keep our trading system as simple as possible. For example, when the market is going up, it may be good to buy low and sell high, but this strategy alone will not always make our profit. Many other factors must be considered, such as support and resistance levels, MACD momentum indicators, Fibonacci retracements, and potential trend reversals. So, we must add indicators to our trading strategy to avoid sticking to one trading system too much or ignoring some of these critical indicators.

Always have a finish loss and a take profit—in simple terms, having a stop loss means defining at what price we will automatically sell our coins. Having a profit means defining at what price we will automatically buy coins. Having these two levels defined, we will always know the exact amount of cash we can lose. There is no way to avoid losses, but this strategy helps us to understand how much of our investment capital is really at risk and how much money we can earn or lose. Prevent loss and take profit should be placed carefully when the market moves very fast upwards or downwards to prevent unnecessary losses or too big profits.

Do Not Panic.

We have our stop loss and take profit levels, so what should we do when the price goes below our level? Many people would sell at a meager price and book the loss. That's a bad idea. We should stick to our trading system and never sell automatically below our stop loss or take profit levels without analyzing the situation first. If we do that, we will eventually lose all our investment capital. We must be patient and wait patiently for the right time to sell.

WHICH CRYPTOCURRENCIES SHOULD YOU TRADE AND WHY?

Cryptocurrencies To Invest In 2021

The best cryptocurrencies. It's enough to think about such a list to make many of the best investors snicker.

Warren Buffett, the trading rock star, named Bitcoin rat poison, a mirage and useless. He also noted that since "they do not produce anything," cryptos are practically worthless.

Carl Icahn went on record labeling cryptocurrencies as "ridiculous." But at least he also noted that to appreciate them, he may be too old.

The owner of the Dallas Mavericks, Mark Cuban, has said he'd rather have bananas than Bitcoin. At least you can eat bananas, after all. But for more than 150,000 bananas, you could also sell a single Bitcoin. That may not be the funny advice provided by Mr. Shark Tank.

Then there's CEO Jamie Dimon of JPMorgan Chase. He is referred to as a "fraud" in digital currency. He also said that people foolish enough to buy it would pay the price for it in the future. It turns out he was close. Bitcoin investors were paying the price. And a sizeable one at that.

And though it's been a few years. And "the fools" who jumped in on Bitcoin have seen a return on their investment during their 2017 highs. And it was even luckier for those who waited until the 2017 crypto frenzy died down.

If something has been proved in the past year, cryptocurrencies have far more staying power than the naysayers assumed. And that it is most definitely a worthwhile effort to list the best cryptocurrencies.

Close to 6,000 separate cryptocurrencies are out there. And the space they take on your hard drive isn't worth a whole bunch of them. For instance, take internet darling Dogecoin. This altcoin was developed in 2013 and cracked into uncharted territories only recently when worth an entire cent.

But this also helps to clarify part of the cryptocurrency draw. There are plenty of people out there who threw a few hundred bucks at it when it was worth a bit of a cent a while ago. A single Dogecoin was worth $0.001774 in March of 2020.

Less than a year, fast forward, and a buy-and-hold strategy (or hold, if you will) would have brought upwards of 460% returns. No matter what type of investment it is, that's a solid return. That takes us to the best cryptocurrencies to pick up and hold for the near future.

The Highest Investment In 2021 Cryptocurrencies:

Bitcoin (BTC)

Sure, it's one of the most obvious. But for a good reason, that is. There's something to tell, after all, about the cryptocurrency that started it all. With a market cap of over $600 billion, it's the most prominent cryptocurrency out there, without question.

But it keeps many potential investors on the sideline with its steep price. But the situation doesn't need to be that. I just happened to have $17 worth of Bitcoin picked up in my Robinhood account.

Sure, that just scored me a Bitcoin number of 0.00046577. But I am introduced to the tiny holding stills of the most popular and one of the best cryptocurrencies out there.

Ethereum (ETH)

There's a Robin for every Batman. And while Bitcoin leads the crypto roost, Ethereum is a solid second fiddle with lots of upside potential. Like Bitcoin, enthusiasts regarded Ethereum as an alternative to fiat money. But the blockchain technology (AKA database) is more oriented than digital currency on decentralized applications. But that did not slow the rapid increase in value of this AltCoin.

It allows decentralized applications to be designed and run without fraud or third-party intervention when running as a software platform (take that Apple and Google). With its cryptographic token, the applications run on its platform operate. That makes this crypto a sought-after one within this network by developers looking to build and run apps.

Ethereum is also one of the few cryptos that can buy other cryptocurrencies on exchanges. Though its market cap pales next to Bitcoin's, it has steadily made headway. And with momentum on its hand, Ethereum is a simple option for one of the finest available cryptocurrencies.

Litecoin (LTC)

This crypto, which former Google employee Charlie Lee created, has several similarities with its big brother, Bitcoin. It was designed to increase transaction times (approximately 2.5 minutes) and lower transaction fees. It has a block generation rate considerably faster than Bitcoin. And the number of merchants accepting Litecoin is increasing rapidly, unlike most cryptos.

As the use of Litecoin becomes more popular, it is fair that its value will only increase. Whether you want to keep it and watch it grow or use it as a form of payment, that makes this one of the best cryptocurrencies out there.

Bitcoin Cash (BCH)

Bitcoin Cash will hold a unique position in cryptocurrency history forever. It's one of the earliest rough Bitcoin forks. And the most effective, up to now.

Since cryptos are decentralized in nature, no changes can be made without a consensus when there is controversy about potential problems to its underlying code. If miners and developers do not reach an agreement, it is possible to break the digital currency or fork it.

There was a heated discussion about Bitcoin's scalability in this situation. The same Bitcoin remained. And with changes to its code, Bitcoin cash was developed. This code shift increased the size of blocks from one megabyte to eight. That caused transaction times to be much faster.

While it still has some catching up to do with some of its rivals, the scalability of Bitcoin Cash could cause the value to accrue much faster than most of the competition.

Binance Coin (BNB)

Binance is the world's biggest volume-based crypto-currency exchange. And it's not near either. Of course, the official token of the Binance trade is Binance Coin. It enables users with smooth efficiency to trade in other cryptos. Transaction payments may also be simplified by Binance Coin and pay for products and services. The Binance Card is also available now. It encourages people to pay for stuff just as they would with their standard credit card. The sole distinction is that they load up the card with Bitcoin or Binance Coin and pay for groceries or a new brutal crypto wallet.

Binance Coin is undoubtedly one of the best available cryptocurrencies based on usability alone. And it is also the most accessible, as of right now.

To Date The Not-So-Great Cryptocurrencies

Two of the biggest cryptos that didn't make this list skipped it for two significant reasons. One is under inquiry. The other still doesn't exist.

For years, Ripple (XRP) has become one of the most commonly recognized cryptos. It has had similar ups and downs in value, much like the others. But while many are growing upwards, in a significant way, Ripple is floundering. Ripple scored a big hit at the end of 2020, and it's unclear how long the harm will last. But it'll be for a while, in all probability.

At the end of 2020, the Securities and Exchange Commission (SEC) filed suit against Ripple Labs Inc and two of its managers. The claims are that, through an unregistered digital asset protection offering, $1.3 billion was raised. It is a big no-no. And Ripple's price has been falling significantly. Is it going to rise to its former heights? To be seen, that remains. But investors should steer clear for now. Or be exceedingly weary at the very least.

There's Diem, then (formerly known as Libra). Perhaps it's the most hyped-up crypto ever. Heck, Congress is responsible for attempting to wrap its collective brain around precisely what cryptocurrency is. While it is no shock that our politicians are still mainly in the dark, the opportunity allowed the future cryptocurrency of Facebook to be in the spotlight for a lot of time. And it wouldn't be too surprising if name recognition rewards early adopters when it's published later this year.

RESOURCES FOR PERSONAL PORTFOLIO MANAGEMENT

What Is A Portfolio In Cryptocurrency?

A cryptocurrency portfolio is a collection of cryptocurrencies that an individual holds. It may be a diversified investment vehicle, or it may be used to track the holdings' values to determine profit and loss.

What Are The Different Types Of Cryptocurrency Portfolios?

There are two types of portfolios: Technical Analysis Portfolios and Fundamental Analysis Portfolios.

Technical Analysis Portfolio

A Technical Analysis Portfolio is created by buying a certain number of coins based on price charts. Typically, technical analysis involves price patterns that indicate whether the cash will increase or decrease. Technical charts are popular among people who use bots to conduct arbitrage trading. An arbitrage trader simultaneously buys and sells an asset to profit from the mismatch in the price across exchanges.

Fundamental Analysis Portfolio

A Fundamental Analysis Portfolio is created by buying certain coins because you believe in their fundamentals. Fundamental analysis involves looking at the history of a currency or an investment and determining the reason for its price.

For example, you might buy Bitcoin. After all, you believe it will be accepted as a form of payment or own Litecoin because you think it will be used as a payment form.

How To Build A Portfolio?

There are three steps to building your portfolio in cryptocurrency:

- Create an account on an exchange

- Purchase your first coins

- Start investing your coins.

Where To Create An Account On An Exchange?

Each exchange has a different process for creating a new account. If you are using Luno, then click here. On Coinbase, click here. On Poloniex, click here. If you are using Binance, click here. Our recommendation is to use Coinbase or Poloniex—these two exchanges process thousands of transactions per minute and have a simple user interface with similar functionality across each platform. They also have the most trading pairs for Bitcoin.

How To Use An Exchange?

Exchanges can seem daunting with so many features and functions, but there are essentially only four things you can do on a discussion:

- Deposit. Deposit Bitcoin into your fund by heading to the "Balances" page, searching for and clicking the bitcoin icon, then clicking "Deposit." This will bring up a wallet address to send bitcoins from your wallet or exchange account.

- Note that you can deposit bitcoins from an exchange account or your wallet.

- Buy. To buy BTC, you need to go to "Exchange," and enter the BTC amount you want to buy, and click "Buy." Also, suppose your country doesn't support Bitcoin. In that case, you can always purchase it on a different exchange with a foreign currency by clicking the currency symbol (the yellow one) for Bitcoin, then clicking "Buy."

- Sell. If you want to market your coins, then go back to the "Balances" page, find the bitcoin icon, and then click "Sell."

- Withdraw. If you want to withdraw your cryptocurrencies to a personal wallet, click "Withdraw."

At this point, you're ready to start investing in cryptocurrencies!

Keeping Track of Your Portfolio Value and Profit/Loss

Since crypto coins are volatile, it is essential to track your portfolio's value as time passes. You could follow the fiat currency value (USD) or cryptocurrency (BTC or ETH). We will look at both tracking methods here and recommend which one you should use.

WHAT IS THE BLOCKCHAIN & WHY IS IT SO DIFFERENT?

Looking About The Hood: Blockchain Technology

I f you have been conscious about online activities, you must have heard the term "Blockchain" or "Blockchain Technology" one time or the other.

Trading crypto coins requires a deep understanding of Blockchain technology and how it works. Blockchain is an I.T. computing technology that makes digital currencies possible.

Think of Blockchain as the functioning system of a computer. Without an operating system, you can't install software or other programs on your computer. The computer will be blank and useless without an O.S.

Blockchain is the operating network behind digital currencies. According to market reports globally, the demand for crypto coins has risen by over 35% since 2016. It's hard to trust anything digital, but Blockchain technology has consistently proven valuable, reliable, and secured.

Many digital agencies and companies worldwide are beginning to integrate blockchain networks into their daily activities. Although certain aspects of the Blockchain are still mystified, time will undoubtedly expose the unknown benefits of the system and how it can be harnessed.

A block is a unit or structure containing transactional data. Thousands of obstructions having a history of transactional data are linked together to form a chain. The result is a system known as the Blockchain system. This block can be likened to a digital ledger containing all the platform's transactions. The log is such that it records all transactions, debit, or credit that occur digitally, working like a highly organized financial system.

A block must be created to kickstart the process to start a transaction. There must also be authorization from the sender before any transaction can occur digitally. That makes the Blockchain system a very safe and secure platform for transacting.

The Blockchain ledger is similar to a google spreadsheet that contains an unending array of blocks or linked computers. There are millions of blocks containing transactional data. As transactions continue to take place, more and more blocks are created.

It means anyone can view a transaction history but cannot alter, change, or copy it. How cool is that?

Yes, Bitcoin and altcoins rely on the system to function. However, Blockchain isn't just a complex system supporting digital transactions. Blockchain has multiple other uses, some of which have not been discovered yet. Industries like: manufacturing, production, finance can also use the Blockchain system.

According to some sources, Blockchain is capable of replacing the internet. The possibility of this happening is not known for now. The advances of the system are still young.

Transactions on the Blockchain System

In the physical world, transferring funds requires having the recipient's bank details, routing, ABA, account number, and other private information before you can send funds. Once you send funds successfully, a transaction I.D. is generated. This ID contains all the necessary details of the transaction. However, this system has a particular flaw. The security system cannot be trusted, especially when dealing with massive amounts. The system can also be tampered with and influenced.

The most frustrating of all is that.

This system can be manipulated by governmental bodies involved and hijacked by fraudsters. This flaw is one of the reasons the Blockchain system of the transaction was established.

How Is The Blockchain System Different?

100% Security

The Blockchain system uses a secure and incorruptible algorithm to transact. You can view a user's data, but you can't make changes to it. To send funds, you need the authorized signature of the sender.

Decentralization

The Blockchain features a 100% decentralized system. The Government, bank, or financial bodies cannot interfere with the system. The transaction is based on mutual agreement between the sender and the recipient. The decentralization of this system means unrestricted, accessible, and unlimited transactions.

Automation

Going to the bank, standing queues are tiring. On the blockchain system, transactions can be automated. This means that you can trigger and program transactions to operate according to specific rules under certain requirements.

How Coins Are Formed

There are hundreds of digital coins in the market, with only a few in the front line, including Bitcoin, Ethereum, and Litecoin. Coins are shared digital records or assets that have a digital value. What this means is they exist virtually as a record or data.

Coins are formed through a process called "mining." To get the picture clearly, juxtapose mining to minting, the production of hard currency. Only the Central Bank of a Nation is licensed to produce hard cash. Coins are produced by a technical computing method known as mining in the digital world. Anyone with the resources and skill can mine coins.

Factors Affecting The Cryptocurrency Market

Like every other market, the crypto market dances to the tune of supply and demand. However, this market is not lopsided like the usual traditional market. Economic activities, political operations tend to influence traditional markets. The factors altering the crypto market are different.

Below are some characteristics that influence the price of coins in the market:

- Availability and supply of crypto coins. The total coins available daily affects the market. The rate of mining and creating currencies (pump rate) and the rate of lost and destroyed (dip rate) affect the market.

- Capitalization of the market. That is simply the accumulation of crypto coins in the system, the total accumulated value daily. The market's capitalization; the coin's value at specific periods affects trading.

- The media and press. Whatever the media portrays to the public becomes the principal opinion. That also can influence the price of coins.

- For example, Bitcoin spiked 20% after Elon Musk added #bitcoin to his Twitter bio (https://www.cnbc/2021/01/29/bitcoin-spikes-20%-after-elon-musk-adds-bitcoin-to-his-twitter-bio.html).

- Crypto integration systems. Sometimes, crypto demand becomes so high. Other times, it could become low. Some vendors require crypto coins to transact physically. For instance, in e-commerce, you can make payments using Crypto. Integration of crypto coins into existing infrastructure also influences the market.

- Actions within the system. Many things happen within the crypto space. Security updates, coin exchange, etc., all influence the crypto market. Whatever it may be, it somehow affects the market.

ALTCOINS

What Is Altcoin?

Altcoins are cryptocurrencies that don't include Bitcoin. The word 'Altcoin' combines two words, where alt means 'alternative' and the word coin means 'cryptocurrency.' Together, they include a cryptocurrency category, which is an alternative to Bitcoin, a digital currency. They share characteristics similar to Bitcoin but are different in other ways. For example, some altcoins use a different mechanism to produce blocks or verify transactions. Or, they differentiate themselves from Bitcoin by offering new or additional abilities, such as low-price volatility or intelligent contracts.

There are almost 9,000 cryptocurrencies as of March 2021. According to CoinMarketCap, altcoins will be considered for over 40% of the total crypto market in March 2021. They are derived from Bitcoin; Altcoin price changes tend to copy Bitcoin's trajectory. Most altcoins that have been released are built on the same blockchain technology that spreads bitcoin. This technology is already assisting more efficient and secure business transactions and transferring assets.

In the last few years, the altcoin market has been full of choices because of the expansion of cryptocurrency and the wave of programmers and developers looking to turn into cash in the rise of alternative payment systems.

How Do Altcoins Work?

There is a blockchain or a recording ledger in a cryptocurrency such as Altcoins. Generally speaking, altcoins work more like the original Bitcoin. Using a private key, users can send a payment from their digital wallet to another user's wallet. The transactions are publicly and permanently recorded, so exchanges can not be denied or altered after the fact.

This blockchain is secured through mathematics proofs which should confirm transactions in blocks.

Different Kinds Of Altcoins.

Depending on their features and consensus mechanisms, altcoins come in different categories. Below is a summary of some more essential Altcoins:

Mining-Based

Mining-based altcoins, as their name indicates, are mined into existence. Such coins are not developed by an algorithm but are issued before being listed in crypto markets. Most mining-based altcoins use Proof-of-Work (PoW), in which systems produce new coins by solving complex problems to create blocks. Examples of mining-based altcoins include Litecoin, Zcash, and Monero. Top of the altcoins dropped into the mining-based category in early 2020. Ripple's XRP is a sample of pre-mined cash.

- Stablecoins

Cryptocurrency use and trading have been noticeable by volatility since launch. Stablecoins aim to decrease this overall volatility by fixing their value to a basket of goods, such as precious metals, fiat currencies, or other cryptocurrencies. The basket acts as a reserve to reclaim holders if the cryptocurrency faces problems fails. Price variations for stablecoins are not directly meant to increase a narrow range.

Facebook's Diem, a social media behemoth, is the most famous example of a stable coin. Diem is a dollar-backed coin. Other examples of stablecoins are MakerDAO and USDC.

- Security Tokens

Security tokens are as similar as securities traded in stock markets. Security tokens resemble traditional stocks, and they frequently promise equity, a dividend pay-out to holders, or ownership form. The possibility of price appreciation for these tokens is an essential draw for investors to invest money into them. Besides, they have a digital source. Security tokens are generally provided to investors through the initial coin offerings or ICOs.

- Utility Tokens

Utility tokens are used to give services within a network. For example, they possibly used to redeem rewards or purchase services. Unlike security tokens, utility tokens are not part of an ownership stake or pay-out dividends. An instance of a utility token is Filecoin, used to purchase storage space in a network.

Is Altcoin Good Investment?

The market of altcoins is just beginning. In the prior decade, the number of altcoins listed in crypto markets has quickly multiplied and attracted a crowd of retail investors, excitedly betting on their price changes to amass short-term profits. But these investors do not have the necessary capital to generate adequate market liquidity.

In the case of Ethereum's ether, consider, which reached the highest value of $1299.95 on Jan 12, 2018. Not more than a month later, it was decreased to $597.36, and at the end of the year, ether's price had further crashed to $89.52. The record prices of Altcoin reached above $2,000 two years later.

But the problem is, the cryptocurrency markets are not mature yet. There are no defined investment standards or metrics to estimate cryptocurrencies despite several attempts. Most parts of the altcoin market were driven by speculation. Majority of the cases of dead cryptocurrencies, those which failed to gain adequate traction or disappear after gathering investors' money, exist.

Therefore, for investors, the altcoin market is ready to take on the massive risk of operating in a deregulated and known market prone to volatility. They should also be able to control stress arising from wild price swings. Cryptocurrency markets offer significant returns for these investors.

Advantages

Altcoins are "greater versions" of Bitcoin because the purpose is to plug the shortcomings of cryptocurrency.

Like stablecoins, altcoins can potentially accomplish Bitcoin's original promise of a means for daily transactions.

Certain altcoins, such as Ripple's XRP and Ethereum's ether, have already obtained traction among recognized institutions, which results in high valuations.

Investors can choose a wide range of altcoins that carry out different functions in the cryptocurrency economy.

Disadvantages

As compared to Bitcoin, altcoins have a comparatively smaller investment market. Bitcoin has a 60% share of the cryptocurrency market as of April 2021.

The regulation and explained criteria for investment mean that some investors and low liquidity characterize the altcoin market. As a result, as compared to Bitcoin, their prices are more volatile.

It is not always easy to distinguish between different and relevant altcoins, use cases, making investment decisions more complicated and confusing.

Various "dead" altcoins result in sinking investor dollars.

Top 10 Altcoins For 2021

There stand thousands of cryptocurrencies, from Bitcoin and Ethereum to Dogecoin and Tether; this can be overwhelming when first entering the crypto world. Following cryptocurrencies are the top 10 based on the market capitalization or the total value of all coins currently in circulation.

- Bitcoin (BTC)

Market cap: Over $641 billion

Bitcoin (BTC) is the first original cryptocurrency created in 2009 by an unknown person, Satoshi Nakamoto's pseudonym. As with many cryptocurrencies, BTC operated on a blockchain or a ledger register transactions distributed over a network of thousands of computers.

Bitcoin has become a family name; its price has soared. Five years ago, someone could buy a Bitcoin for about $500.But now, a single Bitcoin's price is over $33,000.

- Ethereum (ETH)

Market cap: Over $307 billion

Ethereum is a favorite for program developers, both a blockchain platform and a cryptocurrency, because of its possible applications, like the smart contracts that automatically carry out when conditions are met and non-fungible tokens (NFTs).

Ethereum has also experienced enormous growth. In just five years, its price proceeds from about $11 to over $2,500.

- Tether (USDT)

Market cap: Over $62 billion

Unlike other forms of cryptocurrency, Tether (USDT) is a stablecoin, which means it's backed by fiat currencies more like the Euro and the U.S. dollars and supposedly keeps the value equal to one of those denominations. That means that Tether's deal is expected to be more stable than other cryptocurrencies and is favored by investors who are very cautious of the excessive volatility of other coins.

- Binance Coin (BNB)

Market cap: Over $56 billion

The Binance Coin is a structure of cryptocurrency that a person can pay fees and trade on Binance, one of the world's largest crypto exchanges.

Since this coin launch in 2017 has spread past, ultimately facilitating trades on its Binance exchange platform. Now, it is used for payment processing, trading, or even booking travel arrangements. It can also be exchanged or traded for other cryptocurrencies, such as Bitcoin or Ethereum.

Its price was just $0.10 in 2017; by June 2021, it had increased over $350.

- Cardano (ADA)

Market cap: Over $51 billion

Later to the crypto scene, Cardano is noticeable for its early acceptance of proof-of-stake validation. This method accelerates transaction time and reduces energy usage and environmental effect by removing the competitive, problem-solving factor of transaction verification in platforms like Bitcoin. To enable decentralized applications and smart contracts, Cardano also works as Ethereum, which is powered by its native coin ADA.

Cardano's ADA token has had relatively slow growth compared to other major crypto coins. ADA's price was $0.02; in 2017, its price was $1.50, as of June 2021.

- Dogecoin (DOGE)

Market cap: Over $44 billion

Thanks to billionaires like Elon Musk and celebrities, Dogecoin has been a scorching topic. In 2013 famously started as a joke, Dogecoin quickly became a well-known cryptocurrency option, thanks to creating memes and a dedicated community. Unlike Bitcoin and many other cryptos, there is no limit on the Dogecoin numbers that can make, which leaves the currency sensitive to devaluation as supply increases. In 2017 price of one Dogecoin was $0.0002. By June 2021, its price had risen to $0.32.

- Ripple (XRP)

Market cap: Over $40 billion

XRP, created by similar founders as Ripple, a payment processing and digital technology company, can facilitate exchanges of various currency types, including fiat currencies and other famous cryptocurrencies.

The price of XRP at the beginning of 2017 was $0.006. As of June 2021, its price was at $0.92.

- USD Coin (USDC)

Market cap: Over $23 billion

USD Coin (USDC) is a stable coin like Tether, and, andU.S. dollars back, the goal is 1 USD to 1 USDC ratio. Ethereum also powers USDC, and users can use USD Coin to settle global transactions

- Polkadot (DOT)

Market cap: Over $21 billion

Cryptocurrencies may use several blockchains; Polkadot goals to merge them by creating a network that connects the different blockchains to work together. This combination may facilitate how cryptocurrencies are managed and have encouraged impressive growth as Polkadot's launch in 2020. Its price grew from $2.93 to $20.95 between September 2020 to June 2021.

- Uniswap (UNI)

Market cap: Over $13 billion

Uniswap (UNI) is an Ethereum-based token powered by Uniswap, a decentralized cryptocurrency exchange that uses an automated liquidity model for trading. That means no central facilitator, as a broker-dealer or bank. Instead, it is powered by smart contracts and pooled user resources. Uniswap's platform is open source, so anyone to creates their exchanges can use the code.

Difference Between Bitcoin And Altcoins

- Safety Tips Investing in Altcoin

The process of investing in cryptocurrency has been more straightforward over the last few months. Below are some important factors that investors must think about before buying a cryptocurrency:

- Location

To find out where and how to buy cryptocurrency is essential for investors to check their country's regulations.

- Payment Method

The most familiar and accepted payment methods include bank transfer, credit card, or even cash for buying cryptocurrency. Different exchanges accept different payment methods, so buyers need to choose a business that agrees with the payment method they want to use.

Type of Cryptocurrency

All cryptocurrencies are not available to purchase on every exchange. The buyer will have to find first a business that sells the cryptocurrency that he wants to buy.

Cost of Fees

Each exchange has different fees. Make sure how much will be fees cost before setting up an account.

TRADING PSYCHOLOGY

Trading With Emotions

It is common for traders to have their emotions and feelings jumbled up when day trading, from the highs and the lows they experience from the market. This is a far outcry from the confident self that a trader usually poses before the markets open, bubbling up with excitement over the money and profits they intend to make. Emotions in trading can mess up and impair your judgment and your ability to make wise decisions. Day trading is not carried out without feelings but rather as a trader. You should know how to work your way around them, making them work for your good. A precise level headed, and stable mind should be kept at all times, whether your profits are on the rise or a losing streak. That does not mean that you are supposed to disconnect from your emotions as a trader. A person cannot avoid feelings, but in the face of real market scenarios, you have to learn how to work on and around them. The personality type plays a considerable role in determining which kind of a trader they are. When opening up trades, the cautious traders are controlled mainly by fear, while the risky type is in the greed-motivated bandwagon. Fear and greed are such huge motivators that they go a long way in the layout of losses and profits.

Greed

A trader may be fueled to earn more money by checking their balances in their accounts and seeing it be as of a low level. While this may motivate them to work hard, some traders take it too far, earning a lot of money right then. They make mistakes while trading that have reverse effects than the intended ones. Such errors include an overtrade, taking unnecessary risks, among others.

Taking Unnecessary Risks

Greed for more money will convince the trader to take risks that are not worth it to achieve a specific financial threshold in the trading account. These will most likely end up in losses. The risky traders may take risks such as high leverage that they hope will work in their favor, but at the same time may have them making huge losses.

Making An Overtrade

Due to the urge to make more and more money, a trader may extend trading over long periods. Commonly these efforts are futile because the overtrading through market highs and lows put a trader in a place where their accounts can be wiped out due to greed—disregarding the time to trade and dive into opening trades without analysis will most likely result in a loss.

Improper Profit And Loss Comprehension

Wanting to earn a lot of money within a short period, a trader will not close a losing trade, maintaining the losses, and on the other hand, overriding on profit-making business until a reverse in the market happens, canceling out all the gains made. It is advisable to maximize and specialize in a prosperous trade and close a losing trade early enough, avoiding significant losses.

Fear

Fear can work in both directions, as a limit to an overtrade or a limit to making profits. A trader may close a trade to avert a loss, the action motivated by fear. A trader may also complete a business too early, even when on a winning streak in making gains, fearing that the market will reverse and there will be losses. In both scenarios, fear is the motivator, working in avoiding failure a success simultaneously.

The Fear To Fail

The fear of failing in trading may inhibit a trader from opening up trades and watching as the market changes and goes in cycles when doing nothing. The fear of falling in trading is an inhibitor to success. It prevents a trader from executing what could have been a successful trade.

The Fear To Succeed

This type of fear in trading psychology will make traders lose out their profits to the market when there is an opportunity to do otherwise. It works in a self-harming way in market scenarios. Such traders in this category fear to have too much profit and allow losses to run while they are aware of their activities and the losses they will make.

Bias In Trading

There are several market biases that a trader may tend to make that may be as a result of the emotions play, which traders are advised against. They include the tendency of overconfidence, confirmation, anchoring, and loss. In the psychology of trading, these biases may influence a trader to make unwise and uncalculated trading decisions that may prove to be loss-making ones. Even when the trading biases are in focus, as a trader, you have to be aware of your emotions and come up with ways to keep them under control and maintain a cool head in your trading window.

Bias In Overconfidence

It is a common occurrence with traders, especially new traders, that when you make a trade with huge profits, you get in euphoria in the state of winning. You want to go on opening up businesses with the belief that your analysis cannot go wrong, boiling down to the profits and gains you've made. That should not be the case. You, as a trader, cannot be too overexcited and overconfident in the analysis skills that you believe you cannot make a loss. The market is volatile, and therefore, the cards can change at any given time. When they do, the overexcited and overconfident trader now turns into a disappointed one. Get your market analysis right before opening up any trade, regardless of the former works, whether they were a loss or gain.

Bias In Confirming Trades

In trading psychology, the bias in confirmation of a trade you have already made, justifying it, is one factor that wastes a lot of time and money for traders. This type of bias is mainly associated with professional traders. After making a trade, they go back in evaluating and analyzing the work they just made, trying to prove that it was the correct one, whether they sailed according to the market. They waste a lot of time digging for the information they are already aware of. They could also prove that their mistake in opening an unfair trade and making a wrong move was correct. Nevertheless, the bias in confirmation occurs when a business they made turns out to be accurate, which strengthens their determination in their research skills, further pushing them to waste time proving to themselves already known facts. They could also lose money in the process, and it is, thus, advisable against this form of bias in trading.

Bias In Anchoring On Obsolete Strategies

This type of bias in the psychology of trading applies to the traders that rely so much on outdated information and obsolete strategies that do more harm than good to their trading success—anchoring on the correct but irrelevant information when trading might make the trader susceptible to making losses, a blow to the traders who are always lazy to dig up a new statement on the market. Keeping up with the current events and factors that may impact the market is critical for a successful trading career. Lazy traders will tire of keeping tabs with the ongoing economic and even political situations whose influence is exerted on the foreign exchange market. An example is that some traders will have a losing trade, but they hope that the markets will reverse their assumptions based on obsolete information and strategies. Carry out extensive research, be mindful not to be too time-consuming, and ensure you make trades with the correct data.

Bias In Avoiding Losses

Trading to avert losses usually boils down to the factor of fearsome traders whose trading patterns and their trading windows are controlled by fear of making losses. Having gains and making profits is not a motivation to them when fear hinders them from opening trades that could have otherwise been profitable. They also close pas trade too early, even when making profits in a bid to avert the losses, their potential losses. After carrying out a proper and detailed analysis on the market, go for making profits without being deterred with the bias of avoiding to cause a loss, for that holds many traders. Come up with a plan for your day trading to deal with doubts about the trades you are to make.

Psychology Affecting Traders' Habits

Psychological aspects affect habits in trading, the mistakes, and the winning strategies that a trader comes up with. Explained below are the negative habits that many traders make, with the influence of psychology on their practices.

Trading Without A Strategy

With no trading strategy and plan, a trader will face challenges with no place to refer to the expected result. A trader should draw a proper approach to be a referencing point when facing a problem in trading in the market. It should be a constructed plan detailing what to do in certain situations and which trading patterns to employ in different case scenarios. Trading without a strategy is akin to trading to lose your money.

Lack Of Money Management Plans

Money management plans are one of the main aspects of trading, and without solid strategies in this, it isn't easy to make progress in making gains in the trades opened. As a trader, you have to abide by certain principles that will guide you in spending your money in the account in opening up trades and ensuring that profits ensue from that. Without money management plans, a trader would be trading blindly with no end goal in mind, risking the money in non-profitable trades.

Wanting To Be Always Right

Some traders always go against the market, placing their desire for what manner they would like to behave in. They do not follow the sign that the market points to, but rather their philosophy, not doing proper analysis and always wanting to be correct. Losses ensue from such psychological habits. When the trading window closes, the market will always overrule the traders. Thus, a trader's want to be always proper against the market is overruled.

Looking At The Analysis

It's essential to understand how to perform a proper technical analysis to determine the value of a particular option and make sure you don't scare yourself away with any specific number. You might see a dip in a chart, or a price projection lower than you hoped, immediately becoming fearful and avoiding a particular option. Remember not to let yourself get too afraid of all the things you might encounter on any given trading chart. You might see scary projections that show a particular stock crashing, or maybe you see that it's projected to decrease by half.

Before you trust a specific trading chart, make sure you understand how it was developed. Someone that wasn't sure what they were doing might have created the display, or there's a chance that it was even dramatized as a method of convincing others not to invest. Always check sources, and if something is particularly concerning or confusing, don't be afraid to run your analysis as well.

THE BASICS OF CRYPTOCURRENCY TRADING AND INVESTMENT

The crypto market's volatility is why many people are interested in trading cryptocurrencies. Trading a crypto asset can give you a much higher ROI than you will get from traditional investments with the right timing.

As such, cryptocurrencies are generally high-risk investments. You need to know the fundamentals to trade them without losing your capital. It would aid if you also had a trading plan suited to your style. There are several trading strategies, but investors need to determine what works for them the most.

Usually, the goal of a cryptocurrency investor is either to accumulate a specific coin or to profit in the US dollar. In a bull market, you can quickly increase the value of your portfolio in USD. However, you will find it challenging to increase Bitcoin's value.

Since you stand the risk of losing your entire portfolio to the market through active trading, you are better off investing or holding (holding) – a concept which means buying a particular coin and holding on to it for a long time until the value is considerably increased.

Before starting, know that it's easier and much safer to invest in cryptocurrencies with solid use cases and a strong team behind them. You can obtain these details by reading the coin's white paper. That will provide insight into the intended use of the crypto and how it works.

Some of the hottest altcoins in 2021 so far run on decentralized finance blockchains. Defi tokens are those built on Ethereum's blockchain. Cryptos like Uniswap, Compound, Pancakeswap, etc., have increased over 500% in value in the past months.

If you are a risk-averse investor, staying away from the crypto market is better due to the high and constant price fluctuations. Sometimes, the prices fluctuate over 20% in a single day. But if you welcome risk and are looking for high ROI, follow the steps below to start trading.

Step 1: Register On A Cryptocurrency Exchange Platform

The first step is to create an account on a reputable crypto brokerage or exchange; Coinbase, Binance, and Gemini are the best exchanges. All three offer an easy-to-navigate user interface and a wide variety of altcoins to buy and sell.

To register an account, you need to provide your personal identification information. It is the same as opening a stock brokerage account, and some required information includes your social security number, email address, home address, and date of birth.

Step 2: Fund Your Account

Once you've signed up on the exchange, you will be requested to connect your bank account for trading. Most businesses allow you to find your account through wire transfers and debit cards. Since wire transfer is the cheapest funding option, you might want to consider that. Some exchanges even allow you to wire transfer with no charges or fees.

Step 3: Choose Altcoins To Trade Or Invest In

Most new and active traders allocate the most significant portion of their capital to Bitcoin and Ethereum since they are generally more predictable than the other altcoins. Predictability means that you can easily trade BTC or ETH with technical indicators.

A small portion of your capital should go toward altcoins with a smaller market cap. Although smaller markets have higher risk levels than large-market cryptocurrencies, their upside potential is more elevated.

Many altcoins have increased by 1000% in a matter of weeks or months, making them perfect for risk-tolerant traders or investors.

Step 4: Choose A Trading Or Investment Strategy

There are several market indicators, and most investors evaluate varying factors before buying and selling crypto. Experienced traders have one or two strategies that work for them. If you have a background in trading, you likely have a plan for stock trading.

Most of the strategies used in stock trading are also effective for the cryptocurrency market. One of the best strategies is the Elliot Wave Theory that uses the psychology behind market sentiments to analyze the market and trade. It is particularly effective for speculative assets, under which cryptocurrencies fall.

Step 5: Store Your Digital Currencies

If you want to be a vibrant trader, you must store your funds on the exchange to access them anytime you want to buy and sell. But if you plan to buy and hold for a while, you need a cryptocurrency wallet.

A few paragraphs back, you learned that you need a strategy to trade or invest in cryptocurrencies. Trading strategies organize the countless ways of profiting crypto into different coherent frameworks. You only need to find a framework that is suited to you.

When choosing or building your trading strategy, there are two things to consider: Technical Analysis (TA) and Fundamental Analysis (FA). Each trading strategy employs either of these two schools of thought. It's essential to understand what differentiates the two before moving further in your investment journey.

A trading strategy is an extensive plan or framework to guide you in your trading activities and endeavors. Its purpose is to mitigate investment risks by eliminating all unnecessary decisions. With a trading strategy, your chances of achieving your investment and trading goals are much higher.

While it isn't mandatory to have a trading strategy, it is lifesaving for people who are just getting started in the crypto market. When an unexpected event rattles the market, your system will define your reaction. That way, you won't have to react with emotions.

Essentially, a trading strategy or plan is a preventive measure against hasty, rash decisions that can cause substantial financial losses for a crypto trader. A typical system should include:

- The cryptocurrencies you want to trade
- The setups to take
- Tools and indicators
- Triggers for entries and exits
- How to record and evaluate your portfolio's performance

Additionally, the strategy may even contain some guidelines that are specific to you. For example, you might decide never to trade the market on Thursdays. In that case, you need to include that in your strategy.

The best way to create an effective trading plan is to combine multiple strategies instead of sticking to one.

Active Trading Strategies

Active trading strategies require you to monitor the market constantly and manage your portfolio. Therefore, they need plenty of time and attention from you. So, these strategies may not suit you if you are a busy person. But if you think you can dedicate the time and attention needed, you can try any of these strategies.

Day Trading

A common misconception in crypto is that all active traders are automatically day traders – that isn't true. Day trading is all about opening and closing positions within 24 hours. Day traders capitalize on the intraday price swings, meaning price movements within a single trading day. That is probably the most utilized active trading strategy.

The term itself originates from the traditional trading markets, where one can only open trades within specific day hours. Traders in such markets don't open positions overnight when trading is paused.

Most cryptocurrency trading platforms remain open 24/7, 365 days a year. So, the context of day trading is slightly different in crypto markets. It describes a short-term strategy where traders open and close positions within 24 hours or less.

Day traders use technical analysis and price action to form their trade ideas. They also use other techniques to detect market inefficiencies. This trading method is highly profitable for some, but it is also demanding, stressful, and subject to high risk. As such, it isn't recommended for you or any other amateur trader.

Swing Trading

Unlike day trading, swing trading is a longer-term strategy that involves entering and holding positions for longer than 24 hours but usually not longer than a couple of weeks or a month. The swing trending method is a hybrid between day trading and trend trading.

Generally, swing traders take advantage of waves of volatility that play out over several days or weeks. They may combine technical and fundamental analysis to formulate trade ideas. Typically, essential factors or changes take longer to reflect, where fundamental analysis comes into play. Technical indicators and chart patterns also play critical parts in a swing trading plan.

This strategy is considered by many as the easiest and most convenient for beginners, mainly because it takes a longer time to play out. Still, the trades are short enough to prevent losing track of the market.

With this strategy, you have enough time to evaluate your trading decisions carefully. In most cases, you have sufficient time to react to the unfolding of the trade. You don't need to make decisions hastily and irrationally.

In contrast, day trading requires you to make and execute decisions speedily, which is not ideal for anyone learning about the market.

Trend Trading

Trend trading or, as it is also called, position trading involves holding positions for at least a few months or longer. As evident from the name, trending trading involves analyzing directional trends to formulate trade ideas. A trend trader may enter a long position in a downtrend and a short one in an uptrend.

Typically, trend traders utilize fundamental analysis, but this isn't always the case. Still, basic research focuses on events that play out over time, exactly how trend traders take advantage of the market.

To make a trend trading strategy, you must assume that the crypto asset will continue moving in the trend's direction. You also have to consider potential trend reversal. Other factors such as technical indicators, trend lines, and moving averages should go into creating your strategy. That will mitigate risks and increase your chances of success.

If you do your due diligence and manage risk appropriately, trend trading can suit you as a beginner.

Scalping

That is one of the fastest trading strategies for the crypto market. Scalping doesn't involve taking advantage of drawn-out trends or big moves. Instead, it focuses on repeatedly exploiting small movements, for instance, profiting off liquidity gaps, market inefficiencies, or bid-ask spreads.

Scalpers don't hold long-term positions. It's pretty standard for scalp traders to enter and exit positions in seconds, which is why scalping is mentioned with High-Frequency Trading. Scalping is a particularly lucrative trading strategy with consistent market inefficiencies to exploit.

Every time you find an inefficiency to exploit, you can make small profits that cumulate over time. This technique is ideal for cryptocurrencies with high liquidity, where you can enter and exit positions smoothly and predictably.

Due to its complexity, scalping isn't recommended to new traders. You need in-depth knowledge of market mechanics to use this strategy. Other than that, it is perfect for large-volume traders, a.k.a. whales.

Apart from trading strategies, there are strategies for those looking to invest rather than trade.

Dollar-Cost Averaging (Dca)

Dollar-Cost Averaging is an investment strategy where an investor allocates a sum of their capital to build a position consistently over time. If you receive a salary monthly, this might be the best investment strategy for you.

Not all people in the crypto market have access to vast amounts of cash. However, this is an easy way to invest in crypto assets for those who budget their investments. This strategy allows you to invest weekly, monthly, or quarterly.

HOW TO ADVANCED CRYPTO TRADING WITH SUCCESS

There's one other thing you need to learn before you plunge into the cryptocurrency world: how to receive cryptocurrency.

In the cryptocurrency industry, there are many ways to make money. First, you should thoroughly familiarize yourself with them and select the one that best fits your lifestyle, financial situation, preferences, and other factors. You can also choose multiple coins and cleverly combine them. You would have a greater chance to diversify your risks and gain more in this situation.

In today's cryptocurrency industry, there are a variety of ways to profit:

- Long-term investment
- Trading
- Mining
- Participating in ICO
- Reselling cryptocurrency.

Here's a short rundown of each of these approaches. After that, I'll go over each strategy in greater detail.

Long-Term Investment

If you choose this method of benefit, you should have the following:

- A one-to-two-year duration (invest a sum of money you can quickly "freeze" for several years)
- A significant sum of money (if you can invest in parts only, this too can be viewed as a long-term investment) Preparedness for danger (which are higher than in the banking sector).
- In the long run, you benefit from substantial capital gains.

Trading

If you prefer this method of benefit, you should have the following:

- The passage of time (not the time for waiting as with long-term investment, but the free time you can devote daily to trading)

- A modest sum of money
- Perseverance and diligence are required.
- Intelligence created by machines (as you have to work with numbers and charts)
- It's possible to keep an eye on things and track what's going on.
- To potentially make money quickly and earn recurring profits, you beat the market and take risks (the higher the possible gain, the higher the risk).

Mining

Mining is the procedure of making new bitcoins or cryptocurrencies. If you're interested in making money with cryptocurrencies, you'll need to determine if you want to do it as a hobby or go into professional mining.

You'll need the following items for hobbyist mining:

- Mechanical intelligence (or a mechanically intelligent friend or advisor)
- Support for new companies (usually up to six mining farms)
- Preparedness for technological issues and disruptions
- Equipment protection from external influences (pets, children, etc.).

In mining, you make money by making a small but consistent profit. You also have the option of trading and managing the market.

If you want to go into technical mining, you'll need the following items:

- Investments or startup money
- Locations
- a group
- Availability to take on responsibility.

You will make a regular and consistent profit by running your mining farm; you can also control the market rather than just trade in it. Furthermore, you will have the potential to own something concrete and sell your company in the future.

Icos (Initial Coin Offering)

Many people have taken part in so-called initial coin offerings (ICOs) (Initial Coin Offering). In a nutshell, this is a different take on the crowdfunding model, close to an IPO. Participants contribute money to the construction of a project in exchange for potential benefits, although there are no guarantees.

An initial coin offering (ICO) is when a project issues vouchers or tokens that can be used to pay for site services with cryptocurrencies in the future.

A venture fund, i.e., an investment fund that works with creative businesses and ventures, has a lot in common with an ICO (startups). A venture fund invests in stocks or shares in high-risk or reasonably high-risk companies with the expectation of exceptionally high income.

In general, 70 percent to 80 percent of such initiatives fail to pay off. The benefit from the remaining 20% -30%, on the other hand, covers all losses.

If you think you're courageous enough to fund a project with no promises, consider the following:

- Am I willing to take on additional risks?
- Is there a capital cushion for diversification in my portfolio?

You make money with an ICO by taking considerable risks in exchange for a chance to make a lot of money.

Reselling Cryptocurrency

Trading and reselling cryptocurrencies have a lot in common. You can benefit from currency fluctuations here as well, but unlike trading, it's a game between wholesale and retail rates rather than the market or exchange rate.

If you're interested in creating money this way, you should:

- Do not take risks
- Operate in small sums only
- Understand that income depends on your turnover.

So far, we've just scraped the surface of the simple ways to benefit from the cryptocurrency sector. Let's take a closer look at each approach now.

Making Long-Term Investments: A More In-Depth Look

You may remember Warren Buffett's first rule: never lose money. That is particularly true for long-term investments, where the goal is to retain the money rather than lose it.

Let's go over some of the foundations of making a long-term investment:

- Do not lose money; reduce risks
- Do not make a fuss
- Reap benefit in future

That is how you can set up your cryptocurrency portfolio for long-term investment.

Blue coins are the more stable currency at the moment. The blue color denotes more moderate and stable positions but may be less lucrative. The green color indicates places that are riskier but also more promising.

BUILD A CRYPTO STRATEGY THAT MATCHES YOUR GOALS

Every new step requires proper planning to have smooth execution, which holds for cryptocurrency. It is unwise to get into an area without any functional knowledge, especially when it is entirely new to you. The volatility in the price value and unexpected fluctuations in the market could turn your financial status topsy-turvy within seconds if you went with a blind approach. Therefore, it is vital to develop a strategic plan with a proper and systematic technique before making money using cryptocurrencies.

Choosing long-term or short-term goals becomes quick when you have a strategic plan in place.

Strategic Planning With Cryptocurrencies

When there is a defined strategy, the decision is primarily right, thus helping a smooth implementation process without any bottlenecks. The below-mentioned steps can be followed to devise a strategic plan for choosing the right cryptocurrency strategy to help achieve your financial target:

- Write down the goals.

- Identify if the goal benefits are short-term or long-term.

- Determine the objectives required to fulfill the goals.

- Sketch the plan outline.

- Compare the theoretical plan with practical possibilities, i.e., capital money, the period of waiting, expected profit, estimating the unavoidable losses, financial stability, etc.

- Categorize the possibilities.

- Choose the right cryptocurrency strategy based on the drafted plan.

- Get ready to implement the devised plan.

- Asking the following questions of yourself will help in choosing the right strategy to gain better profits with minimal risk:

- Have you already decided on the cryptocurrency you want to use to earn that extra money?

- Do you know which technology cryptocurrency works on and the concept behind the same?

- Will you want to make fast cash, or are you going to wait for the right moment to enjoy long-term benefits?

- Do you want to go with the long-term investment strategy or short-term trading strategy (sell the coins whenever there is a price hike)?

- Have you decided on the 'capital amount' you want to invest in the cryptocurrency?

- Is your wait-time decided (months or years you will be holding to the coin)?

- Do you have complete knowledge of the cryptocurrency exchanges available in the market, and have you decided on the one you want to go ahead with?

- Have you taken the necessary steps to store the purchased crypto coins in a secured manner by choosing the right cryptocurrency wallet (preferably offline or hardware wallet)?

- If you have convincing answers to all the queries mentioned earlier, you are ready to get to the implementation phase.

Cryptocurrency Failure – An Example

A virus called 'WannaCry' attacked systems (computers) of key companies across 150 countries in May 2017. The computers under the attack of the virus had popup messages that said— "Oops! Your files have been encrypted." It was alarming as many vital files were compromised, and unfortunately, cryptocurrencies were one among them. Hackers had the upper hand, and they demanded 'big money' to open the encrypted files. They wanted $300 in Bitcoins from all the computer owners whose computers had been hacked. The owners were given three days to arrange the money, and in case they failed to do so, the locked files would be deleted. Since Bitcoin transactions are anonymous, it was impossible to track the cyber hackers.

Though it is not attainable to predict such incidents, this won't have affected cryptocurrency owners if they had taken additional steps to keep their local system double-safe by installing the best anti-virus software onto their systems (preferably buying the best ones instead of using trial versions) especially when they had their crypto coins stored on the PC. When it comes to cryptocurrency strategy, the most important thing to be remembered is to ensure the purchased cryptocurrencies are stored in a secured manner (with a backup)

Importance Of Strategic Planning

Having a proper strategic plan is essential to ensure the money flow is smooth with good profits and there are no significant setbacks when withdrawing funds. When your objectives are clear with set priorities, the process is easy, allowing you to achieve your moneymaking goals as you desire.

The significant uses of having a proper and calculated plan for your cryptocurrency strategies are as follows:

The sole intention of attaining the objectives is fulfilled.

Focusing on the idea becomes more accessible when the plan is appropriately devised.

It permits the investor to use his money, resources, and time in a precise manner based on the plan.

Implementation is never a difficult task when the entire plan outline is structured clearly with all the required details.

When you choose a sensitive market such as cryptocurrency, it becomes your responsibility to make sure that you know the ins and outs of the chosen cryptocurrency, the underlying technology it uses, the financial benefits it offers, and the threats it can pose during the entire cycle.

Benefits of an innovative strategic plan:

- When the framework is set, it is easy to choose the method which best suits you based on your set goals.
- You can quickly decide which cryptocurrency strategies you want to go ahead with from the available choices:
- Investment
- Trading
- Mining, etc.

When the decision is made, you can focus your concentration and start to travel towards a 'set' direction.

Managing the risk will not be a challenging task if you have already made the right plan (based on long-term or short-term goals)

Your decision-making skills will have also improved dramatically as you are aware of the entire cycle, thus allowing you to take the right decision spontaneously.

Things To Remember When Choosing Cryptocurrency Strategy

The below-mentioned points will be of help to finalize the cryptocurrency strategy that suits based on your requirements and goals:

Understand the history behind cryptocurrencies and the reasons which led to the invention of the virtual currency

Be aware of the underlying technology that cryptocurrencies use –blockchain technology. (If you are someone who invested in crypto coins but has no clue about blockchain technology, then you are in the wrong place. It is essential to know everything about the stock you are investing in.)

Be careful not to repeat the 'famous' mistakes (Don't invest based on the price value. Don't compare the characteristics of altcoins with Bitcoins and dream that it will become big the same way Bitcoin made it big.) don't be in haste to sell your crypto coin when you see a price hike. Don't invest in a crypto coin if you don't have plans to hold on to the cash for a minimum period – at least three years.

Diversify your investment plans, and don't get drawn entirely into cryptocurrency day trading, as it can become a dangerous mistake.

Last but not least, ensure your crypto coins are securely stored in suitable wallets. Have a backup of the private key and seed.

WAYS TO EARN MONEY WITH CRYPTOCURRENCIES

In this crypto market that is currently booming, the chances of making a profit for investors interested in crypto assets are wide. The investor can choose between the variety of cryptocurrencies and the different ways of generating money even without any investment. Learn the possibilities that the crypto market gives you and join those who have succeeded before.

Cryptocurrency Trading

In the versatile world of cryptocurrencies, trading is one of the best ways to generate income online. But we must also consider the high risk of loss in the operations carried out. As digital financial markets expand, several brokers dedicated to crypto assets have emerged. Today, anyone who has a bank checking account, credit cards, payment processors, and cryptocurrencies in wallets can enter the brokers and start with active crypto trading.

In the case of deciding to deposit money to a broker of your choice, it is always advisable to investigate a little to know which broker is the one that best suits the needs of the "trader." Many brokers can potentially be a scam and illegally take over their clients' money. It is advisable to invest in those controlled and regulated by international financial organizations and that comply with the corresponding financial regulations to avoid fraud.

Several brokers offer free demo accounts to practice without risking real money in operations. These demo accounts are efficient and have the same technical functionalities as real ones with cash, or in this case, with cryptocurrencies. The rookie trader will start learning a strategy that can begin to deliver dividends, testing the different technical signals that the graphics and tools offered by the broker platform will give you for good management.

The trader must be patient and not get carried away by emotions when he suffers losses. This type of attitude is the same as playing in a casino; you will only lose your money.

Start to operate correctly by constantly learning from experts who offer tutorials, books, videos, and much information circulating on the subject. This vital information will give you excellent knowledge of how to profit from online cryptocurrency trading.

I have obtained excellent results in investments as an amateur trader. For this reason, if you are interested in starting cryptocurrency trading, you need to practice in a free demo account until you become familiar with trading, its tools, graphics, and statistics. But that entails a period of practice, error, and learning.

Once we have learned to trade in the demo account offered by some brokers and decide to open a real account, it is advisable to start investing small amounts and try the strategy we have practiced in the demo account. With time and experience, we will begin to receive good dividends from operations. But don't risk more than you don't want to lose since you can quickly lose all money.

That is why it is recommended to be well informed of the digital asset in which we decide to invest the money. Read news and information regarding cryptocurrency and monitor the price of your help daily before starting your trading session.

Professional traders earn a lot of money in brokers, but they also invest and risk large amounts. Many of them invest in specialized computer programs with artificial intelligence, giving them the technical signals to enter the market and when to exit it. You can make large amounts of money with the excellent information applied and lose everything if you act by being carried away by feelings and emotions when performing operations.

Whether in cryptocurrencies or in the traditional way, deciding to be a trader requires good information, preparation, and patience to get good results. Maybe trading is the best way to earn reasonable amounts of money quickly. But it would help if you did not forget the risks involved in the trader's lack of information and preparation in the operations carried out.

Cryptocurrency Arbitration

With the expansion of digital crypto active markets, a series of platforms and exchanges are created to purchase and sell online crypto assets. This procedure is known technically by arbitration and can be performed in the various cryptocurrency exchanges that currently exist. Lately, it has become a very profitable business for many investors in crypto assets worldwide, but little exploited for strangers on the subject. Opportunities arise daily for interested investors.

But for those who do not know the concept of arbitration in the financial world, this is related to the anticipated speculation of the asset's price. That means that when comparing the cost of some cryptocurrencies in the different exchanges, there are price variations that allow the investor to buy at a price and then sell at a higher value.

That price difference in our favor is what generates the utility we get. These opportunities arise but do not hold for long until the markets match their prices for supply and demand.

It is a way of trading, but more controlled and with fewer risks than in a broker. Before deciding to invest in these sites, you should know very well the prices and commissions charged by exchanges for operations. Since in this aspect, the same fees vary between different businesses. Once you have all the details you need and feel confident in performing the operations, apply what you have learned in your strategy and start making money with cryptocurrencies.

Bitcoin Hodl

It all started as a meme through the internet, which quickly became the most common way people invest when they acquire bitcoin. The term HODL has to do with people who buy bitcoin but do not make any movement in 1 year or more.

This class of investors hopes that the cryptocurrency will increase its value significantly, as it did in December 2017 when it reached $ 19,900 and obtained good benefits. This practice is well known, and being bitcoin the cryptocurrency pioneer, this type of investment has been made for many years.

Every 12 months, the amount of cryptocurrencies that have not moved is measured. In this last measurement in bitcoin, a new record is established with more than 10.7 million bitcoins, which have not moved over the former 12 months or longer. The company responsible for making this measurement is Digital Assets Data, which creates cryptographic data feeds. This type of investment is made in the long term, hoping that the price of the crypto active will reach a higher price than the purchase price.

Many do not move their cryptocurrencies because they bought the crypto asset when it had a high value, and they don't want to lose money in the operation. When bitcoin attained its all-time high of about $ 20,000, many bought BTC at that price.

But BTC later gradually lost its value. For that reason, they do not move their cryptocurrencies, waiting for BTC to recover and reach new historical importance, which will allow them to recover their investment and obtain the highest possible profits.

Now that the next bitcoin halving is approaching in May 2020, many more investors will do HODL, expecting the cryptocurrency queen to increase its value, as many expert analysts and successful businessmen have predicted. Bitcoin HODL can be an excellent way to invest in the long term and wait for the forecasts that place bitcoin at exorbitant prices come true.

Create Your Cryptocurrency

Suppose you have computer skills and how blockchain technology operates. In that case, you have the necessary capital or are interested in investing in your crypto project; this would be an exciting way to obtain financial results, which could generate the financial freedom dreamed.

Blockchain technology is versatile, and large crypto projects can be undertaken through this system. But this way requires hard and well-organized work. Many are the young entrepreneurs who carried out their crypto projects, and that over time, they have become trendy, transforming them into millionaires.

The possibilities are many, but knowledge is essential to develop an exciting project to convince potential investors. In addition to being able to intelligently manage the marketing associated with the crypto project, to make it known to as many people as possible, the new crypto project, in this case, would be initiated as an ICO to obtain the necessary capital.

The approach should be to develop a cryptocurrency with the best features, which can be sustained over time and with a solid structure. Suppose you have the necessary knowledge to create a cryptocurrency and get potential investors for your project. In that case, this is the best option you have to get benefits in the crypto world.

Faucets That Give Free Cryptocurrencies

For all those interested in cryptocurrencies but have not yet decided to invest real money for fear of losing, there is a way to earn cryptocurrencies for free through multiple faucets that operate online. By enrolling in them, they give away bitcoin satoshis or satoshis of the most popular altcoins to their users. Formerly, it had already been commented on some faucets that gave away bitcoin satoshis, but the variety of this type of faucets is large.

That is an excellent way to get acquainted with cryptocurrencies and generate profits. Although the yields are meager at the beginning, over time and with the knowledge and management done in the faucets, through their referral system, they can generate non-negligible profits and in a passive way. It all depends on the commitment and the strategy used to get the most out of these websites.

Generally, the minimums needed to make withdrawals from these websites are incredibly low, and we will only need to have our cryptocurrency wallet to receive payments. It should be noted that wallets or purses for storing cryptocurrencies are accessible to anyone without discrimination, and opening an account is entirely free.

Only commissions, as explained above, are incredibly low paid when making withdrawals or shipments. That is the best option for those who want to get acquainted with the crypto world without risking capital.

Receive Cryptocurrencies As A Means Of Payment

Cryptocurrencies are gaining ground in more and more business and service provisions. Currently, many online businesses receive cryptocurrencies as a means of payment. If you want to acquire cryptocurrencies in the case of developing an electronic business model, you can choose to have your clients pay you through this form of payment.

The most used cryptocurrencies for electronic commerce are mainly bitcoin, ethereum, bitcoin cash, and litecoin, generally the best known and highest market value. But also, other cryptocurrencies are being implemented in online commerce due to their characteristics and speed of transactions.

If you have an online store or business, in addition to receiving payments through traditional systems, you can also include cryptocurrencies as a means of payment. This way, you can reach more people worldwide and expand your business.

In several Asian countries, cryptocurrencies are prevalent, and even some taxi drivers receive them as a means of payment. In addition, more and more small businesses accept cryptocurrencies. If you have a physical business in a country where cryptocurrencies are used, you can also accept payment through this system and adapt to the future economy.

E-commerce and the provision of online services are expanding more and more and require different means of payment. But cryptocurrencies can bring advantages or a disadvantage. Volatility is a risk, but it can also lead to additional profits.

INTRODUCTION TO MINING CRYPTO

Crypto mining is a technique that might aid you in obtaining cryptocurrency without any investment. You may question, "How are bitcoins and other cryptocurrencies generated, and how can you obtain them without purchasing them on a crypto exchange?" Initially, most individuals were interested in bitcoin and other cryptocurrencies because their values increased. Cryptocurrencies like Bitcoin, Ether, and Dogecoin very much intrigued people in the early months of 2021. Crypto exchanges are where you may purchase cryptocurrencies as well as trade them. But you may manufacture or mine these tokens on your PC. The idea of being compensated with Bitcoin is a big incentive for many miners. To be clear, you do not need to be a miner to hold bitcoin tokens. You can buy cryptocurrencies with fiat currency, trade them on an exchange like Bitstamp with another cryptocurrency (for example, Ethereum or NEO to buy Bitcoin), or earn them by shopping, writing blog posts on platforms that pay users in cryptocurrency, or even setting up interest-earning crypto accounts.

What Is Crypto Mining?

Crypto mining is a method in which cryptocurrencies are minted by utilizing high-power computers to solve challenging mathematical equations and riddles. Data blocks are verified and recorded on a digital ledger in this procedure. A Digital ledger is referred to as a blockchain. Complex mathematical approaches are utilized to keep the blockchain safe. Cryptocurrencies employ a decentralized system that aids in distributing and validating transactions. Cryptographic algorithms are used for this purpose. Here there is no central controlling authority that watches over the transaction. Also, there is no central ledger. To get additional coins, complicated mathematical challenges are completed to verify digital currency. All this information is uploaded to the decentralized ledger. The miners get money for this entire procedure. New coins come into circulation because of this mining process.

Working Of The Process:

In mining, complicated mathematical problems are solved utilizing high-power computers. The one who can break the code has the power over the transaction. The miners earn a tiny quantity of bitcoin for the process of mining. After the miner can verify the transaction, it is subsequently put to a public record on a blockchain.

How Can You Start Mining?

For your crypto mining, you need a high-power computer. Not solely that, but you will also need a digital wallet to store your bitcoins and trade them as well. You may become part of a mining pool where you will receive additional options for making earnings. Mining pools are simply organizations for miners to boost their mining power. The money earned from the mining process is split equally among all those a part of the pool. Through these mining pools, miners have a chance to work together and fight more effectively. The algorithm collects many coins, including Bitcoin, Ethereum, and Dogecoin. It ensures that no one authority grows so dominant that it begins to rule the show. This mining activity is a vital aspect of adding new blocks of transaction data to the blockchain. A new block is only added to the blockchain system if a miner comes with a new winning proof-of-work. What happens after every 10 minutes on the network. Proof-of-work tries to prevent users from printing additional coins they didn't earn or double-spending. Mining the bitcoin may be pretty intriguing and rewarding as well. The bulk of the nations is not really into the crypto area since the mining procedure may be very pricey. But a few countries promote crypto mining, and you will come across fantastic prospects for your crypto mining. But where do you start? Below is a list of a few nations where you may begin your path of crypto mining. But before we go additional into that, let's take a look at some of the variables that make a nation an ideal site for mining.

Critical Reasons For Successful Crypto Mining Operations

There are dozens of elements to be considered if you want to try your hand at crypto mining, but here are some of the more frequent ones you need to be aware with:

Advanced And Specialized Mining Machines

As considered formerly, crypto miners excavate BTC's digital cave to acquire fractions of this digital currency. If gold miners utilize complex rock equipment to dig out nuggets of precious metals, Bitcoin miners create their machines with pricey specialist software and robust mining rigs. Crypto miners use this technology to tackle complicated mathematical problems that are difficult to answer with pen-and-paper and mental techniques. After identifying the answer, BTC miners will be paid with a freshly minted currency and amounts from the transaction fee—but that's a tale for another time.

Fast And Stable Internet Connection

Besides the pricey and powerful equipment, you'll also need a high-speed and steady Internet connection to operate the mining activities. Of course, this service also comes with costs which vary upon the area of the globe that you reside in.

Lower Power Prices

It takes up a lot of power to mine crypto. That is why certain nations do not consent to have operations like such taking place in their border perimeter. If you intend to mine cryptocurrency, opt for a place where the power is accessible at reduced rates.

Suitable Climatic Conditions

You need to select a nation that has an overall colder climate. That is because the computers that mine Crypto operate 24/7. An area with milder weather might minimize the overheating of this machinery. It also reduces the cost of power used by systems to cool the machinery.

Country's Economic Condition

The economic state is vital if you search for a location to mine crypto. That might aid you in calculating how inexpensive or costly mining activities for the cryptocurrency will be. It would be best if you had pricey equipment and qualified people to assist you in monitoring them. The money they earn in exchange for their labor is determined based on the country's cost of living. Moreover, you will have overhead costs. The location to position your machines would add to your overall expenditures.

Government's Attitude On Crypto-Related Activity

The resources needed for the mining of cryptocurrencies influence the environment and the electricity consumption rate of the nation. Some authorities remain skeptical about digital currency. That is why you need to seek countries that do not find it offensive to mine cryptocurrencies and consider it favorable.

Ideal Sites To Mine Cryptocurrency

A few places are fantastic to mine crypto and supply you with various options together. The nations that are good for mining crypto are given below:

Georgia

Georgia is a nation that is both bitcoin and blockchain technology-friendly. It ranked 109th in October 2020. It has a broadband download speed of 26.80 Megabits per second (Mbps) (Mbps). The price of electricity in Georgia is 0.056 USD per kilowatt-hour (kWh) (kWh). Also, its temperature is adequate to cool the mining machinery.

Estonia

Estonia ranks 50th in the worldwide ranking list. It provides a broadband download speed of up to 74.73 Mbps. The price of electricity in Estonia is 0.174 USD per kWh. Not only that, but there are hundreds of blockchain and crypto startups in the nation. It looks at Crypto as "value reflected in digital form."

Canada

Canada ranked 17th on the list. It boasts the best broadband download rate of 149.35 Mbps. The power price in Canada is 0.174 USD per kWh; cryptocurrency mining flourished in Canada back in 2018 due to the low electricity costs and frigid weather. They allow digital currencies, but they aren't regarded as legal cash.

Norway

Norway closely follows Canada and ranks 18th on the list. Norway has an Internet speed of 146.53 Mbps. In Norway, energy is created utilizing hydropower. It snows mainly, and the weather is typically frigid. It makes it an excellent spot to cool the equipment used for mining. Norway neither outlaws nor recognizes Crypto. On the contrary, the Norwegian Financial Supervisory Authority (FSA) established money laundering restrictions on persons who conducted virtual currency conversion locally.

Kuwait

Kuwait ranked 34th on the list. Kuwait has an internet download speed of up to 110.33 Mbps. The price of power in Kuwait is 0.029 USD per kWh. It covers the cost of electricity, distribution, as well as taxes. Kuwait has severe regulatory difficulties. The Ministry of Finance of Kuwait does not recognize cryptocurrencies and the Central Bank of Kuwait restricts crypto trading for official transactions. In 2018, CBK declared releasing an e-currency that they would oversee. If you choose Kuwait for Bitcoin mining, you have to maintain its regulatory rules.

Iceland

Iceland's rank on the list is unclear, but the good thing is that Iceland produces its power from geothermal resources. That is because Iceland has over 200 volcanoes and many hot springs. That offers masses of subsurface water to be transformed for electricity generating.

Switzerland

Switzerland ranked 4th on the list. It has an internet download rate of 186.40 Mbps. That is the quickest among the list of nations stated below. The power price in Switzerland is 0.228 USD per kWh which is a tad pricy. In Switzerland, the legislation regulating cryptocurrency is pretty permissive. They are classed as assets or properties. Switzerland is a nation that promotes Crypto.

Finland

Finland ranks 35th on the list. It has an internet download rate of 108.84 Mbps. The price of electricity in Finland is 0.183 USD per kWh. Finland has a generally cooler climate.

Sweden

Sweden ranked 14th on the list. It has a download speed of 158.73 Mbps. Electricity costs in Sweden are 0.179 USD per kWh. However, these rates vary from region to area and rely upon where you reside.

Latvia

Lastly, Latvia ranks 35th on the list. It has a download speed of 115.22 Mbps. The price of electricity in Latvia is 14.2 euro cents per kWh. This rate is believed to be the lowest price in Latvia since 2014.

Coin Mining in India

In the last few years, the mining of Bitcoin has substantially risen. Many firms give facilities for crypto mining and blockchain development in India. However, mining Bitcoins in India is a costly and dangerous enterprise. The reason for such is that the struggle for currencies in India is excellent and challenging. To mine Bitcoins effectively, significant processing power is necessary.

For this reason, considerable power is needed, and the prices of energy in India are very high. The power price in India fluctuates from Rs 5.20-8.20 per kilowatt-hour. That is about equivalent to 7-11 cents. The total power necessary to mine the coins is 67.29 terawatt-hours a year. That is as per the estimate of the Cambridge Bitcoin Electricity Consumption Index. Not only that but there is also a lack of equipment in India. To have the whole equipment necessary to mine Bitcoins, it needs to be imported from China. That further raises the expenditures and diminishes earnings. Besides that, India also does not have any defined guidelines regarding cryptocurrency. Due to these factors, India is a dangerous location to invest in. The government of India and the central bank have an uncertain connection with cryptocurrency. GOI did recommend creating their digital currency in the interim period. In 2017, India issued a restriction upon the import of ASCI equipment. These machines are intended to mine Crypto, which forced Bengaluru-based blockchain technology startup AB Nexus to stop mining Bitcoin and Ethereum.

CRYPTOCURRENCY PARAMETERS TO ANALYZE IN INVESTING

Value And Price Are Not Synonyms

I f you google "Bitcoin price," you'll see its current value expressed in any currency you choose. This information is helpful to know how much capital you need to make an immediate purchase. Apart from that, present price data is essentially useless. To be genuinely useful, you need to know the potential value in the context of former and future (or possible future) prices.

The price of bitcoin was $0.10, which means an increase to $10,000. Either seems like an extremely high price to pay for the same thing or, if you happen to own some, a phenomenal return on your investment. However, if you know that the price was $20,000 in 2017, $10,000 looks like an intimidating loss. Out of context, a fee is just a number that doesn't tell you anything useful.

If you sift through a bitcoin chart, you will see that the price has (if you negate short-term volatility) consistently increased over the long term. That is true of all the major cryptocurrencies, including ether and XRP. It is even more apparent if you examine the price action on a logarithmic rather than a linear chart.

These charts enable you to see the long-term increase in the price of an asset such as bitcoin as the number of users rises over time. You can operate this to your edge and buy when the price is contextually low against the backdrop of this constant price increase.

As more people start using bitcoin, the volatility will also increase so that each "wave" of the chart will be larger than the former one. That is illustrated in the diagram overleaf on page 64. The boxes represent almost identical price action, but the proportions are more significant, reflecting the market's growth. That means we can expect the subsequent price increase to be proportionally more important.

This data suggests that, so long as you take the long-term view, purchasing bitcoin at any price below $20,000 is justified for as long as the adoption trend continues (i.e., Bitcoin continues to be a technology that people want to use).

A Logarithmic Btc Chart All Time

A linear BTC chart all time

If investors knew with certainty that the price of bitcoin was going to increase to $500,000 over a specified period, things would be very different. Every investor would be extremely eager to enter the market with their investment capital. None of them would question a purchase price below $20,000 (or even $400,000) because they would be sure of making a very healthy return. While it's true that nothing in life is inevitable, we can use data, former price action, and statistics to help us determine the most probable outcome.

When valuing new companies with little or no trading history (and, therefore, no agreed price), investors derive a valuation from what are called "fundamentals." We can define these as "usually intangible qualities likely to result in the company's value increasing or decreasing over a specified time."

Fundamentals include factors such as the caliber of the directors or senior management team, historical sales amount, and staff retention rates. If any of these are of concern (for example, if staff keep leaving because of toxic management), investors tend to avoid investing in the company's long-term growth or may even bet against it. Thousands of analysts worldwide, who pride themselves on their ability to value companies, are working with fewer data than cryptocurrencies can provide to the diligent investor. The investor has to know where to look and what to look for.

Same Price Action, Proportionally Larger Waves

Value investors don't follow the latest fad in technology, fashion, or entertainment. Instead, they invest in companies with solid fundamentals whose brands permeate the fabric of society, such as Apple, Coca-Cola, and Microsoft. Value investors attempt to purchase their shares when the fundamentals are opposed to the share price or the dividend yield the company is offering. By holding the stock over decades, they plan on both the share price and the dividend yield increase over the long-term, when the market increases the cost, in line with the fundamentals (value). When the discrepancy between the share price and the value of the fundamentals becomes smaller, they may sell to invest in a new company with a more significant difference.

Investing (which focuses on long-term potential and profits over a timeframe measured in years) rather than trading, which takes a short-term perspective (hours to days). An investor only sells when they feel their investment has reached maturity and parity with the long-term fundamentals, rather than reacting to short-term price action caused by volatility.

Examples of solid fundamentals for a company such as Google would be the number of daily searches and growing or dropping. A strong fundamental of Virgin is a dynamic, ambitious CEO with a track record of success. Many fundamentals are subjective, but they can help you make good decisions, especially when a lot of information is not available or missing.

Investing in strong, fundamentally supported cryptocurrencies is less risky than investing in new technology companies. Not only can you use fundamentals to significant effect, but you also have historic price data to work from. By looking at the historical data, you can discover what a cryptocurrency was worth at any point in the past and use this to arrive at an informed decision. You never have all the data you'd like to have, and it's never 100% reliable. Nonetheless, putting all the available information together can give you a better idea of your risk, expected return, and potential loss.

Countless fundamentals could be relevant to the value of any given cryptocurrency and therefore affect your investment decisions. Here are the essential ones you need to know about and consider when planning your investments.

Market Capitalization

That is the total amount of capital invested in the cryptocurrency at any given time and is usually, though not necessarily always, measured in US dollars. However, there is a trade-off regarding the potential for highly profitable returns. The higher the market capitalization, the stronger the cryptocurrency. The stronger the cryptocurrency market capitalization, the more limited its upward potential.

Market Share

That is the percentage of the total cryptocurrency market devoted to the cryptocurrency. It indicates how much the marketplace is adopting or using a particular cryptocurrency. In other words, it gives you a good indication as to how many people find valuable cryptocurrency. The higher the percentage, the stronger the cryptocurrency. By way of example, Bitcoin is usually above 50%. Small projects with less than 1% of the market can still be worth investing in, but they carry a greater risk of long-term failure and loss of capital.

Transaction Volume

That refers to the number of transactions occurring within a given period. In general terms, the higher the number of transactions, the more viability the cryptocurrency is said to have. Low transaction volume doesn't necessarily mean a cryptocurrency is worthless. It may not yet be widely adopted (though this could change). On intense trading days, this metric can be deceptive. Traders can initiate transactions worth millions of dollars without using the cryptocurrency for its intended purpose, so this fundamental is only valid when viewed with other real solid reasons to invest.

Development Team And Update Cycle

If the cryptocurrency has a specific development team, who is the leader, and what credentials do they have that would help to develop and strengthen the cryptocurrency? How many people are on the expansion team? It can be a challenge to get good information about this fundamental for cryptocurrencies that, like bitcoin, have no employed developers but rely on thousands of volunteers instead.

Generally, the more experienced and suitably qualified the development team behind a cryptocurrency project, the more potential it has as a viable investment opportunity. You can also check how frequently a cryptocurrency project is developed and monitor its progress via a website such as GitHub. Projects that have not had an update for a while (months) may indicate that the project is performing poorly and are to be avoided as viable investment opportunities.

Partnerships With Financial Institutions

Does the cryptocurrency have partnerships in place with pre-existing non-crypto financial institutions? Furthermore, are these institutions supporting or using the cryptocurrency for its intended purpose and deriving a direct benefit? In both cases, if the answer is yes, this is a very favorable fundamental. The greater the number and quality of these partnerships (for example, with a significant technology company or financial institution), the more likely it is that the cryptocurrency will still exist in ten years and be trading at a substantially higher price than today.

Extent Of Adoption

Are people using cryptocurrency to solve the problems it was intended to solve? Is it starting to fulfill its purpose rather than just being hoarded by speculators keen to sell out as soon as the price increases? Bitcoin is being used in genuine transactions every day; some other cryptocurrencies are not. If a cryptocurrency is unlikely to grow in real-world adoption and traction, it would most likely be replaced by another cryptocurrency that performs a similar (or superior) function and has a more significant number of real-world users.

Number Of Users

How many people are holding or using the coins? The more users a cryptocurrency has, the higher that cryptocurrency's investment potential. It's also worth asking if the cryptocurrency project has significant support from "HODL" investors.

A note of explanation: "HODL" is a misspelling of "hold," which appeared on the Reddit website in the early days of cryptocurrency investing. It has since come to mean "Hold on for Dear Life" and refers to investors who will never sell their coins except to make extremely high returns. In theory, these investors would not only keep their investment if Bitcoin returned to $1 but would buy substantially more. This practice contributes to a steady increase in the price of significant cryptocurrencies over time as more and more people "HODL," a particular digital currency.

This list of fundamental properties is by no means exhaustive. There are many more that an investor could consider before deciding whether to purchase any given cryptocurrency. Not all cryptocurrencies have the same fundamental properties, and any real strength, which is always at least partly subjective, is constantly fluctuating. The critical point is that the greater the number of fundamental solid properties a cryptocurrency has, the more likely to increase the price and the less risk that you will lose your capital.

It is also worth mentioning that these fundamentals are variables—they can change during a cryptocurrency's life. Assessing fundamentals is one way to evaluate whether a currency represents an excellent potential investment. However, some cryptocurrencies are all "smoke and mirrors" and never a good investment. You'll need to know how to avoid them.

Avoiding Scamcoins

Unfortunately, scams are part of the cryptocurrency story, as with any new technology or investment opportunity. Investors have lost billions of dollars by believing scammers and not being sufficiently diligent with their investment decisions. However, before you invest in any crypto project, you can perform some straightforward checks that will increase your chances of avoiding scam artists.

WHAT IS A VIRTUAL WALLET?

A cryptocurrency wallet is a protected mobile wallet used to store, send, and receive digital currency like Bitcoin. Most coins have an official wallet and a few officially recommended third-party wallets.

Like a traditional wallet carried in a pocket, a Bitcoin wallet is used to store money. The difference is that instead of keeping a collection of bills and cards, a Bitcoin wallet holds a group of Bitcoin secret keys. Usually, a wallet is encrypted with a password or protected from unauthorized access.

Working Of Cryptocurrency Wallet

In the wallet, a private key (secure digital code known only to you and your wallet) stores ownership of a public key (a public digital code connected to a certain amount of currency). Thus, the wallet stores private and public keys, which allows for sending and receiving coins. It also shows a personal ledger of transactions to the user.

Security Of Cryptocurrency Wallets

Cryptocurrency wallets are all created to be secure, but the same protection differs from wallet to wallet. Generally, apart from usernames and passwords, the security of wallets comes from two-factor authentication, such as using a mobile phone to authenticate login or transaction on the exchange.

Recently, Google Authenticator has been used for extra layers of protection, thereby encrypting one's wallet. Also, users can use multi-signature transactions.

Types Of Wallets

There are many different wallets you can use to hold your Bitcoin and other cryptocurrencies. These include online, offline, mobile, hardware, desktop, and paper wallets. Each type refers to the medium the portfolio is stored on.

Some wallets offer additionally than one way of accessing the wallet. For instance, Bitcoin Wallet is a desktop application and a digital app.

Desktop Wallet

Desktop Wallets are one of the most common forms of wallets. They are hosted on a personal computer (desktop) rather than stored on a company's servers.

However, the wallet's security is highly dependent on the safety of the personal computer. Thus, if you decide to get a desktop wallet, it is vital to secure your computer with anti-virus protection and be cautious of any download from unknown sites.

Mobile Wallet

That is a wallet that operates on a smartphone or tablet as a mobile app. While not as secure as full-client desktop wallets, some mobile wallets retain high-security features.

Further, having the app on your phone is essential if you plan to use cryptocurrency for purchases at any brick-and-mortar store. Some mobile wallets support NFC (Near Field Communications) payments.

People can use these as a tap-and-pay kind of system, sending cryptocurrencies directly to the seller that accepts this kind of payment.

Online Wallet

The online wallet is a web-based wallet hosted on a real or virtual server rather than on a downloaded app. The good thing about web-based wallets is that you can access them from any device.

However, it is also a disadvantage, as using a web-based wallet requires you to trust a third-party company to take care of your coins.

Hardware Wallet

Dedicated hardware wallets, such as USB devices, are specially built to hold cryptocurrencies and keep them secure. These devices can also be accessed online to make transactions, retrieve data, and be taken offline for transportation and security.

Paper Wallet

You can print out a QR code for both public and private keys, allowing you to send and receive digital currencies using a paper wallet. This can allow you to avoid storing digital data about your money entirely.

WHAT ARE EXCHANGES?

Cryptocurrency trades are websites where you can buy, sell or exchange cryptocurrencies for other digital currencies or traditional currencies (US dollars or Euro). There are several aspects that you need to consider before choosing an exchange.

Reputation

It would help if you looked at the reputation of exchanges by going through evaluations from individual users and popular industry websites. Additionally, you can also ask questions on forums like BitcoinTalk or Reddit.

Fees

There are fees associated with trading on most exchanges. The prices can differ substantially depending on the business you use. You should understand the deposit, transaction, and withdrawal fees on their website's fee-related information page before joining.

Payment Methods

Users should explore the payment methods available on the exchange. The payment methods available on a website may vary from credit and debit card, wire transfer, PayPal, among others.

Users must ensure that the available payment methods are suitable, or it would inconvenience them to operate on an exchange with limited payment options.

Proof Of Identity

The purchase of cryptocurrencies will usually require identity verification. Further, payment by credit cards may come with a premium price as there is a higher risk of fraud and higher transaction and processing fees.

In addition, the purchase of cryptocurrencies via wire transfer may take significantly longer as banks take time to process.

The extensive majority of the Bitcoin trading platforms in the US and the UK require ID verification to make deposits & withdrawals. Verification may take a few days, protecting the exchange against scams and money laundering.

In several geographical locations, the exchanges are mandated to have KYC (Know Your Customer) requirements by regulators.

Geographical Restrictions

Certain exchanges can limit specific user functions to only be accessible from individual countries. It makes sense to ensure that the deal allows full access to all platform tools and features in the country you currently live in.

Exchange Rate

The exchange rate used by different exchanges may vary. The prices of purchasing Bitcoin will change due to varying exchange rates.

The Best Cryptocurrency Exchanges

There are many exchanges to choose from to buy and sell Bitcoin and other cryptocurrencies, but not all businesses offer the same kind of services. The experience on each sale may range in criteria such as user evaluations, user-friendliness, accessibility, fees, and security.

Coinbase

Coinbase exists as one of the most famous and well-known brokers and trading platforms globally, backed by trusted investors and used by millions of customers globally.

The Coinbase platform makes it easy to buy securely, use, store, and trade digital currency. The users can purchase Bitcoins, Ethereum, and Litecoin from Coinbase through a digital wallet available on Android and iPhone. The trading with other users can happen with other users on the company's Global Digital Asset Exchange (GDAX) subsidiary.

GDAX does not now charge any transfer fees for moving funds between your Coinbase and GDAX accounts.

The exchange has an excellent reputation and is highly secure. The fees charged are reasonable and have a beginner-friendly interface. Coinbase insurance also covers the stored currency.

However, the exchange has limited payment methods and country support, and GDAX is only suitable for technical traders.

Kraken

Founded in 2011, Kraken is a prominent Bitcoin exchange in volume and liquidity. The business lets you buy and sell Bitcoin and exchange between bitcoins and Euros, US Dollars, Canadian Dollars, British Pounds, and Japanese Yen.

It is also feasible to deal with digital currencies other than Bitcoin, including Ethereum, Monero, Ethereum Classic, Augur REP tokens, ICONOMI, Zcash, Litecoin, Dogecoin, Ripple, and Stellar/Lumens, among others.

Additionally, for the more experienced users, Kraken offers margin trading and a host of other trading features.

The exchange has a good reputation, decent exchange rates, and low transaction fees. The business also charges minimal deposit fees and has excellent user support. The best part about the exchange is that it is secure and supported worldwide.

However, the exchange has limited payment methods and may not be suitable for beginners due to its unintuitive user interface.

Cex.Io

Cex.io supplies a broad range of services for using Bitcoin and other cryptocurrencies. The platform lets users quickly trade fiat money for cryptocurrencies and vice versa.

The outlet offers personalized and user-friendly trading dashboards and margin trading for professional traders.

The Cex.io website is secure, intuitive, and cryptocurrencies can be stored in safe cold storage.

The exchange has a solid reputation, an excellent mobile product, and supports credit cards. Also, the business is beginner-friendly, has a decent exchange rate, and is supported worldwide.

However, the exchange has a lengthy verification process, and depositing is quite expensive, especially with credit cards.

Shapeshift

ShapeShift is one of the leading exchanges that support a variety of cryptocurrencies, including Bitcoin, Ethereum, Monero, Zcash, Dash, Dogecoin, among others. It is an excellent exchange for those who want to make instant, straightforward trades without signing up to an account or relying on a platform to hold their funds.

However, ShapeShift does not allow users to purchase cryptos with debit cards, credit cards, or other payment systems. The platform has a no-fiat policy and only allows for exchanging Bitcoin and the other supported cryptocurrencies.

The exchange has an excellent reputation and is beginner-friendly. The number of cryptos available for trade is vast, and the business provides reasonable prices.

Poloniex

Established in 2014, Poloniex is one of the world's ruling cryptocurrency exchanges. The exchange shows a secure trading environment with more than 100 different Bitcoin cryptocurrency teams.

The exchange also offers advanced tools and data analysis for sophisticated traders. Users will permanently close a trade position as one of the most popular trading platforms with the highest trading volumes.

The fees on the exchange may vary from 0.10 to 0.25%. There are no fees for withdrawals above the transaction fee required by the network.

The exchange allows for expedited account creation, high-volume lending, a user-friendly interface, and low trading fees.

However, the exchange has slow customer service and no fiat support.

TECHNICAL ANALYSIS FOR CRYPTOCURRENCY TRADING: THE FUNDAMENTALS

Since the cryptocurrency market is unpredictable, you'll need a trading strategy to keep you on track. Many cryptocurrency traders use technical research to aid in developing their plans. This form of study will provide insight into cryptocurrency's past trends, allowing you to forecast where it will go in the future.

Technical Analysis: What Is It And How Does It Work?

It would help if you first grasped what technical analysis is before using it in your cryptocurrency trading. Technological forecasting is the process of predicting the future of a business using real-world data. It entails looking at historical data on the cryptocurrencies in question, such as volume and movement.

Fundamental analysis is another popular approach for determining the cryptocurrency's intrinsic value. On the other hand, the specialized analysis looks at patterns and analytic charting methods to see the crypto's strengths and limitations, holding them in mind for potential designs. Traders also use technical analysis in more conventional assets such as stocks, currencies, commodities, futures, and forex. Using technical research on all of those properties would be remarkably close to using it on cryptocurrencies.

The Basic Ideas Technical Analysis Is Based On

A few concepts are part of the Dow Theory and serve as technical research foundations. To begin with, the theory suggests that market pricing takes into account all factors. That "all" in cryptocurrencies includes present, future, and past demand, legislation, trader expectations, trader awareness of the cryptocurrency, and more. Traders use technological research to look at the price to see what it means regarding market sentiment.

Regarding crypto pricing or patterns, technical research operates under the premise that history repeats itself. Technical analysts use this information to make assumptions about consumer psychology and cryptocurrency.

Technical analysis is often based on the notion that price fluctuations are never random. Instead, these price changes are guided by short- or long-term patterns. When a cryptocurrency follows one way, it almost always follows the opposite trend. Traders using technical analysis will attempt to isolate these movements to benefit.

In general, technological research is more concerned about what is happening than with why it is happening. Instead of thinking about millions of factors that drive price movements, the emphasis is on supply and demand.

How To Read Candlestick Charts

A candlestick chart or graph is the most common graph used by crypto traders for technical analysis. It can seem overwhelming at foremost, but it's pretty simple to comprehend once you get the hang of it.

Candlestick gets its name because each action point on the graph compares a candlestick. They're red (or pink) or leafy rectangles with a bar arriving out of the top or bottom, comparable to a candle's wick. The length and line of the candlestick, as well as the color, reveal essential details.

The opening and closing prices of the cryptocurrency for that day are at the top and bottom of the central rectangle of the candlestick. The opening price is at the bottom, and the closing price is at the top, indicating that the crypto has increased value. The opening price of the crypto is at the top, and the closing price is at the bottom, as shown by red (or pink) candlesticks. Green is a good color since the coin's value has risen.

Both ends of the candle will have wicks coming out of it. These are the cryptocurrency's lowest and highest values for the same period. In other words, the wicks indicate how volatile the market is right now.

Getting The Basics Out Of Candlestick Charts

Candlestick charts can be used to see how a cryptocurrency performed in the past and make projections for the future. For example, if the wicks are long, this means a highly volatile market. As a result, cryptocurrencies have a higher risk of causing you substantial losses or gains throughout the relevant era. Furthermore, given the market's high uncertainty, this could be corrected tomorrow.

When the candlestick's wick is short, however, it means that the demand might be changing. When the top wick is short, the cryptocurrency's highest price that day was most likely notable in the coin's history. A longer wick at the top suggests that the cash was considerably more costly at some stage during the day before traders profited from selling it. This pattern can suggest a bearish market that is about to fall.

A short wick on the bottom means that the coin is still being sold. As a result of the increased availability, the cryptocurrency price is expected to fall even more. On the other hand, a longer wick suggests that the price has formerly dipped and that no further decline is anticipated. In other terms, traders want to purchase cryptocurrency at its lowest price, which they believe is now. That might guide to more improvements in the future.

Understanding And Using Trend Lines

Trend lines are one of the first elements of technical analysis that traders can learn. Trend lines show how the cryptocurrency is moving, but determining them needs some study. That is especially valid given the brief existence of cryptocurrencies. Because of this instability, the technical analysis must identify the underlying trend moving up or down among the smaller peaks and lows. Trends can also shift sideways, adding to the complexity. A cryptocurrency with a sideways pattern has not gone dramatically up or down.

The majority of cryptocurrency trading and monitoring tools will have built-in trend lines. These can be automated, but you can also draw your trend lines for a more precise result. Your forecasts would be more accurate if the trend line is accurate.

The procedure for drawing a precise trend line varies depending on the research software you're using. In most cases, the trend line is drawn directly over the candlestick's lowest price. The bar is then approximately extended until it reaches the lowest point of the next candlestick. You should be able to open the line from there automatically. Make the appropriate changes to ensure you get the same lows for both.

Understanding Support And Resistance Levels

Support and resistance are other important concepts to grasp in technical analysis. These are two horizontal lines that you can draw on your trading chart to understand the cryptocurrency better.

The sponsorship level is the price at which traders are willing to buy large portions of cryptocurrency. In other words, there is a lot of demand because traders believe the crypto is undervalued. When the cryptocurrency reaches the support level, there will be a surge in demand, usually stopping the decline. It can even shift the momentum upward in some cases.

The levels of resistance are the polar opposite. In this case, there is a lot of supply but not a lot of demand. Buyers believe the cryptocurrency is currently overpriced and are hesitant to purchase it. If the cryptocurrency price approaches this resistance level, it will encounter an overabundance of supply, causing a falling price.

Cryptocurrency technical analysts will occasionally notice variations on this. In these situations, buyers may congregate near the support lines, and sellers may sell near the resistance lines. When it comes to lateral movement, this happens more frequently.

A breakout of support or resistance levels in your technical analysis most likely indicates that the current trend is strengthening. If the resistance level becomes the support level, the pattern is maintained further. Remember that false breakout can happen, in which case the design will remain unchanged. As a result, technical research necessitates the examination of several statistics to identify patterns.

Getting To Know Trading Volumes

A cryptocurrency's trading volume will help you decide whether or not a pattern is essential. A high trading volume usually indicates a significant trend that you should pay attention to. On the other hand, the low trading volume suggests a poor trend that may fade quickly.

If the price of a cryptocurrency falls, check the trading volume to put this information to use. In the decreases, look for low volume, and in the rises, look for higher volume. That would mean that the cryptocurrency will likely be on a positive trajectory with long-term development. If, on the other hand, the amount during those declines increases, the upward trend will most likely come to an end prematurely. Volume can also provide similar details, but it can give the opposite in a downtrend.

TOKENS - THE DIFFERENCE BETWEEN COINS AND TOKENS

In the world of cryptocurrency, the terms' coins' and 'tokens' are frequently used interchangeably. That is perfectly natural, but it is also technically incorrect. Another term that can be bracketed with coins and tokens is 'digital assets, and it's essential to understand the difference between these three aspects of cryptocurrency.

That makes it possible for a community to enforce the system's transparent rules. These three terms are related to the blockchain and cryptocurrency, but they have subtly different purposes and definitions.

Crypto Coins

Coins are essentially units of exchange that are associated with blockchain networks. While blockchains have no obligation to be associated with currency, it is undoubtedly the case that most existing blockchains have their coins. These can then be used for payment, effectively digital money. The most notable example of coins in this sphere is Bitcoin, although many others.

Cryptocurrency coins share many characteristics with traditional fiat currency. They are easily distributed, widely accepted for payment, portable and durable. They differ from traditional currencies in the limited supply available, which is one of the defining characteristics of the cryptocurrency niche.

Bitcoin has an entire supply of 21 million coins, intended to protect against inflation. This inflation is an inbuilt characteristic of the monetary system due to the inevitable degradation of economic value caused by the increasing supply of credit. Essentially, when older adults make misty-eyed comments about some decades ago have been able to catch the train, enjoy a cheeseburger and fries, watch a movie, ride home, and still have changed from a quarter or tuppence, this is a manifestation of inflation. That is not some inbuilt law of nature, such as the sun rising in the morning or the tide rushing to shore. It is not inevitable. It is absolutely a function of the monetary system. The supply of money continues to expand due to monetary policy and the fact that there are no such limits on the amount of currency and debt in circulation.

Fungibility

Another important aspect of cryptocurrency coins relates to a word that you will frequently encounter in this field, but which can be a little baffling to the uninitiated. Cryptocurrency coins are fungible. That means that crypto coins can be easily exchanged for something of equal value. There is such a thing as non-fungible tokens, and we will discuss this further as the book develops.

In cryptocurrency, coins are inevitably related to the public and open blockchain. That means that all community participants are invited to join the network and acquire the cash. Cryptocurrency coins can also be sent and received. In most cases, they can be obtained by mining or another similar process, although this doesn't apply to all cryptocurrency projects. As the supply of cryptocurrency coins is also usually finite, there is also a theoretical point in the future when it will no longer be possible to mine the coins.

Crypto Tokens

Conversely, tokens, also frequently referred to as crypto tokens, are units of value built on top of existing blockchain networks by the developers and organizations associated with the projects. There are often links and compatibility between tokens and coins on cryptocurrency networks, but they should be viewed as an entirely different digital asset class.

Cryptocurrency tokens are created by the platforms constructed on the blockchain network. The tokens can then serve a range of purposes on the blockchain, as is reflected among the many great cryptocurrency projects that have been developed. For example, ether's native token is associated with the hugely influential Ethereum blockchain. But many other different tickets can also be built on the identical blockchain, particularly as the structure of Ethereum has become hugely influential and admired. Many blockchains are associated with currency, but blockchain has other possibilities, with content creation becoming one of the most popular areas.

It's also important to know that many different standards are used for cryptocurrency tokens. ERC-20 has become the most popular, operating within the Ethereum ecosystem. At the time of writing, Ethereum looks extremely well-placed to establish itself as the most widely used of all blockchains, even including Bitcoin. Still, the crypto space continues to evolve rapidly, and this is by no means inevitable.

ERC-20 isn't the only standard available. There are also thousands of ERC-721 tokens in circulation, and it is believed that many other bars and token platforms will become popular in the foreseeable future.

Smart Contracts And Programmable Tokens

Cryptocurrency tokens are strongly related to smart contracts, which are involved in defining the features and functions of the token in question and several parameters associated with the network. Smart contracts are significant in cryptocurrency and have an inherent relationship with tokens. Any successful cryptocurrency token should be programmable, permissionless, free from trust issues, and completely transparent. These are fundamental qualities associated with cryptocurrency projects and tokens and must be delivered if a platform is to meet the approval of the discerning cryptocurrency community.

Another critical aspect of cryptocurrency tokens is that they tend to be programmable. That means that they can be run on software protocols composed of smart contracts that outline the features and functions of the token and rules of engagement associated with the network. This programmable quality means that tokens are highly flexible and can be potentially used for multiple purposes. Tokens are also accessible for anyone participating in the system, without any exceptional credentials being required, while roles associated with the protocol should be viewable and verifiable by all participants.

Cryptocurrency tokens can represent virtually anything. Already, there are tokens available that are associated with physical assets, digital assets, real estate, art, processing power, digital storage, and even abstract concepts! In short, if something has value, it can be represented in a cryptocurrency token. It could be a painting, and it could be a currency, it could be a powerful computer server, it could even theoretically be a sportsman or woman! There is no limit to the utility of crypto tokens, which makes them such an exciting concept.

That is where the term 'digital assets' comes in. Cryptocurrency tokens capture a digital asset. As the niche continues to mature, it is expected that these digital assets will only continue to expand and evolve. As more people understand how cryptocurrency operates, the number of use cases and community requirements will grow, leading to more flexibility and diversity in the cryptocurrency space. The simple fact will inevitably exacerbate that cryptocurrency and the blockchain are almost infinitely less restrictive than any traditional currency platform, as the digital world is based on intangibles. Cryptos can become anything to anyone and everything to all people. That opens up an array of new social and economic possibilities, one of the most compelling arguments for the blockchain.

Types Of Token

Another distinction that needs to be briefly covered is the difference between security tokens, equity tokens, and utility tokens (there are also payment tokens, but these do not differ significantly from coins). The majority of cryptocurrency tokens are security tokens, particularly for those platforms that ran initial client offerings (ICO). These tokens derive their name because they are a form of security, a type of financial investment. In this respect, cryptocurrency security tokens are treated similarly to traditional securities.

By contrast, equity tokens offer stock or share in the company that issues the token. These are pretty rare by comparison, making the ICO process considerably more complicated. Finally, utility tokens are sometimes referred to as application tokens and provide access to products or services. In this regard, tokens can have completely different purposes, contributing to the diversity of the concept.

There can be confusion over whether a token fits into a particular criterion, but legal precedent provides a guide. In 1946, the Securities and Exchange Commission engaged in a landmark case with W. J. Howey Co.,[1] which is now considered the benchmark for deciding whether transactions should be regarded as investment contracts or securities. That, therefore, has an impact on cryptocurrency tokens as well.

Suppose a cryptocurrency token is considered a security. In that case, it must be derived from an investment of fiat currency, it must support a joint enterprise, and investment must be made with an expectation of future profit. This last characteristic, in particular, does not necessarily apply to all tokens, as some can have more practical purposes.

TOKENS AND DAPPS

Another critical aspect of tokens is that most are designed to be used with decentralized applications (dApps). These are apps for programs that run on a blockchain network rather than utilizing a single computer network. By using this approach, apps operate outside the control of a single or central authority, meaning that they are more democratized and evolve as part of community activity. Many examples of tokens serve some function related to dApps; for instance, Musicoin enables users to gain access to music and streaming via the Musicoin platform. And the Binance token reduces fees on the Binance platform by 50%. That is another aspect of tokens fundamentally different from coins, as the latter are merely instruments of exchange.

BLOCKCHAIN BUSINESS MODELS

Another example of exciting development is WePower, which allows users to buy and sell electricity on the blockchain via smart contracts. The WePower token represents a certain amount of energy, which can fluctuate based on training. The business and use cases associated with tokens are almost limitless.

Because the blockchain is highly flexible and completely decentralized, the technology delivers a broader range of potential business models than have existed formerly. The blockchain makes it possible for all businesses to shift their entire operation into a decentralized platform, altering how users interact with the system and how transactions are conducted.

A vast innovation advantage can be stored inside the blockchain and never tampered with. That offers security advantages, but it also means that companies can leverage the transparency of the blockchain to improve the way that their supply chains work. Blockchains are also frequently combined with artificial intelligence and machine learning, creating smart and organic platforms that can achieve tasks in entirely different ways than were envisaged formerly and offer increased flexibility.

One of the most compelling business models associated with the blockchain is the utility token. Ripple and Stellar are great examples of this model, in which their tokens drive the functionality of the business. Both Ripple and Stellar have become closely affiliated with banks and financial institutions, which can then arrange for fund transfers via the use of the XRP or XLM tokens. That is faster and considerably more cost-effective than any other formerly accessible form of transfer, which is now being widely recognized by mainstream financial entities. Hence, Ripple is often advocated as an ideal cross-border payment system.

BLOCKCHAIN-AS-A-SERVICE

The Blockchain-as-a-Service (BaaS) model allows businesses to outsource some of their more onerous backend operations, ensuring that they can focus on their shop-floor business. BaaS providers tend to offer user authentication, database management, remote updating, push notifications, cloud storage, and host. These can be handled more efficiently than with any form of existing technology. Google Firebase and Microsoft Azure are compelling examples of this approach.

By employing the blockchain in this way, the technology effectively manages and solves all infrastructure and maintenance issues, enabling companies to focus on improving their core website functionality instead of constantly tweaking glitches and bugs.

CRYPTOCURRENCY VERSUS THE FINANCIAL MARKET

Suppose you are new to the cryptocurrencies world. Then again, cryptocurrencies have become a mainstream phenomenon in the financial market. Right now, the total value of these digital currencies has swelled up to more than $2. As a result, investors are questioning the place of stocks in the market. Still, you have significant experience with stocks, understanding the primary difference between crypto, stocks, and other traditional investment plans can help decide which one to invest in.

Nearly half of the investors in the market are now considering investing rather than plunking down their money into their stock. The reason for that is not far-fetched. The benefits one can accumulate in crypto are far more than what an investor can ignore. But many of them are swarming into this digital world rush. They are investing with a lot of hope yet little knowledge.

Apart from individual investors, companies are rolling out funds to the digital world, despite its ups and downs. The reason for this is not far-fetched, either. Its rapid appreciation and hype are enough to make one invest in expanding one's portfolio.

However, a big challenge with crypto is how investors perceive it. Most new investors do not know the difference between digital currencies and stocks. As a result, they ended up getting everything twisted.

That will help you know certain things about it and help guard your decision on how to invest.

To consider the differences, you must understand that the significant difference between the two can be seen in how you value them as an investor. So, as an investor, you probably need to know the value of each of them.

More so, you need to understand that a stock is an ownership interest in a business. That is backed by the company's cash flow and assets of the major. In contrast, digital currencies are not supported by anything at all. Not with cash flow or a company's assets.

Like I have said, stocks have legal backing. They are used by legitimate establishments that are expected to turn to profit. They include physical assets, such as silver, gold, and others, as part of their valuation. That makes it easy for investors to calculate the value of a stock in the financial market.

Digital currencies, however, don't have such features. They are not lawful tender, nor are they backed by any company's assets. Instead, they are valued based on the popularity they get from people.

You should understand what you want to buy if you're purchasing digital money. More so, you should be able to compare traditional investments, such as stock, which always have a solid long-term record, and others and digital monies.

A Question You Should Ask

It is important to want what you are investing in as an investor. Knowing this will help you adequately see the investment you are about to make. In addition, you will be able to familiarize yourself with it so much that both the risk and the reward are well understood.

Risks and rewards are cogent information every investor must seek to know before investing their money into the business. That is because they are the critical factors that determine and drive an investment's success.

So, you should ask yourself, "Between virtual currencies and stocks, which should I invest in?" This question will be a driving force that will propel you to seek specific information about the investment. If you don't have adequate information on both the risks and the rewards, you can't make the circulation. You can't be successful in any investment if you have not calculated both. If you have one without these two essential things, you are probably investing in something more like gambling.

Below are some basic things about financial markets and virtual currencies.

Other Financial Markets

First, you must understand that we refer to bonds, precious metals, and stocks when we talk about another financial market. These are not the same as crypto, even though they have some areas of similarities.

Stocks

Like I have briefly explained earlier, a stock is a fractional ownership interest in any business. Don't lose sight of this. The wiggling prices and benefits you can derive from the market might make you overwhelmed. On the other hand, as the owner's stake in the business, stocks enable shareholders to claim a portion of the company's assets and cash flow. The two possibilities substantiate your investment and provide a basis for its valuation and approval.

The Nature Of Stocks

Perhaps you have been wondering why stocks rise and fall. Here is the answer: A movement of stock's price guarantees the business's future success. That gives the investors access to the future of the company. While investors may be expecting the best in a short time, the stock price overly depends on the company's ability to increase its profit for the long term. That means that the success of a stock company depends on how stocks rise over time.

Cryptocurrency

Though we have stable coins, there is an exception to that cryptocurrency's possibilities. Unlike stocks, crypto has no backed hard assets. But this may not be the point with popular cryptos such as Ethereum and Bitcoin.

Crypto allows you to perform various functions. You can use it to send money to another investor through smart contracts that automate carrying out the transaction once you have reached an agreement.

The Nature Of Cryptocurrency

Like stocks, virtual currencies also have unstable prices. It is not a legal commodity because the movement of prices is instigated upon speculation driven by sentiments. That means it's impressive for the cost to move when feeling changes. That may not be too fast, but drastic. Inform your understanding that digital monies are driven by the idea that investors will need them more in the future. That is why many investors will buy certain currencies into this wallet then leave it for a while until there are excessive demands in the market. That is done with the hope that someone will buy it for a higher amount in the future. That is what investors refer to as the "greater fool theory of investing."

To make earnings in the crypto world, you need to get someone who will buy more than the price you got it. The market must be more optimistic about it than are.

Stocks And Cryptocurrency. What You Should Consider

If your goal is to invest and maximize the potentials in both crypto and stocks, you probably need to take the time to consider your risk tolerance. You should ask yourself if you truly can handle the volatility of both investments. As you know, both are market-based investments with huge volatility rates. So, it's important how well you can respond to losses and gains. More so, you need to ask if you want to handle the volatility of these kinds of assets.

Below are things you probably have to look into before plugging your money into any of these investments.

Safety And Risk Management

As market-based investments, both platforms involve some level of risk tolerance. As you have read earlier, the volatile nature of both might not give you access to predict when and how much you should earn within a short period. That means, even as an investor, you might not be able to predict the price of stock nor that of a digital currency due to its unstable nature.

Spot The Difference!

Unlike digital monies, a stock's level of volatility is higher. That is because there is a high possibility that many stocks can rise to 100% or more within a financial year and may fall just as quickly.

Also, as an investor, you can sell a stock and push down the price if you don't like it. Nevertheless, a company has to go out of business for a store to be worthless.

The stock market is an effective and robust way to invest with a track record of successful transactions that you can bank on.

You can own your fund if you don't want to buy individual stocks, like those based on the Standard & Poor's 500, which gained more than 10% per year on average over time.

Long-term performance on stocks depends on the underlying company's success.

The Cryptocurrency

Unlike stocks, virtual currencies are not backed by a company's assets or cash flow. Instead, it relies on sentiment to push up its price.

Volatility is not instant; it is drastic, with the price rising or falling fifty percent more in a commonplace year.

As a result of the lack of legal sanctioning, countries can ban it for life. China and other countries have done that already.

Because of its relatively new nature, the market is not firmly established yet. So, virtual currencies can't be regarded as an asset class.

Though stocks are a risky type of business, cryptocurrencies even can be more speculative.

Time Horizon

Another critical thing that must form part of your consideration is the time horizon. That implies the time you need money from an investment. After investing in a business, you probably have the time to expect your business to maximize profits for you. That is what is referred to as your time horizon. However, you must know that the shorter your timeline, the safer your asset should be. When it is safer, it will be there when you need it. More so, you should know that the more volatile your investment is, the less suited it becomes for those who may likely need it.

More often than not, experts recommend that investors with risky assets, such as stocks need at least three years to ride out the volatility.

Below are what you should know about the time horizon of each.

It would help if you had it formerly. Individual stocks have more volatility than portfolio stocks, which are primarily designed to benefit from diversification. They are often volatile but not too volatile, like crypto.

You enjoy more stocks if you are the type who can leave the money alone and refuse to access it, even when you have the urge to do so. This comes with a huge benefit—the longer you leave it, the better.

Stocks can also be more volatile than others. For instance, value stocks or dividend stocks fluctuate less, like growth stocks.

On stocks, you enjoy the privilege of shifting from one difficult (growth stock) to the safer one. Investors approaching their retirement time make use of this because it allows them to tap their money when there is a need to do so.

Virtual Currencies

While we consider stocks to be volatile, virtual monies are ridiculously explosive. For instance, in 2021, Bitcoin lost more than half of its value yet regained it within a few months. Such a volatile nature makes the business unsuited for the short-time investor since they might have to wait a while before maximizing the profits in the market.

With that, we can agree that cryptocurrencies are suited for investors who would like to invest for a long-time purpose. These traders can leave the money tied up and patiently wait until it is recovered. Such traders won't be bothered about the fall of the price since they are in for an extended period. They think of years rather than months and weeks.

PLACING BUY AND SELL ORDERS

Cryptocurrencies are destined to be in a perpetual state of price discovery, with the price of coins on exchanges in flux as they are bought and sold. The collective perception of the value of coins changes as new information enters the cryptosphere. But other factors influence the price that you should be aware of before deciding how to purchase crypto.

Most exchanges are fully transparent with their order books, viewed within the user trading panel. The numbers constantly change as old orders are filled and new orders are placed. You will notice a green segment and a red segment, with the current price landing somewhere in the middle. The green part shows the bid price: the price at which different buyers are willing to purchase coins. The red segment offers the asking price: the price at which sellers are willing to sell their coins. The distinction between the request and ask price is the spread. Spreads depend on liquidity.

Limit Vs. Market Orders

Liquidity is a standard of the ease of buying and selling an asset. To create liquidity, buyers and sellers use limit orders or offers to buy and sell coins at specific prices. The more limit orders on the books, the higher the liquidity, and the quicker orders can be filled.

Anyone who places a limit order on the books is considered a market maker since they are adding liquidity and therefore helping to stabilize the price of an asset. On the other hand, market orders are instant buy orders that are executed at the current market price, removing liquidity. A market taker is someone who uses a market order to take away liquidity by either buying or selling. Day traders who need to make immediate trades would be one example. Market makers pay lower fees than market takers since they narrow the spreads by adding liquidity to the order books. Market takers pay a premium for the convenience of instantly having their orders filled.

Understanding liquidity is essential since different exchanges have different spreads based on available liquidity. Lesser-known businesses will have higher reaches, which means you risk paying more than you would on other trading platforms.

Another factor to consider before placing orders is the illiquidity of lesser-known coins across exchanges. Less supply and demand means there will be fewer orders on the books. That creates slippage that can be especially problematic with larger market orders. A 1% slippage on a $10,000 market order means the total cost for the asset will be $100 different than expected.

As another example, say you have illiquid coins that are suddenly plummeting. You may plan to sell them, but there is such a discrepancy in the spread that your orders aren't filled, leaving you stuck with your bags. The less liquidity for a coin on an exchange, whether buying or selling, the more unstable the price. When in doubt, navigate to the specific trading pair for the business you use on CoinGecko and take a look at its spread.

#	Exchange	Pair	Price	Spread
*	eToroX Sponsored			
*	Crypto.com Sponsored			
1	Gate.io	AR/USDT	$59.17	0.05%
2	Binance	AR/USDT	$59.28	0.15%
3	HitBTC	AR/USDT	$58.98	0.36%
4	Huobi Global	AR/USDT	$59.20	0.85%
5	MEXC Global	AR/USDT	$59.33	0.19%
6	Binance	AR/BTC	$59.23	0.02%
7	MEXC Global	AR/ETH	$58.94	0.3%
8	BitMart	AR/USDT	$59.39	0.57%
9	Binance	AR/BUSD	$58.27	0.33%
10	CoinBene	AR/USDT	$58.93	0.78%
11	Hoo.com	AR/USDT	$58.17	0.64%
12	CoinEx	AR/USDT	$58.06	0.09%
13	Huobi Global	AR/BTC	$59.07	3.85%
14	Binance	AR/BNB	$58.22	0.68%
15	Bittrex	AR/BTC	$59.03	0.74%
16	BigONE	AR/USDT	$58.12	0.84%
17	CoinEx	AR/BTC	$57.67	7.69%
18	BHEX	AR/USDT	$57.67	1.25%

Notice the difference in price and spread for AR/USDT across different exchanges. CoinEx has a 7.69% spread!

Limit buy orders are bids that you place below the current market price, hoping the cost of the coin will drop and your order will be filled. For example, if I want to purchase $100 worth of RUNE for $11.11, but the current price is $12.36, I can place a limit order with $11.11 as the price I'm willing to pay. Limit sell orders work on the same principle, except the asking price you are ready to sell will be higher than when you purchased. For example, after my limit buys order is filled at $11.11, I could set a limit sell order which would fill when RUNE hits my ask price of $27.36.

The risk with boundary orders is that the price may continue to run up or down, leaving your bid unfilled. The reward is that if the price drops to your offer, you will receive a discounted price. Likewise, you will sell at a profit if it rises to your request.

All limit orders will show up in your trade history as open orders. The money you have in your account will be docked for limited buy orders until the order is executed. In other words, you won't be able to use those funds until the order is either filled or you cancel it manually. To cancel an order, it's usually a matter of clicking a checkbox on the far right in the "open orders" panel.

Note that certain crypto apps such as crypto and cash app don't give you the option to place limit orders. Crypto wallets such as Trust wallet and Ledger also offer quick buy options, but with the same caveat. You also may not be capable of using ACH or wire transfer to onboard your fiat. With credit card fees as high as 10%, this is something to consider before registering. In all of these cases, lack of functionality is the sacrifice you make for convenience and simplicity.

Instantly buy and sell trading apps are crypto convenience stores. They'll get you your quick fix without all the bells and whistles, but you're likely going to pay more due to larger spreads and higher fees. If you buy more significant amounts over time, you will save a lot more money using a vetted exchange. FTX, Kucoin, Kraken, and Binance have great apps with full functionality and lower fees.

Take Profits And Stop Losses

3Commas is a command center for all types of trades. It links to many top exchanges through APIs and can execute trades on your behalf without you even having to log in to your business (s). It will also tell you exactly how much money you are up or down on each trade, which is sadly absent on deals. There is even a mobile app for those who need to track profits and losses and make trades on the go.

The best feature of 3Commas is smart trading. You can set limit orders, take profits, stop losses, and more. Take profit is an order for a trading platform to automatically close part or all trade on your behalf at a predetermined price.

Stop losses are similar to taking profits; only they prevent losses rather than lock in gains. When you set a stop loss, the trading platform will automatically execute a sell order for part or all of your position once the price drops to the preset level.

While you can also stop losses and take profits through traditional exchanges, 3Commas will allow you to create different tiers where a specific percentage of the coin is bought or sold. As an example, let's say you purchased RUNE for $7. You could then set the following profit levels: sell 20% at $10, sell 45% at $15, and sell the rest at $20.

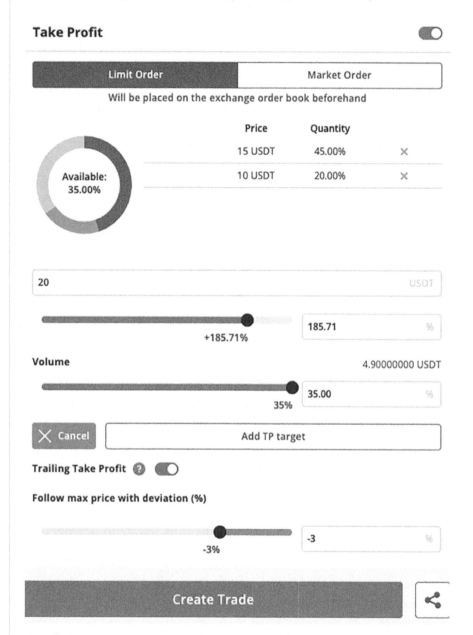

Image 22: Setting profit targets for RUNE using 3Commas. Notice that "Trailing Take Profit" is activated for the last mark at $20, with a 3% follow max price.

Another great feature is setting trailing to take profits and stop losses. Let's say that for your last take profit tier in the example for RUNE above, you put a trailing take profit of 3% at $20. Once the $20 strike price hits, the trailing take profit is activated. If the price suddenly drops 3%, the sell order is executed. But if RUNE continues to rise, your coins won't be sold until the price drops 3%. Theoretically, this means that RUNE could skyrocket to $33.3, and you could still be in the trade, given that there were no 3% pullbacks along the way.

Trailing stop losses are similar. If you bought RUNE at $7, you could then activate a trailing stop loss at -10% after setting all of your take profit targets. That would sell your position if the price dropped to $6.30. Then as the price rises, the stop loss will rise as well, so that it always remains 10% below the current price. If RUNE rises to $10, the trailing stop loss will close your position if the price drops to $9.

The stop loss feature on 3 Commas. Here a trailing stop loss of -10% is used.

Paper Trading And Ai Trading Bots

3Commas also offers a paper trading account with a balance spread out over various cryptocurrencies so that you can practice trading with paper money. The option to give your trading strategy a dry run can save you boatloads of money when it comes time for the real deal. You can use all the standard features of 3Commas, the only difference being you can't cash out when all is said and done!

Professional traders use paper trading accounts to test out AI trading bots that they have developed. Trading bots are computer programs that execute trades for you based on your set parameters. As opposed to intelligent trading, trading bots will continue buying and selling different cryptocurrencies as long as they remain active. As an example, 3Commas has grid bots used when the price is consolidating in a specific range. The grid bot will create buy and sell orders as the price rises and decreases in that range.

AI trading bots are increasing in popularity since they remove emotion. At the same time, they require constant monitoring and aren't practical for long-term investors. Bots execute hundreds, even thousands of smaller trades, complicating taxes and creating higher trading fees on exchanges. Everyone is different–if you want to see how they work, try them out using a paper account on 3Commas.

Sticky Trading Pairs

You will notice that most coins have multiple different pairs. A trading pair consists of two assets that are traded together. BTC/USD is the simplest example since it shows the price of bitcoin in terms of dollars. Almost every major coin can be paired with BTC and ETH. It can be unclear to use specific trading pairs because the value is relative to the two assets in the team. For example, if you search for XMR/BTC, you will see the price of 1 XMR in terms of BTC. Since

1 BTC costs exponentially more than 1 XMR, the price becomes a small fraction. As of this writing, 1 XMR costs about 0.00734 BTC.

Trading pairs are helpful when you want to rotate gains directly from one coin into another. For example, if BTC recently rose 30%, and you see that ATOM is showing signs of going stratospheric, you can use the ATOM/BTC pair to sell your BTC directly into ATOM, saving you the fees from having to convert to USD first.

For most other trading scenarios, it's easier to start with either USD or a stablecoin. Stablecoins are important cryptocurrencies pegged to a fiat currency such as USD, another cryptocurrency, or a commodity such as gold. They are backed by reserve assets and offer general price stability in an otherwise volatile market. Tether (USDT) is a stablecoin that stands pegged to the dollar. 1 USDT = 1 USD, with minor variations depending on supply and demand.

MAKING LONG TERM CRYPTO INVESTMENTS

More people will be curious to learn how to collect crypto coins in the future. People like your friends and family will want to know what they can do to accumulate cryptocurrencies, and now you'll be able to refer them to this book.

Generally speaking, if you hold a well-diversified cryptocurrency investment position over a longer time, you may begin to introduce a few more slightly speculative investments into your overall portfolio mix. That's because you could (theoretically) tolerate a tiny bit of fluctuation in market value with the hope that over time the good times will balance out for your profit. But what if the market value does not perform according to your expectations? In that case, you would either need to cut your losses or re-evaluate your entire strategy. Fortunately, by diversifying in a variety of top Altcoins plus the Bitcoin King and by implementing an effective dollar-cost averaging process, you are more than likely to come out ahead over the long term.

One of the difficulties with speculative long-term investments like new ICO altcoins is identifying when they might outperform the market in terms of performance. It is important to remember that these are dynamic, constantly changing, and subject to significant changes in the current environment. A portfolio designed to take advantage of recent market fluctuations will probably not fare well in years to come. That is why you must have some way of gauging how these investments are performing. Fortunately, this is not as difficult as it seems with a good cryptocurrency broker such as Binance, Binance.us, or Coinbase. Just check your account statements regularly to ensure that cryptocurrencies are performing as expected.

Of course, some categories of long-term investments are much riskier than others. For example, speculative ICO altcoins are considered to be a high risk but potentially high return investment, so this is something that you want to avoid as a beginner. Nevertheless, as you become more proficient and understand more about the different kinds of novel crypto coin investments you are interested in, these speculative investments can play a vital role. If you do choose to invest in speculative ICO altcoins, then be sure to limit their weighting in your crypto portfolio so that, ideally, they do not exceed more than 10% of all your crypto. It is recommended that the remainder of your portfolio consist of top-performing, well-established altcoins as well as Bitcoin.

It's also essential that you think about your retirement planning and the time horizon in mind for retirement. If you are looking to make long-term investments in the crypto market, you will undoubtedly want to use the right crypto exchange broker to do so. However, not all crypto brokers can provide you with access to all of the crypto currencies available in the markets you want to invest in. In addition, some exchanges only offer a small selection of the many different types of cryptocurrencies that are available and might not provide all of the information you need to make an informed decision. A sound investment strategy will always involve having a long-term investment plan in place and being knowledgeable about your own retirement goals, in addition to using a reputable crypto exchange such as those considered earlier.

Once you have taken the time to learn about the various types of long-term crypto investments that you should and shouldn't invest in. You have developed a solid investment strategy; you should have a better idea of what types of long-term investments you should be making. Knowing these types of investments will go a long way in ensuring that you always stay invested in the crypto markets.

Remember also to check www. coinmarketcap regularly to see which altcoins are challenging for the #1 spot currently held by the Bitcoin King. As with any investment, knowledge is critical. Keeping yourself informed and up-to-date about all of your crypto investment choices will ensure that you make the right decisions about where to put your money.

Benefits Of Investing In Cryptocurrencies

There are now over 5,000 Altcoins cryptocurrencies out there. While, in general, you can use Cryptocurrency to purchase items, most wise folks generally only treat it as an investment. Hopefully, this book has helped guide you through the process to help ensure you have a positive experience.

Many experts agree that investing 5 to 10% of your portfolio in cryptocurrencies is a wise investment for the long term.

Keep in mind that some altcoin cryptocurrencies are unpredictable, and some can become worthless.

It is unlikely that the top 15 considered in this book will become worthless, but it's a necessary precaution to keep in mind that no one knows what the future holds exactly. So don't risk investing more than you can afford to lose.

If you invest in altcoin cryptocurrencies carelessly, you could lose your shirt, so be careful. However, if you invest wisely (for example, by rereading this book carefully), top altcoins and bitcoins can have the potential to make you a fortune in the years ahead.

There are many benefits to supporting Cryptocurrencies such as Bitcoin, Ethereum, Cardano, Binance Coin, Ripple, Dogecoin, Polkadot, Solana, Uniswap, Bitcoin Cash, Litecoin, Chainlink, among other top altcoins. Many of these cryptocurrencies function very much like traditional money. They are backed by digital assets and mathematical algorithms and, therefore, secure just as gold and silver coins are. One big difference between Cryptocurrencies and traditional investments is how they are traded. Unlike stocks and bonds, which usually trade on stock exchanges, cryptocurrencies can only be bought or sold on specialized crypto exchanges that are either centralized (like Binance or Coinbase) or decentralized (like Uniswap).

That means that instead of trading shares, you are trading digital coins. That also allows you to leverage your investment because you can control a great deal of value at any given time. Investing in Cryptocurrencies might not be suitable for those who are new to the markets or uncomfortable with the technology and computer science behind these currencies. For example, if you are interested in putting money into stocks, you would need to understand the mechanics of the stock market even to start considering investing in currencies. The exact can be said of investing in cryptocurrencies.

On the other hand, there are many benefits associated with investing in cryptocurrencies for beginners, intermediates, or advanced investors who have read this book. In many cases, with the blockchain technology involved in crypto investments, it is much faster and easier to get up to speed on Cryptocurrencies than it would be to understand, use and manage some traditional assets. Many Cryptocurrencies are also highly liquid, making it easy even for novices to get in (or out) of the market almost whenever they want.

There are many benefits of funding in Cryptocurrencies, including their relatively low cost and diversification of investment risk. Also, due to the distributed nature of these cryptocurrencies, there is very little possible hacking which can be a significant concern for companies and governments. In addition, with the rising number of users, anyone can start investing in the future of Cryptocurrencies which also provides investors with a wide range of opportunities. In general, by using the distributed ledger technology behind blockchains, it is possible to enjoy the benefits of ICO along with the cost efficiency and diversity of investing into most of the top fifteen most traded Cryptocurrencies.

Bitcoin will always hold the title of the first and original Cryptocurrency. However, as we've seen throughout this book, it does have some challenges for the number one spot. Bitcoin currently has the advantage of name recognition and market prominence, but some potential competitors can displace it in the future. No one knows whether Bitcoin will be replaced or which Altcoin will take. Since the end is continuously printing at the hard right edge of your cryptocurrency trading charts, it remains unknown until the future arrives.

In the meantime, it may be a wise decision to diversify your portfolio with a variety of Altcoins considered in this book and just let the future marketplace decide who emerges the victor.

In the end, if most of the cryptocurrencies in the top 15 market capitalization continue to increase in value against the fiat currencies of the globe, then dollar-cost averaging of a diverse portfolio of top Altcoins in addition to the Bitcoin King could very well be the best investment strategy.

As we've seen throughout this book, bitcoin and altcoins have a variety of uses and features. Ultimately, over time the marketplace will determine each of their actual values. And the Altcoin that proves to be the most valuable to the market could someday displace the Bitcoin King. Until then, the future of Cryptocurrency continues to look promising, although the future remains unwritten.

THE 5 MOST PAID WORKS IN THE WORLD. WILL CRYPTO ARTWORKS BE ABLE TO SURPASS THEM IN PRICE?

I want to share with you some statistics, including the one about the five highest-paid traditional works in the world. The highest-paid crypto artwork reached a record $70 million. The next question is, "Will the next works of crypto art make record prices surpass these five overpaid works?"

Salvator Mundi By Leonardo Da Vinci

I vividly remembered the day of Christie's auction in November 2017 and the hundreds of articles in all languages read, compared, and reread by the more curious like me. One had to find out who would buy it, at what price, if the work is original, where it would end up. To date, the answers to these questions are not all specific. It is known that it was sold by Dmitry Rybolovlev, a Russian businessman who is the president of the soccer team of the principality of Monaco. It is understood the price at which it was sold 450 million 300 thousand dollars, a record that has made it both the most paid work in the world and the most paid work bought at auction in the world.

It is not known precisely who bought it and where it is now. Immediately after the auction, it was thought to have entered the collection of Prince Badr bin Abdullah, Minister of Culture in Saudi Arabia. Then it was rumored that he had bought it for Prince Mohammad bin Salman, heir to the throne of Saudi Arabia, with the idea of exhibiting it in 2018 at the Louvre in Abu Dhabi. That was not the case, as the work never made it to the museum. Finally, from a couple of articles that have appeared recently, it would appear to be stored in a vault in Switzerland.

Regardless of the allure of buying this work, what makes it unique, of course, is the artistic component. It is the last Leonardo in a private collection and represents one of the symbols of Christianity. In the guise of man, the son of God is presented as the Savior of a transparent world that holds in his left hand, while with the right hand blesses through the sign of the Cross. An undisputed masterpiece of art history that could not fail to become a record also in terms of economic value.

Interchange By Willem De Kooning

It paid $300 million by two figures in the art world, namely American mogul David Geffen and millionaire Kenneth Griffin. It is, in fact, one of the works that were part of the 2015 exchange and sale in which Number 17A by J. Pollock, one of the significant action representatives painting, was involved. But what drove up the value of the work, in this case, was its history and importance in the artist's journey. The painting is important because it was made in 1955, during a transitional period within De Kooning's entire career, after the Women series of the early 1950s and before his color field paintings around 1960. It is in one of the artist's earliest abstract landscapes. Finally, another assessment to be made in this case is related to the size of the work. Usually, the size can affect the final value in private buying and selling. Given the prices, we do not talk about coefficient anymore, but if you compare two works of the same period, of the same artist, and with the same subject, one of the superior dimensions could be worth more. In this case, the work is almost 6.56 ft x 5.57 ft in size. I want to share and appreciate the sale of such important works of art by such famous collectors because the results do not then remain in vaults in Switzerland but are displayed in museums that could not otherwise acquire them. For example, in this case, Interchange is on display at the Art Institute of Chicago.

The Card Players By Cezanne

This work has also had a lot of international attention, and the news of its record sale has gone around the world. The buyer, in this case, should be the sister of the Emir of Qatar Sheikha Al-Mayassa. It was thought to have been sold by the Greek tycoon George Embiricos to an American collector for 225 million dollars. Instead, it was later discovered that the price paid by Qatar in 2011 was $250 million. That is four times more than the price at auction for a work by Cézanne, whose record was set by a sale at Sotheby's in 1999 for Curtain, Cruchon, and Compotier.

After all, this artwork is one of the artist's most famous for the geometric composition of the figures and for having laid the theoretical and compositional foundations and inspired another fundamental movement of 20th-century art: Cubism.

It was also made in 1893, thus work from Cezanne's defined mature period. But interesting that it was so highly paid as there are four other versions of it, all different but with the same subject.

Nafea Faa Ipoipo By Paul Gaugin

The translation of the title from Tahitian would be "When will you get married?"

The work was purchased for $210 million by the sister of the Emir of Qatar Sheikha Al-Mayassa from one of the most famous historical European collections: that of Rudolf Staechelin. Staechelin was a Swiss businessman known for collecting works by the Impressionists and Post-Impressionists in the first half of the 1900s and then turning his attention to Asian art, which ultimately influenced those movements. Some of his pieces were displayed at the Kunstmuseum Basel for years, and Nafea faa IPO is one of them. The first reported price for the sale was $300 million. Then due to a lawsuit overpayment of the commission of broker Simon de Pury, an auctioneer for Sotheby's who also works as an art dealer, the work was reported to be worth $210 million. Until 2015, however, when it was sold.

Again, the work's aesthetic value, along with the historical importance of the artist and the movement, contributed to the matter in connubial with the collection of provenance and the buyer's desire.

Number 17a By Jackson Pollock

The painting was sold along with another from the same list in 2015 for $200 million by American magnate David Geffen to millionaire Kenneth Griffin.

The seller of the artwork is known in the art world for being the most prominent collector of post-war American works. His collection is filled with Pollock, De Kooning, and Rothko. The collector who bought the job, on the other hand, is famous for being a promoter of American art through loans and contributions to the most important museums in his city, Chicago. But this work that, to the eyes of a naive observer may seem a simple dripping of the famous American artist, has something unique compared to other similar ones. It is dated 1948—the year of Pollock's first-ever exhibition of drip paintings at the Betty Parsons Gallery in New York. And, the year after the invention of this technique, which began to be used by the artist in 1947. Even the title, which is not accidental but linked to the numbering of the works Pollock creates, makes us understand how this is one of the artist's first works.

The value is therefore established by the rarity of the work, by the artist's curriculum, by the collection of origin, but also by the curriculum of the work itself that has been exhibited in major museums and by the desire of the buyer, and finally by the American tax benefits. All of this has resulted in it becoming one of the top 5 highest paid works globally.

THE CRYPTOCURRENCY REVOLUTION

Few American developers can match the success of Henry Ford, who, when asked about how public demand factored into his automotive success, quipped, "If I had asked people what they wanted, they would have said faster horses."

There's no denying the power to understand what a customer base needs and deliver it to them. Still, Ford's genius was seeing beyond the restrictions of what was and creating something completely different that not only inspired the marketplace but fundamentally changed how society was composed.

Ford's well-known quote resonates well with the current state of the cryptocurrency industry. Crypto has risen in an era where people were looking for something new without knowing what it was. Crypto combines elements of a currency that frees users from the big banks, a payment system without fees, and an investment vehicle that fits perfectly into the ever-evolving dimensions of the digital age.

Ford didn't construct the Model T in a day and started mass producing it the following week, with one in every driveway the next month. It took a course from the inside out to persuade the masses to put their horses back in the pasture and turn to the wonders of the automobile.

Cryptocurrency & the blockchain technology that powers it stands every period as revolutionary, but at the same time foreign, as the Model T and mass production lines for cars were 110 years ago. That progression is a powerful metaphor for the present cryptocurrency conditions. By learning from former world-altering innovations, we can better position ourselves to capitalize on the ones of today.

The Trouble With Transitions

Although it's glazed over in most textbooks, the move from the horse to the automobile was long and arduous. It took almost 50 years for the latter to replace the former entirely and forced a change in multiple industries and environments, from the condition of roads to the advancements of maps to a wholly new segment of laws, including local, state, and federal. If that sounds familiar to cryptocurrency users, it comes as no surprise. Completely new rules are slowly but surely being implemented to mandate every facet of cryptocurrency. It's a time-consuming process that requires research and bureaucratic red tape at every step. The transportation system of getting funds to and from users to platforms and back is entirely new and constantly upgraded and refined. And the gradual transition for many from relying on fiat currency and traditional investments to digital money and assets that can change by the second is going to take some getting used to, just as many Americans struggled to get into the car rather than onto the horse.

New Industries Born

The number of new industries born because of the automobile's advancement is almost too many to comprehend. Consider before the dawn of the automobile; no one had ever considered a car stereo, a body shop, tires, a car wash, or even a gas station. Mr. Ford's genius idea that came rolling faithfully off that assembly line has created billions upon billions of jobs and produced a global industry. Cryptocurrency and blockchain provide the same opportunities as the industry begins to expand and take shape. From websites to platforms to digital IRAs, that's just the end of the iceberg. As more and more enterprises become pleased with the security and effectiveness of blockchain, it will be one of the more sought-after technologies.

While the intermediate person might believe Henry Ford invented the car (he didn't) and the mass presentation assembly line for cars (he didn't do that either). Instead, he was taking what had been done before, seeing where it had failed, and producing a new version that was not only less expensive but also faster and better. Ford's product might have angered his competition at first, but it was the best kind of angry, the kind that makes you push yourself to be even better—the kind that drives innovation and competition. The same will hold more than a century later and has already begun to happen digitally. While Bitcoin is the most recognizable name in cryptocurrency, this book and the market, in general, will help you realize that it is far from the case. Other companies have stood on Bitcoin's shoulders to innovate and make remarkable strides in many industries. Think about the modern Tesla compared to the Model-T. Both can fetch you from Point A to Point B on four tires, but most similarities end there. One was meant for short drives with the top down; the other quietly ignored gasoline laws and cruises long distances.

Every person who got into a Model T those first few years was guaranteed one thing: an exhilarating ride on a bumpy road. The comparison is striking to the early days of cryptocurrency, where most companies and investors were fumbling around in the dark, trying to find the light. There are joys and lows associated with the industry, but excellent opportunities are not only here now but also visible just over the horizon.

What's Behind Bitcoin's Big Bounce?

Still, if you're paying attention even a little bit to recent world events, you know that Bitcoin has exploded in price in the first part of the 2020s, defeating all expectations again and again.

The original cryptocurrency first broke the elusive $1,000 price in February 2017. By the fortune of that year, it had risen to $14,000 before tumbling back down to about $3,200 around a year later. Since then, it has started to climb relentlessly, with even the catastrophic news of the coronavirus unable to staunch its flow. It was nearly up to $10,000 in February 2020, then tumbled to less than $5,000 in the early confusion of the COVID-19 pandemic. It regained the $10,000 platform in the summer of 2020 and has since been shattering records day after day. It jumped $2,000 to breach $20,000 in December 2020, but that was quickly old news. $30,000 was surpassed on the second day of 2021; five weeks later, it fell to $40,000. A remarkable $7,000 was gained over two days later that month, and the price has been as high as $54,000 into March 2021. So what in the world is causing such a massive explosion in the price? If you put $5,000 into bitcoin in February 2017, you could sell those five coins today for $270,000. That's a return on investment of 53,000%.

So what's the mystery formula behind this historic rise? Here is a rare of the top ideas.

Institutional buyers hedging versus inflation: Institutional buyers are often companies or organizations committed to investing money for others. They typically take the form of pensions, insurance companies, or mutual funds. In this, they generally are looking for long-term stable investments and can weather the storm of the up-and-down trends of the current volatile market. These buyers are often thought of as the whales of Wall Street, meaning they buy massive quantities of stocks, bonds, and other securities they believe will last a long time at a premium value. What drags them down is inflation, such as when the Federal Reserve tries to stimulate the economy by printing more money, when all that does is weaken the dollar. The Fed can print more money, but by the original network programming of bitcoin, there can never be more than 21 million coins produced. A limited capacity of a highly sought-after commodity will cause its price to go up and stay up. In January 2021, Investment banking firm JPMorgan put a long-term target price for bitcoin at a staggering $146,000 and called it an alternative currency to gold. This is the same JPMorgan, mind you, whose CEO Jamie Dimon labeled Bitcoin a fraud back in 2017.

The dollar's downturn internationally: The US Dollar is the most crucial currency globally. Its index gauges its value against other significant currencies, such as the Japanese yen or the EU's euro. A lot of that has to do with a reason stated above, the US Federal Reserve has printed more than $3 trillion over the past year, in an era where people are using cash less in an attempt to kickstart an economy that went on lockdown with the rest of the world for much of 2020 due to the coronavirus global pandemic. Even without the presence of COVID-19, it's been a rocky time in the US from the outside looking in. The 2020 Presidential election was a bitter feud that included incumbent Donald Trump insisting the election was rigged and that he was the victim, culminating with thousands of his supporters illegally entering the US Capitol in January on the day that the Congress was due to certify the election results and officially declare Joe Biden the winner. Trump going out and Biden coming in doesn't guarantee sudden stability either. The Democratic leader has promised new stimulus packages for COVID relief and other large spending plans that have good chances of passing since the Democrats also have the majority control of Congress. So much spending might be significant for the people directly affected by it. Still, when those US dollars are put to work without any fiduciary return, the dollar becomes weaker. If your traditional currency isn't looking appealing, its alternatives become more attractive.

Retail Purchases: It's becoming easier and easier to use bitcoin to buy everyday items, mainly once PayPal got on board with the cryptocurrency in 2020. Of course, buying with bitcoin at the present date feels a little like selling your gold bars to buy stuff —sure, it's as effective as money, but why would you in the world? When it was hovering below $1,000/coin for years, the novelty was undoubtedly there to purchase from local merchants trying to expand into cryptocurrencies by accepting them as payment. But if you made a $100 purchase in 2017 with bitcoin —about 1/10th of a coin back then, you're now living with the grief that the $100 you spent has now grown into $5,000 of value. We're guessing the item you bought has not likewise appreciated in the past three years.

Halving: Halving is a process coded into Bitcoin since the beginning that functions as its escrow mechanism. We have spoken at length about how miners get a reward for their work processing transactions. The prize is cut in half every four years, meaning it is a law of diminishing returns for the miners. That means the inflation rate is reduced by half every four years and will continue until all bitcoin in the escrow are released. What will happen when Bitcoin caps at 21 million coins. There are presently about 18.5 million in circulation. Despite appearing near capacity, the timeline is a good deal more complicated. Since the halving keeps taking place, the rewards for mining a new block will continue to go down significantly. When Bitcoin was first launched, the prize was 50 bitcoins. In February 2021, it existed down to 6.25 bitcoins. Most estimates say the last bitcoin won't be mined until the year 2140, meaning there's quite a bit of time to get in on the action if you're an investor.

CRYPTO WINTER TO THE NORTH, CRYPTO SUMMER TO THE SOUTH

The first video show of this discussion was recorded at the Bitcoin Argentina Meetup in Collaboration with the Bitcoin Embassy in Buenos Aires, Argentina, in January 2019. Video Link: https://aantonop.io/CryptoWinter Oh my god, everybody came! Ninety days prior, I gave a discussion in Seattle, a major venue with 700 seats. I was hopeful since I had had enormous crowds formerly. It is Seattle. They will come. Microsoft, Amazon, every one of these tech organizations is there. But in eight weeks, we did not even sell three hundred tickets. Since in Seattle, it is crypto winter. Not simply winter, crypto-winter. Many individuals who turned out to be highly energized in October 2017, for inexplicable reasons, turned out to be exceptionally unexcited in March 2018 for similarly strange reasons.

But not here. Here in Buenos Aires, it is a crypto-summer. All seats sold out in five days! Give a significant round of acclaim to Rodolfo and over twenty volunteers who met up to assist me with getting this going. Many thanks to those who upheld and endeavored to make this occasion conceivable. Obviously, to the patrons too. All of the work we do this evening will go towards charity.

The Seasons Of Crypto

Let's begin with these ideas of crypto-winter and crypto-summer. What number of occasional varieties of the unpredictable digital currency markets have you experienced until now? What number of individuals have experienced four air pocket cycles? Two or three hands. Three air pocket cycles? Two air pocket cycles? Also, amateurs, one air pocket cycle? Relax, there is another coming!

In crypto-markets, similar to any innovation, there are these influxes of excitement and hypothesis. Then people forget and move away. They return later with the following cycle. Why? Since most individuals getting involved today, don't require it. They use crypto because it is something worth discussing to conjecture. They are not intrigued by how cryptographic money can help their lives today, however in the capability of its worth expanding because of what it means for the existence of another person, at some other time.

That isn't the demeanor in Argentina, South America, Southeast Asia, or South Africa. In those spots, the worth of cryptographic money isn't tied in with something that happens later. It's unnecessary to focus on, assuming that my administration unexpectedly became terrible, in case my bank began taking our benefits, our discourse was blue-penciled, our affiliations limited, and our ideological groups detained. If, if assuming, but it's anything but an "if" in those spots. These things are, as of now, happening there.

Americans struggle to get this. They have the advantage and extravagance of strength, yet their conditions are excellent. In a significant part of the world, degenerate state-run administrations and banks attack benefits reserves and detain the resistance. There are dropped races and races with a 96% larger part vote. Those things happen the whole way across the world. That is the everyday human experience. That is the motivation behind why crypto is so essential.

They are frameworks that permit us to track down new, 21st century methods of getting sorted out cultural foundations, rather than nineteenth-century ways that have neglected to scale.

What Does Success Look Like?

When we have this blast of interest in cryptographic forms of money, large numbers of us wind up conversing with individuals who appear to be taking an alternate language.

They are incredibly keen on the cost and which shitcoin will be the following enormous thing. They are keen on seeing how they can counterfeit it until they cause it to be too successful.

When I am gotten some information about cryptographic forms of money and blockchains, and they educate me concerning their "superb new venture," I ask them, "What is an accomplishment from your point of view? Suppose that you succeed. What does your organization accomplish? Portray accomplishment to me." Inevitably, they neglect to respond to that inquiry. By and large, they haven't pondered what achievement will resemble, other than, "We will make heaps of money!"

That is a vital inquiry to pose: what does achievement resemble you? "We will fabricate the best item that rules the market and make us bunches of cash!" Who does that assistance? "Me." Okay, amazing. But that is not enough people. Would we be able to ponder how we can help more individuals? Your current marketing strategy is tied in with aiding four individuals. Would we be able to build the scale a bit?

Can We Contemplate Helping More People?

When the business sectors flood this space is abruptly overwhelmed by outcasts, astute individuals who show up because they read an article in The Wall Street Journal or the magazine in the seat pocket of their flight, or because their associates are telling them: "This will be the following huge thing like AI and quantum figuring!" They result in these present circumstances space and bring a series of expectations.

The Zero-Sum Game

One of the suppositions is the thing that I need to discuss today, and that is the presumption that markets work as a lose-lose situation. It is a strong presumption. It would be best if you were extremely mindful of seeing it. At the point when you have a business conversation, when you are conversing with your companions about the most recent crypto project they are keen on, the ramifications under a large number of these discussions is the idea of a lose-lose situation. They will not let you know this because, occasionally, they don't realize that is the thing that they are thinking.

A lose-lose situation is where one party wins, provided that the other party loses. It's anything but a circumstance where the two players win, or everyone wins. In a lose-lose situation, you succeed to the detriment of others.

It's unnecessary to focus on making an ideal world, a particular item, a superior market, or expanding contest. That is a poisonous presumption that exists in each pattern of business. It is basically what procuring an MBA is tied in with, showing you how to play the lose-lose situations and pulverize your opposition. It is tied in with discovering the guidelines, sorting out ways to take advantage of those principles, and building a fence around your licensed innovation, your items, and your market specialty. It's tied in with figuring out how to keep anybody from rivaling you, figuring out how to catch clients not procure, catch clients, group them into this fenced region, and concentrate as much cash as possible. That is a current business in a nutshell.

This poisonous presumption in each pattern of business comes from some significant contemplations. The primary variable is the shortfall of open economies. In an unregulated economy, you don't play a lose-lose situation, and you can't prevent contenders from entering. In an unregulated economy, assuming you make a genuinely new thing, others will arise to expand on it and bring new clients, new freedoms, and market specialties so that everybody can appreciate it and win. In unregulated economies, it's anything but a lose-lose game.

So then, where is this idea coming from? It comes from the fact that most celebrated capitalists in the world have never seen a free market in their entire lives! They operate in an environment where they own the regulators and write the rules. Their essential objective is to trick enough to guarantee that nobody can prevent them from gaining the sacred goal of business: a restraining infrastructure. When you have a restraining infrastructure, you can attempt to keep anybody from breaking into it and concentrate on your client's as much worth as possible. It isn't about rivalry, further developing business sectors or the world. It is tied in with building up syndications. They carry that mentality into the crypto space and begin spreading it like a toxin in each business.

Rules Without Rulers

If you focus, you'll see these presumptions surrounding you. "We can't find opensource our wallet! Assuming that we open-source it, our rivals will duplicate it." "We want to discover who the controllers are. Indeed, we should welcome them to direct our industry. Then we will know what the rules are." What else do you have to be familiar with the principles? The standards are essential: one square-like clockwork and 21 million coins. They seem like pretty basic guidelines. We know what the regulations are. They are authorized by network agreement. The savvy agreement will execute, the symbolic will be given under these conditions. The guidelines are clear. For what reason do you want specific rules?

"Gracious, because we can't fix those principles to help us. But we can fix the human rules with lobbying. We need to release our NDAs (non revelation arrangements) on the lookout. We need to gather together all potential clients and make a decent, comfortable restraining infrastructure, a lose-lose game."

The maximalists think, "Our crypto can't win except if their crypto loses!" If that is the situation, it turns out vital to call attention to every one of the ways the other crypto project isn't sufficiently unadulterated, how it isn't the first vision of the originator, how it isn't developing the right way. That is the lose-lose thinking contaminating our industry.

It doesn't hurt you if another digital currency fabricates something great in an open-source industry like our own. Duplicate it. It is open-source. Dive more deeply into it. This is a delightful climate where each creation made in the whole biological system becomes one that everybody can use.

It isn't only the victories that are important. In business, much more significant than a triumph is a disappointment that didn't cost you anything to learn. Likewise, each blow is an example, an illustration another person took in the most challenging way possible, so you don't have to.

Our Creative Commons

Our current circumstance has an alternate arrangement of rules. We are not experiencing the awfulness of the center. We have an imaginative lodge. The open-source culture isn't simply innovative; it's not our PC code. It is an open culture of creative individuals, which has generally shown up at this particular crossroads in history and consented to one primary reason: this may be an ideal way.

These individuals are, as of now, on our side of the fence. The opposite side of the wall is a lose-lose situation, with the bad state-run administrations, banks, and restraining infrastructure frameworks that make monstrous disparity, financial disappointment, and squandered ability worldwide.

Shitcoins

So assuming your companion has, at last, moved over to this site, with the possibility that there may be something better, and there may be a better approach for getting things done, how will you respond? Will you go to them and say, "You purchased what? That is a shitcoin, you apostate!" No! Purchase shitcoins, assuming you need. Additionally, you presumably shouldn't buy that shitcoin. But while you're here, maybe, I can teach you about the technology instead of just buying. You could find out how you can manage it and how to e. You can become familiar with specific instead of buyingyingn abilities and using them in a business. You can investigate heaps of conceivable outcomes and not simply treat this as a venture. You should say, "Welcome, old buddy.

INTRODUCTION TO THE VIRTUAL REALITY

Virtual means not physical, and it means experiencing things, living life via our computers that do not exist. It is simply experiencing a world that is not real. If you saw an image of some paintings that date back to the war era and you begin to visualize yourself having a feel of those paintings, you probably experience the sounds of the guns shooting into the air and so on. It is also the same for music; if you listen to classical or instrumental music with your eyes shut, and you begin to dream about things, that's some virtual reality. What about imagining the events that took place in a movie or a book? It seems like it is some form of virtual reality. But it isn't. When you read books, watch a movie, or imagine the events around a painting, it only remains in your thoughts or head; you don't get to feel it or get involved in the activities in the book.

Virtual reality is an interactive 3D world created by the computer that you can experience and explore to the extent that you feel everything there physically and mentally. In virtual worlds, you have to believe that you are in a different world, and you must keep thinking that, or the representation of this virtual reality will fade off. You also have to be very interactive; the VR world moves everywhere with you as you go about. You can read a book and be transported to the sea without having an authentic experience, which is not interactive enough. A virtual world has to be very large and filled with details so you can have lots of things to explore. And it should be engaging. It should be very interactive and believable, engaging your body and mind. War artists' paintings can give us a view of what conflict is like, but they cannot deliver the sound, sight, taste, smell, and how it is like to be involved on the battlefield. You can play a VR game that will make you lost in the feel of a warm, so natural, and interactive experience for about two hours.

With everything I said above, we can agree that looking at some paintings, reading your favorite novel, or watching a movie cannot be the same with virtual reality. All of them will give you a partial glimpse of a different reality, but each of them is not explorable or interactive. Suppose you are watching a movie, staring at a big picture of a battle in front of you, and you turn your head to do something. In that case, you will discover that you are still on earth, and the illusion will disappear if you see something that you find eye-catchy on the screen, you won't be able to reach out to touch it or walk to where it is again. That illusion will fade off. So, watching movies is somehow passive activity as you cannot be engaged in what is going on in the film.

Virtual reality is different. It offers you this misconception that you live in the world; it is interactive; as you respond to the things you see and touch, they will also react to you, changing your direction to another place; what you see or hear will change match the new perspective.

Types Of Virtual Reality

There are so many types of virtual reality. Virtual reality is often used as a marketing word for introducing interactive video games, television programs, and 3D movies. But none of them can be said to be a virtual reality as they don't fully immerse you as a partial or entirely virtual world. It is not all the virtual reality that will give you the experience you need.

The Fully Immersive Virtual World

Suppose you want to enjoy a total virtual reality experience. In that case, you should have a gadget that you can use to enjoy this complex virtual world, and the computer should be able to detect anything that is going on and even adjust to your experience each time. The hardware linked to your computer must fully immerse you into the virtual world as you move around. If you genuinely want to enjoy these virtual realities, you will need a head-mounted display with stereo sound and two screens. You will like to wear one or two sensory gloves. You can also move about in the room, with a loudspeaker around you so the images can be projected from the outer side.

The Non-Immersive Virtual World

Suppose you have a highly realistic flight simulator on your personal computer. In that case, it will work perfectly for a virtual reality that is not so immersive, mainly if the game uses a wide screen with sound or headphones that surrounds you and a real joystick and some controls. It is not everybody that needs or wants to be immersed in reality. Virtual reality can make you play some games in the reconstructed building, but you won't be taken to the thousands or hundreds of years to create the smells, sounds, and taste of the history of the building that was reconstructed.

The Web-Based Virtual Reality

Some virtual reality games are available on the web. But most people would instead search for ways to play virtual reality games rather than the virtual reality that can be played on the web.

The Augmented Virtual Reality

Augmented reality emanated from the idea that people can play from their smartphones. Augmented reality connects the real world to the virtual world of data that has been created on the internet.

There are some types of equipment you can use to play virtual reality.

The Head-Mounted Displays

Remember that in VR, you will always have to look at your screen; the 3D images change as soon as you change your direction. That was possible because of the head-mounted display on your head, which seems to look like a big welding visor or motorbike helmet, but it had two tiny screens; there is one at the front of each eye. A blindfold prevents the light from distracting you from the real world. These two screens are a bit different. There is an accelerometer or sensors to detect the extent to which you move your head or body; it knows when you want to move your body or head. But these tools are a bit heavy so you cannot wear them for a long time as they will make you uncomfortable. You can buy the ones that are not so expensive.

Immersive Rooms

You can stay in a room where the changes in the images on the walls are being projected from outside. As you move about in your room, the image will also change.

Data Gloves

While exploring the virtual world, you may see something you like, and you want to reach out to it and even touch them. With the datagloves, you can do that. You can hold virtual objects and use your datagloves; they are simple gloves with sensors around them to detect your feature motion and hands. Each cable has a tiny cut of line in it, so as you move your fingers to and fro, little or plenty of light will escape from it. A photocell at the edge of your cable measures the extent to which light gets into it, and the computer makes use of that to find out what the fingers are doing.

Wands

A wand looks like a stick, and you can point to something or touch an object. It has a motion sensor called an accelerometer built into the rods and a mouse-like button or a scroll wheel. The wands are wired into the VR computer so that they are wireless.

IS THE METAVERSE THE EXACT AS VIRTUAL REALITY?

Are the Metaverse and computer-generated reality indeed the very same? Or then again, would they say they are unique? Stand by, do they cover? That is what you want to know.

In October 2021, Imprint Zuckerberg reported that Facebook would be changing its name to Meta.

Meta is a descriptive word that implies an article is alluding to itself. Be that as it may, it's additionally short for something many refer to as the Metaverse.

This declaration was met with interest, doubt, and the conspicuous inquiry, "What precisely is a metaverse?" It seems like computer-generated simulation and joins augmented reality. However, it's not precisely a similar thought.

What Is A Metaverse?

The idea of a metaverse is not a new composition. It is, nonetheless, something that many people are presently finding out about interestingly.

The term was initially utilized in the clever Snow Crash, originally distributed in 1992 by Neal Stephenson. The Metaverse novel is a virtual common space that consolidates computer-generated reality, expanded reality, and the web.

The case of a metaverse declared by Facebook and other tech organizations gives an impression of being exceptionally like this image. While the specific purpose seems to rely upon who is talking, it's fundamentally another rendition of the web that puts a more central accentuation on virtual universes.

Rather than seeing sites using a program, you will get to data by exploring a virtual world with the choice of using both virtual and increased reality.

The Metaverse versus Computer generated Reality: What's The Distinction?

If you read anything regarding the Metaverse, the similitudes to computer-generated reality are hard to overlook. There are, nonetheless, a couple of significant contrasts.

Computer-generated Reality Is Clear cut; the Metaverse Isn't

The most remarkable contrast between computer-generated reality and the Metaverse is that while VR is currently indeed known, the Metaverse truly isn't.

As per Imprint Zuckerberg, the Metaverse is "an exemplified web where rather than simply seeing the substance you are in it." A new Microsoft declaration portrayed it as "an industrious computerized world that is possessed by advanced twins of individuals, spots, and things."

These portrayals are quite ambiguous when contrasted with our comprehension of computer-generated reality. It's likewise possible that even the tech organizations themselves don't have a total definition.

As shown by Facebook, the choice to rebrand was a vital piece of building the Metaverse. They needed a name that better managed what they were going after. In any case, it's unquestionably not by any means the only conceivable reason for doing as such. Facebook has a picture issue.

It's also conceivable to contend that the Metaverse is just a trendy expression to portray innovative enhancements in the current web.

Facebook Doesn't Possess Either Innovation.

One more possible inquiry regarding the Metaverse is who really will characterize it.

As the proprietor of Oculus Fracture, Facebook assumes a significant part in improving augmented reality. And yet, they are solely one player in a vast industry.

Facebook might have modified its name to Meta. The equivalent is valid for the Metaverse. However, they are by all reports not the only organization included. Microsoft, for example, as of late declared Microsoft Lattice, their form of a blended reality stage in with likenesses to the Metaverse and its different definitions. Moreover, a new Facebook articulation insinuates how they consider themselves to be building a piece of the Metaverse rather than the Metaverse itself.

The Metaverse Incorporates A Common Virtual World

The Metaverse is a virtual space that clients will want to use on the web. Once more, this is something that VR headsets clearly as of now permit you to do.

Clients are relied upon to be recognized by close-to-home symbols that connect in virtual areas. What's more, they will want to buy or fabricate virtual things and conditions, like NFTs.

The essential distinction is that while existing virtual universes are restricted in size, the Metaverse seems to give admittance to the whole web.

The Metaverse Will Be Available In Augmented Experience

The Metaverse won't desire you to wear a VR headset. Yet, it's accepted that enormous pieces of the assistance will be open to headset clients.

That implies that the line between riding the web and utilizing augmented reality will probably become obscured. VR headsets might begin being used for undertakings typically performed utilizing cell phones.

If the Metaverse becomes as well known as Facebook expects, VR will probably become undeniably, to a lesser degree, a specialty item.

The Metaverse Won't Be Restricted To Vr Tech.

Notwithstanding, following on from the last point, the Metaverse won't be restricted to augmented reality. It will be open both by expanded reality gadgets and any gadget you use to associate with the web.

That makes way for different highlights unrealistic with computer-generated reality alone. For instance, the increased fact will permit the Metaverse to be projected into this present reality.

Virtual spaces will likewise be planned to get to anyplace, no headset required.

The Metaverse Is Conceivably A Lot Greater Than Vr.

Computer-generated reality is currently utilized for instruction, treatment, and sports. Yet, it is still seemingly most famous as a sort of diversion.

The Metaverse, basically as far as scale, sounds significantly more like a better than ever web form. It's relied upon to change how individuals work, access online media, and even surf the web, implying that while many individuals have disregarded augmented experience, the equivalent will probably not occur with the Metaverse.

Will The Metaverse Supplant The Web?

Augmented reality hasn't had an incredible impact on the world that specific individuals anticipated. There's a breaking point to how long individuals need to spend wearing a headset.

The Metaverse won't have this issue, open to those with and without admittance to a VR headset. Specific individuals anticipate that it should have a lot greater effect subsequently.

Simultaneously, the Metaverse is profoundly improbable to supplant the web completely. VR headsets give an intriguing option in contrast to PC screens. The Metaverse will provide a fascinating opportunity in comparison to the web. In any case, neither one is intended to go about as a substitution.

AUGMENTED REALITY

While virtual reality is an exclusively digital environment created by one or more computers or applications that simulate actual reality, augmented reality (AR) represents the real world enriched with virtual objects or details that lead to improving or "increasing" the experience.

It is based on the expansion or integration of the surrounding reality with computer-generated 3D graphics images, which modify the original environment without affecting interaction possibilities.

In essence, augmented reality transforms vast masses of data and analytics into images or animations, a digital level that is superimposed on the physical world by integrating with it.

What Does It Take To Create Augmented Reality?

Not being as immersive as virtual reality, it does not necessarily need specific viewers for which everyday devices such as smartphones or special screens can be used (as in the case of car accessories).

How Does Augmented Reality Work?

Augmented reality starts from a device equipped with a video camera - such as a smartphone, tablet, or smart glass - on which AR software has been loaded. When the user indicates the device at an object and looks at it, the software recognizes it through computerized vision technology, which analyzes the flow of images.

Then the device downloads the object information from the cloud, just like a browser downloads a page via the URL. The critical difference is that AR information is presented in a 3D experience superimposed on the object rather than on a two-dimensional page that appears on a screen.

What the user sees, therefore, is partly natural and partly digital. At this point, we must introduce the overlay principle: the camera reads the object in the frame, the system recognizes it. It activates a new level of communication that overlaps and integrates perfectly with reality, enhancing detailed data about that object.

Headsets are the critical technology for both virtual and augmented reality. It is, thus, not unexpected that some of the best-known names in the traditional IT market have thrown themselves into the construction of this equipment which, depending on the model, can be destined for different types of uses (gaming and more).

Google Glass is a trademark of smart glasses developed by the Mountain View company, a pair of glasses equipped with augmented reality through which you can access various information: you can read websites and news online, check social networks, view maps and driving directions through Google Maps, participate in video conferences, take photos and shoot videos, all without the use of hands (hands-free). Perhaps due to the too-high price, probably because it arrived too early (with the official debut in mid-2014), Google Glass had a reasonably tepid welcome from ordinary consumers, also for issues related to usability, as well as protection of privacy. Google, therefore, withdrew the product from sale, which - despite some relaunch rumors - has never seen the light again.

Augmented And Virtual Reality Viewers

The Oculus Rift, produced by the company of the same name then acquired by Facebook, which, starting from 2016, has quickly established itself as one of the most popular virtual reality viewers for gaming, has been decidedly more fortunate. To contend with the priority, there are other viewers produced by names such as Samsung (with its Gear VR), which needs the latest generation smartphone to work and which is to be inserted inside the mask of the viewer, and Huawei with VR2 (first model released in 2016 and then updated in 2018) which can be connected to a PC to use it with games designed for machines with higher computing power than the integrated one.

Mixed Reality Viewer

In the business field, however, at least for the moment, Microsoft's Hololens (created in 2015 and updated in 2019) has captured the most interest, a viewer for mixed reality, specifically designed to bring value to enterprise projects, i.e., in all those work processes that can benefit from a minimum of digital interaction and in which there is a need to experiment with something new.

Growth Market With Ar In The Lead

The global VR and AR market reached a value of $6.158 billion in 2017 and is expected to travel at a growth rate of 58.1% between now and 2023. The growing penetration of smartphones, along with advances, will drive the market in connectivity and information technology, in addition to the significant investments and innovations conducted by technology giants such as Apple, Google, and Facebook, including tools, platforms, and services.

Virtual reality accounts for about 60% of the total turnover, but by 2023 things should be reversed: AR will travel at a development rate of 73.8%, higher than virtual reality. The demand for sectors such as tourism and retail should be driving AR. According to analyses by Statista, IDC, and Goldman Sachs, by 2020, more than 1 billion users will use AR applications and services, helping to fuel a market that is estimated to exceed $215 billion within two / three years.

A parallel statement can be created for the hardware-software division: at the moment, about 65% of the sector's turnover is the prerogative of hardware devices, such as virtual reality viewers. But the demand for software solutions is set to travel faster, approaching these percentages. The USA, which represents the dominant country of this new market, is destined to maintain this leadership position in the following four years, even if Canada, Central Eastern Europe, and Western Europe will experience higher rates of development.

Despite analysts making market growth estimates by unifying virtual reality and augmented reality, developers believe that augmented reality will drive the growth trends of the next few years: "where virtual reality reproduces the real world to create spaces digitally, augmented reality understands and includes the real world; AR superimposes virtual images on real environments, spaces, and images, creating a potential for customer experiences that are very different from those possible with VR," Digital Trends reports.

VR environments, by their nature, require the utmost attention from the user (who is immersed in a reconstructed environment within which he can move and interact only "digitally"), which makes the technology inadequate for real social interaction outside of a digital world.

Instead, AR makes it possible (and this is precisely where its strength lies) because it has the potential to act as an on-demand "co-pilot" in everyday life, integrating perfectly into the daily interactions that users have in the real world.

Interactions that can range from gaming to entertainment, from sports to the shopping experience, up to coming into play in business and work contexts: 64% of American consumers in the United States, even believe that augmented reality will bring benefits to the workplace, for example by facilitating collaboration between teams located in different locations or by accelerating design and innovation processes.

Companies are also in favor of these situations. That is confirmed by research recently carried out by Capgemini entitled "Augmented and Virtual Reality in Operations: A guide for investment," conducted on about 700 executives in the automotive, manufacturing, and utility sectors.

82% of companies currently implementing these solutions believe the benefits exceed their expectations. In comparison, a good 46% of respondents expect AR and VR to become mainstream within the next three years, while a further 38% expect this transition within the next three to five years.

In general, augmented reality is considered more applicable in the company by supporting a more splendid series of innovative uses precisely because of its ability to interact with reality. Some virtual reality solutions are considered capable of positively impacting businesses.

45% of companies use AR, while the percentage drops to 36% for companies that have implemented virtual reality (the rest are still in the experimental phase).

The extent of the investments and the areas of application of augmented reality

When Augmented Reality Began: Origins And Evolutionary Scenarios

The first condition of augmented reality dates back to 1968 when Ivan Sutherland developed the first AR glasses. Also, in the same year, the origin of the first VR viewer can be traced back when Ivan Sutherland, together with Bob Sproull, developed a primitive solution with wireframe graphics similar in design to the cumbersome mechanical machinery called Sensorama of 1962, the earliest known example of immersive multisensory technology by Morton Helig.

In the 90s, virtual time reality was coined by Jaron Lanier so that an organized vision of how portable devices, the Internet, and GPS can come together to give life to devices capable of increasing or enriching the level of information in the real world.

Even if the first projects were not very successful, in those years, the foundations were laid that allowed:

in 2015 to see tools such as Samsung Gear VR, Google Cardboard, and Oculus Rift on the market, technologies that will enable us to be catapulted into another world, into another room, into an environment different from the one in which we are physical;

in 2016 to witness the mass diffusion of AR, mainly thanks to the Pokémon Go game, which allowed us to understand the novelty and the difference with VR: bringing digital content simply and immediately into the physical world.

However, the phenomenon has exploded in recent years and has turned the spotlight on the new big trend, Mixed Reality (MR). Defined by analysts as the combination of virtual reality and augmented reality aimed at producing new settings and visualizations where digital and physical objects coexist and interact in real-time, Mixed Reality has a market that:

will arrive in 2024 to generate a turnover that will touch 6.86 billion dollars (according to analysts of Grand View Research).

Much more technologically advanced than VR (because it combines the use of different technologies, sensors, wearable devices, very advanced optics, and ever-greater computing power for data analysis), Mixed Reality allows you to raise AR to a superior experience enabling people to experience increasingly vast, realistic scenarios within spaces and times that become unlimited.

Giants such as Facebook, Samsung, Sony, and Nintendo are not the only ones to invest in AR-VR technologies, given that even the panorama of startups dedicated to this area is gradually expanding.

A lot is being supported in AR and VR. The application frontiers are comprehensive. Soon, there will be business opportunities in many areas, from the world of gaming to events, from health to insurance through Retail, Education, Sport, and Live Entertainment.

Augmented Reality In Marketing

Augmented reality is, in fact, a form of visual content management 2.0 that allows companies and organizations to engage customers through innovative ways: in fact, it adds new levels of information in real-time and with a high rate of interaction using mobile devices of any type, including wearable technologies.

Not surprisingly, the first experiments were in entertainment, exploiting that effect capable of capturing attention through surprise and virtual magic, making the experience with the brand as immersive and engaging as possible.

Exclusivity, personalization, and uniqueness are advantages of integrating augmented and virtual reality into the broader customer experience strategies to allow consumers to interact with the brand in a new way. People love to feel special in the eyes of brands and appreciate exclusive services; whether it's an app that allows them to try out new furniture in the apartment they live in, or that offers tips for the perfect makeup based on their skin type, the important thing is that they are personalized.

BIG TECH IN METAVERSE

The Metaverse will require a critical mass of related technologies, including:

Virtual Reality

This is an experience that simulates realistic conditions. Real-life use issues include gaming, social networking, education, and on-the-job training.

Unity predicts that AR-VR headsets will be as standard as gaming consoles by 2030. And, regarding ARK Invest, VR headsets could contact smartphone adoption rates by 2030.

At that point, accessories like full-body haptic suits and VR gloves will likely explode in popularity.

There are already several outlets that allow you to connect with other VR users:

Facebook Horizon lets you research virtual worlds where you can connect with people worldwide, participate in fun challenges, and even create your virtual worlds.

Facebook Workroom is a collaboration experience that allows people to work in the same virtual room, regardless of physical distance.

VRChat offers an endless collection of VR social experiences created by a community of 25,000 people.

And you can use AltspaceVR to participate in live shows, meetups, classes, and more with people from all over the world.

The most fantastic VR products include Oculus Quest 2, HTC Vive Cosmos, Sony Playstation VR, and Valve Index.

Artificial Intelligence

This sector will benefit the Metaverse in numerous ways, as stated by Eric Elliott in an article on Medium:

Realistic-looking intelligent AI beings could roam the Metaverse and interact with us and others. They could be programmed with their own vitality stories, motivations, and goals. Depending on the virtual world, we could participate in pre-planned scenarios with these characters or create our designs. The Unreal Engine's MetaHuman Creator could play an essential role in creating these characters. And if and when these characters can exhibit general artificial intelligence, the results could be surprising and surreal.

AI can help us simplify the creation of metaverse assets such as characters, landscapes, buildings, character routines, and more. We could see a future where advanced AI capabilities are integrated with Unreal Engine game engines to make this possible.

AI can automate software development processes to build increasingly complex assets within the Metaverse with less and less effort.

AI can create, control, and protect intelligent contracts on the blockchain. Fundamentally, smart contracts allow for trusted transactions and agreements without the need for a central authority or legal system.

Augmented Reality

That is an experience where designers enhance parts of the users' physical world with computer-generated input.

Communication lenses and AR glasses could be utilized to augment the world around us and promote virtual assistance with the help of sophisticated artificial intelligence.

This artificial intelligence would help us navigate both the real and virtual worlds.

The Microsoft HoloLens & the Magic Leap One are the many impressive augmented and mixed reality headsets in the market. They are mainly used for business purposes, but we will see more AR headsets sold to the general public as their prices drop.

Blockchain Technology

Blockchain technology would be an ideal aid in facilitating fast and secure digital transactions in a decentralized metaverse.

Although blockchain technology originated with Bitcoin, blockchain has far-reaching potential outside of cryptocurrency. Blockchain is a transferred database that permits multiple parties to access and verify data in real-time.

Brain-Computer Interfaces

Control of avatars and digital transactions would occur through brain signals sent through computer interfaces.

Initially, this technology is expected to spread to the video game and productivity markets.

Some adopters, by the mid-2030s, could begin using brain-computer interfaces to connect to their neocortex.

Internet Infrastructure

In this case, we are referring to wireless technologies and Web 3.0. First, we talk about 5G and 6G.

5G allows for extremely high frequencies in the millimeter-wave spectrum, which opens up possibilities such as VR experiences that include the sense of touch and AR experiences that will enable visitors to have in-depth conversations with AI characters in real-time.

Eventually, 6G will replace 5G. 6G is not yet available, but several countries have already established research initiatives.

Some aces estimate that it could be 100 times faster than 5G, which equals 1 TB per second. You could download 142 hours of Netflix films in one second at that speed.

According to one study, 6G would make it possible for cyberspace to support human thought and action in real-time through wearable devices and micro-devices mounted on the human body. Sensory interfaces would handle and examine just like real life.

Next, let's talk about Web 3.0. With Web 1.0, content creators were scarce, and most users acted as consumers of content.

For the most part, we are currently in the Web 2.0 era. Web 2.0 has brought us the "Web as a platform," where software applications are built on the Web instead of just desktop computers.

That has allowed masses of users to create content on social networks, blogs, sharing sites, and more. However, Web 2.0 gives a lot of power to centralized tech giants and allows for surveillance and advertising exploitation.

One of the main advantages of Web 3.0 is its ability to enable a decentralized blockchain protocol, which would allow individuals to connect to an internet where they can own and be compensated appropriately for their time and data. That is more beneficial than a network where giant corporations take the lion's share of the network and can divert large percentages of profits to themselves.

In addition, Web 3.0 is expected to enable computers to understand the semantics or meanings of sentences so that content can be generated, shared, and linked through search and analysis. Web 3.0 will help facilitate excellent connectivity between data sources with semantic metadata.

Mobile Processors

Attracting audiences to augmented reality will require giving functional glasses an everyday look.

That would require small, super-fast mobile processors mounted on normal-looking glasses.

VR devices will also need processors to handle hyper-realistic graphics, high refresh rates, low latency, high frames per second.

We could also see the introduction of optical components alongside traditional silicon components. That would lead to a 100-fold increase in data transfer rates.

Lightmatter is a start-up founded at MIT and is working on a chip that works using light.

Metaverse Companies

So far, the technologies we have talked about would not be possible without research and development. Research and development that small start-ups will undoubtedly do but that, in all likelihood, will be carried out mainly by the current technological giants that, just as obviously, will buy the best players that will arise with the rise and during the development of the Metaverse.

A critical aspect for the Metaverse to work is that one company cannot control it. It must be a decentralized system with many companies supporting it. The companies that will likely bring it to life permanently are as follows.

Facebook. Facebook already has a pair of products that will bring us nearer to the Metaverse: Facebook Horizon and Facebook Workrooms that we just mentioned earlier.

In addition to its famous Oculus virtual reality headset, Facebook is also working on augmented reality headsets.

Epic Games. It is famous for various products such as Fortnite, Roblox, and MetaHumans. Fortnite and Roblox, in particular, have elements similar to the Metaverse, such as their creator economies and the ability to use a single avatar in multiple virtual worlds.

Microsoft. One of Microsoft's most profitable ambitions involves giving Microsoft Azure developers the ability to create digital twins of our physical world connected to our world in real-time. This would allow us to run simulations in those virtual environments, analyze trends in real-time, and form very accurate predictions that we could apply to the real world.

Microsoft also proposes the HoloLens, a holographic and mixed reality device specifically intended to improve productivity and training efforts in various industries such as manufacturing, healthcare, and education.

Microsoft also has Microsoft Mesh, which gives users an AR and VR meeting space to interact with other users and 3D content.

In addition, Microsoft has Xbox Game Pass and Xbox cloud gaming, which could help facilitate efforts to use the software-as-a-service business model for some Metaverse components.

Google. It could also release hardware to facilitate augmented reality, such as an updated version of Google Glass. Likely, Google will also explore advanced virtual and mixed reality headsets.

Apple. It already offers widely used frameworks for developing AR experiences such as ARKit and RealityKit. And it provides creative tools like Reality Composer and Reality Converter.

Nvidia. Nvidia has an Omniverse service that helps companies bring various digital assets into one virtual environment. Omniverse allows companies to work with many file formats and collaborate with third parties using different technology stacks.

Amazon. Amazon doesn't have an advantage in the major hardware and software components of the next Metaverse. Amazon Alexa could also work seamlessly with augmented reality, virtual reality, brain-machine interfaces, and other technologies in the metaverse ecosystem.

METAVERSE VERSUS MICROSOFT

Microsoft has branched out towards bringing the Metaverse to office life, in the latest sign that irrefutably, the best tech associations see the blending of the high level and real universes as one of the super ongoing prevailing fashions in handling. The US programming goliath said that in the vital portion of the following year, customers of its Teams composed exertion programming would have the choice to appear as images — or invigorated child's shows — in video get-togethers.

Remote workers can, in like manner, use their images to visit virtual workspaces, which would eventually join propagations of their administrators' working environments. Microsoft's first moves to blend the virtual and real universes are modest appeared differently about the broad vision that Facebook spread out last week when it changed its name to Meta to reflect its new focus on the Metaverse. Regardless, Microsoft's plan relies upon essential advancement, known as the Cross area that it uncovered as of late to manage certainly seriously bewildering virtual associations on different kinds of hardware, from PCs to expanded reality headsets. In like manner, Microsoft pioneers said they believed the gathering of individual images to be the underlying stage in a development that would see workers become dynamically okay with new sorts of virtual collaboration that might give off an impression of being unfamiliar to them now. 'With 250m people all through the planet using Gatherings, the introduction of images will be the head real Metaverse part to give off an impression of being authentic,' said Jared Spataro, the head of Teams.

Teams have transformed into the item through which various workers talk with partners and access Microsoft's more comprehensive game plan of effectiveness instruments. The association said it would organize its other helpfulness programming into its new virtual experiences — allowing workers to do things like view PowerPoint presentations in the Metaverse. Spataro said a massive piece of the motivation for introducing further cutting-edge correspondence came from the hardships associations are looking at with creamer working, as specific agents return to the working environment after the pandemic. In contrast, others choose to work in a good way. Microsoft said that its assessment showed that using individual images passed on a sensation of 'presence' that made get-togethers genuinely enthralling while simultaneously freeing workers from having to appear before a camera consistently. The association said that workers who had been in a social affair where someone else displayed as an image were similarly more open to using genuine advancement. Appearing as an image 'has all the earmarks of being essential, it seems like just one phase, yet that is the kind of step I think people are ready to make,' Spataro said. 'Maybe it's even kind of lighthearted at first.' The association said it would use re-enacted knowledge to make an image's lips appear to mouth the verbally communicated words and add looks and hand signals. The gradualist way of managing familiarizing workers with the Metaverse stands apart from the past Facebook's more moderate vision for the possible destiny of office social occasions. The electronic media association showed a whole expanded re-enactment office experience, with people wearing VR goggles to sit in a virtual room nearby images of various subject matter experts.

FACEBOOK BECOME META

One is consistent among the numerous concerns about Facebook: it is simply too huge. That is why some opponents and regulators want to shrink it by compelling Mark Zuckerberg to divest himself of large purchases, like Instagram.

According to data portal Pitchbook after a brief pause in 2018, when the Cambridge Analytica issue broke, Facebook has continued to make significant acquisitions – at least 21 in the former three years.

Many of the agreements have been reported since December 2020, when the US government launched its first antitrust complaint against the Business, accusing it of illegally monopolizing social networking via acquisitions and destroying competitors. The initial case and an amended one seek to compel Facebook to divest Instagram and WhatsApp.

In the last couple of years, Facebook's thirst for deals has ranged from Giphy, a service that allows users to include animated GIFs in your social network postings, to Customer. This commercial software startup caters to Facebook's corporate clientele. However, most of them have been focused on a single area: gaming and virtual reality. That makes sense, given Zuckerberg's explicit announcement that gaming and virtual reality, collectively dubbed "the metaverse," are the future of Facebook.

As a result, the company's name was changed to Meta. What's more significant is that Facebook has committed to deploying thousands of personnel to the endeavor and anticipates losing $10 billion this year alone and much more "over the next many years."

The day after Facebook revealed the name change, the corporation announced an agreement to acquire Within, the Business co-founded by virtual reality pioneer Chris Milk and best known for the Supernatural fitness program. According to people familiar with the transaction, Facebook spent more than $500 million on the acquisition.

Other Metaverse-related purchases announced this year include Unit 2 Games' acquisition of Crayta, a "collaborative game production platform"; Bigbox VR's acquisition of a popular game for Facebook's Oculus VR goggles; and Downpour Interactive's acquisition of another VR game producer.

The government does not have to win a lawsuit or enact legislation to stifle or halt Facebook's goals.

These transactions raised questions even before Facebook proclaimed that it reflected its future. What, then, should we make of them now?

That is if you believe that the 2021 Facebook should be broken up in part to reverse earlier acquisitions such as Instagram ($1 billion, 2012) and WhatsApp ($19 billion, 2014), shouldn't you also be concerned about the deals Zuckerberg is making today to establish the 2031 Facebook?

A Facebook representative was more than pleased to explain the distinction to me: Unlike a decade ago, Facebook is not the leader in virtual reality/augmented reality/whatever you want to call it – a slew of large, well-capitalized firms are investing significant time and money on it. And, as Zuckerberg has made clear, he envisions a future in which Facebook is only one of the numerous corporations operating in the metaverse.

The following is the company's on-the-record statement to Recode outlining the thesis:

"The secret to success is investing in and developing things that customers desire. We cannot construct the metaverse without the assistance of developers, creators, and specialists. As we invest in the metaverse, we recognize that we will encounter stiff competition along the way from firms such as Microsoft, Google, Apple, Snap, Sony, Roblox, and Epic."

In the short term, Facebook is pleased that Snap continues to sell sunglasses that record video and interact with your phone, as they are potential competitors to Facebook's sunglasses that record video and communicate with your phone. Additionally, next year, Facebook will be pleased when Apple is expected to introduce its virtual reality headset, which will compete with Facebook's Oculus.

However, it's impossible to believe that Facebook believes Apple, Snap, and everyone else will always be formidable rivals. After all, one of the primary reasons Zuckerberg is interested in the metaverse is because he believes it would enable him to communicate directly with his consumers without relying on Apple and Google's phone duopoly.

Facebook's purchase spree also demonstrates how tough it is for antitrust enforcers to keep up with a fast-paced and unpredictable sector. Even the most vigorous antitrust enforcement actions we've seen in recent years are intended to go back in time and correct alleged faults.

Or they're fixated on the here and now, such as a proposed regulation that would prohibit large platforms like Facebook from entering businesses where they presently dominate.

So how can you predict that Facebook — not Google, Epic Games, Roblox, or another business you've never heard of — will ultimately dominate the metaverse? Especially when the metaverse does not exist, may never exist, or may exist in a completely different shape than Zuckerberg, science fiction writers, and tech executives and investors see today?

I've asked the Federal Trade Commission, which is currently suing Facebook over its Instagram and WhatsApp deals, what they think of Facebook's metaverse ambitions and acquisitions. Still, I'm not expecting a response — partly because the agency is embroiled in a lengthy legal battle with Facebook, but also because it likely doesn't know what they think.

It's essential to note that the government does not have to win a lawsuit or approve legislation to stifle or halt Facebook's goals. According to some Internet investors I've spoken with, Facebook is - at least temporarily — out of the market for social networking acquisitions simply because the scrutiny and difficulty are too great.

"It simply feels like it will be tough for Facebotoughr to buy anything in the social area," says a venture capitalist who has formerly sold firms to Facebook.

And that may be true not just of large-scale acquisitions but also of small-scale "acquires" — arrangements with lackluster firms solely to bring their programmers and other workers into Facebook's payroll.

Washington has already indicated a desire to pay greater attention to tiny transactions: In September, the FTC issued a study of 616 transactions done over the former decade by Facebook, Google, and other significant technology corporations that did not prompt regulatory supervision.

However, the report's existence demonstrates that authorities believe they should be monitoring more transactions, not fewer. FTC commissioner Rebecca Slaughter put it succinctly: "I view repeated acquisitions as a Pac-Man strategy," she stated when the report was issued. "While an individual merger may appear to have little influence on its own, the cumulative effect of hundreds of smaller purchases might result in monopolistic behavior."

You may dispute whether Facebook has a monopoly on social networking today — the corporation is happy to point up TikTok's near-overnight popularity as evidence that it does not. However, there is no doubt about its vast riches and power. The fundamental question is this: Will we allow it to utilize those resources to maintain its current level of dominance in the future?

Mark Zuckerberg put out our vision of the metaverse as the successor to the mobile internet today at Connect 2021 - a collection of interconnected digital environments that let you perform things you can't do in the real world. Notably, it will be defined by social presence, the sense that you are physically there with another person, regardless of where you are in the world. In keeping with that ambition, he also announced the launch of a new brand for our organization, Meta, that more accurately reflects our future direction. That is an exciting new phase for the organization, and we're looking forward to contributing to the realization of the metaverse.

While the metaverse is still a long way off, some of it is already here — and more are on the way. We consider what we're developing to better virtual and augmented reality as we know it now, as well as the actions we're taking to help achieve the metaverse's full social potential in the future, during today's keynote.

Horizon Residence

We unveiled Horizon Home, our initial concept for a metaverse home base. When you put on your Quest headset, this is the first thing you see. It was named Home recently due to the absence of social interaction. Soon, you'll be able to invite friends to join you in Horizon Home, where you'll be able to socialize, watch movies, and jump into games and applications together.

Horizon Home is the newest component of Horizon, our social platform for creating and interacting in the metaverse. Horizon Worlds, which is presently in testing, and Horizon Workrooms, our flagship productivity solution, complement each other. And now Horizon Venues has joined the fray. Horizon Venues, your all-access pass to concerts, sports, and more, allows you to experience the excitement of live events from the comfort of your own home. NBA games will resume in early November; keep tuned for further information.

Messenger Calls In Virtual Reality.

We debuted Messenger functionality in VR earlier this year, allowing you to send a brief message to pals from within the headset. However, why type when you can speak? We're introducing Messenger audio calls to VR later this year. You'll be able to initiate audio calls with pals from any Messenger-enabled platform and ultimately meet up or go to virtual reality places together.

Playing

From augmented reality chess with long-time friends to fierce skirmishes with new acquaintances, gaming is guaranteed to remain as popular in the metaverse as it is now. We announced during the Connect Keynote that Beat Saber just exceeded USD 100 million in gross lifetime sales on the Quest Platform alone — and teased some interesting new enhancements coming in the coming months.

We have already announced the production of the Rockstar Games classic Grand Theft Auto: San Andreas for Quest 2. Discover a fresh viewpoint on Los Santos, San Fierro, and Las Venturas as you revisit or discover one of gaming's most renowned open spaces. That is a multi-year endeavor, and we can't wait to share more with you.

Additionally, we announced several new games and improvements, including a partnership with Vertigo Games on five titles and recent events for the virtual reality combat royale POPULATION: ONE. Visit the Oculus Blog for further gaming news.

Fitness

Many of you are complementing or even substituting VR exercise for your traditional gym regimen these days, and we want to ensure that your Quest 2 is the most excellent piece of gym equipment possible. Next year, we're launching a new accessory package, the Active Pack for Quest 2. The Active Pack features improved grips for the Touch controllers that will help you maintain control while sweating and an exercise-optimized facial interface that will make cleaning up afterward easier, ensuring that you can continue to meet your Oculus Move objectives for years to come.

If you're skimming for some variety in your routine, fear not: Plenty is coming before the end of the year, including the recently added Boxing mode for Supernatural, a new FitXR fitness studio, and hand-tracked bodyweight exercises in Player 22 by Rezzil, which has aided in the training of skilled athletes across a sort of sports.

THE TOP 7 METAVERSE STOCKS TO INVEST IN

In late October, Facebook Inc. (NASDAQ: FB) made news by announcing that it would change its corporate name to Meta as part of a new focus on establishing a "metaverse." The idea is to create integrated virtual online habitats for individuals to live, work, and play in. A real-life version of "The Matrix" may appear science fiction, but ideas like the internet and self-driving vehicles once did. According to Bank of America, the global metaverse market might rise between $390 billion and $800 billion by the mid-2020s. Here are the top seven metaverse stocks to purchase right now.

Meta (Ticker: Mvrs)

On December 1, Facebook stated that it would change its company name to Meta and its stock symbol to MVRS. According to CEO Mark Zuckerberg, the metaverse is a version of the internet that people can enter rather than merely see. "Today, we are visited as a social media company, but our DNA is a firm that produces technology to link people, and the metaverse is the next frontier, just as social networking was when we started," Zuckerberg said at a media event. Facebook's virtual reality companies Oculus and Horizon will undoubtedly play a crucial part in its metaverse drive.

Microsoft Corp. (Msft)

Microsoft is attempting to establish itself as a forerunner in the professional metaverse. IN OCTOBER, Microsoft CEO Satya Nadella explained the metaverse notion in an interview with Harvard Business Evaluation. "I believe that the core principle of the metaverse is this: As we embed computing in the real world, we can further incorporate the real world in a computer," Nadella stated. Using avatars or holograms, the metaverse could transform the way professionals meet, communicate, and interact online, according to Nadella. Microsoft's mixed-reality smart glasses, the HoloLens, and Xbox game consoles could also play a role in the metaverse user interface.

Unity Software Inc. (U)

Unity Software holds one of the two main 3D game engines, which allows game designers to modify how players move and interact in their games. The Unity engine is used by 94 of the top 100 game production teams. Unity CEO John Riccitiello stated on the company's second-quarter earnings call that the company will "support and define the metaverse," emphasizing "content creation, cross-platform access, and shortening the distance and lowering friction between creators and customers." Unity could play a key role in assisting businesses in creating unique metaverse presences, which are today's equivalents of websites or social media pages.

Roblox Corp. (Rblx)

Roblox is an online entertainment platform that comes the closest to a social metaverse that exists today. Roblox is a computer game with 43.2 million daily active users, a digital currency, and various unique virtual events, including a live digital concert by Lil Nas X in 2020. Outside developers continuously create new games and content to integrate into the core game, which acts as the metaverse's foundation. In 2021, the platform's 1.3 million developers are expected to earn a total of $500 million from their work.

Amazon Inc. (Amzn)

Finally, Amazon Web Services will almost certainly play a significant role in developing and maintaining metaverse infrastructure. For years, Amazon has been working to turn its e-commerce platform into an "ecosystem," bringing together shopping, entertainment, and cloud services for its customers. Amazon is the most popular online shopping site, and it'll likely try to create a metaverse version of an "Amazon mall" where users can connect and buy digital goods. Amazon's Vince Koh, who oversees the company's global digital commerce, recently wrote a blog post about how innovations like virtual try-on, virtual pop-up stores, and a virtual avatar economy are transforming the retail scene.

Autodesk Inc. (Adsk)

Layout software for architecture, engineering, and construction, or AEC, accounts for over 70% of Autodesk's revenue. Engineers and architects use Autodesk's software to design virtual reality 3D structures and infrastructure projects. Autodesk currently offers a suite of solutions specifically built for creating virtual reality and augmented reality 3D animations and buildings, making them ideal for metaverse development. Autodesk's AEC segment revenue increased by 21% to $397 million in the second quarter, while its media and entertainment segment revenue increased by 10% to $53.3 million. It's easy to see why Autodesk is famous among early metaverse developers.

Nvidia Corp. (Nvda)

Nvidia makes graphics and video processing chips for high-end servers, supercomputers, artificial intelligence, and virtual reality. Nvidia chips will be critical in supplying the vast amount of processing power the metaverse requires. Nvidia is also developing Nvidia Omniverse, its metaverse platform. Nvidia Omniverse is a virtual universe platform that connects 3D worlds into a single virtual universe. According to the business, Omniverse may be utilized for a wide range of enterprise applications, including design collaboration and real-world architecture modeling. Nvidia also claims that Omniverse is a valuable tool for robot training.

Metaverse And Nft Video Gaming

There is a lot of precedent for what the metaverse will look like in the realm of video games.

Gaming in the future might look and feel different. Still, at its foundation, it's likely to be similar to how players currently immerse themselves in a game's world and atmosphere. So, what will be different? The main difference is in monetization.

So, what will be different? The NFTs, in the metaverse, will be applied to everything that can be tokenized, including in-game assets.

The gaming sector is a prime target for the "endowment effect" of NFTs.

Game creators and publishers have long leveraged gamers' desire to acquire extra powers, features, and assets as a means of selling their games. It's a historically effective strategy.

However, players may get frustrated when they realize their "purchases" only last as long as they keep playing the game they've "purchased" it in.

Your dazzling virtual objects disappear when you start a new game. NFTs are considered a solution to "address" the problem of players believing they "own" their in-game assets by making them sellable to others and transferable from one game to another.

Tokenized game asset exchanges are available. The misconception that a digital asset may be converted into a traded well using NFTs must be dispelled. Whether or not an in-game asset can be sold to another player depends on whether the game publisher supports the idea of traceability and has put in place the required infrastructure in-game to keep it.

In theory, a games publisher that allows in-game asset trade may not need to tokenize its assets on the blockchain to do so.

Just because something is more complicated doesn't mean it's necessarily better. In addition, game publishers would be able to commission each sale and continue to monetize their assets, albeit from a new aspect, if they controlled their in-game marketplaces.

This in-game solution would significantly align with what happens when players "buy" and "sell" in-game assets.

In-game assets cannot be sold independently from their intellectual property, as stated in the NFTs segment, and game publishers are not in the business of selling their intellectual property lightly.

The in-game assets also include licenses, not sales, as we said when talking about non-financial transactions in art. As explained in the game's terms and conditions, they grant you access to the object for a specific period and within a particular context.

Will in-game assets never be traded on NFT marketplaces because of this decision?

Probably not. NFT games are currently generating a lot of hype. Still, caution is advised because licenses are more difficult to sell than property rights.

That could lead to the demise of NFT games due to a lack of value.

A prime example of items that will eventually be traded in the Metaverse gaming NFT marketplace is portable game assets.

The ability to use your leveled-up rare sword, for example, from one game to the next, would be fantastic.

Can Nfts Make This A Reality?

Again, there's more to this story than meets the eye. Unlike in the real world, you can't easily pack up your blade and go on a trip with it. If the sword isn't in your host game, good luck using it to sever the heads of your foes. What's the point of creating a "foreign" word if the publisher already has some perfect ones available for you to use within their game world? You can't utilize a sword made for a video game in any other capacity. Nothing is more assured until the two corporations agree to make portability possible. There is little doubt that firms will notice that gamers' demand is strong enough. However, we believe that in-game assets (including characters) will only be transferred between games developed by the same company for the foreseeable future. It's important to remember that most gamers don't give a hoot about the legal ramifications of their purchases if they can have a fun time playing the game.

According to the endowment effect, there will undoubtedly be a widening gap between what games are composed of and what people believe they are.

That is a precondition for the metaverse to be a viable alternative to the real world; it should closely resemble it.

The metaverse gaming prospect relies heavily on advanced technology.

Fortunately, corporations do not have to spend as much money on infrastructure.

Processor and graphics technology advancements have been spurred on for years by a booming video game sector. Today, we are getting ever closer to photorealistic gaming experiences. It is just a matter of time before intellectual property and licensing issues take center stage in the gaming industry. There is no way around the inherent limits of that approach when applied to a notion of interoperability imposed by video games as a prototype for the metaverse.

Problems with NFT and related tokenization are more manageable than those connected to the metaverse's underlying infrastructure, in specific ways at least. Why should we assume that the metaverse would look like a single planet where everyone on it can connect and interact in all of these ways: love, hate, fight, reconcile, exploit, and heal?

Multiple metaverses, segregated at the very least by platform configurations but maybe also by content, genres, and publishing rights, are significantly more likely due to the intellectual property and the accompanying license.

The financial motive that has fueled technological growth is the construction of barriers between competing worlds. Metaverse's paradigm as a video game hints at the limitations built into the infrastructure that would create the virtual world. A metaverse that spans jurisdictions and platforms may exist. Still, it will be shattered by intellectual property laws, antitrust laws, privacy regulations, and the capitalistic ethos that has driven the video game industry for decades. When it comes to power, the metaverse's infrastructure will once again raise concerns about the amount of energy needed to run the CPUs and graphics chips.

Video games and the companies building the infrastructure that will support future generations of fun and perhaps even a metaverse can serve as helpful guides. People who want to make video games more immersive will need to be environmentally responsible (both energy usage and sustainable construction materials). Sustainability and energy saving will be essential differentiators for organizations vying for market share in video games and platforms.

Game developers must consider green alternatives instead of simply creating more massive and voracious appetites for the earth's resources.

That is especially important since public opinion appears to be shifting toward a shared goal of preserving our planet.

Metaverse Gaming And Laws

Modesty has its bounds when it comes to the nature of human beings. Online video games and the platforms that host and market them teach us another important lesson: if left unchecked, they may degrade into hazardous environments.

Already countries around the globe are beginning to regulate the Metaverse gaming system.

For example, the EU Directive 2010/13/EU amendments seek to align nonlinear service regulation with linear TV restrictions to protect minors and harmful content and include specific video-sharing platforms (VSP) requirements to protect children from harmful content.

Other European countries are also beginning to step up their web regulation.

Children (under 18) focus on the new ICO Age-Appropriate Design Code in the United Kingdom, which went into effect in September 2021.

The code recommends specific default settings for services that are likely to attract children, including considering children's best interests when designing any data processing in services.

A new German law, the Federal Protection of Young Persons Act (Jugendschutzgesetz - JuSchG), which took effect on May 1, 2021, aims to protect children and young people from harm caused by media consumption and ensure that media is only distributed or made available following the applicable age classification.

The various types of media and other publications that fall into this category include immoral and violent content; the detailed presentation of violent acts, murder, and massacre; and the recommendation of "the law of the jungle" to obtain 'justice.'

The French government has also enacted several laws that regulate online behavior.

One stands out: the pending French audiovisual reform draft law, which would combine the Conseil Supérieur de l'Audiovisuel (CSA) and the Haute Autorité pour la Diffusion des Oeuvres et la Protection des Droits sur Internet (HADOPI) into a single entity.

Among the many new powers that would be granted to this new "super-regulator," known as the Audiovisual and Digital Communication Regulatory Authority (ARCOM), would be the ability to regulate online platforms and combat harmful content on the Internet, and improve the fight against piracy.

It is uncertain if governments can successfully control and promote the moderation they now do in video games in the metaverse. Yet, it is possible in the real world.

If the idea of "platform" becomes nebulous, what liability might be imposed on a developer that does not implement anti-online harm moderation requirements on their platforms?

Would the regulators be required to interact with the public in the virtual world, like Agent Smith in The Matrix?

These issues will unfold as the metaverse is continually being developed in the coming years. All enthusiastic fans and loyalists of the concept can do is wait.

SIX WAYS TO INVEST IN THE METAVERSE

With all the exciting opportunities to play, earn, and invest in the metaverse, your head may well be in overdrive at this stage.

If you want to participate fully in the metaverse, you may consider investing in the essential equipment. For VR, you will need a headset and hand controllers of some type. For AR, you only need a smartphone or tablet to get started. For a decentralized world purchase, such as a plot of virtual real estate, you'll need a cryptocurrency wallet such as MetaMask. To participate in play-to-earn schemes, you may also need to buy a cryptocurrency coin or token required to play in a particular world or casino.

However, what if you want to go beyond that? How can you make money in a big way? What type of projects would pay off the best and provide the quickest ROI (return on investment)? Here are six options.

Invest in individual projects such as Decentraland or The Sandbox by buying their native token, virtual land, NFT collectibles, or creating a business inside their world such as an exclusive networking venue, business meeting venue, coworking space, etc. With this virtual land, you can flip the land or build a structure for your sole use, rent or lease it, or construct a unique design such as one of the Seven Wonders of the World that you charge a small admission fee for visitors to explore.

You don't necessarily need to learn to build yourself. You can help forge the metaverse economy by hiring an experienced designer, and there are already many professional 3D and voxels designers. You can easily find these people by joining Discord servers dedicated to a specific world and asking for help or finding designers advertising their services. You can also find professional virtual service providers on the web, including Voxel Architects, Landvault, and Polygonal Mind, as well as individual freelancers listed on Upwork.

Create games inside metaverse worlds as an independent game developer and charge gamers the local currency token to play. Most virtual gaming platforms, for example, use a utility token similar to that of Linden dollars (Second Life), which has no value outside the virtual world but can be converted to fiat on a secondary exchange. Many children make their games on such platforms, so you can, too. You can launch and develop your small game within existing worlds such as The Sandbox and Decentraland, as Zynga achieved with their first breakout game FarmVille hosted on Facebook. Roblox, too, provides a great starting point for indie game developers to build their skills using the building tools offered by Roblox.

Create wearables, avatars, skins, or art of various types and sell them as NFTs in the metaverse on existing marketplaces. You can either list your NFTs on native marketplaces inside these worlds or an independent, standalone marketplace, such as OpenSea, a host point for sales of many virtual worlds NFTs.

To create an NFT, you must pay a fee to write it to the Ethereum blockchain, making its authenticity and ownership paperwork. The official ownership is sold over the blockchain when you sell it from an entity like OpenSea. Some of the more significant sales from NFTs include the artwork of music artist Grimes, which has sold for millions of dollars. Many more affordable options also exist, such as CryptoCats and Kitties.

If you want, you can wait until Shopify debuts its new NFT platform. Since it already has a lock on e-commerce and its founders created the Shopify site to host businesses, its NFT sales platform should provide an easier to use method than writing an NFT to the ETH blockchain and listing it on OpenSea.

Take the "sell picks and shovels" approach to earn money by providing a service to landowners such as land leasing, creating a scholarship program like Yield Guild Games did in Axie Infinity, a virtual construction company like Landvault has for The Sandbox, or an elite investment package as Republic Realm has done with virtual land in Decentraland, which allows investors to profit from land appreciations and revenues derived from virtual worlds.

Many pieces of the metaverse didn't exist just twelve months ago, so the field remains open to innovation. You may come up with a novel idea that other companies have yet to consider, as was the case for the original inventors of Oculus. Facebook's purchase increased the company, and it now stands to contribute a significant technology to the metaverse. Your service, for example, could include designing in the virtual world for those without the inclination and talent, or you might take your business online to a metaverse platform. Moreover, many virtual worlds offer a marketplace so that you can open a virtual shop like your bricks-and-mortar one or an existing 2D website.

Many solutions to using a new technology start in a skeuomorphic way, which means that you take something you are familiar with and apply that approach to the latest technology, such as building a twin music concert venue or a luxury store in the metaverse. However, the real exciting use cases in the metaverse will be business models that experiment with the new technology and create new and innovative experiences. In this way, we can think of a clothing store like Nike, allowing users to walk into their metaverse store and design their clothes using a range of virtual materials rather than stacking their metaverse store with mannequins and prefabricated clothing and apparel.

Invest in metaverse-related companies by purchasing stock. You can use the traditional stock market as a convenient method for investing in metaverse-related stocks. As the metaverse is comprised and powered by multiple different technologies, you have plenty of stores to choose from. You can save yourself some time, though, by evaluationing stocks highlighted by the ETF Motley Fool and Fidelity. A brief overview of the significant metaverse-related stores is listed here for your convenience.

Roundhill Ball Metaverse ETF (META): An exchange-traded fund (ETF) option offers you significant utility as an individual investor, as it allows you to invest in multiple different stocks at once and without needing to make personal decisions on which stocks to back. Futurist and venture capitalist Matthew Ball created the fund to represent the variety of options among metaverse technology companies fully. Launched in June of 2021, it consisted of 50 stocks and had $104.6 million in assets under management at press time. The majority of the stocks, about 70 percent, consist of computing components, cloud solutions, and gaming platforms. These include Microsoft (MSFT), Nvidia, and Tencent (TCEHY). META averages a 30-day daily volume of about 250,000 shares, which means it took off rather quickly. However, it has an expensive annual fee of 0.75 percent per $10,000 invested ($75). Other similar metaverse-related ETFs, Life Multisector ETF (IWFH) and iShares Virtual Work, only charge 0.47 percent per $10,000 ($47) in expenses.

Autodesk (ADSK): Next, software company Autodesk and its well-known AutoCAD software provided a core virtual and augmented reality technology element. It went public in the 1980s, making it one of the most established metaverse-related companies. Valued at $62.7 billion, it is also more valuable. Traditionally, the software program was used to design infrastructures, such as buildings or physical products among academics, architects, designers, and engineers. The game design community recognized the value of ADSK, too, and now use it to design and build virtual worlds. The company responded with a software suite for rendering 3D animation, constructing and launching virtual buildings, and creating inside AR and VR environments. Now, providing its software tools under a software-as-a-service (SaaS) model, the company has increased its profits and provides an essential cornerstone for metaverse development.

Fastly (FSLY): Data-intensive processes take time to load, and participants often experience lag or latency over an online connection. That's where Fastly steps in to provide a much-needed infrastructure solution called infrastructure-as-a-service (IaaS), which brings the servers and other related equipment to the data creation source. The platform scoots 145 terabytes of data every second across 28 countries to reduce lag time. FSLY has a market value of $4.8 billion, and the decade-old company has experienced rapid revenue growth, growing 14% year-over-year in the second quarter of 2021. The metaverse requires edge computing solutions such as Fastly to deliver AR, VR, and decentralized data.

Meta (formerly Facebook) (FB): Facebook, the company, changed its name to Meta in November of 2021 while retaining Facebook's dominant social product. Meta, the parent company, provides some of the cornerstone hardware and apps of the coming metaverse. This mega-firm currently has a market value of $956.9 billion. Its founder, Mark Zuckerberg, discovered an early building block to the metaverse when he created Facebook. He has added to its capabilities with the purchase of VR-start-up Oculus in 2014. It is out of Oculus that his company made Horizon Workrooms. With the growing trend toward remote work due to COVID-19, VR tech may have found its time. Its VR competitor, Snap, also develops goggles called Spectacles. Whether the two companies will create compatible hardware and software remains to be seen. The same company, Meta, also owns Instagram and Portal, a standalone device for virtual meetings and entertainment. Facebook makes an excellent choice for more conservative investors.

Microsoft (MSFT): The company founded by Bill Gates still leads the pack in developing hardware and software. The firm's Xbox gaming system provides the hardware for many to access the Internet and metaverse. The company also invests heavily in cloud gaming. Minecraft's game/platform also bears some resemblance to Roblox, where you can play and build inside a voxel-based world. Of course, Microsoft owns a version of most software programs, from word processing to database creation and maintenance. They also make computers and tablets now and briefly forayed into smartphones. As far as core metaverse stock options go, Microsoft is a worthy bet with a current market value of $2.52 trillion.

Nvidia (NVDA): Nvidia brings infrastructure to metaverse technologies and the metaverse as a whole. Your computer likely has an Nvidia part, and its chipsets pervade many systems. At the time of writing, it plans to purchase ARM Holdings from SoftBank Group (SFTBY), a move likely to increase its market value by $516.2 billion. ARM will allow it to end-to-end its ecosystem. As a semiconductor stock, it ranks at the top of the list. Nvidia has also entered the artificial intelligence (AI) market, and its chipsets feature prominently in edge computing platforms. Even without the buyout mentioned above, it provides a vital component of the hardware of the metaverse, necessary for high-speed computing and the calculations required for the decentralized computing of the blockchain.

Roblox (RBLX): The video game platform Roblox provides a child-safe area on the metaverse. This metaverse technology began as Dynablocks in 2004, but Roblox replaced it. If you're surprised to learn the gaming platform has existed for more than 15 years, you're forgiven. Most people first heard of it during the COVID-19 pandemic when their child or teen discovered it and began playing. This virtual platform has quietly amassed a market value of $43.5 billion to date. Roblox has attracted significant players, including fashion house Gucci, which held an exclusive event in its confines and licensed its products to allow users to re-create virtual versions.

THE MOST IMPORTANT PROBLEM TO SOLVE

The Coming Battle Over The Metaverse

Well before the web entered famous cognizance, there was the Data Interstate. The name became famous in the mid-1990s to depict the computerized spine that was used to turn into a course for interchanges, diversion, and trade. The media and broadcast communications monsters wandered off in the fantasy land of controlling this unavoidable organization. What at long last arose, looking like the web, was an undeniably more open organization of organizations, preparing for an entirely new class of online go-betweens. Many years later, some in the tech world accept they can see another data domain sparkling not too far off: the Metaverse. A completely vivid, computer-generated simulation world is where individuals will want to seek vicariously after all parts of life, as though in an equal computerized universe. Like with the Data Expressway, early dreams of the Metaverse will probably be a flawed estimate of what an absolute reality will resemble. What structure it takes and what its first "executioner applications" will be involved guess.

What's more, in particular, it isn't yet settled who will set the standards and gather the benefits — however, the present web goliaths are in shaft position. Mark Zuckerberg has unquestionably put down his bet. Toward the end of last month, the Facebook CEO proclaimed that his organization would one day be seen not as an informal community but rather as a "Meta-verse organization." Given the political strain Facebook has been under, this may appear to be an endeavor at the interruption. Yet, attempting to shape thoughts of things to come has consistently been a significant way for tech organizations to set up the market for what they intend to sell straightaway, and Zuckerberg has been working on this for some time. It has been long since he purchased the computer-generated reality organization Oculus. He might need to stand by some time longer to profit from these speculations. To many, directing a portion of your most significant individual and social collaborations through a computerized symbol in a virtual world inspires a distant and not especially appealing science fiction future. However, after the social separation imposed on a significant part of the total populace by the pandemic, getting away into an utterly computerized space no longer appears as freakish. If laborers took to Zoom so effectively, why not assemble in an automated office?

Furthermore, this is certainly not a go big or go home undertaking. Rather than diving clients straight into a full VR world, the Metaverse could well come to fruition all the more steadily.

Utilizing expanded reality to extend parts of the Metaverse onto the actual world, for example, would see it come to fruition first as an incomplete computerized overlay. The eventual outcome could be an extreme "walled garden," where a solitary organization benefits from the complete inundation of clients. If Facebook and other substantial web organizations construct their own — and especially assuming that they each offer their exclusive equipment to get to these zones — then, at that point, the outcome could be an assortment of detached universes, constraining computerized residents to pick where they invest the central part of their energy.

Then again, the Metaverse could involve a bunch of all the more firmly interconnected universes, some of them controlled altogether by their clients. That would be where individuals could take their information, computerized merchandise, and most loved administrations with them as they move from one spot to another. It is enticing to see the web monsters as the present form of the telecoms and media powers of the mid-1990s, longing for molding and possessing the following cycle of the web-based medium. In this correlation, it is likewise enticing to see blockchain innovation and digital forms of money as the decentralizing powers of the early web. Crypto fans see individuals claiming their edges of a more divided Metaverse, rather than tossing every one of their information in with a couple of massive stages.

However, restricting the force of the predominant tech organizations won't be simple. It will rely vigorously upon the current worldwide push for more viable guidelines. It will likewise rely upon whether the advancements basic the crypto transformation brings about new encounters and better approaches for collaborating that are not accessible through the present mass internet-based administrations. Precisely what those could be is still difficult to tell. As things stand, the current web powers are in a decent situation to overwhelm a future Metaverse. Assuming that occurs, they will wind up with undeniably more ability to shape the internet-based existences of billions of individuals than they have now. What might turn out badly?

HOW TO GET INTO METAVERSE AND HOW IT LOOKS LIKE

Mark shared his audience to bring users closer to the mental perception of how to deal and coexist within metaverses. He likened it to turning the Internet into a community that surrounds you with a three-dimensional feature. Then the users will enter this world to find themselves inside a group of endless and interconnected virtual worlds, as well as meeting and dealing with a large number of other users; Furthermore, the virtual community is not limited to social transactions only; you can also play, work and hold business meetings.

Glasses And Headphones To The Metaverse:

Augmented reality and virtual fact headsets and glasses, as well as some smartphone applications, this is all you need to enter the virtual world so you can shop online and closely inspect the product offered to purchase, play a game or meet with your friends, or hold business meetings while you are leaning on your sofa.

Horizon Workrooms

Meta company "Facebook formerly" launched an application to enter the virtual "Horizon workrooms," the user needs Oculus VR virtual reality glasses, the next step comes in determining the appropriate body for your character using the correct "avatar" for you, to discover the excellent features of the virtual world.

Emotions In Metaverse

To achieve emotional communication, this emotion needs a headset with a new sensor that reflects facial expressions and eyes on the avatar in the Metaverse; as Mark formerly revealed, the cost of the virtual headset reaches $ 300, its high price will not stop the purchase of it because people will be curious about it and want to try this technology.

As for whether the user will become a part of the virtual world or not, experts of communication and information predict that if the headset and VR glasses are provided with fast Internet shortly, let's say the 5G; the technology will change in its ways of dealing with the user to turn from a user to an integral part of this life using the headset and VR glasses.

This type of integration will help humans engage and communicate interactively; for example, we can attend a meeting with audio and video today. In Metaverse, we will be able to participate in it using 3D technology with the help of our movements of the face and hands. Just like we exist in reality, we will dance, listen to music, and communicate with other users.

Lastly, let's answer some common questions that may arise about the metaverse world: Is it possible to tell the time?

It is possible to know the time through the glasses, where the time appears on the screen of the glasses, or we can ask them directly about the time.

How to attend a movie, news, series, video, or YouTube?

Also, through glasses.

How to attend a football or basketball match?

1. Through glasses.

How to buy a match attendance card?

2. Through glasses.

How to pay for the card?

3. Through glasses.

How to go to the stadium and sit in a particular place in the grandstand?

The stadium and the audience will be presented and demonstrated with glasses.

How to make a family visit, a business visit, or an acquaintance visit?

4. Through glasses.

How will the people who appear in front of us look like through glasses? Or what would it be like for the people who would see us through glasses?

, we will draw a character very similar to us, and we will choose clothes through glasses; we will be able to buy clothes for our character through glasses borrow and lend some clothes through glasses.

Is the world ready to start using virtual reality or augmented reality?

In general, no, the technology is still under development, although it has begun to be tested in more than one field, such as games, virtual tours, or even virtual meetings, all using glasses. On the other hand, despite the progress of the Internet, the speed and quality of communications currently will be an obstacle to entirely using the Metaverse. But with the spread of 5G connections, in which the connection is high-speed, and with the Internet space via fiber, the speed and quality of the Internet connection will significantly allow the possibility of singing the Metaverse.

When is Metaverse expected to spread or to start relying on virtual reality?

Experts imagine that in light of the speed of technical development, and light of the vast amount of new technology, and in light of the naive madness of people and companies to rely on technology, Metaverse will spread during the next few years, especially with the start of the recovery from the Corona pandemic and the return of life to normal.

To conclude, if we want to get into the Metaverse, or simply the advanced virtual world, we will only need VR glasses supplied with other advanced technologies like headphones.

THEY WILL MAKE SOMETHING TOGETHER

Online Partying And Concert Participation

In different ways, it is simple than real-life partying and is one of the popular ways to earn money in the Metaverse. Although it may lack the look and feel of a good party, you are making money from the party, unlike when you go to a walk-in party you only have fun, but you cannot make money from it. The Metaverse has been trying to connect the chasm.

On the Ethereum blockchain, investors like the sandbox have allowed users to buy land, build properties, and host any activity they prefer. For instance, Rapper Snoop Dogg has reconstructed his mansion in the sandbox metaverse and is now giving people VIP tickets to any of his live shows. You can create a party or be a part of a concert and earn some money. Another thing you can do to make money is to participate in competitions. Some metaverse platforms allow users to participate in contests to earn money, such as art design, song contests, drawing contests, etc.

The portrait award sponsored by BP is one of the reputable competitions in the portrait painting class. It is one of the avenues for creative artists to display their talent on a metaverse platform. Each submission is expected to be made in Acrylic, tempera, or oil on a canvas or board. Any work submitted on watercolors, paper, or pastels will not be accepted. For you to participate, you must be 18 years and above.

Artists who are experts in acrylic works can also contest on a popular website called www. artists network. It is a powerful platform for artists from different walks of life to share and collaborate on ideas and concepts. Acrylic works became 8th this year, and the organizers created a platform for the best Acrylic works painter to show their talents. The competition is a beautiful way for artists to create an impactful presence in the community. The theme for this year is "color and light." The organizers hope that artists will show their creativity so you can contest too to earn some money and recognition.

Online Digital Property Ownership

In the real-life, parcels of land and art pieces of land have gotten the interest of investors. A considerable portion of the population has a new stake in the Metaverse; at least a few people now know about the benefits of land in the metaverse world. Buying land is one of the significant ways to make money in your internet world.

Land Brokers

Just like in the real world, you can become a land broker in the Metaverse, assist people in purchasing and selling land in the Metaverse and take a particular percentage of successful deals. There might be many whales that own plenty of plot in the Metaverse. If you become a metaverse land broker, you can assist the whales in selling their plots of land at a high rate and getting a particular percentage as commission. Purchasing land in the Metaverse like MANA and SAND and then selling them for a profit is an easy way of making money in the Metaverse.

How To Buy Land On The Decentraland

The Decentraland project was first opened for public use on August 26, 2017. It went ahead to create a decentralized metaverse. A few months back, Facebook announced the rebrand to Meta, and the virtual reality cryptocurrencies building a metaverse have skyrocketed. MANA has been traded for pennies from the beginning of last year. As of November 2021, MANA trading has gone above $5 per one coin.

Being the first decentralized Metaverse, asset ownership in Decentraland has been controlled by smart contracts on Ethereum's network. Like second life and Minecraft, there is no goal in Decentraland; instead, users can communicate in an open-world game. Users now have the option to buy land within the game. The games are tokenized as NFTs, and the ground can be monetized and developed. Decentraland games have created a virtual casino in the Decentraland where users can gamble in the Metaverse, and landowners can earn money from their land anyhow they want it.

MANA is a crucial term in Decentraland – it is the Decentraland's cryptocurrency. MANA is a token that lets holders have rights in the future over the future of Decentraland's protocol. It is also an ERC-20 token that you can be employed to buy parcels of land and pay for goods and services in the platform's Virtual reality world. You may also invest in MANA tokens in the cryptocurrency exchange.

When you purchase land, Decentraland burns your MANA to acquire the land. In Decentraland, the team sold a lot of ground for 1,000 MANA. But now that we have other markets, the land prices differ. Currently, the cheapest land in the game is being sold for about 6,000 MANA; in dollars, it is $30,000. But the land is situated in prime locations, and big parcels can attain up to six digits. Top sales of land sold in the Decentraland go for over a million dollars.

Decentraland operates by allowing people to interact with your land. The land is a digital asset that cannot be replaceable, and you can buy it in the game. The platform lets the landowners create applications, games, creative 3D scenes, gambling services, and anything the landowner can think about. As a result of the limited amount of virtual real estate in the game, a plot area has been estimated as 16 x 16 meters. There is no limitation to the height of that land.

Different lands have their regions, and they can be termed as small communities having a common theme. Decentraland works the same way most blockchain project works. The agreement comprises three layers; consensus, land content, and real-time.

Decentraland was the first to use Ethereum as its smart contract to manage and track land ownership certificates. The second layer uses a distribution system that presents shared content in a virtual world. The third layer is in control of providing peer-to-peer connections (remember I talked about the peer-to-peer connections in cryptocurrency) for users to interact without external interference within the game.

So, Decentraland is one of the platforms you can trade lands, buy lands with MANA and sell to people.

HOW DOES IT CHANGE EVERYTHING

Top Ways To Innovate In The Metaverse

The way individuals connect online is evolving, with younger populations already accustomed to purchasing and interacting virtually via social media augmented reality filters, video games, and interactive, real-time content. We are experiencing a consumer behavior transformation fueled by a virtual renaissance.

The Metaverse promises something new, something that merges the digital and physical worlds. Metaverse opens the door of immense opportunities and possibilities for individuals and entrepreneurs alike.

With the introduction of LiDAR 3D scanners on smartphones, the mainstreaming of virtual reality headsets, and over 7 billion gadgets able to produce high 3D experiences rapidly, businesses now have a tremendous opportunity to excel in the Metaverse. They are potentially lucrative business ideas to profit from the Metaverse. We will share important trends that businesses can rethink and adapt to create a niche in the Metaverse space.

Why would you want to make a virtual reproduction of a Canada Goose store since you could shop for a new Canada Goose coat within an Arctic expedition experience guided by Iditarod champion and Canada Goose ambassador Lance Mackey in the Metaverse? There, you can learn firsthand about the garment's basic features and performance, buy it, and have it shipped to your real-world address. In the Metaverse, you can buy a new automobile while having an adrenaline-pumping test drive on the racetrack of your choice rather than from a stationary showroom of cars. You can obtain beauty tips from a personal advisor you bring into your living room from the Metaverse. Why on earth would we adopt our industrial-era version of retail as a paradigm for the future in a world where everything is possible? Advertisers, store owners, retailers, and others will have to change their minds about what a "store" is.

Eventually, virtually all of us will spend time interacting, learning, working, and relaxing in the Metaverse. In contrast, some people may spend nearly all of their waking hours there, considering the world is tedious, limiting, and inefficient. The ratio between the virtual and real items we own will substantially grow as we spend more time in the Metaverse. Who wants to go to two different digital events on the same digital weekend?

Brands will utilize this desire by developing an ever-expanding range of virtual goods at real-world pricing. Status symbols such as the digital house you own, the digital dress and jewelry you put on, and the digital cosmetics you use will become just as essential as physical-world purchases and assets as we spend more time in the Metaverse. Indeed, the amount of time spent in the Metaverse as opposed to the physical world might be considered a status symbol in itself.

For example, Obsess creates computer-generated landscapes and experiences for big fashion and beauty companies. Ikea, for example, is already utilizing augmented reality technology in its Studio app to allow users to build their environments. L'Oréal, the world's largest cosmetics company, has created a complete range of virtual cosmetics. Gucci has also started selling virtual clothes, unveiling the Gucci Virtual 25 shoes, designed by Gucci creative director Alessandro Michele, and retailing for $12.99 per pair.

Each of these items represents a tiny step toward the Metaverse, despite the limitations imposed by today's technology and protocols. Growth will be sluggish and gradual until, like with the internet, enough technology, developers, and users come together to produce a tipping point.

Innovative businesses will acquire virtual real estate and pay builders to expand their brand presence and experiences, selling virtual and physical items to individuals who spend time in both realms. Laggard businesses and organizations will be trapped in the physical world, and worse, in the ghetto that the legacy internet will morph into.

Virtual Stores

As physical stores and shopping centers struggle, metaverses — or the underpinnings of such — are thriving. Stores are supposed to be friendly and entertaining, but virtual worlds play these roles more than ever due to the pandemic. Consider meeting up with a buddy in a Minecraft-like environment to chill out and shop at digital stores instead of going to a single retailer's website.

So, where do we go from here? E-sports applications and merchandise are becoming more popular, indicating a logical progression toward the Metaverse. Virtual goods, for instance, which were first promoted by gamers (primarily through character skins), have subsequently expanded into the fields of fashion, real estate, art, and even pets, resulting in a $190 billion industry. Customized virtual avatars, promoted by Snapchat-owned Bitmoji, Apple's Memojis, influencer, and celebrity-focused Genies. Most recently, Roblox's purchase of avatar firm Loom.ai has found a presence beyond games such as The Sims in the former five years.

These developments show how the internet and the natural world are rapidly converging on a larger scale. Metaverses will, among other things, offer the spontaneity that is frequently lacking in e-commerce encounters. Aglet, for example, a "Pokémon Go for sneakerheads" app that allows users to acquire virtual shoes while walking, promises to let consumers and companies open their virtual retail stores in the app in the future. These are potential opportunities for brands to keep an eye on and an opportunity for tech organizations to design platforms for virtual stores.

And we believe the opposite will be accurate in the future. We are headed for Nike and Adidas to create things in the real world and then incorporate them into games. People will make their brands in these virtual environments later in real life.

Once the technology is in place, the economic implications are enormous since the Metaverse provides users with unparalleled access and absolute immersion, thereby establishing a virtual "third space."

As a result, businesses and retailers can:

- Work in a market that is less fragmented than the internet.

- Avoid "marketplace cut" from third-party discovery or selling platforms altogether.

- Allow greater cross-franchise or fan cooperation rather than separate business marketing opportunities (e.g., each business has its application or website). The Metaverse's open universe enables businesses and followers to pioneer a more interactive experience.

Big tech businesses are the most probable challengers to develop the Metaverse beyond gaming platforms like Fortnite and Roblox. Directing this endeavor will take vast amounts of capital, engineering skill, and a desire for dominance. Given each company's perseverance in holding a significant chunk of the online job economy, social graph, and e-commerce architecture, tech giants such as Microsoft, Meta, and Amazon, will double down on this in the nearest future.

Offering virtual items may be fashionable in 2022. Still, in the next five years, the trend will most likely shift to creating more detailed, fleshed-out virtual environments that provide an interactive shopping experience.

The First Virtual Store

The official launch of Metajuku, a shopping area in the Decentraland metaverse space, was announced by Republic Realm, a metaverse real estate development and investment business, with DRESS X being one of the first virtual-only enterprises to build a store within the area. Additionally, digital artist Hanne Zaruma has developed three NFT artworks inspired by DRESS X collections devoted to SpaceX launches.

Metajuku is a 16,000-square-foot project featuring a pedestrian-friendly open area in the heart. Metajuku has its origins in Harajuku, a Tokyo neighborhood recognized for being the epicenter of Japanese street fashion.

As stores transfer more brands online, physical-world shopping centers are sitting half-empty. Complex virtual malls being developed in the Metaverse led to a new sector termed 'de-commerce.'

Customizers And Configurators

With the Metaverse becoming the reality of commerce, businesses must act now and incorporate new tools, concepts, and software to avoid being left behind.

Consider allowing a customer to check if a couch, desk, or table looks nice or even fits in their space before purchasing and installing it. Consider how, if it doesn't, they may make changes to assure that it does. That, and more, is achievable with Product Configuration and 3D configurator software on the Metaverse.

Users may create bespoke things using a product configurator tool, which enables them to design and pick various features before applying them in real-time. That removes the human element's experimentation and effort while still allowing requirements, adaptations, and processing on the manufacturer's end.

Why You Need Product Configuration

One of the key reasons to use product configuration, as mentioned above, is to present all conceivable combinations of all your items. Nevertheless, there are several other advantages to using this technology for your brand.

Customer Satisfaction And Customization

The use of product configuration technology in the Metaverse eliminates the element of surprise from virtual shopping. It offers the buyer confidence and comfort that the customized product is completed and completed correctly. They increase sales by offering consumers high-quality, immersive images that help them grasp many product possibilities. Customers may modify or pick the choices they want for a given product using a product configurator, which provides them with a unique and exciting shopping experience; in the end, everyone wins from using product configurator technology.

Customer Interaction

Product Configuration involves the customer by including them in the process and personalizing it, resulting in a more engaged feeling and increased sales. After implementing this technology, Nike saw a 32 percent increase in sales and an 84 percent increase in virtual sales.

Teamwork

The pandemic has altered how we purchase and how we interact with colleagues. You may now use configurator software to bring your team together virtually. Website asset management, marketing, and product creation may benefit from 3D configuration technology.

This discussion of the Metaverse and a virtual environment may seem intimidating. However, product configurators may be a straightforward approach to adapt your brand to the Metaverse.

Gamified Commerce

As commerce became more immersive and social, many of the enjoyable, participatory, and social aspects of shopping vanished. It did, nevertheless, open up a whole new range of other entertaining and exciting activities that may render shopping even more addicting than before – only this time from the comfort of your own home, where you can attain your win-states much more frequently.

That is when e-commerce Gamification enters the picture. Most e-commerce gamification instances have successfully increased sales and conversions by quadruple in the correct direction, and some have even assisted e-commerce sites in becoming billion-dollar corporations!

We have put up a list of fantastic e-commerce Gamification examples that will inspire intending entrepreneurs and change how we purchase.

Ebay's Bidding And Feedback System

When it comes to great early gamification, few could rival eBay's potential to bring out our Core Drives. If you were only thinking about starting an e-commerce business, having a competitive bidding system, real-time feedback, and stars for leveling up that eBay offered would not seem necessary.

The exciting thing about eBay is that, unlike other e-commerce sites, buying products on eBay is more than simply a "buy" as you feel like you WON! Even though you spend 10% more than you intended to spend, you feel like you had beaten the other scumbags who were bidding against you, securing your win. That is a fantastic example of Core Drive 2: Development & Accomplishment.

Woot's Daily Deal System

Woot, a virtual merchant, only provides one original product per day. Limited numbers are available at a discounted price. A new product will be released when the initial product's stock has been depleted. People will look forward to the product being removed, usually around midnight.

BLOCKCHAIN FOR THE METAVERSE

Blockchain and its development in the new frontier of METAVERSE

During the pandemic, the Metaverse concept grew in prominence as lockdown measures and work-from-home rules drove more people online for business and pleasure. The phrase includes a wide range of virtual worlds, from business applications to games and social networking sites.

Many of the new platforms are built on blockchain technology and employ bitcoin and non-fungible tokens (NFTs) to enable the creation, ownership, and commercialization of a new type of decentralized digital asset.

What Is Blockchain?

A blockchain is a distributed database that a network of computers may access.

Once a record has been counted to the chain, it is complicated to change it. The network runs regular checks to ensure that all database copies are identical. Blockchain has been used to back digital currencies like bitcoin, but many other uses are on the horizon.

Without getting into the nitty-gritty, blockchain is a highly complex database. It is tough to hack because it is not stored in a single area. This decentralization also eliminates the need for an intermediary. It's open, which fosters consumer trust and empowers them. And because every modification is documented, no one can sneak in and change entries to suit their purposes.

So, how does this assist us? Accounting systems that are impenetrable to tampering would reduce fraud. Transactions conducted without the need of intermediaries will be less expensive and faster. Furthermore, decentralization has the potential to improve trust and security.

Furthermore, A blockchain is a distributed database shared across nodes in a computer network. It is a database that digitally stores data. Blockchains are well-known for their crucial function in maintaining a secure and decentralized record of transactions in cryptocurrency systems such as Bitcoin. The blockchain's distinguishing feature is that it keeps data record integrity and security while fostering trust without relying on a third party.

A regular database and a blockchain have pretty different ways of structuring data. A blockchain divides data into "blocks," each containing a set of information. When a block's storage capacity is reached, it is closed and linked to the preceding block, forming a data chain known as a "blockchain." All additional information added after that newly added block is compiled into a new block, which is then added to the chain after it is filled.

A database arranges data into tables, whereas a blockchain, as the name implies, organizes data into chunks (blocks) that are strung together. This data structure creates an irreversible data chronology when implemented decentralized. When a block is filled, it is added to the timeline and permanent. An accurate timestamp is assigned to each block when added to the chain.

Key Takeaways

- A blockchain different from the traditional database is considered a shared database in how data is stored: information is stored in blocks that are then linked together using cryptography.
- New data is inserted in a new block as it arrives. Once the league is filled with data, it is chained onto the former block, resulting in a chronological data chain.
- A blockchain can hold various data, although the most popular application so far has been as a transaction ledger.
- In the case of Bitcoin, blockchain is employed in a decentralized manner, meaning that no single person or group has power, but rather all users collectively do.
- Decentralized blockchains are immutable, meaning that the data input cannot be changed. That means that transactions in Bitcoin are forever recorded and accessible to everybody.

Who Are The Big Players?

In general, the metaverse can be classified into two types of platforms.

The first includes creating a blockchain-based metaverse using NFTs and cryptocurrencies. On sites like Decentraland and The Sandbox, anyone may buy virtual plots of land and construct their settings.

The second group used the word "metaverse" to characterize virtual worlds in general, where people may interact for business or pleasure. Facebook Inc. announced the development of a metaverse product team in July.

Gaming platforms such as Roblox, Fortnite, and Minecraft fall into this category because they allow players to compete and create their games.

How To Buy Into And Make Money In The Metaverse

Although many metaverse sites offer free accounts, anyone buying or selling virtual goods on blockchain-based platforms must use cryptocurrency.

Several blockchain-based platforms, such as Decentraland's MANA and The Sandbox's SAND, require Ethereum-based crypto tokens to buy and sell virtual assets.

In Decentraland, users can trade NFT art pieces or charge for a virtual show or concert attendance. They can also gain money by selling land, which has increased in value significantly in recent years. Roblox users make money by charging other Roblox users to access their games.

The Future Of The Metaverse

It's uncertain how realistic or long it would take to construct an entire metaverse that reflects real-life precisely.

Many blockchain-based metaverse systems are still developing augmented reality (AR) and virtual reality (VR) technology that will allow users to immerse themselves in their surroundings fully.

In anticipation of the industry's growth, Facebook Inc., Alphabet Inc.-owned Google, Microsoft Corp, and other companies invest in cloud computing and virtual reality startups?

PLAY-TO-EARN GAMES

Play-to-earn games are popular ways to make money on the Metaverse. Game players in southeast Asia earn a way of living by playing "play to earn"; they are blockchain-based games. Games such as Axie Infinity have made players make about 3000-5000USD per month. There are so many games on Metaverse that do fundraising to launch. You can go ahead to play games in the Metaverse and also earn money.

Play-to-earn NFT games have gained so much popularity in 2021. The users have a lot of access to personalization and control of the game's ecosystem's entities like characters, skins, virtual lands, weapons, and more. Users can quickly be paid for spending more time and energy playing the games empowered by the blockchain network. The use of NTF tokens and the standard gives developers more opportunity to maintain the uniqueness and rarity of some of the collectibles in NFT games; as a result of this, some games assets operated by the blockchain are more costly than other game assets.

Play-to-earn NFT games are blockchain-based games that users can play and earn money by acquiring, playing, and trading game-related assets. Suppose the users want to maintain their power over digital access; each player is expected to play strategically by breeding or creating new game characters, purchasing digital collectibles on third party or native platforms. The players can have more ownership and control of the digital collectibles. Users can also decide to unlock the games to earn new items. The players can select to sell the NFTs or share them and receive funds from the trade wallets – which is why the game is called play to earn. Now that you have more information about what play-to-earn NFT games are all about, let us address five top NTF games that you can play to make money.

1. God's unchained

2. Axie Infinity

3. The sandbox 3D

4. Splinterlands

5. Spaceport

God's Unchained

This game does not cost players to enroll in it. The game is a card trading one, where your players collect cards by purchasing them from winning players or other players vs. player battles. The gaming skills of players and the quality of the players' cards are the major factors that can determine how they win.

More emphasis is placed on the player's skills and strategy as it shows the ranked game mode, where players can be matched in ratings. The cards are created and sponsored by an ERC-721 token, and they can be exchanged on the game's native marketplace or in the virtual world open market. Immediately the cards are sold, players will get a payment in the form of GODS – its native token.

The axie infinity

Axie Infinity used a gaming system similar to the one used on the popular game Pokemon Go. The game is operated on the Ethereum blockchain network, where each player is expected to collect and breed digital creatures referred to as axies. The characters have their weaknesses and strengths that form individual characteristics. The features are genetic and can be transferred to the offspring.

Axies can be used to battle other players on the game platform. The axie infinity was founded by Tu Doan and Trung Nguyen. To start playing this game, the Ayers is expected to purchase a minimum of three axies. For each player vs. player battle (PVP) and the adventure mode, the player will receive a smooth love portion (SLP) as a gift (it is the platform native ERC-30 utility token). In this game, axies infinity shard (AXS) is another ERC-20 utility token that can be earned in the game, and it is used for governing and anchoring the platform. The game's creator aims to include new features like axie battle and axie land in future games.

However, the Axie Infinity game is not free; players are expected to pay to play the game and earn from the competition.

The Sandbox 3d

The Sandbox 3D is a blockchain-based gaming system, and it is one of the powerful active NFT gaming platforms where the players are permitted to create and sell virtual assets. The players are allowed to monetize and manipulate the voxel assets. The Sandbox 3D is a blockchain version of popular bakes like Roblox and Minecraft.

The game platform gives animate and build items and later sells them. Users can also create and play games customized on the forum. Players can purchase in-game items by using tokens as currency on your platform's marketplace. Sandbox 3D also launched SAND, an ERC-20 token and the native token of your Metaverse that runs on your Ethereum blockchain network. Other NFT tokens like LANDS are considered one of the most valuable assets most searched for in the sandbox gaming ecosystem. As of April 2021, a record of about $8.5 million in land sales was reached.

The Splinterlands

The splinterlands are like God's unchained. The game is referred to as a card trading game. To begin with splinterlands, the player has to buy a starter pack or cards, register to have a new system account, and reveal the purchased cards on the splinterlands. Some players get lucky and can receive rare cards with their first bought set of cards.

If the player receives multiple copies of similar cards, they can mix up similar cards and choose to hike up their power or purchase one of the cards for payments in the form of cryptocurrencies. The moment players get used to the game and cards, they can fight against other players or be a part of the quests. The outcome of the tasks will determine if players can earn more cards or lose.

The Spaceport

The spaceport is a space-based play-to-earn money game dependent on the BSC blockchain. It is one of the significant market caps to play to earn games. You can make at most 10% of the holding per day. You can go ahead to earn money based on the high score you have without twenty-four hours. The more the score, the more money you can get. You can begin with a low amount.

NFT FOR METAVERSE

Nfts And Our Virtual Lives

It is easy to ignore that the World Wide Web has only been around for 25 years. In those 25 years, digital technology has grown tremendously, considering its importance to our existence. It's also important to mention that this has radically altered our lives. We have progressed from a small network of users accessed via massive desktop computers at about 30 kbps to a large percentage of the world having easy access to the entire human knowledge carried on a smartphone in our pocket.

The flow of technological progress, on the other hand, continues. Our daily lives are becoming engulfed by the digital world. As a result, the Metaverse, a concept long confined to science fiction, is beginning to shape.

Many investors and futurists characterize the Metaverse differently, but the basic notion remains the same. The Metaverse is a paradigm for living a very interconnected life. Of course, we are all interconnected right now via our smartphones, laptops, and desktop computers. The Metaverse will develop when more products, services, and capabilities connect and blend. Even in today's highly connected society, this will join us in ways that would seem unfathomable.

Most people, including Mark Zuckerberg, view the Metaverse as the point at which VR can perfectly mimic social interactions. That would allow two individuals from different parts of the world to connect in a virtual space, explore the environment, and play games together. Of course, the notion of internet gaming is not new. The Metaverse is the concept that internet interactions may connect all aspects of our lives.

Nft Technology: The Key To Metaverse

As a result, existing nonfungible token applications are only scratching the surface of the innovation. In the Metaverse, everything will keep being simulated. That implies that products for sale, online items, and even online land and property must all be ownable, sellable, and transferable inside the metaverse space.

Holders of nonfungible token technology get full ownership of digital assets. You will begin to comprehend how NFTs may create a metaverse that connects society worldwide once you realize the security that possessing a digital purchase on the blockchain provides. As shown by the amount paid for many digital art pieces, the notion of NFTs giving ownership over digital assets has already been embraced by the masses. The Metaverse is just the virtualization of that idea.

Some NFT initiatives are already going more and more into the Metaverse world. Most people consider blockchain gaming to be the model for an all-encompassing metaverse. Most of the principles in the Metaverse have already been tested and modified in blockchain gaming.

Axie Infinity is the biggest game project in the area right now and one of the most significant nonfungible token projects generally. Players adopt, train, and battle in Axies, which are comparable to Pokémon. On-chain, each Axie is denoted by an NFT. As the Axies gain experience, they grow stronger and, as a result, costlier. It is possible to buy Axies and in-game products to improve Axies skills. In the realm of Axie Infinity, players will combat and interact with one another. Axie Infinity is a virtual environment where individuals worldwide communicate through digital objects. In some ways, it is its own constrained form of the Metaverse.

Another product that dabbles in the Metaverse is Xplorer's Studio, a collection of 10,000 nonfungible token astronauts. An Xplorer NFT can be used as a digital ticket to get access to a set of online tools that will assist in the creation of an online identity. Zoom backdrops, an entire store, a digital community wallet, and other unique features are among the functionality available. In addition, and maybe more importantly, when the NFT transactions are completed, Xplorers Studio will acquire land in a metaverse.

The purchase of virtual land in most NFTs projects is a significant step forward for the metaverse paradigm. It demonstrates that value can be derived from online real estate and adds to blockchain technology another aspect of our offline lives. This dedication to broadening horizons is exactly what Xplorer Studio attempts to instill in their community and NFTs.

The Metaverse is still in development. It is only now that the technology on which it will be constructed is being developed. The Metaverse will start to shape when VR advances, the internet becomes more widely available worldwide, and blockchain gains widespread use. This new perspective is already being included in NFT projects.

Role Of Nfts In Metaverse

NFTs assist the Metaverse in achieving three of the seven fundamental criteria stated by Matt Ball in his metaverse blog:

- Mass Participatory Medium: The Metaverse will be a hugely interactive technology that will run simultaneously and be driven by the creative effort of millions of individuals.

- An Independent and Fair Economy - The ideal future Metaverse will be based on an autonomous economy, which is open and decentralized, allowing for worldwide job opportunities.

Individual and Collective Agency - The Metaverse will fluidly enable individual agency (i.e., you develop and produce an action) and collective agency (i.e., people collaborate toward a common goal, such as in a mass movement), giving you a feeling of control over your metaverse experiences.

Large firms will undoubtedly impact the Metaverse by creating environments, entertainment experiences, games, and the system that supports them. On the other hand, the Metaverse will be a lot more diverse and creative media than we are used to. While social media networks make it possible for anybody to create content, they are pretty limiting. They decide who has access to them, what content may be generated, and who benefits from the creators' efforts.

The Metaverse enables anybody to engage as an essential member of the Metaverse and actively shape its appearance. Users in the Metaverse choice can develop things that are greatly valued in that Metaverse, define their experiences, and help define the actual appearance and feel of the Metaverse.

NFTs will be a crucial component of realizing that creative participative future. In the future Metaverse, NFTs can generate meaning, economic activity, and offer utility.

Mass Participatory Medium

NFTs can bring millions of people into virtual environments, but it is vital to remember that the Metaverse is still a tiny participatory medium. Aside from Fortnite and Roblox, most metaverses, particularly decentralized ones, have just a few thousand daily active users. In May, over 150K-250K people registered into the Dapper Labs NFT Platform of NBA Top Shot daily, whereas Axie Infinity had around 350K daily active users (DAUs).

Even though NFT ownership exceeds metaverse involvement, it is worth noting that the former can be a crucial facilitator for the latter. That is because most NFT owners (for example, Axie + TopShot Collectors) are accumulating passive digital assets that, unknown to them, maybe interactively experienced and employed in the Metaverse. We predict NFT owners to have a more robust understanding of the flexible character of the digital space as a more accessible metaverse evolves, allowing for more creative applications within virtual environments. In the metaverse space, nonfungible tokens are currently being used to showcase digital art galleries as membership tokens for exclusive access to events, virtual fashion, digital sporting events, and interactive infrastructures.

Luckily, the nonfungible token space's technology and innovation assist in onboarding and evangelizing NFT ownership regardless of one's cryptocurrency knowledge or expertise. The tools for creating, discovering, acquiring, showcasing, and selling NFTs are crucial onramps into the larger NFT space. Still, they may also be used to enroll digital citizens into the Metaverse.

NFTs will ultimately become ubiquitous in gaming and metaverses. You will reach a point when you do not even notice using a nonfungible token in the virtual environment. To arrive here, we will need early testing from metaverses like ours and continuous technical improvement, but we are well on our way.

These Instruments Can Be Divided Into Four Groups:

Minting Platforms

Systems that facilitate the creation of digital assets in the form of nonfungible tokens are known as minting platforms. Bitski and Art Blocks are two minting platforms that enable companies and creatives to mint and sell primary Nonfungible tickets.

Marketplace

Marketplaces are where NFTs may be found, posted for sale, and bought. Rarible and OpenSea are open platforms that accept any approved protocol NFT, whereas MakersPlace and SuperRare are curated marketplaces.

NFT Social Networks

These are decentralized online social networks for displaying and discovering nonfungible tokens. NFT Bank enables users to track and get alerts on collectors' nonfungible token wallets and changes creative monetization.

Wallets

Wallets are a central hub and storage location for their nonfungible tokens. Wallets may one day become the virtual identity that may be transported from one Metaverse to the next. Collectors can display and send NFTs and cryptocurrency using wallets like Rainbow and Phantom.

Independent and Fair Economy

The future Metaverse will include a vibrant economy that will revolutionize resource allocation while allowing members to locate a "job" via virtual labor. Virtual economies arise in games like World of Warcraft and Fortnite, but they are often centralized, closed, proprietary, and extractive. People could be restricted (or worse, removed) from economies, standards can be modified unilaterally, and players' financial circumstances (such as currency supply) remain hidden. Users in Fortnite, for instance, have no practical method of determining a skin's actual scarcity.

As a result of leveraging NFTs, the Open Metaverse (s) will feature virtual economies that can increase size and complexity while also infiltrating the virtual and real worlds. NFTs provide players in virtual economies property rights enforced by irreversible code. The value of a digital asset or the tokenomics of its coin will be visible and understood to users, allowing for economic predictability that will encourage creativity, development, and resource allocation in support of a healthy virtual economy.

We anticipate open metaverses to profit from quicker development, higher innovation, and more effective use of limited resources, as in the physical environment economies that tilt their arc toward openness.

Nonfungible tokens that give actual user utility and function as an incentive for metaverse users who give back to the Metaverse they occupy will be created to help mainstream in this virtual economic space. The play-to-earn gaming category, NFT DeFi, and DAOs are examples of this coming to reality.

Play To Earn

ZED RUN, a virtual gaming startup that enables participants to purchase, trade, breed, and race NFT horses in the play-to-earn sector, is at the front line. NFT-based games allow metaverse users to earn virtual environment currencies and items exchanged for other digital assets or fiat currency. Participants may profit from their horses (which can cost anywhere from $130 to $45,000) as their worth rises by breeding them and winning races. With a quickly growing group of 50,000 participants in ZED RUN, we believe the next Bob Baffert will be discovered training and racing NFT horses on digital racetrack across the Metaverse that will be televised on Twitch rather than at Churchill Downs preparing 1,000-pound horses for NBC.

Animated horse racing has existed for years, but what ZED RUN has accomplished via digital ownership has profoundly altered the dynamic. ZED RUN includes a captivating play-to-earn element and NFTs that show great value in response to user actions. A racehorse that routinely wins races, for instance, will undoubtedly gain in weight and develop a more powerful emotional bond with its owner.

PROS AND CONS OF THE METAVERSE

Pros Of Metaverse's Virtual World:

First: the 3D virtual world provides the ability to live, fly and see the world within and takes the user away from the real world.

Second: It provides the user with an opportunity to achieve all its high accuracy skills and allows users to raise their level of concentration and mental ability.

Third: In the virtual world, many things and measures are similar to the real-life of the user, such as the natural shape of the human being and similar sizes.

Fourth: The virtual world enhances the stereoscopic image of sensory perception in the human brain.

Fifth: The virtual world provides the ability to move through time and take you on a trip around the world; in addition to that, it sometimes contributes to re-presenting situations that happened in the past or that may happen to you in the distant future.

Sixth: Users of the virtual world can also use local and global networks and information. It also allows sharing a different environment with users from the rest of the world, increasing users' social links.

Seventh: The virtual world displays fictitious images, but when viewing them, the users can feel that they are living in a virtual environment, and this world is enhanced by non-virtual technology that is visual and auditory.

Eighth: Users of virtual world technologies can have a completely secure virtual environment, providing platforms through which time and space are difficult to obtain.

Cons Of The Metaverse's Virtual World

First, in recent times, the virtual world is expensive, and no one can contribute to its innovation, and the reason behind this is the high cost of the hardware used.

Second: The use of the virtual world is considered very harmful to human health, as most children and young people spend a lot of hours in front of technology screens every day, and they do not use any of their five senses except sight, hearing, and touch.

Third: There are some platforms and programs in the virtual world that are contrary to our religion and our customs, as there are many immoral programs, such as criminal games or programs that include sexual scenes.

Fourth: Continuing to watch virtual world programs through stereoscopic science fiction leads to eyestrain, specifically the retina, and sometimes the user's vision is blurry, and the doctor must be consulted to prescribe the appropriate treatment, and eventually some people may have to wear glasses in most cases.

Fifth: Some technologies in the virtual world are used by particular types of computers. These computers can display moving pictures, which may sometimes exceed sixteen frames per second, and looking at these screens leads to dizziness, nausea, and headaches. It may sometimes lead to problems in the eyes, and according to recent studies, most cases of myopia in the world are due to misuse of programs in the virtual world. The world has witnessed a twenty-five percent increase in myopia compared to the seventies of the last century.

CRYPTO IN METAVERSE

The payments infrastructure is one of the most critical components, and it will surely be one of Metaverse'sMetaverse's cornerstones. The ability to purchase, sell, and, most crucially, own things in the MetaverseMetaverse may be the most revolutionary aspect of this new era. As a result, decentralized ledger technologies, such as blockchains will become the most viable, if not the final, solution for value exchange and storage. Because this is indeed building a new universe where users will connect, transact, own, trade, and share economic value, the prospects for economic development will be incomprehensible.

That opens up a whole new universe for cryptocurrencies, which authorities are currently trying to regulate in the actual world; how can they be governed effectively in the MetaverseMetaverse? The reality that we have already transferred our lives to the digital realm has been highlighted by Covid-19: we work, do commerce, and communicate online. The next step will be to exist within the digital world around us.

Crypto In The Metaverse

Cryptocurrencies skyrocketed after Facebook CEO Mark Zuckerberg announced the company's rebranding as Meta. Digital money will recreate a vital role in the MetaverseMetaverse because they share a fundamental operational principle: decentralization of fiscal ownership, which allows for verifiable and immutable ownership of virtual assets.

Your digital avatar may require some fancy attire to attend the digital concert. So, what kind of monetary exchanges will take place in the virtual world? Cryptocurrency is the answer to blockchains, and cryptocurrencies will dominate the metaverse dominated by blockchains and cryptocurrencies. Transactions will be cryptographically secured on a blockchain.

NFTs, which are essentially unique digital goods—pieces of art or in-game items, for example—where the ownership and other information are recorded into the token, have sparked interest in digital properties. Currently, gamers can establish their virtual casinos and use cryptocurrencies to monetize them.

NFTs will allow users control of their characters, in-game purchases, and even the ability to register virtual territories in their names in the MetaverseMetaverse. Cryptocurrencies will become legal cash in the virtual economy, and all intangible objects will be NFTs.

Crypto is a requirement because of its ease of use, fueled by developing technology and the demand for transparency. People will be more confident in making more and better investments and trade due to this. That will be accomplished by combining cryptography with virtual reality and augmented reality technology. With the help of NFTs, it might become the only tender for use in the MetaverseMetaverse.

The New Gaming Universe

Within the metaverse frontier, the game business is advancing at full speed. It paves the path for a more realistic gaming experience that seamlessly integrates engagement and interaction and allows users to modify their virtual world naturally.

Simple games, which developers are reintroducing, have a higher level of involvement. The goal of metaverse gaming is to create connections. That is accomplished through the use of advanced digital avatars and holograms. It encourages the formation of active communities. One feels wholly involved in the digital environment when using virtual reality and augmented reality technologies.

Musical concerts are conducted during the games to attract spectators and generate a lot of money. Blockchain technology enables virtual trading, with digital games being one of its most valuable assets.

By designing games, gamers have become active participants. There are also 'live service games,' which constantly stream new updates and downloadable material.

Changing technology, such as 5G, will give the additional speed required for this digital transformation to progress.

Will Artificial Intelligence (Ai) Take Over The Metaversemetaverse?

As commented at the start of this book, creating human-looking Android machines that will take over the actual world may be difficult. However, in a world where everything is digital, it will not be challenging to create intelligent, self-replicating agents that can send and learn from their environment and evolve to take over their environment. That is precisely what the MetaverseMetaverse will give.

Our cognitive processes and cognitive architecture are not confined to one single region and are not independent processes; they are the aggregate behaviors of numerous deeply embedded concepts that our minds are capable of, as described by AI's Godfather, Marvin Minsky, decades ago. Intelligence may become a curse to humanity if it is tainted by undesirable tendencies such as greed, avarice, and vindictiveness.

Given that our brains are tremendously intricate networks of hundreds of billions of neurons in continual communication with one another, this is not a novel concept in the domain of AI, but it assumes excellent relevance. It is what enables humans to comprehend what is occurring. Neurons begin to trigger and respond to various fast-paced stimuli, forming patterns in the brain that determine the course of actions that our mind and body will take in perfect harmony. Artificial neural networks (ANNs) had been used in the past by AI researchers to try to recreate this process, but this was just software-based trickery to simulate the human brain.

The advancement of Neuromorphic computing, in which traditional semiconductor architectures are disrupted and re-engineered to mimic the structure of the human brain, where processing and memory are combined in one unit, the neural network created by Marvin Minsky, and many other systems are slowly becoming a reality from a hardware standpoint, is changing this rapidly. As a result, AI is becoming faster, better, and more general. That is quite intriguing because, if applied correctly, it will yield highly innovative applications that may eventually surpass human-level general intelligence.

That is especially true in the MetaverseMetaverse, which will be a place where avatar-wearing humans interact with other avatar-wearing humans in a virtual 3D space and the first place and a chance for artificially intelligent agents to exhibit quasi-human behavior without the physical constraints of building a real-world humanoid robot. We may soon see a metaverse where an AI is indistinguishable from a human, thanks to advances in AI, particularly Neuromorphic computing, which is hastening the approach of artificial general intelligence (AGI).

METAVERSE INVESTMENT

Investing in the Metaverse may be one of the unique opportunities for savvy investors out there to create a hell of a lot of money. After Facebook's current rebranding to meta to create out their vision and interpretation of the Metaverse, it picked the interest of investors worldwide on how they can potentially invest early into this space and capitalize from what could be a perfect investment opportunity.

Indeed, there are many different and exciting ways to invest in the Metaverse, which goes beyond just investing in stocks. As the Metaverse evolves more ingrained into our daily lives, it becomes something that we engage in more and more. It certainly lives in what could be a little bit more of a virtual world, and I suspect the investment opportunities surrounding it will only enlarge over time. So let's talk about some of these before investment opportunities.

Stocks

The first investment opportunity I wanted to talk about is investing in products. It's the bread and butter of most asset portfolios, including mine. There are many different companies out there who are actively contributing to the Metaverse and the infrastructure in building out the metaverse ecosystem.

We already know that Mark Zuckerberg has outlined his intention to build out his Metaverse and stake his insistence on developing social connectivity. But what's fascinating here is that the Metaverse in itself goes far beyond just what one company can build because the infrastructure to build out a metaverse and the activities going on within it is a little vaster.

It contains everything from gaming with friends in a virtual world, seeing live events and entertainment, getting personal training without going to a gym, working with colleagues and meeting in a virtual office, or even going shopping in the Metaverse. Imagine all the different companies already operating, establishing, and having a physical product they could transfer into a digital or virtual product and placed into the Metaverse.

You've got gaming companies like agreement software and Roblox fitness companies like Peloton, Video conferencing companies like zoom and Microsoft, e-commerce companies like Amazon and Shopify. There are endless possibilities for all of these companies mentioned. Due to that, there are many opportunities to invest and gain exposure to some of these stocks within your investment portfolio. It will undoubtedly be interesting to see which stocks actually look to make a bit of a move and start investing in the business to gain some exposure into the

Metaverse and actively look to gain some market share. I suspect the first-mover advantage into this space will be huge.

The market opportunity or the forecasted market possibility for the Metaverse is expected to be 825 billion dollars by 2028 and grow a compounded annual growth rate of 43.3% per year. So there are plenty of opportunities to invest in companies that capitalize from massive levels of growth in their business simply from investing in the Metaverse and having some virtual product within it.

Metaverse Token

These are the following few investment opportunities that get a little more interesting. So we're going to start by talking about metaverse tokens. If you go onto a website like coinmarketcap, you can scroll across and click into the metaverse tab, bringing up some of the top metaverse cryptocurrency tokens.

We have tokens like axie infinity, Decentraland, Enjin coin, and the Sandbox. All of this has varying market capitalizations, especially with axie infinity and Decentraland, which is between close to six to nearly nine billion dollars of market cap. These aren't any tiny tokens. They are tokens that have a lot of people actively investing in them. These tokens are essentially the kind of currency you would use for the corresponding virtual metaverses they've built.

I guess you could compare spending great British pounds in England to buy things. The same goes for these virtual or metaverses, as you could call them. For example, you've got axie infinity with the AXS token, Decentraland with the MANA token, and Sandbox with the SAN token.

Investors are investing in these tokens. They're using the tickets to buy things within their corresponding Metaverse and looking to invest in this token as a pure investment opportunity. They believe that the corresponding Metaverse may be the next big thing. What's interesting is how much these metaverse tokens have gone up in value since Facebook announced its rebranding. Even when you look at the Decentraland pass and put it on a kind of one-year time chart, you can see that the price of this token went from 75% up to a market peak of $3.56, and even as of current market price, it is still trading around $3.17 per token. We're talking about a 300 to 400% growth rate over the past three weeks.

By investing in these metaverse tokens, you're essentially relying on the popularity of the corresponding Metaverse to increase over time. With the increase in demand, you can buy things within the Metaverse, pushing up the price over time.

That is where some subjectivity comes into play when investing in some of these metaverse tokens. Decentraland has a present market value of six billion dollars, though what exactly defines that?

But underpinning an underlying value to some of these tokens is still pretty tricky. It all comes down to supply and demand as well as potential competition within the space as well. Nonetheless, with the predicted growth of some of these crypto-built metaverses, the upside potential could be huge, in my opinion.

Land And Property

I don't point to land and property in the physical feel when I say land and property. I mean land and property in some of these metaverses currently being built. You literally could buy pixels that depict land and ownership within these metaverses.

We all know the excellent investment Disney made a few decades back when he bought 27000 acres of land in Orlando, Florida, for only $182 an acre. Today, that ground itself is worth several billion dollars, and the same potential opportunity appears to be available in the Metaverse. You'd likely be surprised at just how much cash some of this land is currently selling for. If we look to buy some ground on the sandbox metaverse, click the buy land button, it will then take you over to where lots of people buy NFTs and all kinds of different digital assets. You can see just how pricey some of these lands are. It's just pretty absurd.

If you go to recently sold, you can see that the legitimate land is selling for anywhere between 1.5 to 2 ethereum, based on a theme. That probably has a current market price of roughly about $4500.

This price of land has upwards possibility of about nine thousand dollars just for a few pixels on a screen. Then once you've gone bought the ground, it appears over on the metaverse map where you see many companies with different icons of individuals who have bought land within.

Atari stands out in the image above. Another video game company appears to have bought land within the sandbox metaverse. You can see hundreds of other individuals and potential companies who have bought land within the sandbox metaverse.

So I guess you might ask how investing in this land and buying this land within these metaverses is a kind of investment opportunity. As I said earlier, as more and more people use this Metaverse and use its tokens, the land on sale becomes scarce because many people have already bought it. It then becomes a focus of supply and demand. When you have a limited supply, people can demand whatever price they think they'll sell their land.

What's interesting is that you can build upon that landing that you've brought as well. The land with more infrastructure would attract people, which you could place more charge for that if you were going to sell it at a later point in time. If you desire yourself as a pretty savvy landowner and investor in some of these metaverses, then be sure to go and check out some of the marketplaces on many of these different metaverses.

Nfts And Wearables

Non-fungible tokens are things people argued to have no value whatsoever in the real world but could potentially have much value if you use them and apply them in the virtual world, especially if you are transitioning as a human species to place less value on your physical assets and items, and start to place more value on your digital assets and things in which you own.

You could potentially be the exclusive proprietor of an NFT. You could put in your virtual property to sit on the virtual land in your Metaverse, where people currently flex with their designer clothes and expensive cars. You could potentially see the same kind of thing in the Metaverse with NFTs and wearables. It's an exciting concept and one that's undoubtedly a little bit mind-blowing to think about.

Market Opportunities In The Metaverse

Most of the time, I think it'll just be a bunch of 12 years old will use these metaverses and run around with their avatars in the virtual worlds, but the reality is quite different. The money spent on these platforms is absolutely astronomical and simply mind-blowing to think about.

To give you an example over on axie affinity, the most costly item ever sold at the moment was 300 ethereum which, founded on today's current market price, would be roughly 1.35 million dollars or the equivalent to about a million quid.

The money being spent on some of these digital assets is insane. We've seen it in the NFT space, and now we're starting to see it over in these metaverses too. I guess this is where there is a potentially huge investment opportunity if you know what you're doing and know which assets are the right ones to invest in because some of them certainly have a tremendous amount of value. On a similar note, also in these virtual worlds, you have something called wearables.

Let's take Metaverse's marketplaces to show what I mean. Let's say you have an avatar in a virtual world. You will need to put clothes on that avatar in the form of different accessories and unique items exclusive to that avatar.

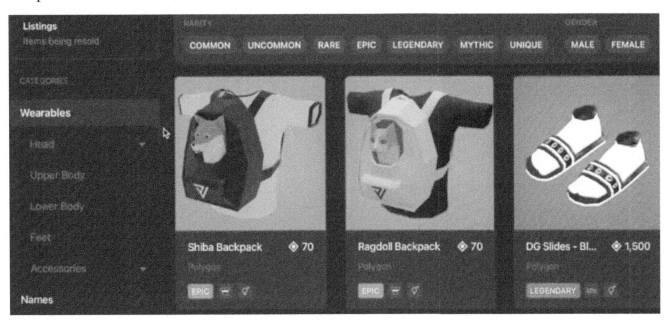

If you go into the Decentraland marketplace, you can see all kinds of NFT, wearables, and collectibles that you can actively put on your avatar.

You can see the different prices for the other variables from 70 tokens to 1500 tokens down to five tokens. Mainly speaking, the value of these various digital assets depends on the rarity in which they are. So you've got down from common assets in which you can buy way up to unique ones, which are one-of-one collections, like the one below, an ethereum dusk ghost helmet priced at 2500 tokens, which would be roughly about seven and a half thousand dollars in real money.

TOP METAVERSE TOKENS

With time, Metaverse Coins are predicted to continue to rise in popularity. Surprisingly, Metaverse Coins have been slowly growing in price over the last few months. Metaverse Coins are also more secure in comparison to other cryptocurrencies. It is more stable, and your investment is less likely to be lost. You will optimize your income if you start investing in Metaverse Coins early. So, if you're interested in digital investment (metaverse coins), don't wait to get started! Keep checking back for additional information on the most popular Metaverse Coins.

In no particular order, the following are the top metaverse tokens.

Axie Infinity (AXS)

The Axie Infinity game's governance token is AXS. This token, unlike AXS, is not used for voting; instead, it is used for breeding and may be obtained through winning fights and adventures in the game. Holders of AXS tokens will stake their tokens to earn additional AXS and even vote on governance ideas. Smooth Love Potion is another symbol in the Axie world (SLP). Binance, Mandala Exchange, OKEx, FTX, and Huobi Global are the top exchanges to trade Axie Infinity on right now if you want to invest in this Metaverse Crypto Coin.

Bloktopia (Blok)

Bloktopia is a more recent project than the others on our list, but it has already attracted top-tier game investors (Animoca Brands). Like KuCoin and Coinmarketcap, several big crypto exchanges launched virtual offices within Bloktopia as part of the initiative. It's also a metaverse project, meaning the Polygon network drives it. The game employs the industry's most potent real-time 3D creative engine, allowing users to create and partake in stunning visual effects in virtual truth. Spawning, Level One, and Auditorium stand some of the major zones in the game's 21 levels. Bloktopia, like different metaverses, has a marketplace where users may acquire BLOK real estate via the NFT method. With a staking scheme that pays up to 60% in yearly return, the BLOK tokens become more valuable.

Decentraland (Mana)

Decentraland was one of the first initiatives to establish a decentralized virtual reality platform using the Ethereum blockchain. Anyone may acquire LAND chunks and develop them into anything they want in this fascinating metaverse game.

Enjin Coin (Enj)

Enjin Coin is an Enjin-created ERC20 coin. It's an online gaming platform with over 250,000 gaming communities and 18.7 million users. Developers may use the Enjin Coin to create one-of-a-kind money for a gaming community that can be utilized on any platform. Binance, Mandala Exchange, OKEx, FTX, and CoinTiger are now the most delicate exchanges for trading Enjin Coin if you want to invest in this Metaverse Crypto Coin.

Epik Prime (Epik)

Compared to other blockchain-based game initiatives, Epik offers a unique economic strategy. It facilitates enterprises' licensing and production of immersive blockchain-powered in-game experiences and NFTs. Epik is widely considered a frontiersperson in enabling early-stage games and driving them into the mainstream gaming demand. It has over 300 clients and has performed with some AAA game firms. In 2018, Epik was another earlier adopter of NFTs. To debut its NFT bar, it cooperated with several brands, corporations, and worldwide leaders. Epik is unusual because it is both an NFT technological platform and the world's premier digital agency, delivering unique in-game drops worth millions of dollars.

High Street (High)

High Street is another metaverse that permits users to make cash by playing games. This concept is fantastic since it is based on a hybrid virtual background, half digital and half material. It's the world's foremost commerce-centric metaverse, and it'll bring shopping to new heights. NFTs are also current in the virtual worlds of High Street. The platform uses smart bonding curves to provide token holders with quick liquidity.

Meta Hero (Hero)

In some parts, the utility of these tokens is best compared to that of others. It becomes simpler to get up companies and utilize their products as NFTs since users can purchase real-life objects. Aside from that, players may spend time playing the game and earning in-game tokens by completing objectives.

The 4K HD scanners are presently operational, but the team is examining to upgrade to 16k ultra-HD shortly. HERO is a utility token mainly used to pay for scans and royalties on the NFT marketplace.

Netvrk (Ntvrk)

Network solves several industry difficulties by focusing on virtual reality and providing a diverse range of income options. This project's target audience is people of all ages and professions. The VR experiences built by Netvrk may benefit anybody from content providers to developers. Because brands and businesses seek new ways to interact and advertise, we predict that such concepts will take off shortly. And what better way to do it than with a low-cost virtual interface? Netvrk's customization options are what make it so unique. Users may make games, develop in a virtual world, and sell them to other gamers or turn them into NFTs. That expands the metaverse's capabilities, giving it a superior option to other top projects.

Redfox (Rfox)

Red Fox Labs is a technological firm actively developing a virtual shopping environment. It aspires to be a stand-alone metaverse that combines gaming aspects in RFOX VALT and Callinova Auction to provide engaging retail experiences. In addition, Red Fox has two tokens that help with operations and other activities in the ecosystem. The RFOX tokens are used to purchase land and virtual assets, while the VFOX token is used to earn incentives. RFOX Finance and RFOX Games are two different products developed by this firm to complement the ultimate metaverse.

Somnium Space (Cube)

Somnium Space has gained a lot of talk in the NFT sector and the gaming community. Anyone, even in VR mode, may use Somnium's WebXR platform to access any segment of the metaverse. Users may create whole sceneries on their land parcels and deploy full-body avatars, making this project unique. CUBE is the token that makes frictionless asset transfers is a fantastic value boost for gamers. Unlike former metaverse initiatives, Somnimum Space chose Polygon to eliminate entrance restrictions for people worldwide.

Star Atlas (Atlas)

Following the release of the teaser, the game has gained a sizable following on social media, with fans anxious to visit the Solana-powered metaverse. Fictional Engine 5 creates the game's cinematic atmosphere and real-time world. Star Atlas is different because of its ability to generate cash flows through staking, battles for obtaining rare in-game objects, and exploration of other planets for building alliances.

The Sandbox (SAND)

Sandbox can overtake Axie Infinity in terms of market capitalization quickly. The explanation is straightforward: improved utility value. The virtual environment developed by The Sandbox is user-friendly and sticks to decentralization's core codes. The Sandbox presents its own NFT marketplace and gaming outlet for user-generated content. The SAND tokens are utilized by users who wish to construct and build a unique game in the metaverse.

Platform access, governance, staking, and essential foundation are the critical use cases for SAND tokens. We should hope the scarcity of SAND tokens increases as the game advances, causing the token price to skyrocket.

PROFITABLE STOCKS TO INVEST IN METAVERSE AND THEIR CATEGORIES

In Metaverse, there are a variety of stocks that can be invested in. Whether you're looking for blue-chip companies with stable income or new tech startups, there's something out there for everyone! Here's a list of the best stock to invest in based on different categories:

Blue Chip Stocks – Financials/ Insurance/ Real Estate

Top blue-chip stocks include SEB, Suntech Power Holdings Co. Ltd., and Kingdee Intl. Software. These companies are typically large-scale financial institutions with solid returns on investment (ROI) that yields steady income for investors.

Major players in the real estate industry include Hengda Real Estate Group Limited, SOHO China Ltd., and Country Garden Holdings Company Limited. They are all well-established firms with a proven track record in the market.

Technology Stocks – It/ Communication/ New Media

Technology stocks are always a hot investment, as they tend to have high growth potential. Some top picks include Alibaba Group Holding Ltd., Baidu Inc., and JD, Inc. These firms are at the forefront of cutting-edge technology and continue to make significant strides in the industry.

Healthcare Stocks – Pharmaceuticals/ Medical Devices

The healthcare sector is constantly growing as medical needs increase around the world. Top stocks to invest in this category include Shanghai Fosun Pharmaceutical Group Co., Ltd., Johnson & Johnson, and Siemens AG. All of these companies have solid fundamentals and are poised for future growth.

Consumer Staples – Food/ Beverages/ Tobacco

Investing in consumer staples can be a safe bet, as demand for these products remains consistent even during tough times. Some suitable options include Procter & Gamble Co., Nestle S.A., and Unilever NV, all of which have a strong brand presence in their targeted industries.

Finance Stocks – Banks/ Financial Services

Investing in finance stocks can be lucrative as many financial institutions outperform other stock categories yearly. Some top picks include Bank of America Corp., JP Morgan Chase & Co., and Goldman Sachs Group Inc. These banks are all well-established and have a significant presence in the industry.

So there you have it! Good luck with your investments! The best stocks to invest in are Metaverse right now. Keep in mind that stock prices can go up or down, so it's essential to do your research before making any transactions.

Steps On How To Invest In Metaverse

There are a few things you need to do before investing in Metaverse. These are:

- Set up a Metaverse wallet
- Buy some Metaverse coins
- Store your coins in your wallet
- Wait for the cash to mature
- Sell your coins on an exchange
- Withdraw your funds from the exchange

Let's go via each of these steps in more detail.

1) Set up a Metaverse wallet

The first step is to set up a Metaverse wallet. You can do this by going to the Metaverse website and clicking on "Create Wallet." You will need to enter a username, password, and email address.

Once you include formed your wallet, you will need to download the wallet client. By connecting on "Download Client" on the wallet page, you can do this. The client is available for Windows, Mac, and Linux.

2) Buy some Metaverse coins

The second step is to buy some Metaverse coins. You can do this on an exchange such as Bittrex or Poloniex.

3) Store your coins in your wallet

Once you have purchased your coins, you need to store them in your wallet. You will need to enter your wallet address into the exchange to do this.

4) Wait for the coins to mature

When the coins have arrived in your wallet, you need to wait for them to mature. You can do this by just leaving your cash in your Metaverse wallet.

5) Sell your coins on an exchange

Once the coins are matured, you will be able to sell them on an exchange such as Bittrex or Poloniex. You can do this by going to your wallet page and clicking on "Sell MVT."

6) Withdraw your funds from the exchange

Once you have withdrawn your coins from the exchange, they will be in your Metaverse wallet. To access them, click on "Balances" (in the top menu) and then "Withdraw." You can then enter the amount you want to withdraw and the address of your Metaverse wallet. Click on "Submit," and your coins will be transferred to your wallet.

Attribute Of Metaverse

One of the essential attributes of metaverse technology is its ability to provide a metaverse environment. This environment is a virtual space that allows for sharing information and resources among users. It also enables users to interact in real-time, creating an online community.

The metaverse environment contains various features that users can access to improve the utility of their online experience. This environment features a customizable avatar or virtual representation of oneself used for all interactions within the community. Avatars are depicted as three-dimensional images created by computer graphics technology. Virtual avatars have long been used in multiplayer video games to create new identities and enable them to interact with other users. The avatar also can change depending on an individual's preferences and can even be used as a form of communication, conveying emotion and nonverbal cues through actions and gestures.

Within the metaverse environment, users can access immersive virtual environments. These computer-generated experiences allow for online interactions between participants who are geographically distant from each other. Virtual spaces, such as chat rooms and virtual reality simulators, enable users to communicate through their avatars. They can even interact in real-time with one another using motion tracking technology that allows them to control their online experience by moving or positioning themselves within the virtual space.

The metaverse environment also contains a variety of different functionalities for social interaction. Forums, or message boards, enable users to participate in online discussions on a particular topic. These topics can range from popular culture to ideas and opinions on various issues within their communities. In addition to forums, the metaverse environment contains other tools for communicating, such as chat rooms and instant messaging. These tools allow users to communicate privately, saving their conversations for future reference.

In addition to these functionalities, the metaverse environment also contains various applications that provide information and resources to users. Wikis are applications that allow for collaborative production, adding new content, or changing existing material by using a web browser. This technology is similar to the traditional encyclopedia in that information is stored online for users to access. Still, anyone with access to the site can continuously update wiki pages, making new content more straightforward and more efficient. Forums are another type of application designed specifically for discussing issues among users. Each topic has its message board within forums where people can discuss the issues at hand. This type of application allows group discussions on a particular case or opinion, making it easy to progress the conversation without distracting irrelevant material.

The creation of virtual spaces allows people from different backgrounds and cultures to become more connected. These technologies provide users with the tools necessary for social interaction and sharing information and resources. The metaverse environment is an essential facet of the online community and continues to evolve with the advancement of technology.

OTHER OPPORTUNITIES TO GET PAID IN THE METAVERSE CREATOR ECONOMY

The booming stock market and the growing popularity of additional or side jobs are two unexpected by-products of "working from home." I'm not saying it's good or wrong, but the current COVID-induced economic instability encourages people to hunt for alternative sources of income to maintain financial stability.

Even high-income workers who already live well have unexpected part-time occupations in their spare time due to the pandemic allowing them to save time from inefficient long commutes, business excursions, and meeting schedules. Working from home will enable you to conserve energy in general.

The metaverse is a metaphysical reality where users can create and be anybody or anything they desire. One of the metaverse's primary purposes is to contribute to the creative economy significantly. Many tech experts have already put money into the game and are assisting more producers in socializing in the metaverse and monetizing their platforms.

More paid online experiences, subscription services, and virtual retail sales will be commonplace in the coming years. It's no surprise that the Roblox gaming app economy has over 10,000 artists making substantial money. A woman in her mid-twenties has sold over 1.3 million virtual things on the avatar software Zepeto. The creative economy is a worldwide concern, not the YouTube or TikTok craziness.

Many businesses and institutions are working to create inclusive and egalitarian cultures that value people from all walks of life. This year, the focus is on diversity, equity, and inclusion (DE&I). DE&I efforts require cross-organizational buy-in from all levels of the company.

However, DE&I culture will not emerge on its own. Culture acts as a glue that ties an organization together in good and bad times. Creating corporate culture during the COVID-19 epidemic, on the other hand, is difficult due to the considerable reduction in human interaction. People are employed and dismissed over Zoom without ever meeting in person.

Zoom video conferences have removed barriers. Zoom does not have a high table. As a result, all delegates and attendees take part in a conference call as equals. In many ways, remote work has leveled the playing field.

In video meetings, we view more junior associates who would otherwise be excluded. It helps employees form a closer bond with their boss as human beings when senior leadership attends a meeting from their kitchen while their pets run about in the background.

No one is perfect, but some care and seek to improve their appearance on Zoom. Lighting is crucial to them. In Zoom, anyone may quickly build up an essential chroma background. It's a little like real estate voyeurism because their natural surroundings reveal a lot about who they are. People frequently dress in bright colors from head to waist, rather than head to toe, with business attire on top and pajamas on the bottom.

People try to locate the most admirable background or virtual wallpaper to appear professional. It is natural for people to use Zoom to expose their faces and increase their online presence to engage in greater human engagement. However, it is possible to have a lot of good things. When a video is required on Zoom, there is nowhere to hide.

Seriously, who cares who you are or what you do when you enter a virtual environment as your avatar? The metaverse, on the other hand, gives you freedom. You can be anybody or anything you choose, and you can customize the texture, background, and mood of your experience. Furthermore, the metaverse will provide an excellent platform for amplifying the diversity and inclusion of various viewpoints.

Platforms in the metaverse can appeal to a wide range of viewers, regardless of gender, age, ethnicity, or sexual orientation. The metaverse brings people together to form social bonds and better understand without prejudices based on looks. We saw firsthand how the metaverse could minimize biases based on race, ethnicity, country, geography, and socioeconomic position during the epidemic.

When people gaze about the metaverse, they notice that everyone appears the same and no attachments are attached. In metaverse, there are no restrictions on creative self-expression. Nonfungible tokens (NFTs) can also be created, and people can be compensated solely for their creative work.

The world of employment will undergo a significant upheaval. Facebook stated that it intends to become a metaverse firm in a recent release. The metaverse is meant to be a fun place to hang out, but it can also be a productive workstation. It has amassed augmented reality (AR) and virtual reality (VR) assets to construct virtual platforms over time.

Microsoft is developing the same thing, although it plans to concentrate on enterprise metaverse rather than a social platform. With our deep social affinities, we're all talking about the metaverse. Many analysts believe that Facebook will eventually bring people together for work, whereas Microsoft may do so for enjoyment.

The good news is that by ripping down borders, constraints, and conventions between distinct material realities, the metaverse could open the way for labor equality. People can now choose to live outside of cities, thanks to the digital transformation, and still actively engage in the high-value creator economy through digital labor, regardless of where they are or how they work.

Avatar economy, which I believe is a precursor to the metaverse economy, where virtual items are sold mainly and traded on a secondary market, is already a tremendous potential boom for the online game business. In the future years, more consumers will move their spending to virtual goods, services, and experiences.

In the actual world, income disparity has been caused by technology, trade, and financial globalization. In the metaverse, there is already a labor imbalance. Mineral mining, for example, is nothing new in multiplayer games like "StarCraft."

People in low-income countries spend their days and nights accumulating digital stuff to sell either within or outside of the game. However, as the metaverse spreads, the value of digital labor will rise, presenting unprecedented opportunities.

In theory, everyone in the metaverse might be treated fairly, and everyone appears to be at the same starting place. Although no one now rules the metaverse, it will be constructed and fine-tuned to satisfy the market's ever-changing needs.

Virtual worlds with economies linked to the real world and the capacity to establish ownership and exchange content within such worlds are crucial Metaverse criteria for you as an entrepreneur. Even further, online avatars and aliases in social media or chat channels might be considered a loose form. That is undeniably present, and there is enough of a Metaverse to be a successful maker.

According to nonfungible, the NFT sales volume has been $2 billion to $3 billion in the last two months.

Though not all NFTs are related, many of the opportunities listed below are directly or indirectly intersected by NFTs.

Virtual Avatars

In many virtual worlds, having an embodied avatar presence provides users with a sense of self. It is a basic need for a human to express oneself through personal style, including everything from hairstyles, colors, make-up, piercings, tattoos, and other physical features to clothing and accessories. In a virtual environment, the physical body and any accessories have significantly more creative potential, and the creation of avatars, skins, and accessories is a rapidly expanding field. Roblox is an example of a world featuring a person-to-person avatar and accessory marketplace.

Apart from avatars in virtual worlds, there is a contemporary trend of generating and selling profile images for use on Twitter or other online platforms. Not only are human images famous right now, but so are photos of other animals. The most popular is the generative art technique, which involves creating a collection of thousands of variations of varied combinations by randomly mixing a set of many different base body types and accessories/modifications. Cryptopunks and Bored Apes are two well-known examples of pfp projects that have jointly sold for millions of dollars.

Cryptopunks have become such a cultural phenomenon that is writing the cheapest punk costs 102 ETH ($391k). Cryptopunks' founder, Larva Labs, has secured an agreement with UTA to represent them in content partnerships for films, games, and other projects. Punks are on the verge of evolving into full-fledged virtual entities. Virtual beings' creative potential is an exciting area considered later in this article. There's a chance to make the identical Cryptopunk shown above a reality.

Pixel art to cartoon-style 2D to sophisticated 3D models with animation capabilities, avatars come in various styles. Through those numerous channels, you have a lot of leeways to show your creativity and specific skillset. The proper technique will depend on where you plan to sell the avatar for use.

Using NFTs to package avatars simplifies creating and selling ownership rights. Games that aren't built on the blockchain have their marketplaces and laws.

Other Virtual Goods

There are numerous options for what a virtual good might be and what types of value it can provide to entice people to purchase it. A single item could fall under more than one category.

People buy virtual objects for various reasons, including creative art, collecting rarities, investment, memorializing and proving involvement in an event, showing support for a cause, or just looking cool.

As with the Cryptopunks, the social capital of being an informed early adopter or a heavy purchase cost believer of a limited release collection has become a new source of worth.

Goods With Game Utility

Aside from just aesthetic or social worth, some emerging experiences go even further in terms of utility. The Sandbox game goes beyond what Roblox or Neon District offers by allowing game makers to create creatures with stats and other creative elements to inhabit their area.

Virtual goods for blockchain-based worlds can likewise be packaged and sold as NFTs, although they usually come with additional world-specific limits. In theory, virtual goods interoperability between worlds is a hot topic, but it has a long way to go in practice. It's best to find out which virtual world you want to make for first and then look into their procedure.

Creator Tools / Creator Training

Most would-be gold miners lost money during the Gold Rush, but those who sold them picks, shovels, tents, and blue jeans (Levi Strauss) made a tidy profit. — Lynch, Peter

While everyone is rushing to generate content in the hopes of a hit, if you have both creative and technical talents, you can develop tools, set up training courses, or create communities to help a large number of people build more efficiently. 2D/3D animation tools are typically sophisticated, requiring substantial experience and expertise, expensive, or both. It's not easy today to rig a model for animation with natural-looking articulating joints and control points. Making more straightforward and purpose-suited tooling or assisting individuals in learning how to get the most out of existing tools with precisely what they need to know has a business opportunity.

"During the Gold Rush, most would-be miners lost money, but people who sold them picks, shovels, tents, and Levi Strauss (Levi Strauss) made a good profit," as Peter Lynch memorably coined.

Remastering Content

Thousands of 2D avatar and profile photo projects compete for attention in an increasingly crowded market.

Give their holders more excellent value and the chance to connect as a community. Many are opting to offer 3D rigged models (annotated with articulation control points) for usage in one or more virtual worlds or games.

METAVERSE'S UNDERLYING ARCHITECTURE-VIRTUAL CURRENCY

The trading of virtual currencies is a very controversial and severe thing, with some countries allowing it to be legal and others explicitly banning it. I have found online that countries like the US, Australia, Canada, the UK, Japan, and Germany currently allow virtual currency trading. Also, they will enable the use of virtual currency for shopping (but it is usually up to the merchant to decide whether or not to charge virtual money), some countries are using Bitcoin as fiat currency, and the US is even adding virtual currency varieties to the futures market; China, Russia, India, Indonesia, Egypt, Pakistan Countries such as China, Russia, India, Indonesia, Egypt, Pakistan, etc. have partially or entirely banned virtual currency trading; more countries and regions are taking a wait-and-see attitude and have not explicitly stated that they ban or allow virtual currency trading.

We mentioned that virtual currency is without physical equivalents, financial institutions, or government endorsement, so what is its value?

In layman's terms, many people currently believe in the value of the existence of virtual currencies. The global liquidity of virtual currencies provides support for their value. This trust of a wide range of users supports the value system of virtual currencies and drives their circulation and trading, even allowing their prices to continue to reach new highs.

There are two types of virtual currencies: the first is the digital currency issued by national financial institutions (the digital RMB issued by China's central bank), and the second is the virtual currency issued by an utterly unsecured institution but traded by the market in spontaneous circulation (such as Bitcoin, Ether, etc.).

Virtual currencies issued by national financial institutions (collectively referred to as digital currencies below) are called digital currencies, which are legally equivalent to national fiat currencies and can no longer be called virtual currencies because they are guaranteed and issued by the state and financial structures with the physical currency or equivalent they own, and may also be directly tied to the user's actual monetary fund account, which the public will more easily recognize and use to do transactions.

However, free virtual currencies like bitcoin and ethereum are very risky because state agencies or financial institutions have no equivalents or guarantees. The value of their currency depends entirely on the hype and the trust and expectations of most users. (Of course, virtual currencies are designed with clever algorithms to make them seem scarce and possess a cost of a generation that seems valuable, but in reality, this cost of age is almost always a pointless waste of resources, such as bitcoin mining, and there are exceptionally few real-world landing solutions that use virtual currencies as an incentive for actual production costs)

On a national level, the generation and management of virtual currencies are almost uncontrolled. We believe that most national institutions will not be willing to endorse them; it would be better to develop official national digital currencies (e.g., China). Of course, some small countries use Bitcoin directly as a transaction currency, such as Savaldo, whose development remains visible.

On a popular level, virtual currencies are virtual items created at will. A few people speculate on virtual items like commemorative coins, and their conversion rates to national fiat currencies often fluctuate dramatically. If a merchant accepts a virtual currency as payment currency for the purchase of goods, they have to bear the risk of the virtual currency going up or down significantly; and merchants who are willing to pay the risk of virtual currency going up or down are usually not people who are eager to do business practically! So really can use virtual currency to buy the goods less and only accept a limited number of mainstream virtual currency shopping payments.

An Amazon insider reportedly said Amazon would accept bitcoin payments by the end of 2021. Still, the exact landing date is undetermined and not officially announced. Still, if Amazon does generally accept bitcoin payments and runs steadily for a while, this could be a significant turning point in developing the virtual currency payments market. Still, it's also more likely that Amazon is experimenting with it on a small scale and counter to the dollar overshoot and devaluation as a hedge against the dollar.

The Metaverse may be an updated version of the current Internet. From this perspective, the Metaverse will inherit most of the application models and functional styles of the existing Internet and then create new models of applications and content. However, from the perspective of the operating model of monetary payment, the future Metaverse is not very different from the current Internet. It will take the digital currency to trade or purchase goods or directly exchange virtual and fiat currency.

Therefore, in the future Metaverse era, the country and the public's perception of virtual currency should not change much. It is challenging to accept virtual currency as a transaction currency.

Investment advice: Digital currencies other than ETFs and BTC are not recommended for investors because of the Metaverse.

AR, VR, AND 5G DATA

We've all heard of virtual reality (VR). Some of us have strapped on headsets and experienced what developers have been working on. With products like the Oculus and PlayStation headsets, the experience is getting steadily better. Whether you want to play a game, use a skydiving simulator, walk on a beach in Hawaii, or visit someone who lives halfway around the world, we've been assured that the technology will be ready within a few years. And our brains will find the VR experiences indistinguishable from the real thing.

Augmented reality (AR) provides an overlay that supplements what we see in the natural, physical world. Google Glass was the first example of this, and the world wasn't ready for it yet (just as it wasn't ready for Microsoft's tablet computer until ten years later when the iPad popularized these devices). In the years since Google Glass flopped, we have become more dependent on technology. Many people have become comfortable using voice commands to interact with Siri, Google, Alexa, Cortana, and virtual assistants. These assistants are growing ever more innovative through the artificial intelligence algorithms that allow them to better understand and focus on what we want. Soon, most of us will be interacting with our smart devices by voice rather than by typing on keypads. And that raises the question of why we need these blocky smartphones as our hubs.

Apple, Google, Facebook, Lenovo, Epson, Microsoft, and others will soon be releasing updated AR "smart glasses." Amazon has a lower-end pair of glasses with no display to talk with Alexa. Qualcomm has a Snapdragon chip that is designed just for AR. These device makers believe that smart glasses will replace cell phones over time.

With AR, we are still rooted in the physical world; the experience is not wholly immersive with VR. But augmented reality can help us by providing the information we need. That could be an arrow in the freeway lane in front of us, telling us to turn right at the next exit. It could be a list of new movies that are playing. It could be a phrase in a foreign language to assist us in an international conversation. Or it could be an overlay for jogging or biking that puts some competitors in your field of vision and turns your trail into an Ironman or Tour de France competition.

There's a good argument that the first successful metaverse worlds might be in AR rather than VR. Indeed, virtual reality is enjoyable for gaming and immersive experiences. But I'm not talking about gaming only here; I'm talking about replacing and enhancing the kinds of functions we currently use on our smartphones. When a person is paying extended amounts of time with this technology, moving around within a world and going from place to place, meeting with friends, enjoying the artwork in a museum, virtually ordering physical pizza, and playing games, how long is that person ready to spend in there with a virtual reality headset? It's a significant change from our phones.

Another strong possibility is that we might end up with mixed headsets. Extended or enhanced reality sets might include some elements of both VR and AR, or they might be capable of both. VR may be used more for games, while AR would be used more for day-to-day roaming through the metaverse worlds.

Will a mixed headset be better, or would people prefer lighter smartglasses for the AR functions? Will most people start with AR or go straight for the full-on VR experience? Will people reject AR glasses if they don't look fashionable enough? We don't know yet. Ultimately, there will be trial and error in the marketplace until users find a comfortable starting point. From there, it can evolve.

5g Will Enable Free Data And 3d Applications

There's another pillar of futuristic technology that is being implemented now. And that's 5G data. Faster, more readily available data will be a key to virtual and augmented reality. We finally moved from phone conversations to video conferencing. Soon, when you are talking to someone on the other side of the world, they can be right there with you as a three-dimensional hologram image. A significant obstacle to 3D imagery has been data: its slow data speeds and its costs.

Pretty soon, those things shouldn't be obstacles anymore. Once 5G is fully rolled out and open on everyone's devices, data essentially will be free. And people will be using a lot of it. It takes some juice to generate a 3D hologram and power the sorts of things we'd like to do using VR and AR devices. It's slightly until someone turns on the microwave and knocks out your Wi-Fi signal (Haha. Hopefully we get past those obstacles pretty soon, too).

THE FUTURE OF NETWORKING: METAVERSE AND HYBRID

Companies have long believed that constant growth is the key to success. That often entails discovering opportunities to reach and broaden target clients, whether through collaborations or new products.

However, when it comes to developing with new technology and future methods, this form of progress can be constrained. Although new collaborations and products typically contribute to increased revenue, focusing on trend tracking and keeping relevant should also be prioritized.

Hybrid events and virtual workspaces are the future of practical business and networking in today's corporate world. Much of this is because a growing number of industry specialists are beginning to provide their skills remotely.

The name came from a pandemic in which 'digital alone' was the primary mode of communication. Digital and physical elements are combined in hybrid events. There is indeed a digital opening, for example, that focuses on content. Then there's a physical activity - perhaps only for a subset of participants. The interaction then proceeds in the digital realm."

But, how is that even possible.

Organizations like New World Events are currently mixing science fiction and modern technology to normalize hybrid events, forever impacting the global workforce's future.

Major Reason Hybrid Events Are The Way Of The Future

Before making a significant investment in technology that may or may not correspond with how most firms now operate, it's critical to consider the larger picture. Aside from incorporating the metaverse further into the corporate sector, there are several reasonable grounds why hybrid events are the most effective approach to expand a company in the future.

1. Working from home is now expected.

By 2025, it is predicted that 70percent of the world's employment will be remote. This significant shift has far-reaching ramifications for how organizations will conduct themselves in the foreseeable future.

Rather than fighting trends, history has repeatedly shown that organizations that remain on top of them and roll out new technology to meet future demands are the most successful.

For example, John D. Rockefeller, the late oil magnate, understood the benefits of oil the decade before automobiles became commonplace consumer goods. He built many of the most influential and infamous commercial empires in human history due to his vision.

2. The Faces of a Company Can Be Found All Over The World

Businesses find it challenging to micromanage customer service and arrange live events where prospective equity investors can interact directly with a company's face in today's worldwide economy.

For situations like this, most companies turn to artificial intelligence. That is accomplished by deploying pre-programmed chatbots to respond to typical questions. But what are almost those of us who choose to communicate with real people?

An executive in India, for example, can communicate with prospective investors and consumers in the United States via hybrid events and virtual reality workplaces. What's the best part? You can speak with a company's face in person, and they will offer you their complete attention.

3. Allow traditional office spaces to be used by remote workers.

There's been a lot of talk about how remote employment will change in the future.

Many conventional leaders are hesitant to give up their personal office spaces, meetings, and other forms of communication.

As workers become more and more distant, this has become one of the most significant controversies we've witnessed. However, organizations like Modern World Events can blend the best of both old and new business technology worlds.

Employers can achieve this by setting up their own digital office space. You still can take attendance, hold face-to-face meetings, and even have personal cubicle areas this way! Best of all, you won't have to worry about obtaining visas for international workers, providing benefits and insurance charges to comply with local labor rules, or purchasing or renting actual office space.

What could the future of work feel like in a hybrid world?

As the globe prepares to open up despite the ongoing uncertainty surrounding the COVID-19 epidemic, executives' at large and small businesses consider when—and if—they will reopen its doors to welcome staff "return" to work. But most of those CEOs, people operations leaders, and corporate leaders end themselves somewhere in the center. Shifting work locations between homes and workplaces, dubbed "hybrid" by many, has been a hot topic of debate.

Is hybrid, on the other hand, the best option?

Many offices worldwide have effectively transitioned their operations to the digital realm. In a year of accomplishment, it's time to confront a fundamental question: "What is the office's mission, anyway?" What's the sense of having actual office space if millions have demonstrated they can produce exceptional, imaginative work outside of a traditional office environment—even one filled with snacks, sodas, coolers, and ping pong? Why aren't teams able to work from whatever location?

What if employees don't want an office that feels like a second home, complete with pinball tables and chefs? It's available to teams when they need it, but it's not required to get work done. Instead, what if they're seeking a location where they can go for a specific purpose, such as a crucial meeting or a brainstorming session? They might use an office space to work on a particularly complex subject, then operate elsewhere when they don't need it.

Companies should start thinking about providing an even more critical resource for work done outside the Office: a reliable, always-available workplace for the work-from-anywhere employee.

The debate and focus point for a heterogeneous workforce must evolve for the future workforce. It's time to stop focusing just on the workplace and begin to embrace it.

The Office has already passed away.

There is a 0% likelihood of everyone returning to work 100 % of the time.

It's impossible to disagree with this viewpoint. I don't believe the workplace will ever return as we once understood it. Before the epidemic, the traditional Office, where everyone commuted to work every day from 9 a.m. to 5 p.m., was on its way out.

You used to go to these accessible workplaces in which people would be sitting at their work stations in front of computers, messaging or emailing the person beside them rather than speaking directly to them unless, of course, everyone had headphones on to drown out the office noise and get some work done.

I recall talking with people who said, "I have to work from home today cause I must get work done," since they couldn't do their best work in the Office.

Despite this friction, few people in a pre-pandemic environment wanted to attract attention to the Asian elephant. Working from home isn't as rare as it once was, now that millions of people have done so and seen the rewards.

As a result, working from anywhere—or doing hybrid work—is possible. We're aware of it. However, we all know that a hybrid configuration isn't ideal.

Challenges

The inability to meet in person, especially abroad, is a considerable downside." This notion isn't exclusive to Hastings.

Numerous employees want a reallocation: to get work done, yes, but primarily to be with each other for those enjoyable and playful interactions. You miss out on a few things when you work from home, notably those fortuitous moments that happen around the Office. Or the buzz you get when you're seated among your coworkers working on a big project.

Consider the time spent with coworkers waiting for elevators when everyone arrives simultaneously. It may seem insignificant, but these simple events contribute to a sense of familiarity with your employees. While you wait for your transport upstairs, you strike up small talk with your colleague's stair-haters and get to know each other. Maybe you'll find out later that your elevator buddy is also your financial business partner. You already have that modest bond and familiarity because you arrive at the workplace at the same time every day and ride the elevator alongside when you need to collaborate cross-functionally.

When you're filling up your coffee cup—or when you're waiting for a meeting to start—you experience similar moments. You miss out on those casual "watercooler" talks that don't make sense in an online environment when you don't see each other every day.

Stronger connections have gotten more vital in the hybrid world. Still, weaker connections have gotten more fragile, and I believe this is because many teams lack a systematic means to make creating rapport and trust a part of their process. You'll miss out on such unforeseen experiences as a result.

However, some businesses have found how to recreate those moments online. Simple exercises, such as online icebreakers, warm-ups, and energizers, can, for example, provide fun to even the dullest meeting. Alternatively, you can provide your team with a "virtual" water cooler where they can share the shows they're watching, the articles they're reading, and the viral memes they're laughing at.

A dispersed workforce does not automatically bring spontaneous fun to scheduled video calls. It's a stumbling block that can be overcome with a bit of forethought and knowledge.

A Business Success

Adopting a distributed or hybrid architecture has a lot of benefits. One advantage of switching to a remote workforce is extending their hiring pool. You can be based in San Francisco but hire people in regions like Kansas or Arizona, where living and employee salaries are much cheaper.

Even's an advantage that Heyward Donigan, CEO of grocer Rite Aid, has noticed, "We have adapted to work-from-home extremely effectively...," he said. We've discovered that we can work from anywhere, and we can now hire and operate a business from anywhere" (Cutter 2020).

Businesses are better positioned for growth with fewer employment expenditures. Moving to an all-remote workforce has the extra benefit of putting all employees on the same footing. When it comes to interaction, whereas there may have been some friction in the past when most of the company's employees worked at the headquarters, that gap vanishes when everyone is remote.

Before the pandemic, one of the most talked-about aspects of working from home was productivity. While I believe it was assumed that working outside the Office would reduce productivity, the contrary has proven true.

Some may argue that great production is due to individuals having nothing to do; however, this is not the case. Remote employees have been taking care of their children and other responsibilities. Still, they also don't have to worry about things like a long, stressful commute, allowing them to concentrate much more.

Remote work is intrinsically more output-oriented than traditional office labor.

Someone may have worked until ten noon. Remote workers are rewarded for maximizing their productivity and completing their tasks. That is different than getting rewarded for putting on a display of hard work by being observed with your head bowed at your office desk. In the past, they wasted time if they spent part of their day perusing the internet. Now, instead of focusing on how much time someone spends in front of their computer, managers focus on what's vital to production.

What is the Office's Purpose?

The fact exists that there is no one-size-fits-all solution for what the Office of the future will look like. What is appropriate for one company may not be suitable for another. For some companies, all-remote—or remote first, as it is at MURAL, where I work—will be the way to go. Others may want a hybrid arrangement where workers come into the workplace a few days a week.

TOP TECHNOLOGIES THAT METAVERSE NEED FOR ITS ADVANCEMENT

The Metaverse is the next stage in the internet's development. It's the intersegment of physical, augmented, and virtual reality in a distributed online margin. The Metaverse is a 4d understanding of our current internet, and it can be referred to as an internet that you're inside of rather than one that you're just glancing at. The Metaverse would need an essential mass of related technologies, including:

1. Virtual Reality: This is an adventure that simulates realistic conditions. Real-life use cases contain gaming, social networking, education, and on-the-job training. Unity's CEO, John Riccitiello, indicates AR-VR Headsets will be as standard as Game Consoles by 2030 & according to ARK Invest, VR headsets could contact smartphone adoption rates by 2030. By then, additions such as full-body haptic suits and VR gloves will likely explode in popularity.

There are already numerous platforms that allow you to connect with other VR users:

- Facebook Horizon lets you research virtual worlds where you can connect with people across the world, participate in fun challenges, and even create your virtual worlds
- Facebook Workroom is a partnership experience that lets people come together to work in the same virtual room, regardless of physical distance.
- VRChat offers an unlimited collection of social VR experiences created by a community of 25,000 people.
- And you can utilize AltspaceVR to hear live shows, meetups, classes, and more with people from around the world. The most notable VR headsets contain the Oculus Quest 2, HTC Vive Cosmos, Sony PlayStation VR, and Valve Index. And according to Grand View Research, the international virtual fact demand will grow from $22 billion in 2021 to $67 billion in 2028.

2. Artificial Intelligence: This will help the Metaverse in numerous ways, as stated by Eric Elliott in this Medium article:
- Humanoid, intelligent AI beings can roam the Metaverse and interact with others.
- They could be programmed with their life reports, motivations, and objectives. Depending on the virtual world they're in, we could participate in pre-planned scenarios with these characters or create our scenarios. Unreal Engine's MetaHuman Creator could

play a significant part in creating these characters. And if and when these characters can exhibit general artificial intelligence, the results can be unique and surreal.

- AI can help us create metaverse assets such as consistencies, landscapes, buildings, character routines, and more. We may witness a future where advanced AI capabilities are combined with game engines, Unreal Engine, to make this possible.
- AI can automate software development processes to seamlessly build progressively more complex assets within the Metaverse.

According to Grand View Research, the synthetic intelligence demand will grow from $94 billion in 2021 to $998 billion in 2028. • AI can create, audit, and secure smart contracts on the blockchain. Smart contracts allow authorized trades and agreements to be carried out without the need for a central authority or legal system.

3. Augmented reality: This is an affair where designers enhance parts of users' physical world with computer-generated input. Eventually, AR contact lenses and AR glasses could be used to augment the world around us and facilitate virtual assistance with the help of sophisticated artificial intelligence. This AR would help us navigate both the real and virtual worlds. Currently, the Microsoft HoloLens and the Magic Leap One are the most notable augmented and mixed reality headsets on the market.

They're primarily used for enterprise purposes, but we'll see more AR headsets sold to the general public as their prices decrease. According to Grand View Research, the augmented reality market will grow from $27 billion in 2021 to $340 billion in 2028. That's a massive 13 times increase in AR adoption, which will make a metaverse emerge sooner rather than later.

4. Blockchain Technology: Blockchain technology would be an ideal currency for facilitating quick and secure digital transactions in a decentralized metaverse. As much as blockchain technology came into existence with Bitcoin, blockchain has more potential beyond cryptocurrency. Blockchain is a shared database that allows multiple parties to access data and verify that data in real-time. According to Grand View Research, the global blockchain technology market will grow from $6 billion in 2021 and to $395 billion in 2028— that's a whopping 65 times increase.

5. Brain-Computer Interfaces: Brain-computer interfaces would control our avatars, various objects, and digital transactions with our brain signals. This technology is expected to gain an initial foothold in the video game and workforce productivity markets. This technology won't play a significant part in the early years of the Metaverse. However, by the mid-2030s, some early adopters might begin using brain-computer interfaces to connect to their neocortexes, according to Ray Kurzweil. Several companies are already developing brain-computer interfaces. Neuralink, NextMind, and Neurable are among the most notable

companies. The global brain-computer interface market is projected to grow from 1.4 billion in 2020 to 3.7 billion in 2027.

6. Internet infrastructure: In this segment, I'll cover wireless technologies and Web 3.0. First, I'll talk about 5G and 6G. The Metaverse would require highly high internet speeds, high bandwidth, and low latency, especially when a user enters a vast virtual world with highly-detailed textures and unbelievably high polygon counts. 5G enables high frequencies at the Millimeter-wave spectrum, which opens up possibilities like VR experiences that include the sense of touch and AR experiences that let visitors have in-depth conversations with AI characters in real-time. Eventually, 6G will replace 5G. 6G isn't an available technology yet, but several countries have already established analysis initiatives.

Some proficients estimate that it could be 100 times quicker than 5G, which equals 1 TB per second. You could download 142 hours of Netflix films in one second at that rate. According to a white paper by NTT DOCOMO, 6G would make it possible for cyberspace to support human thought and action in real-time through wearable devices and micro-devices mounted on the human body. Sensory interfaces would simulate real life. Now, with Web 1.0, it's all about creating and reading content on computer devices. We're presently in the Web 2.0 era. Web 2.0 introduced the" 'Web as a Platform,' where software applications are built on the Web instead of just desktop computers.

One of Web 3.0's primary advantages is its ability to enable a decentralized blockchain protocol, allowing individuals to connect to an internet where they can own and be adequately compensated for their time and data. That helps many people participate in content creation on social networks, blogs, sharing sites, and more. However, Web 2.0 greatly empowers centralized tech giants and enables surveillance and exploitive advertising.

Web 3.0 will help facilitate more excellent connectivity between data sources by Appreciating semantic metadata. That is more advantageous than a web where giant, centralized companies own the lion's share of the Web and can siphon large percentages of the profits. Additionally, according to Rajarshi Mitra at Blockgeeks.com, it's expected that Web 3.0 will allow computers to understand the semantics or meanings of sentences so that they can generate, share, and connect content through search and analysis. As a result, the user knowledge evolves to another level of connectivity that leverages all of the available information on the internet.

7. Mobile Device Processors: For augmented reality to appeal to the mainstream public, we likely need augmented reality to work on normal-looking glasses. That would require small, super-fast mobile processors fitted on normal-looking glasses. VR devices will also need fast mobile processors to handle hyper-realistic graphics, low latency, high refresh rates, high frames per second, and so forth. As processors require more cores and components, we may

also see optical elements that would work with traditional silicon components. That could result in a 100 times increase in data transfer speeds. Lightmatter is a startup founded at MIT, and it's working on a chip that works using light.

MYTHS ABOUT METAVERSE AND REAL-WORLD SAFETY

There is a lot of misinformation on children's safety in virtual worlds. Just as kids can be hurt and even killed by cars, TVs, knives, walking around the street, or any other real-world item which we have let them play with freely, so too can they be hurt (or worse) in virtual worlds. Yet many parents I meet feel that metaverse is "different" and "safer." That leads to this segment about myths about metaverse and real-world safety.

The dispatch media may be to blame for perpetuating some of the myths. That was especially true in the early days of Second Life, when the stories journalists wrote were often laced with a certain amount of sensationalism. As time went on, several incidents and crimes garnered negative media attention even though they had nothing to do with the metaverse. In addition, there is something about virtual worlds that can be misunderstood in a way that gives rise to false fears about them.

Kids spend long hours in virtual worlds such as MMORPGs like World Of Warcraft. It is often assumed that this time can be just as safe (or unsafe) as time spent in the real world, but it's also often believed that virtual safety risks are much scarier than real-world ones. Unfortunately, both sets of assumptions are misguided.

Some people say it's better to keep your children out of the metaverse. But, this is fallacious thinking. Research shows that young people who can participate in virtual worlds are less likely to get involved in drugs or other dangerous activities like alcohol and fast cars.

I've found people's most significant barrier of entry into virtual worlds is their perceptions about the threats and risks of coming into a virtual world. The fact is, your kids' virtual world experiences face virtually the same dangers as their real-world experiences, plus one or two more. The most important lesson to be learned is that there is no such thing as 'safe spaces' online or offline. There are only safer spaces and ways to make your kids safer within those spaces.

The idea that kids - or anyone else - should not be allowed to wander around in virtual worlds without adult supervision seems crazy to most VR veterans. That is because it's ass-backward. It's a holdover from the pre-metaverse world, which judged things by their surface appearance rather than realizing that what got scary on the net was not the tools but the people you met and how they talked and behaved.

The virtual world or the metaverse is a topic that will come up in conversation every once in a while. But it does not come up as much as saying Virtual Reality, perhaps for two reasons. The first reason is that it is still not so commonplace, and only a very few people can experience it. The second reason is that it hasn't received as much media attention yet, although quickly changing.

You are reading this for a reason. That reason is that someone you care about, or maybe yourself, has heard something about the virtual world, which has made them concerned. At first glance, it makes sense. Everything looks so natural. And yet it's animations and avatars where users are free to be whoever they want to be. How could that be safe? How could that be good?

It's worth remembering that life in Second Life is very much like real life, and it would be nice if everyone behaved according to the rules of common courtesy and etiquette.

Many people still think that online games are just for unserious players who sit at their computers all day and won't go outside.

The types of dangers kids face in virtual worlds.

This book focuses mainly on the dangers kids face in virtual worlds - sexual predators, gaming addiction, and bankruptcy.

These are the distinct types of dangers that kids face in virtual worlds: Scams, exploitation, and sharing too much information.

Virtual worlds are a trendy place for kids to hang out. I've been one of them since Second Life came out in 2003. In this article, I will discuss every type of danger and risk they can face while hanging out with friends or strangers in these environments.

At this moment, it should be said that not all adults will have the same reactions to dangers in virtual worlds. Some adults can leave their children to take care of themselves, and some can't. It is also true that your child would typically make different choices at a younger age than you did – this is just as likely to make you proud of them as it is to worry you, so keep an open mind.

The first thing to know is: virtual worlds can be dangerous. Kids' safety in virtual worlds is directly proportional to their interaction with other players.

When the adult message boards started, they were trendy, swamped during those first couple of years. People were reporting how incredibly cool it was to see their kids having fun in a virtual world doing all sorts of stuff they had never seen them do before – playing games and interacting with other players and trading and fighting dragons together. They'd also report how much trouble their kids were having with griefers and trolls and hackers – but unlike their own experience growing up, when the worst thing that could happen was maybe a black eye or, at worst, real-life assault and battery, these online perils could have consequences just as serious as the ones young people face in the physical world.

It's tempting to think that what goes on inside virtual worlds has no connection to the real world. Why should it? But there are also some good reasons for taking kids' safety in virtual worlds seriously. Here are a few of them. The Biggest Reason: Other People. Other human beings populate virtual worlds. These humans act and feel much like the people you encounter in reality. They have the same hopes and dreams, the same fears, the same experiences, and emotions – they can give the same love and lust for life as any human being you might ever meet in your life!

Virtual worlds are evolving increasingly popular among kids, especially during the summer when their school is closed and they have too much time on their hands. Many parents wonder if it is secure to log into such virtual worlds.

Many adults think it is acceptable for children to play online games since their experience in a virtual world could not be different from their experiences while watching cartoons or playing baseball. But there are no safe places on the internet—not even in 'children-friendly' worlds.

As a parent or caregiver, you can't always prevent your child from having problems in Minecraft. If she is determined to show off to her friends, she may find some way of doing it even if you tell her not to. But at the smallest, you can make sure that your child does not put herself in harm's way. You don't have to behave like helicopter parents, who hover too close and take over every aspect of their child's life. But you also should not give in entirely and let your children do whatever they won't either. It would be best if you hit the right balance between taking charge and letting your kids be independent.

> "What's your biggest fear," I recently asked an eighth-grade class. Predictably, they called out every nightmare from abduction to zombification. Then I asked, "What's the scariest thing you've ever discovered in a game?" They considered for a moment and called out, "When another player kidnaps character term."

It's not just a matter of someone being the victim of a clever criminal scam. What if you run across the badlands and get shot by somebody? It felt like you got hit by a player with something better than a starter pistol, so you died and lost some time playing. But since there was no real damage, you don't bother reporting the crime.

CAN THE METAVERSE THE RULES OF OUR SOCIETY?

Besides the world of video games, the Metaverse is deeply embedded in society; it seems that the various confinements have accelerated the digitization process in everyday life and companies.

In 2020, Facebook launched Horizon, a virtual reality, a multiplayer social network that works with the Oculus VR headset.

After the entertainment, the Facebook group is now tackling the world of work with the Oculus Horizon Workrooms project, which proposes to use a metaverse to allow employees to meet virtually in a meeting room, as shown in the video below.

Mark Zuckerberg now employs 10,000 people to work on virtual reality and augmented reality of going even further.

In discussion with the Verge, the entrepreneur said he sees the metaverse internet embodied. Instead of just watching the content, you are in it, so the race to conquer the metaverse end Facebook is careful to get there first.

The Metaverse At The Ground For Tech Giants

Now that he has got the mobile world under his thumb, Mark Zuckerberg has his eyes set on a new realm: the metaverse future of Facebook as a company, assured the manager to his shareholders on the occasion of the last presentation of Facebook's results; but what is the Metaverse?

It is a virtual universe that will seem familiar to the few who have read Neal Stephenson's book, Snow Crash, published in 1992, and to those who, more numerous, have seen Steven Spielberg's film, Ready Player One.

It is, according to the American VC, Matthew Ball, author of numerous articles on the subject, a virtual, live, persistent, and open environment; so that each user can transport their avatar and their belongings from one part of the Metaverse, no matter who manages that part.

We necessarily think of Second Life, this virtual universe that buzzed in the early 2000s, affecting up to 30 million users before falling back into oblivion, swept away in particular by the revolution.

The big difference between the metaverse ebook wants to set up and that of Second Life is the addressable market; it is no longer the prerogative of a few geeks, as numerous as they were in the days of Second Life.

Today, the vast majority of the population can navigate these worlds, the coronavirus has been there and, with it, numerous confinement and social distancing measures that have pushed a whole segment of the population to go digital.

The other difference is the evolution of technology, no connected glasses like Snapchat Spectacles or Facebook Glasses in the Second Life era, or even virtual reality headsets like Facebook's Oculus or Microsoft's Hololens.

Uses are still in their infancy, and manufacturers are still a long way from designing devices that are both easy to wear and technologically advanced. Still, democratization is underway, and with it, that of the Metaverse will only have meaning if you can get there via a device that allows you to navigate it spatially, which is not possible with a computer mouse; Epic Games have recently acquired the platform.

Sketchfab, which contains 4 million 3D assets that can be sold, bought, or edited, should allow the owner of Fortnite to get closer to an open and interconnected metaverse.

Sketchfab allows everyone to get their hands on avatars or environments, such as the 3D version of the planet Mars, which will make it possible to offer experiences in the metaverse giant to the architect of the Metaverse only one step, seems to believe its new shareholder, Epic Games had already begun its transformation into full containment, hosting a concert by rapper Travis Scott. He brought together no less than 12 million users in April 2020.

The American, which brings together more than 350 million players on Fortnite, will have to nevertheless deal with top competitors like Roblox or Minecraft, who also want their share of the Metaverse brings together forty million players every day and has been valued at $ 50 billion since its IPO in April 2021, Roblox has just announced a partnership with the Vans brand, resulting in the creation of an animated universe called Vans World, in which fans of the brand can go skating, wearing their favorite Vans, in a virtual version of their favorite skatepark.

No more Roblox than Epic or Minecraft is, for the moment, able to transpose their users in the Metaverse of being able to offer persistent environments, but they are approaching it very slowly.

It is also a whole economy set up in Roblox's Vans World, with some items that will be free but most of which will be accessible via the local virtual currency, the Robux.

The metaverse gaming, the realm of the freemium model, is a kingdom where you will have to pay to stand out like what is already done in Fortnite, where it is a whole economy of the skin that has developed.

Epic, the gaming giant, had communicated on the sales of skins made last November during a partnership with the NFL, with a total of 3.3 million skins sold for $ 15 each; it made nearly $ 50 million in revenue in just two months.

That is just the beginning as more and more brands are investing in these up-and-coming Metaverse, which also announced a partnership with Roblox last July, allowing users of the gaming platform to dress their avatar in the brand's clothes.

The Metaverse is confined to entertainment; that is what Facebook hopes for with the launch of its virtual meeting rooms, the Workrooms, which can be accessed via an Oculus Quest 2 headset.

From a meeting Zoom, where static cameras limit interactions, to a Workroom meeting, where interactivity would be more robust, there is only one step that many want to take, assured Andrew Bosworth, vice-president of Facebook Reality Labs, on the occasion of the beta presentation.

Fans of remote work will decide, but this first attempt by the Facebook laboratory remains a technological feat when we know that an environment like Workroom must, on its own, allow the capture of participants' hand movements, the flows of their computers, as well as the video and audio that concerns them.

That is only the first step towards a more successful experience; Facebook wants to go further by offering interactions with virtual objects, making it easier to explain things.

The Metaverse is a reality, but many are already claiming its authorship; it must be said that, for gaming giants like Epic Games, Roblox, and Minecraft, it has become a matter of sovereignty; a way out to the Internet as we know it today, where walled gardens like Facebook, Google and Amazon are making more acquisitions to strengthen the thickness of their walls and where an Apple makes it rain and shine.

In the application world, thanks to IOS, by switching to the Metaverse could free themselves from Apple, for example, by controlling everything themselves, where on mobile, they must deal with the rules of the firm at apple and its commissions of 15 to 30%, we can also see in the lawsuit that currently opposes Epic Games to Apple the first battle of a long-term war and should, sooner or later, move to the Metaverse.

Against Big Tech

The boss of Epic has also pleaded that the outcome of this trial would be crucial for the creation of the Metaverse will be very complicated for Epic and the creators to exist in a future where Apple takes a commission of 30%; he assured the judges, the boss of Epic won the first battle. Still, he knows that the road is long.

Epic has made openness and interoperability one of its hobbyhorses; the challenge is not to own the Metaverse provide tools that allow everyone to create their own.e

Meantime, everyone is working on their weapons; gaming players have mastered the language that will make the Metaverse have ten years of experience in social gaming, the GAFA have, for them, almost unlimited resources and a certain mastery of the hardware, the metaverse opportunity for Marc Zuckerberg to justify the $ 2 billion spent on Oculus technology in 2014.

Without really having a return on investment for the moment; for Apple and Google, it is necessary to transpose their patents and the technical knowledge accumulated via their OS and smartphone to new devices: connected glasses, voice assistants, the fight between gaming giants and GAFA, therefore, turns to the eternal hardware duality versus software.

It is challenging to know, at this stage, which of the site managers, the players in gaming, or the holders of the access doors, will have the most power.

Why Build The Metaverse?

The Internet has created new markets and new opportunities, so too is the metaverse ducts and services will emerge, giving birth to companies well-positioned to capitalize on the needs of the Metaverse people who use it; this change may mean that other incumbents may become obsolete if they do not get behind the wheel from the start.

The Metaverse will surpass anything we have seen, and the Metaverse can create an immersive experience in a whole new virtual space.

There will undoubtedly bead throughout the Metaverse ends can go beyond that and help build the Metaverse. Almost all the top internet companies' rank among the most valuable public companies in the world;

Before the Metaverse, it will need a competing infrastructure, and then it will need defined standards and protocols to work; finally, it should be filled with content.

Creating the Metaverse, the capacities of singular people requires resources beyond our reach, the Metaverse to be built by a set of organizations and IT professionals.

The Players

Who will build the Metaverse likely be a combination of businesses and individuals that will help create it, the Metaverse in its infancy, but some pioneers having already made it clear their intention to build it.

Epic Games

If there is currently one leader rising to the forefront of this technological race, it is Epic Games, and as the maker of Fortnite, Epic Games already operates one of the platforms closest to what the Metaverse come; Fortnite started as a game that evolved into a social square with its economy where users can create and monetize their content.

The Metaverse requires an unprecedented level of interoperability to be functional; Fortnite has already demonstrated its ability to bring together competitors in cooperative alliances; this game develops a shared virtual space where brands and players can interact in a way similar to how the metaverse work.

The systems and platforms operated by Microsoft have hundreds of millions of users, coupled with their technical background and infrastructure, the metaverse apple uses the most valuable computing platform and the most significant game store, he has demonstrated his willingness to invest in the Metaverse of his investments; the company has invested money in augmented reality devices that can affect the way we connect with the Metaverse.

If we have augmented reality that adds virtual enhancements to physical reality, we will need a 3D digital map of the real world.

Google is the leader in indexing the digital world and conquering the intuitive ad placement market. Google runs Android, the most widely used operating system; it also has a sprawling investment portfolio.

THE METAVERSE VERSUS COMPUTER-GENERATED REALITY: THE KEY DIFFERENCES

Are the Metaverse and computer-generated reality indeed the very same? Or then again, would they say they are unique? Stand by, do they cover? This is what you want to know.

In October 2021, Mark Zuckerberg declared that Facebook would be changing its name to Meta.

Meta is a descriptive word that implies an item is alluding to itself. In any case, it's likewise short for something many refer to as the Metaverse.

This declaration was met with interest, doubt, and the conspicuous inquiry, "What precisely is a metaverse?" It seems like augmented simulation joins computer-generated reality, but it's not precisely a similar thought.

Anyway, what precisely is the Metaverse, and will you want a Facebook-claimed VR headset to get to it?

The idea of a metaverse is undoubtedly not a new product. It is, nonetheless, something that many people are presently finding out about interestingly.

The term was initially utilized in the clever Snow Crash, initially distributed in 1992 by Neal Stephenson. The Metaverse is a virtual common space that joins computer-generated reality, increased reality, and the web.

The possibility of a metaverse reported by Facebook and other tech organizations gives an impression of being profoundly like this depiction. While the exact definition seems to rely upon who is talking, it's fundamentally another rendition of the web that puts a more noteworthy accentuation on virtual universes.

Preferably than visiting sites utilizing a program, you will get to data by exploring a virtual world with the choice of using both virtual and increased reality.

The Metaverse Versus Augmented Reality: What's The Distinction?

On the off chance that you read anything about the Metaverse, the likenesses to augmented reality are hard to overlook. There are, nonetheless, a couple of significant contrasts.

The following are six essential qualifications if you're attempting to comprehend the contrasts between computer-generated reality and the Metaverse.

1. Computer-generated Reality Is Well Defined, the Metaverse Isn't

The most prominent distinction between computer-generated reality and the Metaverse is that while VR is presently indeed known, the Metaverse truly isn't.

As per Mark Zuckerberg, the Metaverse is "an exemplified web where rather than simply seeing the substance you are in it." A new Microsoft declaration depicted it as "a tenacious computerized world that is possessed by advanced twins of individuals, spots, and things."

These depictions are quite unclear when contrasted with our comprehension of computer-generated reality. It's likewise conceivable that even the tech organizations themselves don't have a total definition.

As per Facebook, the choice to rebrand was an essential piece of building the Metaverse. They required a name that better addressed what they were going after. Be that as it may, it's indeed not by any means the only conceivable justification for doing as such. Facebook has a picture issue.

It's likewise conceivable to contend that the Metaverse is just a popular expression to portray mechanical enhancements in the current web.

2. Facebook Doesn't Own Either Technology

One more expected inquiry concerning the Metaverse is who really will characterize it.

As the owner of Oculus Rift, Facebook assumes a significant part in advancing computer-generated reality. And yet, they are only one player in an enormous industry.

The equivalent is valid for the Metaverse. Facebook might have changed their name to Meta, yet they are not the only organization included by all accounts. Microsoft, for instance, as of late declared Microsoft Mesh, their adaptation of a blended reality stage in with similitudes to the Metaverse and its different definitions. Besides, a new Facebook proclamation suggests that they consider themselves building a piece of the Metaverse rather than the Metaverse itself.

That implies that the Metaverse will be greater than a solitary organization like VR.

3. The Metaverse Includes a Shared Virtual World

The Metaverse is a standard virtual space client will want to get to through the web. Once more, this is something that VR headsets clearly as of now permit you to do.

The virtual space in the Metaverse additionally sounds like what, as of now, exists in computer-generated experience programs.

Clients are relied upon to be recognized by close-to-home symbols which will associate with one another in virtual areas. Furthermore, they will want to buy or construct virtual things and conditions, like NFTs.

The essential contrast is that while existing virtual universes are restricted in size, the Metaverse seems to give admittance to the whole web.

4. The Metaverse Will Be Available in Virtual Reality

The Metaverse won't expect you to wear a VR headset. Yet, it's accepted that vast pieces of help will be available to headset clients.

That implies that the line between riding the web and utilizing augmented reality will probably become obscured. VR headsets might begin being used for undertakings commonly performed utilizing cell phones.

On the off chance that the Metaverse becomes as well-known as Facebook expects, VR will probably become undeniably, to a lesser extent, a thing item.

5. The Metaverse Will Not Be Limited to VR Tech

Be that as it may, following on from the last point, the Metaverse won't be restricted to computer-generated reality. All things being equal, it will be open both by expanded reality gadgets and any gadget you use to associate with the web.

That makes way for different highlights unrealistic with augmented reality alone. For instance, expanded reality will permit parts of the Metaverse to be projected into this present reality.

Virtual spaces will likewise be planned with the goal that they can be gotten to anyplace, no headset needed.

6. The Metaverse Is Potentially Broadly Bigger Than VR

Computer-generated reality is presently utilized for training, treatment, and sports. Yet, it is still ostensibly most famous as a sort of amusement.

The Metaverse, basically as far as scale, sounds much more like a better-than-ever web form. It's relied upon to change how individuals work, access web-based media, and even surf the web, implying that while many individuals have overlooked augmented experience, the equivalent will probably not occur with the Metaverse.

Will The Metaverse Replace The Internet?

Computer-generated reality hasn't had an incredible impact on the world that specific individuals anticipated. There's a cutoff to how long individuals need to spend wearing a headset.

The Metaverse won't have this issue, available to those with and without admittance to a VR headset. Specific individuals anticipate that it should have a lot greater effect, therefore.

Simultaneously, the Metaverse is profoundly far-fetched to supplant the web completely. VR headsets give an Intriguing option in contrast to PC screens. The Metaverse will provide a fascinating opportunity in comparison to the web. However, neither one is intended to go about as a substitution.

We can't conclude what becomes the fate of the internet with the advent of the Metaverse, and we keep our fingers crossed as we watch on to see what mark has in store for us. Until then, let's live with the new technological advancement in Facebook and its impact on our world.

THE HIDDEN STOCKS

One of the most desirable investment themes in the stock market recently has to be the metaverse stocks. The virtual reality space has long been part of sci-fi novels and movies for many years. And thanks to advancements in virtual reality (VR) technology and computing power, that fiction is slowly becoming a reality. Whether we're talking about augmented reality (AR), VR, or digital entertainment, Facebook's (NASDAQ: FB) most delinquent update has sent a shockwave through tech.

In late October, the tech giant made headlines, announcing that it's changing its corporate name to Meta as part of a new focus on building a metaverse. The concept involves constructing integrated virtual online environments where people live, work, and play. Make no mistake, though; the metaverse isn't something that Facebook created. That is something that has been around for years. At its core, it's a realm that would function as the internet we're used to, but one in which our avatars could move through and participate.

The metaverse has plenty of potentials to be as big as the internet. Bloomberg Intelligence estimated that the global metaverse market could reach $800 billion by 2024. That is why many metaverse stocks have become a focus in the stock market today after Facebook's latest news.

Facebook Inc. (ticker: FB) made headlines in late October by announcing that it's changing its corporate name to Meta as part of a new focus on building a "metaverse." The concept involves constructing integrated virtual online environments where people live, work, and play. Facebook plans to establish its Facebook Reality Labs as a separate reporting segment in the fourth quarter. That would provide investors with more in-depth details regarding the overall financial performance on this front. According to Bank of America, the global metaverse market could grow between $390 billion and $800 billion by the mid-2020s.

Now, when it reaches to investing in this area of the tech world, investors can consider a wide array of companies. This ranged from virtual reality (VR) and augmented reality (AR) tech manufacturers to software and consumer tech giants. In its latest quarterly profits called yesterday, the company provided a notable update on its metaverse efforts.

At the exact time, even consumer-focused companies are concentrating on the metaverse now. Take Disney (NYSE: DIS), for example. CTO Tilak Mandadi has emphasized the viability of a "Disneyland composition park metaverse." In idea, this would allow eager park-goers to partake in Disneyland from the comfort of home, significantly expanding Disney's market reach. All in all, the applications and use points for the metaverse are increasing.

It'sGiven the technological hurdles and financial rewards, it's unlikely that a single company will build the metaverse.

The metaverse must be immersive to the capacity that it is preferable to complete in a given instance or a specific use-case. Achieving this will demand technology from a mixture of areas.

It brings a village (or a Valley?) to construct the metaverse.

An actualized version of the metaverse will need high-performance computing, data services, next-gen connectivity, virtual platforms, digital money, and identity services, among countless other technologies.

The Other Ways To Fund In The Stock Market

Individual stocks: You can support individual stocks if and only if you have the time and desire to research and evaluate stocks on an ongoing basis thoroughly. If this is the case, we 100% urge you to do so. An intelligent and patient investor can outperform the market over time. On the other hand, if something like quarterly earnings reports and average mathematical estimations doesn't sound appealing, there's absolutely nothing wrong with taking a more passive approach.

Index funds: In addition to buying particular stocks, you can choose to invest in index funds, which track a stock index like the S&P 500. We generally prefer the latter regarding actively vs. passively contained funds (although there are certainly exceptions). Index funds typically have significantly lower costs and are virtually guaranteed to match the long-term performance of their underlying indexes. Over time, the S&P 500 has produced total returns of about 10% annualized, and performance like this can build substantial wealth over time.

Robo-advisors: Finally, another possibility that has exploded in popularity in recent years is the robot-advisor. A robot advisor is a brokerage that essentially invests your money on your behalf in a portfolio of appropriate index funds for your age, risk tolerance, and investing goals. Not only can a robot advisor select your investments, but many will optimize your tax efficiency and make changes overtime automatically.

NVIDIA NVIDIA Corporation (NVDA) STOCK PRICE (4TH of November) $264.93+

NVIDIA Corporation, global corporation that fabricates graphics processors, mobile technologies, and desktop computers. The corporation was founded in 1993 by three American computer scientists, Jen-Hsun Huang, Curtis Priem, and Christopher Malachowsky. NVIDIA is known for developing integrated circuits used in electronic game consoles to personal computers (PCs). The company is a leading manufacturer of high-end graphics processing units (GPUs).

NVIDIA is headquartered in Santa Clara, California. NVIDIA became a powerful force in the computer gaming industry with the RIVA series of graphics processors launched in 1997. Two years later, the company gained prominence with the release of the GeForce 256 GPU, which offered superior three-dimensional graphics quality. NVIDIA battled with prominent video card maker 3dfx Interactive, pitting the GeForce against 3dfx Interactive's popular Voodoo technologies. NVIDIA eventually prevailed and purchased 3dfx Interactive's remaining assets in 2000. That same year, Microsoft Corporation selected NVIDIA to develop graphics cards for Microsoft's long-awaited Xbox video game console. In 2007, NVIDIA was honored as Company of the Year by Forbes magazine for its rapid growth and success.

Nvidia could surpass Apple in five years as the artificial intelligence economy will be nearly four times larger than the mobile economy that drove Apple. To understand how big the AI economy will be, it was pointed towards estimates of AI adding $15 trillion in GDP once it reaches maturation in 2030 compared to mobile adding $4.4 trillion to GDP in the current year.

Nvidia, the company, has been speaking about its Omniverse platform for several years now, providing a highly graphical 3D environment created for engineering, graphics creation, and collaboration.

OMNIVERSE ENTERPRISE is developed to collaboratively build graphically realistic simulations of real-world devices and systems, making it useful for everything from designing the most delinquent cars to seeing how AI-powered versions of those cars would function in simulated environments. Omniverse delivers the support for Nvidia's Drive Sim actions on autonomous driving, as well as its Isaac Sim robotics simulation outlet.

Omniverse Create is the instrument that leverages its RTX graphics technology to make advanced scene arrangements and virtual worlds with photo-realistic attributes and then transfer them via the Pixar USD setup. (Ironically, while we'll never learn for sure, it could even be that Meta used Omniverse Create to help make its fantastical metaverse "worlds.")

One of the other exciting aspects of Nvidia's approach is its focus on partnerships. As Microsoft is doing with Teams, Nvidia emphasizes Omniverse as an extensible platform that other software companies and developers can leverage, including big-name graphics ISVs like Adobe, Autodesk, and more. In addition, Nvidia is working with various hardware partners to help provide the systems that can power its Omniverse vision. The company is also working with resale members to bring the 3D graphics collaboration capabilities to enterprises.

Nvidia's annual GPU Technology Conference (GTC), an online occasion occurring (November 8-11) GTC expected to draw more than 200,000 attendees, including innovators, investigators, thought leaders, and decision-makers. More than 500 sessions focus on deep knowledge, data science, HPC, robotics, data center/networking, and pictures. Speakers will consult the latest breakthroughs in healthcare, transportation, manufacturing, retail, finance, telecoms, and more.

Competent money managers are always looking for the following hot stock, and NVIDIA has many fundamental qualities that are attractive.

That sets up nicely for the stock going ahead. But how the shares have been trading effectiveness to more upside. As I'll guide you, the Big Money has been constant in the shares all year.

You see, account managers are constantly looking to bet on the following outlier stock, the most useful in class. They spend numerous hours sizing up companies, reading reports, speaking to the analyst, you name it. When they find a business firing on all cylinders, they spring in a big way. That's why I've discovered how vital it is to gauge Big Money demand for shares.

To show you what I mean, have a look at all the significant money signals NVDA has made the last year.

In 2021, the stock has drawn 24 Big Money buy signals. Naturally speaking, current green bars could mean more upside is ahead. Now, let's check out technical action holding my attention: 1-month outperformance vs. Vanguard Information Technology ETF (+17.89% vs. VGT)

Outperformance Is Essential For Leading Stocks.

Next, it's an acceptable idea to check under the hood. Meaning, I want to make sure the whole story is vital too. As you can see, NVIDIA has been increasing sales at a double-digit rate. Take a look:

- 3-year sales growth rate (+22.2%)
- 3-year earnings growth rate (+18.0%)

Source: FactSet

Marrying excellent fundamentals with technically superior stocks is a winning recipe over the long term.

NVDA has been a top-rated product at my analysis firm, MAP signals, for years. That means the store saw buy stress, strong technicals, and developing fundamentals. We have a scalable process that showcases stocks like this every week.

NVDA has a bunch of grades that are drawing Big Money. And since 2015, it's created this checklist 62 times, with its first appearance on 2/17/201 and earning 302.15% since. The blue bars below indicate the times that NVIDIA was a top pick since 2015:

AMD ADVANCED MICRO DEVICES, INC. (AMD) STOCK PRICE (4TH of November) - $137.73+

Advanced Micro Devices, Inc. (AMD) is an American multinational semiconductor company based in Santa Clara, California, developing computer processors and related technologies for business and consumer markets. While it initially manufactured its processors, the company later outsourced its manufacturing, a practice known as going fabless, after GlobalFoundries was products include microprocessors, spun off in 2009. AMD's main

motherboard chipsets, embedded processors, and graphics processors for servers, workstations, personal computers, and embedded system applications.

AMD'sChip designer Advanced Micro Devices has been able to skirt most of the problems. CPU market share raised by 0.46 percentage matters in March, and the company ended the month with 28.97% of the market under its power. Intel controlled the rest of the demand with a share of just over 71%.

AMD is now examining to turn up the heat in the higher end of the PC processor market. Supply chain sources suggest that AMD could increase the production of Ryzen 5000 parts by 20% in the second quarter of 2021 compared to the first quarter. That could help AMD corner more market share, as its high-end processors are reportedly more useful than Intel's competing offerings as per third-party benchmarks. That's not astonishing, as AMD took the gaming CPU crown from Intel after launching the Ryzen 5000 series processors last year because of its technological edge. More significantly, AMD is unlikely to lose its edge over Intel anytime soon.

FEATURES OF THE METAVERSE: CURRENT STATUS AND FUTURE POSSIBILITIES

Realism

We right away qualify our use of period realism to mean, in this context, immersive realism. In the equal manner that realism in cinematic laptop-generated imagery is certified with the aid of using its believability in place of devotion to element (even though absolutely enough diploma of the component is anticipated), realism in the Metaverse is sought in the service of a consumer's mental and emotional engagement in the surroundings. A digital surrounding is perceived as extra sensible, primarily based totally on the diploma to which it transports a consumer into that surroundings and at the transparency of the boundary among the consumer's bodily movements and people of their Avatar.

By this token, digital global realism isn't always merely additive nor, visually speaking, strictly photographic: in lots of cases, strategic

rendering selections can yield higher returns than simply including polygons, pixels, gadgets, orbits infamous throughout the board.

What does stay steady throughout all views on realism is the instrumentation through which humans engage with the surroundings, their senses, and their bodies, primarily through their faces and hands—we. As a result, method realism thru this shape of notion and expression.

We deal with the concern at an ancient and survey stage, inspecting cutting-edge and destiny trends. More excellent technical elements and recognition totally at the (perceived) realism of digital worlds may be discovered withinside the mentioned paintings and educational materials, together with Glencross et al. [2006].

Sight. Not surprisingly, scenery and visuals incorporate the sensory channel with extensive records inside digital worlds. The earliest visual medium for digital worlds—and for all of the computing for that matter—changed into straightforward textual content. Text changed into used to shape imagery in the mind's eye and, to a sure diploma, it stays a potent mechanism for doing so. In the end, however, phrases and logos are indirect: they describe a global and depart specifics to people. Effective visible immersion entails getting rid of this stage of indirection—a digital global's visual presentation seeks to be as records-wealthy to our eyes because the actual global is. The mind then acknowledges imagery in synthesizing or recalling it (as it'd while studying textual content).

To this end, the country of the artwork in visible immersion has till currently hewn very carefully to the land of the artwork in actual-time laptop pictures.

The precise means of actual-time visible notion is complex and fraught with nuances and outside factors, together with interest, fixation, and nonvisual cues [Hayhoe et al. 2002; Recanzone 2003; Chow et al. 2006]. For this discussion, "actual-time" refers back to the simplified metric of body charge, or the frequency with which a laptop pictures device can render a scene. As pictures hardware and algorithms have driven the brink of what may be computed and displayed at 30 or extra frames in keeping with second—a usually ordinary minimal body charge for actual-time notion [Kumar et al. 2008; Liu et al. 2010]— global digital packages have furnished an increasing number of targeted visuals commensurate with the strategies of the time.

Thus, along with video games, 3-D modeling software program, and a certain quantity of 3-D cinematic animation (certified as such due to the fact the actual-time constraint is lifted for the very last product), digital worlds have visible a development of visual elements from flat polygons to easy shading and texture mapping and subsequently to programmable shaders, that can practice adjustments and different computations to graphical factors with high-quality performance and versatility.

Initially, visual richness changed into achieved clearly with the aid of growing the number of facts used to render a scene: extra and smaller polygons, better-decision textures, and interpolation strategies, together with anti-aliasing and easy shading. The constant-characteristic pictures pipeline, so named as it uniformly processed 3-D fashions, facilitated the stabilization of pictures libraries and incremental overall performance improvements in pictures hardware. However, it also restrained the alternatives for turning in targeted gadgets and realistic rendering [Olano et al. 2004; Olano and Lastra 1998]. That served the region nicely for a time as hardware upgrades accommodated the growing bandwidth and requirements that emerged for representing and storing 3-D fashions. Ultimately, however, the use of expanded facts for expanded elements led to diminishing returns because the fee of growing the records (3-D styles, 2D textures, animation rigging) can, without problems, surpass the advantage visible in visual realism.

The arrival of programmable shaders allowed critical quantities of the laptop graphics rendering pipeline to be written in a specialized language, ensuing unprecedented flexibility. Shaders and shader languages additionally supply high-quality performance thanks to accompanying hardware; this is incredibly optimized and often explicitly parallelized for them. Their eventual status quo as a brand new helpful baseline for 3-D libraries, such as OpenGL, represented an enormous step for global digital visuals because it did for laptop pictures packages infamous

[Rost et al. 2009]. With programmable shaders, many components of 3-D fashions—whether or not in phrases in their geometry (vertex shaders) or their very last photograph rendering (fragment shaders)—have become expressible algorithmically, as a result getting rid of the want for large numbers of polygons or textures even as on the equal time sharply increasing the range and versatility with which objects may be rendered or offered. This diploma of flexibleness has produced effective actual-time strategies for several items and scene types. The detachment of vertex and fragment shaders has additionally facilitated conventional procedures regarding geometry and item fashions with photograph-area systems [Roh and Lee 2005; Shah 2007].

Some of those strategies can see instant applicability in global digital environments, as they contain outside environments, together with terrain, lighting fixtures, our bodies of water, precipitation, forests, fields, and the atmosphere [Hu et al. 2006; Wang et al. 2006; Bouthors et al. 2008; Boulanger et al. 2009; Seng and Wang 2009; Elek and Kmoch 2010] or not unusual place gadgets, materials, or phenomena, together with clothing, meditated light, smoke, translucence, or gloss [Adabala et al. 2003; Lewinski 2011; Sun and Mukherjee 2006; Ghosh 2007; Shah et al. 2009]. Techniques for specialized packages, together with surgery simulation [Hao et al. 2009] and radioactive threat schooling [Koepnick et al. 2010], have an area as nicely, due to the fact digital global environments try to be as open-ended as feasible with minimum regulations at the styles of sports that may be finished inside them (simply as withinside the actual international).

Most digital global consumer packages or visitors presently stand in transition be- tween constant characteristic rendering (specific polygon representations, texture maps for small details) and programmable shaders (particle era, bump mapping, at- atmosphere, and lighting fixtures, water) [Linden Lab 2011a]. Virtual global visitors generally tend to lag in the back of different pictures packages together with video games, visible effects, or 3-D modeling.

Real-time lighting fixtures and shadows, for example, had been now no longer carried out withinside the reliable Second Life viewer till June 2011, lengthy after those had come to be pretty popular in different pictures software categories [Linden Lab 2011b], as certainly considered one among its specific dreams, the extension and integration of pictures strategies, together with sensible shadows, the intensity of area, and different functionalities, that take higher benefit of the power afforded with the aid of using programmable shaders.

It changed into said in advance that visible immersion has hewn very carefully to actual-time computer pictures till currently. This divergence corresponds to the kind as mentioned earlier of realism. That is demanded using global digital packages, which isn't always an element but different, primarily an experience of transference, transportation right into extraordinary surroundings, or perceived truth. It may be said that the visible constancy afforded with the aid of using progressed processing strength, show hardware, and pictures algorithms (especially as enabled with the assistance of using programmable shaders) has crossed a certain threshold of sufficiency, such that enhancing the experience of visible immersion has shifted from natural element to specific visual factors.

This diversity of visitors for the equal records area is similar to the supply of a couple of browser alternatives for the Worldwide Web.

One would consider then that stereoscopic imaginative and prescient can be a crucial aspect of visible immersion. That, to a point, has been borne out with the aid of using the current surge in 3-D movies and especially exemplified with the assistance of using the fulfillment of movies with actual 3-dimensional facts, together with Avatar and laptop-lively paintings.

However, a proscribing element of 3-D viewing is the want for unique glasses to completely isolate the imagery visible with the aid of using the left and right eyes. Although such glasses have come to be gradually much less glaring and can, in the end, come to be unnecessary, they nevertheless constitute a problem of sorts and include a version of the "come as you are" constraint taken from gesture-primarily based interfaces, which states that preferably consumer interfaces have to reduce the want for attachments or unique controls [Triesch and von der Malsburg 1998; Wachs et al. 2011].

Sound. Unlike visuals which can be pretty actually "in one's face" while interacting with cutting-edge digital global environments, the function of audio is twin in nature, together with relatively aware and un- or unconscious assets of sound. Like visual realism, the virtual replication or era of sound reveals packages nicely past the ones of digital worlds and may be argued to have had a more effect on society as an entire than laptop-generated visuals way to the CD player, MP3 and its successors, and domestic theater structures.

(1)Conscious or front-and-middle audio in digital worlds is composed typically of speech: Speaking and listening are our maximum herbal and facile varieties of verbal communication, and the supply of speech is an enormous element in psychologically immersing and tasty ourselves in a digital global as it engages us directly with a different population of that surroundings, possibly extra so than studying their (digital) faces, posture, and motion.

This experience of sound immersion derives directly from the aural surroundings of the actual global: we're always enveloped in sound, whether or not or now no longer we're consciously taking note of it. (2)Ambient audio in digital worlds includes sound that we might not consciously method, however, whose presence or absence subtly impacts the experience of immersion inside that surroundings. Such sound gives critical positional and spatial cues, the notion of which contributes drastically to our experience of placement inside a selected state of affairs [Blauert 1996].

For the primary aware shape of audio stimulus, we word that splendid voice chat, which somewhat captures the nuances of verbal communique, is now commonly to be had [Short et al. 1976; Lober et al. 2007; Wadley et al. 2009]. In this regard, the experience of listening to is genuinely beforehand of sight in shooting avatar expression and interaction. Future avenues in this region encompass voice protecting and modulation technology that no longer best seize the consumer's vocal expressions; however, customize the reproduced vocals seamlessly and effectively [Ueda et al. 2006; Xu et al. 2008; Mecwan et al. 2009]. Ambient audio, however, deserves extra discussion.

COMPUTE AND THE METAVERSE

In the hardware and networking categories, I investigated only a piece of the gradual information that will be created, sent, and got as a component of the Metaverse —, for example, haptics, facial checking, and live climate filters. The entire degree will be significant degrees more considerable.

For instance, Nvidia's originator and President, Jensen Huang, see the following stage for vivid reenactments as an option that could be more noteworthy than more sensible blasts or road races. It's the utilization of the "laws of molecule physical science, of gravity, of electromagnetism, of electromagnetic waves, [including] light and radio waves … of strain and sound". Furthermore, similarly, as the virtual world increases, so will the 'genuine' one. Consistently, more sensors, cameras, and IoT chips will be coordinated into the actual world around us, a large number of which will be associated continuously to virtual simulacra that can communicate back. In the interim, our gadgets will fill in as our identifications to a significant number of these encounters and low-maintenance generators. To put it plainly, a large part of our general surroundings will be persistently interconnected and on the web. They are counting on us.

In its entirety, the Metaverse will have the best continuous computational prerequisites in humanity's set of experiences. What's more, the figure is and is probably going to remain amazingly scant. To cite Chris Dixon, general accomplice at Andreessen Horowitz, "Each great processing asset on the planet, ever, has had request overwhelm supply … it's valid for computer chip power. It's valid for GPU power." therefore, the accessibility and improvement of figuring power will compel and characterize the Metaverse (even though end-clients will not understand this). It doesn't make any difference in how much information you can get, how rapidly, or why if it can't be utilized.

Consider the present most famous Metaverse-like encounters, like Fortnite or Roblox. While these stages prevail through mind-boggling innovative accomplishments, they perceive that their fundamental thoughts are a long way from new — they're recently conceivable. Designers have since long ago envisioned encounters with many live players (if not hundreds or thousands) in a solitary, shared reproduction, just as virtual conditions limited by only creative minds.

It was simply by the mid-2010s that a great many buyer-grade gadgets could handle a game with 100 genuine players in a solitary match. That reason enough, server-side equipment was accessible and equipped for synchronizing this data close to continuous. When this specialized obstruction was broken, the games business was immediately surpassed by games zeroed in on rich UGC and significant quantities of simultaneous clients (Free Fire, PUBG, Fortnite, Honorable obligation: Disaster area, Roblox, Minecraft). What's more, these games then, at that point, immediately ventured into such media encounters that were already 'IRL Just' (for example, the Travis Scott show in Fortnite or Lil Nas X's in Roblox).

It would appear that normal DAUs for the fight royale kind currently surpass 350-400MM consolidated.

- More significant than the generally characterized AAA console+PC market by and large
- Pretty staggering accomplishment for what is another game kind. Feels like a newfound social crude.

— Matthew Ball (@ballmatthew) June 25, 2021

However, even four years after the fight royale type arose, various stunts are expected to guarantee it works. For instance, most players are never truly together. All things being equal, they're dissipated across a vast guide. This implies that, while the server needs to follow what each player is doing, every player's gadget doesn't have to deliver them or track/process their activities. Furthermore, when Fortnite unites players into a more bound space for a get-together, like a show, it decreases the number of members to 50 and cutoff points what they can do versus the standard game modes.

What's more, more trade-offs are made for clients with less-amazing processors. Gadgets a couple of years old will decide not to stack the custom outfits of different players (as they have no ongoing interaction result) and, on second thought, address them as stock characters. Entirely, Free Fire, which is versatile just and for the most part played on low-to-mid-range Androids in developing business sectors, is covered at 50 for the primary fight royale mode.

"It makes me wonder where the future developments of these sorts of games will go that we couldn't construct today. Our pinnacle is 10.7 million players in Fortnite — yet that is 100,000 hundred-player meetings. Could we, in the end, set up them all in this common world? Also, what might that experience resemble? There are entirely different classifications that can't be created at this point due to the consistently up pattern of innovation." - Tim Sweeney (2019)

METAVERSE ETF

What Is An Etf?

ETF stands for exchange-traded fund. It is a form of security that tracks an index, sector, commodity, or other asset and can be bought and sold on the stock market like a regular stock. An ETF can track anything from a single commodity's price to a vast and diverse portfolio of assets. ETFs can even be designed to carry out specific investment strategies.

An exchange-traded fund (ETF) is a collection of securities traded on a stock exchange.

- ETF's share prices fluctuate throughout the day as the ETF is bought and sold, unlike mutual funds, trading only once a day after the market's closure.
- ETFs can contain many assets, such as equities, commodities, and bonds; some are only available in the USA, while others are available worldwide.
- ETFs have lower expense ratios and broker charges than individual stock purchases.

Because it is traded on a stock market, an ETF is an exchange-traded fund. ETF's shares price will fluctuate during the trading day as shares are bought and sold on the market. On the other hand, mutual funds are not traded on a stock exchange and trade just once a day after the closure of the markets. Furthermore, ETFs are more cost-effective and liquid than mutual funds.

An ETF might own hundreds or thousands of stocks from various industries or narrowly concentrate on a single one. Some funds are exclusively concerned with the United States, while others are concerned with the entire world. Banking-focused ETFs, for example, would hold equities from a wide range of financial institutions.

Types Of Etfs

Investors can use a variety of ETFs to generate income, speculate on price increases, and hedge or partially offset risk in their portfolios. A rundown for some of the most popular exchange-traded funds (ETFs) currently available is explained below.

Bond ETFs

Bond ETFs are used to offer investors a steady stream of income. The performance of the underlying bonds determines the distribution of their earnings. Examples are government, corporate, and state and local bonds, often known as municipal bonds. Unlike their underlying assets, Bond ETFs don't have a set maturity date but typically trade at discount or premium to the actual bond price.

Stock ETFs

Stock exchange-traded funds (ETFs) are a group of equities that track a particular industry or sector. For example, a stock ETF may follow automotive or foreign stocks. The objective is to provide diverse exposure to a specific industry, comprising high-performing companies and newcomers with growth potential. Unlike stock mutual funds, Stock ETFs have cheaper costs and do not require actual stock ownership.

Industry ETFs

Industry exchange-traded funds (ETFs) are designed to provide investors with exposure to an industry's upside potential by monitoring the performance of companies within it. Industry or sector ETFs specialize in a particular sector. For instance, an energy sector ETF will contain firms that operate in the energy business. The IT industry, for example, has witnessed a recent influx of cash. At the same time, because ETFs do not entail direct stock ownership, the risk of irregular stock performance is mitigated. Industry ETFs are often used during economic cycles to enter and exit sectors.

Commodity ETFs

As their name suggests, Commodity ETFs invest in commodities such as crude oil or gold. Commodity ETFs have several advantages. They begin by diversifying a portfolio, making it easier to defend against recession periods. Commodity ETFs, for example, can become a safety net in the event of a stock market downturn. Second, owning shares in a commodities ETF is less expensive than purchasing the commodity itself due to the former not requiring insurance or storage.

Currency ETFs

ETFs (exchange-traded funds) track the performance of currency pairings that include both local and foreign currencies. Currency exchange-traded funds (ETFs) are helpful in several situations. They may be used to speculate on currency values depending on political and economic trends in a particular nation. And Importers and exporters use them to diversify their portfolios or hedge against the volatility of the foreign exchange markets. Some of them are also used to protect against inflation. Bitcoin has its exchange-traded fund (ETF) (ETF).

Inverse ETFs

Inverse ETFs try to profit from stock declines by shorting shares. Shorting is the practice of selling stock and then repurchasing it at a lower price in the hopes of a price decline. An inverse ETF uses derivatives to short a stock. They are essentially bets on the market's demise. When the stock market declines, the value of an inverse ETF rises in lockstep. Investors must be aware that many inverse ETFs are exchange-traded notes (ETNs), not actual ETFs. An ETN resembles a bond, yet it trades like a bank-backed stock. Talk to your broker to evaluate if an ETN is suitable for your investing strategy.

Metaverse Etfs

"Metaverse" is a word used to describe a future version of the Internet. The goal of the investment is to track the performance of the Ball Metaverse Index before fees and expenditures (the "index"), which is designed to measure the performance of publicly traded equity shares of companies that engage in activities or supply products, services, technologies, or technological capabilities that enable the Metaverse and profit from its produced revenues. Under typical conditions, the fund will invest at least 80% of its net assets in Metaverse Companies, including ADRs or SPACs. The fund has no diversification.

How The Metaverse Etf Thinkers Picked Stocks So You Can Invest In The Metaverse

The Securities and Exchange Commission authorized the ETF, and it now trades on the New York Stock Exchange. Because the technique is designed to be forward-compatible, Epic Games might be included as one of the stocks once it goes public. On the other hand, private companies are not included in the index.

The Metaverse's social pillars are incredibly significant. 'What are the basic pillars that metaverse experiences must have?' is one of the more intriguing pieces. It necessitates a genuine social connection and expressing one's individuality and identity.

Part of the fascinating debate over which equities to include revolves around defining the Metaverse. In a market map, Ball observes seven different types of businesses.

These are some of them:

- payment services
- interchange tools and standards
- Content services and assets.
- hardware, computing, networking, virtual platforms

CHALLENGE OF VIRTUAL REALITY

Metaverse technology is a term used to describe virtual spaces that allow for sharing information and resources among users. These spaces can be accessed through immersive virtual environments and enable users to communicate through their avatars. The metaverse environment also contains various applications that provide information and resources to users. These tools make connecting people from different backgrounds and cultures easier. Metaverse technology is an essential facet of the online community and continues to evolve with the advancement of technology.

The challenges of metaverse range from technical issues to governance and legal concerns. First, the underlying technology metaverse is still in its early stages of development. That means that many unresolved bugs and glitches need to be fixed. In addition, the infrastructure for supporting a large-scale metaverse is not yet in place. As metaverse becomes more populated, new challenges will arise with scaling the infrastructure to meet the demands of users.

Second, there are no effective governance structures for the metaverse. The lack of proper regulation and laws poses risks to its adoption rate. Legal frameworks exist for virtual worlds like Second Life (Blackburn, 2009). However, these frameworks were developed to govern the world as they existed ten years ago and may not be relevant to virtual worlds today. For example, the law that covers theft of intellectual property in Second Life states that if a user steals content from another user's land, both users should be held liable (Blackburn, 2009). Today's metaverse has more complex interactions, including exchanging blockchain currency, thus requiring new laws and governance structures to manage it (Lampe & Moore, 2009).

Third, metaverses are facing issues with online harassment. Harassment in virtual worlds can take multiple forms, including verbal abuse, cyberstalking, cyberbullying, and many others. These behaviors can significantly impact the victim's mental health and well-being. In extreme cases, victims have even committed suicide due to online harassment.

Fourth, there are concerns about the use of metaverse for illegal activities. For example, criminals can use metaverse to commit fraud, money laundering, and other crimes. The anonymity of metaverse makes it a perfect place for criminals to operate.

Lastly, there are concerns about the use of metaverse for terrorist activities. Terrorists can use metaverse to plan and carry out attacks. They can also use it to recruit new members and spread their message.

These are some of the significant challenges that metaverse is facing. As the technology continues to develop, new challenges will emerge. The community needs to work together to address these challenges and ensure the success of metaverse.

As virtual reality technology advances, so too does the potential for creating a metaverse: a digital world in which users can create and interact with objects and others as if they were in the same physical space. While the metaverse offers many exciting possibilities, it also raises several legal issues that need to be considered.

One issue is whether in-world actions could have legal consequences in the physical world. For example, players are "kidnapped" and taken to a digital prison in one virtual reality environment. While this may seem like harmless fun, what if the game developer adds malicious code that causes players' computers to become badly damaged when they try to escape? The developer may be subject to a lawsuit by its players, not just for the virtual damage but also for real-life consequences.

Another potential legal issue is digital rights management (DRM). Most DRM strategies create a license agreement between the user and the product creator, stating what users can do with the product. To maintain control of their intellectual property, creators should establish clear terms and conditions for using their products. If those conditions are not met (for example, if a user tries to sell or steal the virtual item), the creator may be able to take legal action against the user.

The potential upside of these issues is that metaverse technology could have significant benefits in education, healthcare, and environmental protection. For example, future versions of Google Earth could include 3D models that allow students to explore historical sites and natural habitats around the world without leaving the classroom.

BACKEND INFRASTRUCTURE FOR THE METAVERSE - CLOUD COMPUTING

The Metaverse must be built on top of advanced digital infrastructure.

The "immersive," "low-latency," and "anywhere" nature of the Metaverse not only places high demands on VR/AR hardware technology and network delivery systems but also depends on High-performance cloud-side computing power and streaming technology.

As a brand new thing, the growth and development of the Metaverse require massive computing and storage capacity to support.

A more realistic and complete experience also means massive amounts of data production. Real-world computing and storage capacity directly determines the size and completeness of the Metaverse.

As you can see, without solid cloud computing and extensive data capabilities, it isn't easy to take the lead in this Metaverse scramble.

According to media research, the global cloud computing market will reach $265.4 billion in 2021.

As the earliest country, the U.S. has gathered many high-quality cloud computing technology companies. The three cloud computing giants, Amazon, Microsoft, and Google, occupy 63% of the global market share.

With Google, Amazon, Microsoft, Tencent, Ali, Huawei, & different giants to further enhance the market concentration, cloud computing has crossed into a new era; the past few years, the cloud computing model has had a strong impact, the future of cloud computing will have a further evolution, and more technical areas of mutual depth of integration, resulting in a more intense "chemical reaction The future will see further evolution of cloud computing, with deeper integration with more technology areas and stronger "chemical reactions."

As the optimal primary support platform for the Metaverse, cloud computing provides massive low-cost, primary resources.

In the Metaverse scenario, the distributed network connection, ICT resource sharing, rapid, on-demand, and dynamic expansion of elastic services features of cloud computing itself will be further demonstrated and based on its scale effect on resource utilization and higher utilization rate, it makes the lowest unit cost of technology and the highest efficiency of resource utilization.

The whole popularity of Metaverse will mainly benefit from the low-cost procurement of bulk hardware equipment brought about by the scale effect of infrastructure; the decrease in energy efficiency (PUE) of green data centers under the cloud trend, bringing cost savings; the business elasticity brought about by virtualization and other technologies that greatly enhance resource utilization; and additional supporting costs such as disaster recovery, construction, maintenance and personnel costs in the expansion process.

Cloud computing far exceeds traditional IT in terms of cost, stability, security, and efficiency at the infrastructure level.

The ecological advantages built by the original cloud giant's IaaS+PaaS integrated services may be pivotal in the Metaverse era.

The Metaverse is the result of the integrated application of various technologies.

A new computing architecture with the cloud as the core is taking shape at the cloud computing end, with the further integration of cloud-network-end technologies, whatever technology forms will further migrate to the cloud in the future.

This new system is evolving at three levels: First, in the infrastructure layer, the cloud down to define the hardware, self-research chips, servers, operating systems, and other underlying technologies, the construction of the cloud as the core hardware system.

Secondly, the core software is reconfigured based on the cloud. The open-source community becomes the center of innovation and introduces new development methods such as low code, making the cloud easier to use.

Finally, in the application layer, in the future, with the development of 5G networks, computing and data accelerate migration to the cloud, giving rise to new species such as cloud computers, Metaverse, and autonomous driving.

With the development of communication technologies such as 5G, computing and data will accelerate their migration to the cloud, thus giving rise to more new species.

The cloud has gone through the first and second phases, with traditional IT being replaced by the cloud, but the real change is yet to come. Countless new species on the cloud will emerge in the future, and there is already an excellent foundation for such a technology explosion.

We believe that Metaverse must be one area where cloud computing can be heavily empowered. The Metaverse itself needs computing, storage, machine learning, etc., all of which cannot be separated from the cloud. For example, Epic Games, a company that developed the Metaverse game Fortnite, which has 350 million users worldwide, runs almost all of its workload on Amazon Cloud Technologies.

A digital twin is a digital mapping of a material system that can be updated periodically based on the structure, state, and behavior of the real-world objects it represents.

And Amazon IoT TwinMaker makes it easier for developers to combine data from multiple sources and combine them to create a knowledge graph that models real-world environments.

With Amazon IoT TwinMaker, consumers can use digital twins to build applications that reflect the real world, improving operational efficiency and reducing downtime.

With Amazon IoT TwinMaker, creating real-world digital twins is easier and faster.

Creators can connect Amazon IoT TwinMaker to data sources such as device sensors, video feeds, and business applications to quickly build digital twins of devices, installations, and processes.

Also, at the conference, Amazon CloudTech introduced three new Amazon EC2 instances powered by its chips, including a C7g instance, powered by the new Amazon Graviton3 processor; a Trn1 model powered by the Amazon Trainium chip; and an Im4gn/ Is4gen/I4i instances with the new Amazon Nitro SSDs.

These undoubtedly provide Metaverse with advanced infrastructure from hardware to software and help Metaverse gradually move from concept to reality.

Investment advice: the combination of Metaverse and cloud computing, recommended focusing on Amazon's stock.

IS MARK BETTING FACEBOOK FUTURE ON THE METAVERSE? WHAT EXPERTS THINK

As June concluded, Facebook CEO Mark Zuckerberg informed his representatives regarding an eager new drive. The eventual fate of the organization would go a long way past its present undertaking of building a bunch of associated social applications and some equipment to help them. All things being equal, he said, Facebook would endeavor to fabricate a maximalist, interconnected arrangement of encounters straight out of science fiction — a world known as the metaverse.

The organization's divisions centered around items for networks, makers, business, and computer-generated reality would progressively attempt to understand this vision, he said in a remote location to workers. "What I believe is most fascinating is the way these subjects will meet up into a greater thought," Zuckerberg said. "Our general objective across these drives is to help rejuvenate the metaverse."

The metaverse has a second. Begat in Snow Crash, Neal Stephenson's 1992 science fiction novel, the term alludes to an intermingling of physical, increased, and computer-generated reality in a common web-based space. (Epic Games CEO Tim Sweeney has been examining his craving to add to a metaverse for a long time now.) the New York Times recently investigated how organizations and items including Epic Games' Fortnite, Roblox, and surprisingly Animal Crossing: New Horizons progressively had metaverse-like components.

In January 2020, a powerful article by the investor Matthew Ball set off to distinguish critical qualities of a metaverse. Among them: it needs to traverse the physical and virtual universes; contain a completely fledged economy; and deal "remarkable interoperability" — clients must have the option to take their symbols and merchandise starting with one spot in the metaverse then onto the next, regardless of who runs that specific piece of it. Fundamentally, nobody organization will run the metaverse — it will be an "encapsulated web," Zuckerberg said, worked by a wide range of players in a decentralized manner.

Watching Zuckerberg's show, I could not conclude which was more venturesome: his vision itself or his planning. Zuckerberg's declared expectation to assemble a more maximalist form of Facebook, crossing social presence, office work, and amusement, comes when the US government endeavors to split his present organization up. A bundle of bills clearing its path through Congress would possibly constrain the organization to turn out Instagram and

WhatsApp and cut off Facebook's capacity to make future acquisitions — or offer administrations associated with its equipment items.

Also, regardless of whether tech guideline slows down in the United States — generally not a terrible bet — a flourishing metaverse would bring up issues both natural and peculiar with regards to how the virtual space is administered, how its substance would be directed, and how its reality would deal with our familiar feeling of the real world. We're getting our arms folded over the two-dimensional adaptation of social stages; fighting the 3D variant could be dramatically more complex.

Simultaneously, Zuckerberg said, the metaverse will carry gigantic freedom to individual makers and artisans, people who need to work and claim homes a long way from the present metropolitan communities, and individuals who live where openings for instruction or amusement are more restricted. An acknowledged metaverse could be the following best thing to a functioning instant transportation gadget, he says. With the organization's Oculus division, which creates the Quest headset, Facebook is attempting to foster one.

"I don't think that this is primarily about being engaged with the internet more. I think it's about being engaged more naturally."

After I watched his discourse, Zuckerberg and I had a discussion. We examined his vision for an encapsulated web, the difficulties of administering it, and sexual orientation lopsidedness in computer-generated simulation. (The metaverse being inaccessible to us at press time, we utilized Zoom.) furthermore, with President Biden's wild analysis of Facebook's disappointments in eliminating hostile to immunization content in the features, I got some information about that, as well.

"It's somewhat similar to battling wrongdoing in a city," he told me. "Nobody expects that you're truly going to settle wrongdoing in a city completely."

Much obliged, Casey. It's great to be here. We have a ton to go through.

As usual, there's a ton to talk about with you — and the White House is requesting Facebook do more to eliminate antibody falsehood, which I know is on many individuals' psyches at this moment.

CONCLUSION

A distributed software network that is used as a digital ledger and a secure way of transferring assets is known as a blockchain. Blockchain technology initially emerged in the year 2009. The bitcoin blockchain first appeared as a bitcoin blockchain. The bitcoin blockchain is considered one of the most secure and resistant to censorship electronic cash systems. Nowadays, there are several blockchain technologies. Ethereum blockchain is powered by ether (ETH). The non-fungible token is a new concept, which is increasing with every passing day. The digital assets are traded peer-to-peer. That is so no one can change or alter any transactions happening over the network.

Non-fungible tokens or NFTs represent the ownership rights over a digital asset. All the information regarding the ownership of these assets is recorded on the Ethereum blockchain. You can interchange cryptocurrencies with each other, but you cannot interchange the NFTs. That is because the NFTs are unique, and this uniqueness is a factor that makes them scarce as well. If you compare the cryptocurrencies and the NFTs, you may conclude that cryptocurrencies and the NFTs may work on the same blockchain technology. Still, if you look at their uses and purposes, you will find out that they are entirely different from one another. Although the marketplaces where you can buy and sell the NFTs may accept payment in the cryptocurrencies. But creation and uses of the two are entirely different from one another.

The NFT royalty scheme is a good way for the artists who create digital art to generate revenues after selling their artwork. Formerly the artists suffered a lot financially because they could not earn enough from their art. That jeopardized their art careers, but through the NFT royalty scheme, the artists can earn a percentage of the total revenue generated with every resale. When a buyer sells the NFT on a secondary platform and makes sales, the original artist will get the resale's predetermined incentive. That has helped the artists a lot with their financial issues, and they can come up with more creative content.

NFT industries and markets are relatively new, and the markets are highly volatile. Before you make any investment in the NFT market, you need to do all the background research. You need to understand the market well because you never know how would the market be in the coming years. It is growing and flourishing nowadays, but there is no certainty that it will do so in the coming years. NFT markets may be a great way to generate revenue online, but it comes with risks that you cannot ignore.

There have been instances where people earned millions of dollars through the NFTs, but you have to remember that this may not always be the case. It is not required that you would make so much through the NFTs. Certain factors contribute to earning millions of dollars through NFTs. However, you can generate revenue through the NFTs, and people nowadays are doing so. Do all your relevant research and then select a marketplace for the NFT trading. It would be best if you chose a popular and commonly used marketplace. You need to trust the marketplace you are choosing because there have been multiple cases of fraud and theft on unreliable marketplaces. There have been several instances recorded where the cryptocurrencies were stolen from the users' crypto wallets. To protect your digital wallets, you need to have a strong password and a secret phrase that you can use to protect them.

Experts say that NFTs have come to stay and are not going any time soon, and we have seen that. The significant growth that has been seen in these markets is proof that NFTs could indeed be the future if you like it or not!

Made in the USA
Monee, IL
31 March 2022

93858730R00308